Heroes or Traitors?

Reappraisals in Irish History

Editors
Enda Delaney (University of Edinburgh)
Maria Luddy (University of Warwick)

Reappraisals in Irish History offers new insights into Irish history, society and culture from 1750. Recognising the many methodologies that make up historical research, the series presents innovative and interdisciplinary work that is conceptual and interpretative, and expands and challenges the common understandings of the Irish past. It showcases new and exciting scholarship on subjects such as the history of gender, power, class, the body, landscape, memory and social and cultural change. It also reflects the diversity of Irish historical writing, since it includes titles that are empirically sophisticated together with conceptually driven synoptic studies.

1. Jonathan Jeffrey Wright, *The 'Natural Leaders' and their World: Politics, Culture and Society in Belfast, c.1801–1832*

2. Gerardine Meaney, Mary O'Dowd and Bernadette Whelan, *Reading the Irish Woman: Studies in Cultural Encounters and Exchange, 1714–1960*

3. Emily Mark-FitzGerald, *Commemorating the Irish Famine: Memory and the Monument*

4. Virginia Crossman, *Poverty and the Poor Law in Ireland 1850–1914*

5. Paul Taylor, *Heroes or Traitors? Experiences of Southern Irish Soldiers Returning from the Great War 1919–39*

Heroes or Traitors?

Experiences of Southern Irish Soldiers
Returning from the Great War
1919–39

PAUL TAYLOR

LIVERPOOL UNIVERSITY PRESS

First published 2015 by
Liverpool University Press
4 Cambridge Street
Liverpool
L69 7ZU

British Library Cataloguing-in-Publication data
A British Library CIP record is available

ISBN 978-1-78138-161-8 cased
978-1-78138-338-4 paperback

Typeset by Carnegie Book Production, Lancaster
Printed and bound by CPI Group (UK) Ltd, Croydon CR0 4YY

Dedicated to

Jack Hutchison
Robert Taylor
Soldiers of the Great War

and their Great Grandchildren
Natasha, Charlotte, and Rebecca
Always to Remember

Figure 1   Victory Parade Dublin 1919 © RTÉ Stills Library

Acknowledgements

As befits an exercise in history, I start at the beginning. I am indebted to Tony Gynn, a schoolteacher who several decades ago inspired a reluctant pupil with an enthusiasm for history. A business career later, and after early retirement, this latent interest led to an MA in Modern History at University College London. The faith of Melvyn Stokes in accepting an under-qualified applicant earns him my grateful thanks, as does the support of Stephen Conway throughout my MA. I completed an elective at Kings College London under the head of the History Department, Paul Readman. It was Paul who suggested this subject for my dissertation and then took on the onerous task of supervising me. I little thought it would become my focus of research for over five years. I have much to thank him for in suggesting such a stimulating and pertinent topic. The knowledgeable comments of Richard Grayson of Goldsmiths College and John Horne of Trinity College Dublin were so helpful during the early stage of my investigation.

The University of Oxford proved a stimulating and convivial environment in which to complete a PhD in Irish history. The Irish History Seminars of Roy Foster were an invigorating forum through which to expand my knowledge. I am grateful to Jane Garnett, Marc Mulholland, Tim Wilson, Senia Pašeta, Colin Reid, and most of all to my doctoral supervisor, Adrian Gregory, for their help and guidance. Particular thanks to Keith Jeffery of Queen's University Belfast, my external examiner, who encouraged me to seek publication, and to Fearghal McGarry and Marie Coleman, both of Queen's University Belfast, and Timothy Bowman of the University of Kent, whose insightful comments considerably improved the manuscript.

Many thanks for all their assistance to the staff of: the Bodleian library at the University of Oxford; the British Library; the Imperial War Museum; the National Archives of the UK and Ireland; the National Library of Ireland; the Irish Military Archives, Dublin; University College Dublin archives; and the local libraries and archives I visited in Ireland.

My research started as an academic exercise but became something more when I discovered that my grandfather, John (Jack) Hutchison, was an Irish soldier of the Great War. I took time out to research our family history and accompanied his daughter to the battlefields of Flanders where he had served. It was a new discovery for my mother; the War for my grandfather was a silent memory that he rarely discussed with his family. We learnt of a brave man who had fought and was badly wounded at the second battle of Ypres. We discovered that our family originated from Birr, King's County (now Offaly), headquarters of the Leinster Regiment, and joined its Association. The friendship of its members, including David Ball, Sean Cooke, and Ian Lowe, and their recollections of relatives who were Irish soldiers in the War, emphasises that behind such research as mine there is a human story.

Finally, thanks to my ever-patient family for all their support over the last years. Especially to my parents, Robert and Patricia, for the interest they took in my subject and for accompanying me on some of my research visits to Ireland, and my niece Kate, a graduate with a keen interest in history. The critical eyes my sister Marilyn Trask, recently retired after many years as a headmistress, and her husband Roger, cast over my final drafts were much needed and greatly appreciated. If mistakes remain, they are mine.

Contents

List of Tables

Notes on Tables

Most figures in the tables are rounded.

Table 2 shows recruitment figures during the Great War, 1914–18, pro rata to the 1911 census population figures.

Tables 5, 7, and 8 show various incidents of violence and intimidation that occurred during the period of conflict from 1916 to 1923 pro rata to the 1926 census population figures. As the available population data does not exactly coincide with the relevant periods, it should be noted that the population of the 26 counties that became the Free State declined by 5.34% between the census of 1911 (the last one in which Ireland was part of the UK) to 1926 (the first one after the formation of the Free State).

List of Figures

List of Maps

Biographical Notes

Bryan Cooper	Member of the Dáil Éireann, supporter of ex-servicemen
William Cosgrave	President of the Executive Council of the Irish Free State 1922–32
(John) Lord French	British Army Field Marshal, appointed Lord Lieutenant of Ireland in May 1918
(Douglas) Lord Haig	British Army Field Marshal, President of the British Legion
W.B. Hickie	British Army General, President of the British Legion, Southern Ireland
William Redmond	Member of the Dáil Éireann, founded pro ex-servicemen National League Party in 1926
Éamon de Valera	President of the Executive Council of the Irish Free State 1932–37, Taoiseach 1937–48

Glossary

Black and Tans (The Tans) One of two paramilitary forces, the other being the Auxiliaries, both composed largely of British World War I veterans, employed by the Royal Irish Constabulary (Ireland's armed police force) as Temporary Constables from 1920 to 1921 to suppress revolution in Ireland.

British Crown Forces British army, Royal Irish Constabulary, Black and Tans, and Auxiliaries.

British Legion, Southern Ireland The League of Irish ex-servicemen became affiliated to the British Legion in 1925, forming its southern Irish branch. It was referred to by different designations but, for consistency, the term British Legion, Southern Ireland (BLSI) is used. Due to its independent origins it had a very different character, confrontational and aggressive, particularly in the 1920s, from its parent body in Great Britain. When the term British Legion is used it refers to the parent body.

Cumann na nGaedheal Governing Party from 1922. Origins in the pro-Treaty members of Sinn Féin, merged with two smaller opposition parties in September 1933 to form Fine Gael. Led by Cosgrave.

Currency The sterling currency referred to is imperial i.e. pre-1971 decimal, with units of pounds (£), shillings (s), and pence (d). There were 12 pence to the shilling and 20 shillings to the pound. Amounts under £1 were expressed as s/d, for example, 8 shillings 6 pence as 8/6, 8 shillings as 8/, and 6 pence as 6d. Amounts above £1 were expressed as £ s d, for example, for £2, 8 shillings, and 6 pence as £2 8s 6d. Sometimes for smaller denominations of pounds the amount was still expressed in shillings, for example, £2, 8 shillings, and 6 pence as 48/6. Both options are used, following the original text of the sources. Ten old shillings is equivalent to 50 new pence. £100 in 1925 would be worth £4,976 in 2013 based on Retail Price Index increases (Source: measuringworth.com).

Ex-Servicemen   The terms ex-serviceman or veteran when used without further description, refers to soldiers who served in the British army in the Great War and returned to the area that became the Free State. Other ex-servicemen, for example ex-Irish National army, are specifically designated.

Fianna Fáil   Governing Party from 1932. Republicans with origins in the anti-Treaty members of Sinn Féin Party. Led by de Valera.

Great War/First World War   Referred to as the War. Other conflicts e.g. the Anglo-Irish War are specifically designated.

Irish Free State   Consisted of the 26 southern counties of Ireland, established as a dominion under the Anglo-Irish Treaty. Became Éire/Ireland in 1937.

Irish Sailors' and Soldiers' Land Trust (Abbreviated as the Trust)   A body constituted under the Irish Free State (Consequential Provisions) Act 1922 to build and administer houses (not land, despite the name) for ex-servicemen in Ireland as legislated by the Irish Land (Provision for Sailors and Soldiers) Act 1919. The Trust assumed responsibility for the administration of schemes developed by the Local Government Board in Ireland prior to its establishment. Properties built by the Trust were officially called cottages, although some could be more appropriately considered houses. They are referred to as both without distinction.

Irish Republican Army   From the First Dáil Éireann in 1919, the Irish Volunteers changed their name to the IRA, both terms are used. In the Civil War, the anti-Treaty IRA was termed the Irregulars by the Free State Government.

Loyalists   Southern Irish who remained loyal to the British Crown.

National Army   Irish Free State army initially formed to combat the anti-Treaty IRA.

Oireachtas, Dáil Éireann, Seanad Éireann, Teachtaí Dála, Senators, President   The Irish Parliament (Oireachtas) consisted of two Houses: the Dáil Éireann (House of Representatives), whose members were Teachtaí Dála (TDs) or Deputies; and the Seanad Éireann (Senate), whose members were Senators. The Government was headed by the President of the Executive Council until 1937, thereafter by the office of Prime Minister (or Taoiseach).

Sinn Féin   Republican political party; they secured 73 out of 105 Irish seats in the 1918 election but split into pro- and anti-Treaty factions with regard to the settlement with Great Britain.

Statistics   Statistics for Ireland prior to the Free State generally refer to all Ireland unless so noted.

Abbreviations

BL	British Legion
BLSI	British Legion, Southern Ireland
DO	Dominions Office
IFDDSS	Irish Federation of Discharged and Demobilised Sailors and Soldiers
IFS/FS/Free State	Irish Free State
IGC	Irish Grants Committee
IMA/BMH	Irish Military Archives, Bureau of Military History
IRA	Irish Republican Army
IT	*Irish Times*
Land Act 1919	Irish Land (Provision for Sailors and Soldiers) Act 1919
Lavery Committee/ Lavery Report	Committee on the Claims of British Ex-Servicemen, referred to after its chairman, Cecil Lavery, as is its resultant report.
LGB	(Irish) Local Government Board
MoL	Ministry of Labour
MoP	Ministry of Pensions
MoT	Ministry of Transport
NAI	National Archives of Ireland
RIC	Royal Irish Constabulary
SILRA	Southern Irish Loyalist Relief Association
The Trust	Irish Sailors' and Soldiers' Land Trust
TD	Teachtaí Dála
TNA	UK National Archives
WS	(IMA/BMH) Witness Statement

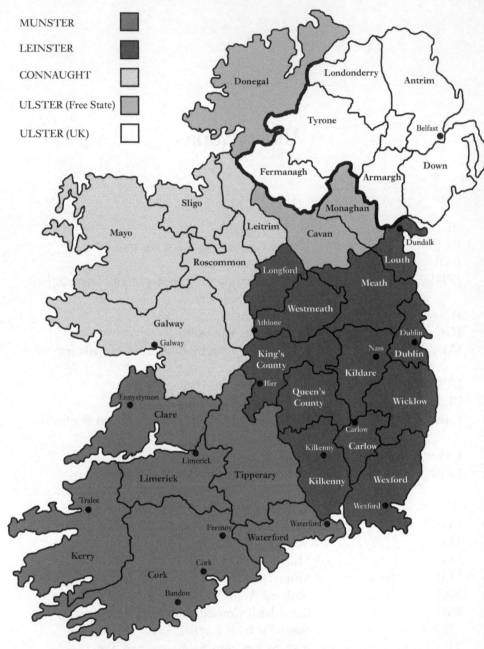

MUNSTER ▨
LEINSTER ▨
CONNAUGHT ▨
ULSTER (Free State) ▨
ULSTER (UK) ▢

Donegal

Londonderry

Antrim

Tyrone

Belfast

Fermanagh

Armargh

Down

Sligo

Monaghan

Leitrim

Cavan

Dundalk

Mayo

Roscommon

Longford

Louth

Meath

Westmeath

Galway

Athlone

Galway

King's
County

Nass

Dublin

Dublin

Birr

Kildare

Ennystymon

Queen's
County

Wicklow

Clare

Carlow

Limerick

Kilkenny

Carlow

Limerick

Tipperary

Kilkenny

Wexford

Tralee

Wexford

Fermoy

Waterford

Kerry

Cork

Waterford

Cork

Bandon

Map 1   Ireland: Provinces and Counties*

* Towns named are major towns or those most commonly referred to in the text. The nomenclature for counties is based on pre 1922 names, i.e. King's County (now Offaly) and Queen's County (now Laois). Even after the formation of the Free State, these were the designations often used, and much archival material refers to them as such. Likewise, in terms of provinces and other counties, Connaught and Londonderry are used rather than Connacht and Derry.

Introduction

Ex-Servicemen and their Place in Irish History

At the onset of the Great War southern Irishmen volunteered in large numbers and marched off accompanied by cheering crowds and the promise of a hero's welcome home. These volunteers, ordinary citizens from all walks of life, became embroiled in the carnage of the first war to be fought on an industrial scale and which affected all aspects of society. Many people today have relatives who were part of what became the largest military mobilisation of Irish manpower. Although within the recent past, the experiences of these soldiers, both during the war and in its aftermath, are often silent and forgotten memories. Attitudes to the ex-servicemen became influenced by the historiography of a republican Ireland and a litmus test of political attitudes. Ireland had long been defined by its ambiguous relationship with England – was it, like Scotland, part of a joint enterprise in building and maintaining a global empire, or a colony and, like India, a source of manpower to maintain British power? The dilemma was epitomised by the ex-servicemen. Were they heroes who as part of the United Kingdom aided their country in its time of need, or traitors who, as Ireland fought off the colonial yoke, wore the uniform of its enemy? This book examines the daily experiences of those Irish soldiers who returned to the part of Ireland that became the Free State, covering the years from the Armistice to 1939.[1]

In 1916, whilst its soldiers fought in the British army, Ireland witnessed an insurrection, the Easter Rising, against British rule. Its violent suppression by the Crown Forces and the intended introduction of conscription changed Irish sentiment against the British Government and meant the soldiers returned

---

1 Northern Ireland (six counties) has been excluded; religion and politics ensured the experiences of the soldiers from north and south varied significantly.

to a much-changed Ireland with increased demands for an independent republic, rather than limited Home Rule. On 21 January 1919, the Dáil Éireann convened for the first time in Dublin. Republican Sinn Féin had secured an overwhelming majority with 73 seats in the general election of the preceding month. Instead of taking their seats in Westminster, they proclaimed their defiance of Britain by establishing an independent Irish parliament. The new assembly was held in Mansion House in the heart of colonial Dublin. With an irony that well captures the atmosphere to which Irish soldiers were returning, 'soldiers from the Dublin Fusiliers, just returned from France, had been lunching in the Mansion House just before the historic inauguration of Dáil Éireann. As they walked out to the tune of "God Save the King", the republicans walked in'.[2] In the Declaration of Independence issued that day, the Dáil Éireann affirmed 'foreign government in Ireland to be an invasion of our national right', and demanded 'the evacuation of the English garrison'.[3] Irish soldiers returned to a country in increasing conflict with an enemy whose uniform they had worn, and the initial reaction to them has to be understood in that context. Sam Hutchinson, convalescing in Dublin in 1918, complained that he and other recovering veterans were jeered and taunted. Jack Campbell, also in Dublin, recalled that two women spat at him, 'that was their way of saying they didn't like British soldiers'.[4] During the Peace Day celebrations on 19 July 1919 to mark the end of the war, black IRA flags were flown in Dublin and Cork.[5]

For the two Irelands, north and south, that emerged after the war, their relationship to Great Britain became the dominant theme. Lyons argues there was not just 'a simple dualism between native (Catholic) and settler (Protestant), but a complex of Irish and Anglo-Irish cultures'.[6] In contrast, the historiographies developed by the respective dominant forces in the nascent political entities of Northern Ireland and the Free State were uncomplicated and non-inclusive. Both new states gave a sense of purpose and identity to their supporters to the exclusion of others. In the north it was Protestantism, Unionism, and loyalty; Protestant soldiers were mythologised, a thread of history created from the Boyne to the Somme.[7] In the south

---

2 Maurice Walsh, *The News from Ireland: Foreign Correspondents and the Irish Revolution* (London, 2008), 58; *Manchester Guardian*, 22 January 1919, 5.
3 Walsh, *News from Ireland*, 60; Ronan Fanning et al. (eds), *Documents on Irish Foreign Policy, vol. I, 1919–1922* (Dublin, 1998), 1.
4 Jane Leonard, 'Facing the Finger of Scorn: Veterans' Memories of Ireland after the Great War', in Eoin Magennis and Crónán O'Doibhlin (eds), *World War One–Ireland and its Impacts* (Armagh, 2005), 93, based on interviews conducted with ex-servicemen.
5 *Irish News*, 21 July 1919, 5.
6 F.S.L. Lyons, *Culture and Anarchy in Ireland 1890–1939* (Oxford, 1979), 26.
7 Gillian McIntosh, *The Force of Culture: Unionist Identities in Twentieth-Century Ireland* (Cork, 1999), 222–32.

after the assumption of power by Fianna Fáil, it was a historiography based upon the idea of republican predestination, defined in opposition to Britain, and marginalising those who had fought in her armies. Boyce argues that those who had fought in the British army found themselves at odds with the ethos of the emerging state and that 'the War was soon perceived as the wrong war, fought in the wrong place, and against the wrong foe'. After the republicans assumed power in 1932, they celebrated the twentieth anniversary of the Easter Rising as a state occasion. The simple 'heroics' of the Rising contrasted with the ambiguities engendered by the returning veterans, and indeed the bitterness caused by the Civil War. The thirteen rebels executed by the British after the Rising were remembered, the thousands who died whilst serving in the British army were forgotten in a sort of Irish 'national amnesia', the cause for which they fought almost regarded as a form of treason.[8] Republican ideology had no room for Irish Volunteers in France, Flanders, or Gallipoli.[9] Father Francis Shaw, writing at the time of the fiftieth anniversary of the Rising in 1966, was one of the first historians to challenge what he called the 'canon of Irish history', that 'condemns as being anti-Irish all who did not profess extremist nationalist doctrine'. He argues that Ireland in 1916 was not a suffering country, but one in which the people were already socially more advanced than at any time since the Union, and were moving to their goal of independence in their own way and at their own pace. Pearse and the Rising inflicted 'three grave wounds on the body of the unity of Ireland': partition, for 1916 closed the door to a peaceful resolution of that question; the Civil War of 1922–23, since the teachings of 1916 was that no compromise could be brooked, and that it was a separate republic or nothing; and the refusal of Ireland to honour those of her dead who fought in the Great War for the honour and freedom of their country. The publication of Shaw's article was delayed until 1972 as it was considered too sensitive.[10] As Boyce writes, 'revising national history is perilous, especially if cherished legends are debunked or heroes pushed off their pedestal'.[11]

---

8 D.G. Boyce, 'That Party Politics Should Divide Our Tents: Nationalism, Unionism and First World War', in Adrian Gregory and Senia Pašeta (eds), *Ireland and the Great War: 'A War to Unite Us All?'* (Manchester, 2002), 191, 201.

9 Senia Pašeta, 'Ireland's Last Home Rule Generation: The Decline of Constitutional Nationalism in Ireland, 1916–1930', in Mike Cronin and John Regan (eds), *Ireland: The Politics of Independence, 1922–49* (London, 2000), 13–14.

10 Father Francis Shaw, 'The Canon of Irish History: A Challenge', in *Studies*, 61 (1972), 113–53; D.G. Boyce, '1916, Interpreting the Rising', in D.G. Boyce and Alan O'Day (eds), *The Making of Modern Irish History: Revisionism and the Revisionist Controversy* (London, 1996), 178–9.

11 D.G. Boyce and Alan O'Day, 'Revisionism and the Revisionist Controversy', in D.G. Boyce and Alan O'Day (eds), *The making of Modern Irish History: Revisionism and the Revisionist Controversy* (London, 1996), 1.

With the advent of the peace process, and particularly the Anglo-Irish Agreement in 1985, the Great War was 'rediscovered' in the Republic and its exclusion from Irish historiography and the attitude of the state towards commemoration of the ex-servicemen questioned. Indeed reconciliation and remembrance became intrinsically linked. In November 1998 on the eightieth anniversary of the Armistice, the President of Ireland, Mary McAleese, and Queen Elizabeth II dedicated a memorial Peace Park at Messines, Belgium, to all the Irish soldiers who had fallen in the First World War. Unionist and nationalist soldiers had fought together at Messines. President McAleese said: 'For much of the past eighty years the very idea of such a ceremony would have been unthinkable. Those whom we commemorate here were doubly tragic. They fell victim to a war against oppression in Europe. Their memory fell victim to a war for independence in Ireland'.[12] This new climate helped encourage research into the experiences of the ex-servicemen. Such studies have mostly focussed on violence towards ex-servicemen during the period of conflict encompassed by the War of Independence and the Civil War ending in 1923. Most have investigated the activities of the IRA or violence towards loyalists generally, particularly in Munster, with ex-servicemen only tangentially referenced as one of the groups targeted. Jane Leonard, one of the first scholars to focus specifically on the experiences of Irish ex-servicemen returning from the Great War, argues that ex-servicemen 'formed a marginalised and unwelcome group in Irish society', were subject to 'extremes of intimidation including beating, mutilation, punishment shooting, prolonged kidnapping, expulsion from Ireland and murder', and of the estimated 120 ex-servicemen killed by the republicans during the civil conflict, 'the vast majority appear to have been killed simply as a retrospective punishment for their service in the Great War'.[13] Peter Hart, in his award winning book *The IRA and its Enemies* (1998) on violence in Cork, concluded that the IRA saw their enemy as 'types', including ex-servicemen and Protestants, killed for who they were, not for what they did. Hart's book, based on a Trinity College Dublin doctorate, provoked a debate far beyond the normal academic cloisters. It challenged one of the long-held tenets of a republican narrative, that ethnic violence and sectarianism were the preserve of Protestant Unionists in the north towards the Catholic minority, and that the IRA, in representing the political will of all the people, restricted its use of violence to military necessity in a war to rid Ireland of British occupation. Hart's assertion that IRA violence was

12 'Island of Ireland Peace Park', http://en.wikipedia.org/wiki/Island_of_Ireland_ Peace_Park.
13 Leonard, 'Facing the Finger of Scorn', 93, 95; Jane Leonard, 'Survivors', in John Horne (ed.), *Our War: Ireland and the Great War* (Dublin, 2008), 218.

motivated by sectarianism, for example in the Bandon massacre in April 1922, in which most of the victims were Protestant, brought a virulent and long-running response from republican historians who questioned his use of sources. Hart was supported by 'revisionist historians' who were willing to question republican orthodoxy through what they considered to be 'evidence based' research and critical investigation, and by influential journalists such as Kevin Myers and Eoghan Harris, who ensured the controversy was played out in the popular media. Myers wrote, 'To understand how mythology has concealed the truth in Irish history, it is obligatory to read Peter Hart's *The IRA and its Enemies*. It is a masterpiece'. Harris called Hart, a 'hero', writing that to him 'fell the grim task of telling us what the IRA did to some of these servicemen's comrades after they came home'.[14]

The perception of the ex-servicemen has been a reflection of changing political attitudes at the point of observation. This book seeks to go back in time and use contemporary sources to better understand their everyday experiences in the interwar years and how this varied chronologically and by geography.[15] Chapters 1 and 2 in Part 1 cover the 'Time of Conflict: 1919–23' encompassed by the War of Independence and the Civil War. Chapter 1 examines the type and frequency of violence and intimidation directed towards ex-servicemen, where it happened and the reasons for it, and whether it was related to war service or for reasons that were applicable to other sectors of the population. The analysis is based on the records of the perpetrators and the victims, those most directly involved.[16] Chapter 2 compares the geographical variation in violence directed towards ex-servicemen to other metrics of republican violence, in order to understand whether it simply reflects the general level of intimidation experienced by other sectors of the population in different locations, or whether they were particularly singled out. It also considers the extent to which Ireland was radicalised and republican and thus hostile to all that was British, including its ex-servicemen, and concludes with an assessment as to whether the evidence shows that ex-servicemen were intimidated as a group.

Few researchers have gone beyond this time, except in the area of remembrance and commemoration. This book takes a more holistic perspective, examining the interwar decades in terms of the practical support the ex-servicemen received from the former imperial power, and their

14 *IT*, 29 May 1998; Eoghan Harris, 'In memory of Peter Hart', *Irish Independent*, 25 July 2010.

15 It should also be recognised that much that was written during this period, especially in the press or by special interest groups such as the British Legion or the Southern Irish Loyalist Relief Association (SILRA), also portrayed a bias, the latter in using ex-servicemen as an example of neglected loyalists.

16 See the Appendix on these and other sources used.

experiences within Irish society. The period can be divided into that under
the Cosgrave administration, in which relations with Britain were reasonably
positive and the Free State functioned as an imperial dominion, followed
by the period of republican government under de Valera, which witnessed
a weakening of formal ties and increasing confrontation with Britain. The
impact of the different dynamics of these periods on the experiences of the
ex-servicemen is assessed. The year 1939, with the outbreak of the Second
World War, represents a suitable cut-off point for several reasons. Irish
neutrality led to restrictions on commemoration of the Great War. Perhaps
more pertinent, the numbers of ex-servicemen had diminished (as evidenced
by the rapidly increasing number of widows occupying cottages built by
the Irish Sailors' and Soldiers' Trust for ex-servicemen) and any residual
political influence had disappeared. Equally importantly, the book is centred
on the everyday experiences of ex-servicemen, an area that has been little
researched. To have continued beyond the Second World War would have
meant an increasing focus on commemoration, which in contrast is well
documented. In addition, other factors come into play, for example, the
attitude to those who returned from service in the British Forces after the
Second World War.

The structure of the following chapters reflects the dilemma of the
ex-servicemen. With the formation of the Free State, they were no longer
domiciled in the United Kingdom but the British Government, due to
their service in the Great War, had an obligation to them. Conversely,
they were citizens of the Irish Free State but its formation was not based
on their sacrifice, indeed it was achieved in conflict with the army whose
uniform they had worn, and therefore the new state felt no obligation to
them. Chapters 3 and 4 in Part 2, 'Britain: Legacy of Obligation: 1919–39',
examine the nature of the British obligation, the reasons for it and the
extent to which it was fulfilled in terms of the provision of schemes for
employment, pensions, land and homes, some of which were only applicable
up to the transfer of power to the Free State Government. Chapters 5 and 6
in Part 3, 'Ireland: State and Community: 1922–39', assess the experiences
of the ex-servicemen in the Irish Free State, both in terms of state apparatus
(government, army and the judicial system), and in the community, and in
both contexts address the question as to whether the ex-servicemen were 'a
marginalised and unwelcome group in Irish society', defined predominantly
by war service. The division between the chapters results in some events
being referred to more than once, albeit from differing perspectives. For
example, the provision and management of houses for the ex-servicemen
by the Irish Sailors' and Soldiers' Land Trust is dealt with in Chapter 4 in
relation to the British obligation. The role the Irish Government played in
the disputes between the tenants and the Trust is dealt with in Chapter 5 in

assessing the Irish State's attitude to ex-servicemen. Similarly, the political motives of the Irish Government in establishing a committee to examine the grievances of the ex-servicemen (the Lavery Committee) are considered in Chapter 5; the findings of the committee in terms of the claims against the British Government of unfulfilled obligations are dealt with in Chapters 3 and 4.

Irish Soldiers: Who Were They?

Perhaps an underlying weakness of much research and comment related to ex-servicemen returning from the Great War has been the tendency to refer to them as a homogeneous group. They were not, politically, socially or economically; neither when volunteering nor upon their return, including after the formation of the Free State. War service did not define them and their motives in volunteering did not distinguish them from the general population. Irish service in the British army in the First World War was a continuation of a long tradition; Irish regiments forged close associations with the areas from which they were recruited. In 1914 the British regular army consisted of 200,000 men of which around 10% were of Irish extraction. The soldiers who were recruited in large numbers at the outset of the war were different. They were volunteers, representative of all classes of society, who joined specifically to fight against Germany and its allies and not for a professional career. Fitzpatrick estimates 210,000 soldiers from all Ireland fought in the war, excluding recruits in Britain; 'the greatest deployment of armed manpower in the history of Irish militarism', a figure all the more impressive as conscription was not enforced in Ireland. An estimated 57% of all Irish recruits were Catholic. Fitzpatrick's figures include 58,000 who were mobilised immediately (including 21,000 regulars, 30,000 reservists and 5,000 naval ratings), and a further 144,000 (134,000 army, 6,000 navy and 4,000 air force), who volunteered after initial mobilisation. Several thousand officers not included in the above statistics made up the total. Some estimates, which include those of Irish extraction volunteering in Great Britain, are higher. Callan's estimate of volunteers is similar to Fitzpatrick's; he also breaks the recruitment figures down by time.[17]

17 David Fitzpatrick, 'Militarism in Ireland, 1900–1922', in Thomas Bartlett and Keith Jeffery (eds), *A Military History of Ireland* (Cambridge, 1996), 386–9; Patrick Callan, 'British Recruitment in Ireland, 1914–1918', quoted in Keith Jeffery, *Ireland and the Great War* (Cambridge, 2000), 7. Based on questionable data and assumptions, Harrison calculated 318,000 Irishmen enlisted, 255,000 of these from what became the IFS. See Henry Harrison, *Ireland and the British Empire, 1937* (London, 1937), 20–36.

Table 1: Recruits raised in Ireland per six-month period

Period	Total
4 August 1914 – February 1915	50,107
February 1915 – August 1915	25,235
August 1915 – February 1916	19,801
February 1916 – August 1916	9,323
August 1916 – February 1917	8,178
February 1917 – August 1917	5,609
August 1917 – February 1918	6,550
February 1918 – August 1918	5,812
August 1918 – 11 November 1918	9,845
Total	140,460

Source: Callan in Jeffery, *Ireland and the Great War*.[18]

Table 2: Geographical analysis of army recruits for the area that became the Free State

Province	Male Population	Recruits	% enlisted	Recruits per 10,000 population
Leinster	582,967	48,000	8.23	823
Munster	526,130	17,500	3.33	333
Connaught	312,089	6,500	2.08	208
Ulster (3 counties)	168,323	5,500	3.27	327
Total	1,589,509	77,500	4.88	488

Source: TNA, PIN, 15/757; Population data from Central
Statistics Office (Ireland), 1911 census.[19]

18 War Office figures obtained by the Ministry of Pensions in 1927 show Irish per annum
    recruitment as follows: 1914 (from August): 44,134; 1915: 46,371; 1916: 19,057; 1917:
    14,023, 1918 (until November): 10,617, totalling 134,202. See TNA, PIN 15/757.
19 According to War Office figures, recruitment for all of Ulster was 62,000. Further
    breakdown is only available by recruitment district and only to the end of 1917. The
    three counties that became part of the Free State were in the Omagh and Armagh
    regimental districts and recruitment figures for them are an estimate based on the pro
    rata percentage of male population within each district. See TNA, PIN 15/757.

Over half (75,342) joined in the first year, recruitment falling significantly thereafter.[20] Over half the volunteers were from the area that became the Free State.

Both in absolute terms and as a percentage of the male population, Munster provided significantly more recruits than the other provinces. Within the provinces there were some significant variations. Cork City and County provided 10,106 recruits, 5.17% of the male population, while Clare, Limerick, and Kerry, provided 5,745 recruits, 2.77% of the male population. Dublin City and County provided 24,276 recruits, 10.72% of the male population.[21] Southern Ireland remained predominantly agricultural and as farmers did well out of the war, rural prosperity may have undermined the economic impulse for enlistment.[22] The volunteers came from 'all trades, professions and classes', according to Ernie O'Malley, contrasting with the pre-war regular army in which only 'scapegoats, those in debt or in trouble over a girl had joined the ranks'. Some 500 students and faculty of the predominantly Catholic University College Dublin volunteered. According to British army recruiters, the agricultural and commercial classes were under-represented among the recruits of 1915 as anti-war Sinn Féin propaganda made special headway among farmers' sons and commercial assistants.[23]

Their motives in volunteering did not distinguish the soldiers from the majority of the population. Bryan Cooper in a Dáil Éireann debate in 1927 on the grievances of ex-servicemen said it was not 'enthusiasm for the British Empire' that caused them to enlist.[24] Pašeta argues that the 'rape of Belgium' had a significant impact on the Irish population. She writes, 'war fever swept over Ireland, not only because of the excitement generated by the Home Rule crisis, but also because of a genuine sense of outrage at German actions in Belgium and sympathy for the country's plight'.[25] The Irish Nationalist Party under John Redmond supported the British Government in the hope

20 As did recruitment in Great Britain. See Jeffery, *Ireland and the Great War*, 6.
21 TNA, PIN 15/757. Based on War Office recruitment figures to the end of 1917, but as 1918 recruitment for all Ireland was, according to their figures, only 10,617, the total would not vary significantly; population data from the Central Statistics Office (Ireland), 1926 census assumes recruits from Cork and Dublin counties enlisted in Cork and Dublin cities respectively; Population data from Central Statistics Office (Ireland), 1911 census.
22 Jeffery, *Ireland and the Great War*, 31.
23 Peter Karsten, 'Irish Soldiers in the British Army', *Journal of Social History*, xvii (1983), 34–7 (quoting IRA commander Ernie O'Malley, *Army without Banners* (Boston, 1937), 21).
24 *Dáil Éireann*, Vol. 21, 16 November 1927.
25 Senia Pašeta, 'Thomas Kettle: An Irish Soldier in the Army of Europe', in Adrian Gregory and Senia Pašeta (eds), *Ireland and the Great War: 'A War to Unite Us All?* (Manchester, 2002), 10.

of securing a Dublin parliament, a decision that caused a split in the Irish Volunteers with the majority supporting him.[26] The war was portrayed as the defence of a small country against a barbaric aggressor and the right for Home Rule, causes with which many in southern Ireland could identify. The Kingdom of Great Britain and Ireland was much united in 1914, only a minority of republicans believed Britain was the enemy. But Ireland's commitment and sacrifice were made in exchange for political reward. The Home Rule Bill had received royal ascent. Its implementation delayed during the war, the promise to do so after it ended secured the support of the majority of nationalists. They also realised that not to participate would endanger this goal.[27] In 1920 MacDonagh wrote that most nationalists believed the causes for which the war was fought were morally right.[28] Desmond FitzGerald, future director of publicity for the Dáil Éireann, wrote that extreme nationalists were without influence and impotent; 'Redmond's exhortations that the Irish people should support Britain, really represented the views of the majority of the Irish people'.[29] According to post-war veteran organisations, the vast majority of the population sympathised with the cause for which men volunteered.[30] A republican volunteer in Galway recalled how 'we tried to break up recruitment meetings but got beaten up ourselves as at least 80% of the population were hostile to Sinn Féin for a number of their husbands and sons were in the English army'.[31] Catholic soldiers marched to war with the support of nationalist leaders, the Catholic Church, and their communities. When the Royal Munster Fusiliers left in August 1914 enthusiastic crowds sang 'Rule Britannia'.[32] Many Catholics were recruited into the 10th (Irish) Division and 16th (Irish) Division. Hugh Martin, a correspondent for the *Daily News* who was extremely critical of Britain's post-war Irish policy, wrote that it was the British War Office's distrust of the loyalty of these formations, in contrast to its support for the Protestant 36th (Ulster) Division, that caused the first impulse towards a new nationalism.[33]

   According to Boyce, 'the news of the Easter Rising was greeted by the

---

26 Nuala Johnson, *Ireland, the Great War and the Geography of Remembrance* (Cambridge, 2007), 23. The Volunteers split, with 170,000 supporting Redmond and 11,000 opposing.
27 Catriona Pennell, *A Kingdom United: Popular Responses to the Outbreak of the First World War in Britain and Ireland* (Oxford, 2002), 171,179, 181–2, 195–7, 229–32.
28 Michael MacDonagh, *The Home Rule Movement* (Dublin, 1920), 282.
29 Walsh, *News from Ireland*, 48; *IT*, 13–18 July 1991.
30 TNA, LAB 2/855, IFDDSS to Prime Minister 17 February 1920.
31 *Freeman's Journal*, 26 September 1914.
32 Martin Staunton, 'The Royal Munster Fusiliers in the Great War, 1914–1919' (University College Dublin MA dissertation, 1986), 23.
33 Hugh Martin, *Ireland in Insurrection* (London, 1921), 32–3.

Irish soldiers with a mixture of incredulity and shame'.[34] R.B. Marshall wrote to his mother, 'I am glad the rebels are getting squashed. The Irish regiments out here would like nothing better than to have a go at them with a bayonet'.[35] Jack Chappell wrote that a nationalist friend, Pat, 'feels very grieved for his people whom he feels sure have been incited by German agents'.[36] R. Venables wrote, 'We heard that there was a rebellion in Ireland, and we were having to send soldiers there instead of the war; we thought this was odd, as we were a lot of Irishmen in the firing line'.[37] In Dublin, Ernie O'Malley, later an IRA commander but then a student, and with a brother in the British army, witnessed different reactions. He met two Leinster Regiment officers who 'had followed Redmond; now they thought by promising Irish help without getting a working measure of freedom in exchange, he had failed. No longer did they believe in what they were fighting for but, in honour, felt bound to return to their battalion in France'.[38] Tom Barry, who upon returning from service in the British army was to become one of the most successful IRA commanders, wrote that through the Rising he was 'awakened to Irish Nationality'.[39] Irish soldiers were on duty in Dublin after the Rising. One told a rebel prisoner that 'he couldn't understand why we should start a rebellion until the lads returned from the Dardanelles'.[40] Another said, 'Why didn't you wait till the War was over, and we'd all be with you?'[41] Many Irish soldiers openly expressed sympathy with the rebel's objectives, although some demonstrated no such ambivalence, and many rebels received brutal treatment from their compatriots; one rebel in Kilmainham jail said, 'the Dublin Fusiliers were the worst of the lot'.[42]

Estimates of the number of Irish soldiers who returned home vary as significantly as those of the numbers who fought. The British Ministry of Labour estimated that the number of discharged men in all Ireland in April 1920 exceeded 100,000.[43] Fitzpatrick calculates that, for all Ireland, 100,000 were demobilised between the armistice and May 1920 (when records ceased). Based on his calculation of war dead (27,400), he estimates 75,000 re-enlisted, demobilised elsewhere, or were invalided out of the army before

---

34 Boyce, 'Party Politics Should Divide our Tents', 198.
35 Liddle Collection, University of Leeds, GS1056, R.B. Marshall, letter to mother.
36 Imperial War Museum (IWM), 1674, Lieutenant Colonel Chappell, letter to parents.
37 IWM, 7421, R.L. Venables, 'The Great War 1914–1918', diary entry, 1916, 33.
38 Ernie O'Malley, *On Another Man's Wound* (Dublin, 2002; original edition 1936), 56.
39 Tom Barry, *Guerrilla Days in Ireland* (Tralee, County Kerry, 1971), 8.
40 IMA/BMH, WS850, Colgan, Kildare.
41 IMA/BMH, WS532, MacDonagh, Tipperary.
42 Fearghal McGarry, *The Rising Ireland: Easter 1916* (Oxford, 2010), 255–7; IMA/BMH, WS1758, Burke, Dublin.
43 TNA, LAB, 2/747, MoL internal note, April 1920.

the armistice.[44] Hickie, President of the BLSI, claimed in a Legion meeting in 1924 that 138,623 had returned to the area that became the Free State by the end of 1920, and 20,000 thereafter (with the disbandment of the five southern Irish regiments).[45] He provided estimates of the ex-serviceman population in major towns, which illustrated that they formed a significant portion of the population.

Table 3: Ex-servicemen pro rata to population (1924)

Town	Population	Ex-Servicemen	Percentage
Dublin	304,802	30,000	9.8
Cork	76,673	16,000	20.9
Limerick	38,518	3,800	9.9
Waterford	27,464	3,700	13.5
Galway	12,255	1,216	9.9
Tralee	10,300	2,116	20.5
Athlone	7,472	1,257	16.8
Fermoy	6,863	800	11.7
Enniscorthy	5,495	640	11.6
Ennis	5,472	700	12.8
Nenagh	4,776	985	20.6
Ballina	4,662	900	19.3
Maryboro	3,270	882	27.0
Cavan	2,961	500	16.9
Total	510,983	63,496	12.4

Source: *IT*, 23 September 1924.[46]

44 Fitzpatrick, 'Militarism in Ireland', 392, 397, 501. Myers estimates 35,000 war dead, see Kevin Myers, 'The Irish and the Great War: A Case of Amnesia', in Richard English and Joseph Morrison Skelly (eds), *Ideas Matter: Essays in Honour of Conor Cruise O'Brian* (Dublin, 1988), 103–4. The 49,400 recorded on the National War Memorial at Islandbridge, Dublin includes non-Irish serving in Irish divisions. Based on questionable data and assumptions, Harrison calculates that by 1919, 199,000 soldiers returned to what became the IFS (Harrison, *Ireland and the British Empire*, 26–31).

45 *IT*, 23 September 1924.

46 Dublin, Cork, Galway, and Tralee were four of the seven recruitment centres in southern Ireland. Galway and Tralee were regimental depots for the Connaught Rangers and Royal Munster Fusiliers respectively. The BLSI had perhaps a political interest in exaggerating the number of ex-servicemen (as did Redmond). Borgonovo

In the debate in the Dáil Éireann in November 1927, leading to the formation of a committee to examine ex-servicemen's grievances, William Redmond said there were 150,000 to 200,000 British ex-servicemen who with their dependents accounted for half a million people. In the same debate, Cosgrave referred to '100,000 ex-servicemen in this country'. The concluding report referred to 150,000 ex-servicemen resident in the Free State.[47] It is unlikely that figures in excess of 150,000 were accurate; nearer 100,000 is more likely. Nevertheless, given that the male population of the Free State was 1,506,889 in 1927, the number of ex-servicemen represented a significant portion of the population.[48]

The choices of ex-servicemen upon their return resulted in them taking opposing sides. According to Fitzpatrick, with their knowledge of firearms and tactics, the ex-servicemen possessed military skills demanded by all sides in the violence that engulfed Ireland until 1923. Unemployment, ingratitude for their sacrifice and a desire for the type of comradeship they had known in the trenches may have encouraged them to join the conflict. As Fitzpatrick notes, 'many ex-servicemen easily lowered one flag for another in their quest for income or happiness', and the 'veterans who changed allegiance found no inconsistency in reapplying their obedience and skill to new masters. They relished the military life, but often cared little for the contending rhetoric of patriotism'.[49] Returning soldiers were subject to suspicion from the British authorities; demobilisation centres were located outside of Ireland to avoid weapons being given to the IRA, which they were advised to avoid by their officers.[50] Many returned home disillusioned; the 'political treachery' of England was much cited at meetings of the Irish Nationalists Veterans' Association (INVA).[51] Large numbers refused to take part in parades organised to celebrate the end of the war in protest at the failure of the British Government to make good its promise of Home Rule. Between 2,000 and 3,000 nationalist veterans declined to take part in the Peace Day celebrations in Dublin on 19 July 1919, the INVA having decided to boycott it three days before. Similar reactions occurred elsewhere in southern Ireland.[52] For some, disillusionment produced a more extreme

writes that in 1918, when Cork City had a male population of 38,000, over 5,500 were serving overseas with British Forces. Even allowing for discharged and retired ex-servicemen already in the city, it is difficult to justify the discrepancy between the BLSI figures and those of Borgonova.

47 *Dáil Éireann*, Vol. 21, 16 November 1927; TNA, PIN 15/758, Lavery Report.
48 Population data from Central Statistics Office (Ireland), 1926 census.
49 Fitzpatrick, 'Militarism in Ireland', 397, 401.
50 IMA/BMH, WS1011, Garvey, Kerry.
51 *Irish News*, 22 December 1919, 5, speech by Mary Sheehy, widow of Tom Kettle.
52 *Irish Independent*, July 1919; *Dundalk Democrat*, 19 July 1919, *Evening Herald*, 17 July 1919; Johnson, *Ireland, the Great War and the Geography of Remembrance*, 65.

response. Fitzpatrick writes that 'several hundred Catholic ex-servicemen found military or paramilitary employment after 1919 under a nationalist flag, despite the hostility which their war service often provoked'. He quotes a Colonel O'Callaghan-Westropp, who wrote that the 'great mass' of demobs had been so disgusted by the government's errors that they were 'ready to throw in their lot with the Republicans where they have not done so already'. Fitzpatrick notes that many of the most efficient and reckless IRA men in Clare had gained their experience in the War.[53] Of the 27 members of the north Longford brigade, four had seen service in the Great War.[54] Michael Brennan, an IRA officer in Clare, refers in a personal memoir to 'practically all' the ex-servicemen being Volunteers.[55] Jackson writes, 'service with the British Army appears as a common characteristic of the IRA'.[56] Leonard comments, 'of the hundreds who joined most served as drill and ammunition instructors or as flying columnists'.[57] The witness statements of IRA veterans contained in the Irish Military Archives (IMA/BMH) refer to 109 ex-servicemen serving in the IRA (the figures exclude ex-servicemen identified only by surname or unnamed). They include 24 commanders (almost all on active service), 34 instructors (at least 15 on active service), 42 other Volunteers on active service, and eight intelligence officers.[58] Ex-servicemen who served in leadership positions in the IRA included Ignatius O'Neill, Frank Carney and Tom Barry, who became the most successful commander of the IRA in West Cork. Patrick Garvey from Tralee, County Kerry wrote that at the outbreak of the War many of the Volunteers, including drill instructors, were called up for service as they were in the British army reserves. After the War they returned to train the IRA in the use of arms, with many ex-servicemen co-operating with the IRA.[59] John O'Riordan, also from Tralee, wrote, 'in 1919 our instructors were both ex-British soldiers'. He recounts how Major McKinnon, the Auxiliaries' Commanding Officer, was shot dead on the golf

53 Fitzpatrick, 'Militarism in Ireland', 400; David Fitzpatrick, *Politics and Irish Life, 1913–1921: Provincial Experience of War and Revolution* (Cork, 1998), 169.
54 Marie Coleman, *County Longford and the Irish Revolution, 1910–1923* (Dublin, 2006), 155.
55 Michael Brennan, *The War in Clare 1911–1921: Personal Memoirs of the Irish War of Independence* (Dublin, 1980), 80.
56 Alvin Jackson, *Ireland 1798–1998: Politics and War* (Oxford, 1999), 250.
57 Leonard, 'Survivors', 218.
58 Steven O'Connor, 'Forgotten Soldiers: Ireland's Great War Veterans in the Irish Revolution, 1919–1921', paper presented at the conference of the French Society for Irish Studies, *Ireland: Identity and Interculturality*, Toulouse 1 Capitole University, 21 March 2014. The figures related to the period from January 1919 to December 1921. The breakdown is based on the 109 named in the witness statements plus seven from other sources.
59 IMA/BMH, WS1011, Garvey, Kerry.

course, killed by two bullets through the head by an ex-British army soldier who was a 'crack shot with a rifle'.[60] A local brewer from Kilmallock, County Limerick told English writer Ewart, 'The IRA used to drill under the instructions of ex-soldiers; some of the hottest Sinn Féiners are ex-soldiers'.[61] The veterans added a professionalism that was previously lacking. Augusteijn writes that 'the importance of experience accounts for high numbers of ex-soldiers among the IRA fighting forces.'[62] Others joined the Crown Forces. Fitzpatrick writes that massive recruitment of ex-soldiers into the Royal Irish Constabulary (RIC) was made possible by a long-awaited award of pay rises in 1919; 300 Irishmen, including many war veterans, joined the RIC in the first two months of 1920. With the formation of the Black and Tans, in addition to the 683 men enlisting in Ireland between June 1920 and June 1921 (8% of the total intake), several hundred Irish ex-servicemen probably enlisted in Britain.[63] Similarly, O'Connor has calculated that 1,500 Irish ex-servicemen joined the RIC from January 1919 to December 1921, of whom 166 were Irish ex-officers in the Auxiliary Division. Based on these figures, Irish ex-servicemen represented 10% of the 14,000 recruits to the RIC during the War of Independence.[64] Upon its formation, many joined the National army, which grew to almost 60,000 men around half of whom were ex-servicemen.[65] They fought on behalf of the new state against anti-Treaty republicans and, in helping to create a disciplined and professional force, they were one of the primary reasons for their defeat.

The ex-servicemen were not a homogeneous group, either when volunteering or upon their return. They came from all walks of Irish society and were not exceptional in their loyalty to Britain; the reasons for which many volunteered, to secure home rule and to fight for small nations, reflected popular opinion. They left with the support of their communities. On their return, they often made choices that put them in conflict with each other.

60 IMA/BMH, WS1117, O'Riordan, Kerry.
61 Wilfrid Ewart, *A Journey in Ireland 1921* (London, 1922), 73–4.
62 Joost Augusteijn, *From Public Defiance to Guerrilla Warfare: The Experience of Ordinary Volunteers in the Irish War of Independence* (Dublin, 1996), 97.
63 Fitzpatrick, 'Militarism in Ireland', 399; Fitzpatrick, *Politics and Irish Life*, 20.
64 O'Connor, 'Forgotten Soldiers'.
65 Bryan Cooper, *Dáil Éireann*, Vol. 21, 16 November 1927.

PART I
TIME OF CONFLICT,
1919–23

1

Violence and Intimidation

Most studies of the Irish War of Independence and Civil War have dealt with the extremes of violence, and the ex-servicemen were but a tangential part of broader research. Their geographical focus has generally been Munster and particularly County Cork, the area of greatest violence. Jane Leonard, however, focussed specifically on the experiences of Irish ex-servicemen returning from the Great War. She writes that they 'often experienced hostility and rejection', and were subject to 'extremes of intimidation including beating, mutilation, punishment shooting, prolonged kidnapping, expulsion from Ireland and murder'. She estimates that 'during the period from 1919 to 1924, upwards of 120 ex-servicemen were killed either by the IRA or by the anti-Treaty republican side during the Civil War', and that, although some of these veterans were acting as intelligence agents for the RIC and military forces, 'the vast majority appear to have been killed simply as a retrospective punishment for their service in the Great War'. Leonard concludes that British ex-servicemen 'formed a marginalised and unwelcome group in Irish society'.[1] Commenting on the motives of the IRA in targeting ex-servicemen she writes, 'within the nationalist community ex-soldiers weakened the revolution's effectiveness by refusing to join Sinn Féin, subscribe to its funds, or obey the rulings of its courts; and also by maintaining economic and social contacts with the British administration and its security forces'.[2] Leonard was one of the first academics to conduct research in this area. Her influential article 'Facing the Finger of Scorn', first published in 1997 and much quoted by later researchers, was 'largely based on (28) interviews conducted with Irish ex-servicemen during the 1980s and 1990s'.[3] Although the oral interviews were an important historical contribution, as they represented one of the last opportunities to record the

---

1 Leonard, 'Finger of Scorn', 93, 95; Leonard, 'Survivors', 218.
2 Jane Leonard, 'Getting Them at Last: The I.R.A. and Ex-servicemen', in David Fitzpatrick (ed.), *Revolution? Ireland, 1917–1923* (Dublin, 1990), 119.
3 Leonard, 'Facing the Finger of Scorn', 88.

comments of some of the ex-servicemen, there is a risk in generalising from
such a limited sample. To support her argument, Leonard referred to a case
in the Irish Grants Committee (IGC) files and wrote, 'Michael Shannon,
a former tailor in (Ennistymon) County Clare found that he "was never
insulted until I returned from the War" and as "an ex-soldier I was not
wanted anywhere."'[4] In fact, the IGC declined his claim as it did not feel
he had provided 'full and acceptable proof'. The Committee investigated 79
cases from Ennistymon and Lahinch in County Clare and found them to be
bogus and for the most part made by republican supporters.[5] It noted, 'these
cases in Ennistymon are almost impossible to investigate; confirmatory
evidence can be obtained in that town for a few shillings'.[6] An unusually high
number of claimants from Ennistymon claimed that they were intimidated
because of their army service.

   Augusteijn argues that the IRA acted only against civilians when they
endangered their operations:

> Only those who openly showed sympathy for the Crown Forces were
> targeted. This was limited to women who associated with soldiers or
> policemen, and to persons who associated with soldiers or policemen,
> and to persons who were clearly friendly towards them. The police
> acknowledged that all civilians shot in Wexford had been overtly
> friendly to the Crown Forces; some of them had even joined in raids
> on Republicans.

The IRA considered civilian spies the most dangerous of all as they were
often locals well acquainted with the IRA men, and the need to cut off
sources of intelligence meant any civilian suspected of collaboration was
likely to be targeted. Augusteijn writes, 'A number of ex-soldiers who
publicly mixed with the Crown Forces were shot. Their previous service to
the Crown and continued association made them prime targets with a high
symbolic value'. But the IRA was prepared to target any they presumed
to have informed. An elderly woman was tied to a lamppost with a note,
'Long tongues beware'. Women had their hair shorn, others had their
property destroyed or were told to leave. A few in Cork were even executed.[7]
Fedorowich writes, 'even associating with serving soldiers and police, or
having a family member in the British army or the RIC, was enough for
the IRA to send threatening letters warning ex-servicemen that reprisals

4 Leonard, 'Facing the Finger of Scorn', 94, quoting from TNA, CO, 762/96/6.
5 TNA, CO, 762/2/Admin.
6 TNA, CO, 762/86/5.
7 Augusteijn, *From Public Defiance to Guerrilla Warfare*, 291–3, 314–5.

would be taken if such contact continued'.[8] In Wexford seven attempts to kill ex-soldiers who had maintained contact with the Crown Forces were recorded by the police between January and April 1921. Similar attacks took place in Tipperary, where eight civilians, mostly ex-soldiers, were killed.[9] Jack Moyney, a Victoria Cross winner, avoided the company of local British servicemen in case he was suspected of providing information.[10] Although both Augusteijn and Fedorowich recognise the risks for ex-servicemen in associating with the Crown Forces, they reach different conclusions as to whether they were exposed to intimidation as a group. Fedorowich writes:

> Like their colleagues in the RIC, ex-servicemen too were boycotted, ostracized and relentlessly targeted by Sinn Féin and the IRA. This was by no means a new phenomenon. Within republican circles there had been an abiding intolerance and resentment of Irishmen who had joined the British armed forces well before World War I. The real difference after 1918, however, was the intensity and ruthlessness of the nationalist campaign, coupled with the high number of ex-service casualties.

Fedorowich acknowledges that there were regional variations: 'The tactics employed against Irish veterans and the intensity of the campaign directed against them varied depending upon the region, as it had with the RIC'.[11]

Hart, in his comprehensive study of County Cork, where the propensity to violence was highest, argues that a 'tit for tat' dynamic of escalating conflict was driven by fear and a desire for revenge.[12] Augusteijn agrees that the execution of captured volunteers and the victimisation of their families caused 'a sharp increase in the attempted killing of members of the Crown Forces as well as civilians who were considered hostile, such as Protestants and ex-soldiers'.[13] Hart writes that much of the violence, of which the war on informers was a part, was based on preconfigured communal animosities related to class, sectarianism and other stereotypes, and that beneath the welter of suspicions and accusations of betrayal, the IRA were 'tapping a

---

8 Kent Fedorowich, 'Reconstruction and Resettlement: The Politicisation of Irish Migration to Australia and Canada, 1919–1929', *English Historical Review*, 114 (1999), 1153.

9 Augusteijn, *From Public Defiance to Guerrilla Warfare*, 182–3; TNA, CO, 904, 151–156, County Inspector of the RIC. Wexford, Monthly Confidential Report 1921; County Inspector of the RIC, South Tipperary, Monthly Confidential Report, 1921.

10 Leonard, 'Facing the Finger of Scorn', 95.

11 Fedorowich, 'Reconstruction and Resettlement', 1152.

12 Peter Hart, *The IRA and its Enemies: Violence and Community in Cork, 1916–1923* (Oxford, 1998), 314.

13 Augusteijn, *From Public Defiance to Guerrilla Warfare*, 242.

deep vein of communal prejudice and gossip' against categories of people of whom such talk was normally confined behind closed doors but which the revolution took into the streets. The IRA saw their enemy as 'types' including 'ex-servicemen, Orangemen, freemasons, tramps, fast women; people who were perceived as falling into such categories were the most likely to be denounced as informers or enemies of the republic and shot, burned out, or intimidated'. Hart argues that informers could be broken into three categories: suspects, informers and victims, and that there was little overlap. That is, those suspected were generally innocent but not usually attacked, the majority of those who informed were never suspected or shot, and those actually punished mostly never informed. In the latter category fell Protestants, ex-soldiers and 'tinkers'. They were killed for who they were not for what they did, in a persecution that went beyond a hunt for informers. Hart claims that Volunteers and respectable Catholics were most likely to give information but the least likely to be punished, whereas Protestants made up the majority of victims but, despite being supposedly loyal to the Crown, did not inform, perhaps out of fear of retribution. Hart calculated that Protestants represented 36% of the victims in County Cork and Catholic ex-servicemen 25%. He also quotes an IRA West Cork report which said that Protestants made up 64% of the victims and ex-servicemen 15%. He argues that Protestants were targeted for being landlords and loyalists even more than ex-servicemen; violence based on historical sectarian animosities caused its population to almost halve by 1922 from pre-war levels. Hart claims that soldiers and their families were harassed upon their return, precluded from employment and, as the conflict escalated, became subject to death threats. He concludes that IRA officers 'routinely insisted that those executed were proven, convicted traitors', though in reality they acted on their own suspicions and without any evidence other than the opinion that the suspect was not for the IRA and of the wrong type.[14]

Borgonovo, who conducted a study of violence in Cork City, questions Leonard's assertion that ex-soldiers were executed because of their previous military service and that they represented a 'soft target' as a comparatively unprotected symbol of British rule, when the superiorly equipped and trained Crown Forces became increasingly difficult to attack. There was a significant body of ex-soldiers in the city, including ex-officers, who had high profiles in society but were left unmolested. This also brings into question Augusteijn's assertion that killing ex-servicemen had a high symbolic value for, if that were the case, high-profile ex-officers would

---

14 Hart, *The IRA and its Enemies*, 291, 300–15; Peter Hart, *The IRA at War 1916–1923* (Oxford, 2003), 136. Leonard agrees that many of the confirmed spies came from within the IRA itself, see Leonard, 'Getting Them at Last', 129.

have been targeted. Borgonovo also contradicts Hart's conclusions, arguing instead that there was little indication that the IRA deliberately targeted ex-soldiers or Protestant unionists as part of a general terror campaign, or as reprisals for republican defeats. Meehan concurs, asserting that Hart refused to accept the possibility that IRA executions had a military connotation as it undermined his theory that their actions were motivated by sectarianism. Meehan also refutes that ex-servicemen were targeted as a group as many had joined the IRA. He writes:

> For Hart, Protestants and ex-servicemen in the South performed the equivalent function of Catholics in the North of Ireland. They were, reported Hart, potential targets because of who they were, rather than what they did. For his theory to have weight, it had to be shown that any Protestants or ex-service personnel killed by the IRA in the course of the conflict were not active combatants. This he failed to do.

Meehan's comments have to be viewed in context. He writes on behalf of the Aubane Historical Society, which opposes what it perceives as revisionism of republican historiography. Republicans have refuted that the IRA targeted particular segments of the population or that executions were carried out for other than military purposes. Hart's assertion that the Bandon massacre in April 1922, in which most of the victims were Protestant, was carried out by the IRA and motivated by sectarianism, drew a virulent response from republican historians, who questioned his use of sources. Murphy criticises 'modern revisionism' as being ideologically led in exaggerating the Catholic sectarian component of separatist nationalism and attributing to it anti-Protestant and Anglophobic values. Republican historians therefore tend to question any proposition that the IRA targeted victims on the grounds of social status, religion or indeed anything other than military necessity. Borgonovo argues that when reprisals occurred there were reasons besides just associating with the Crown Forces. Of the 26 ex-servicemen targeted by the IRA, nine had associations with the Crown Forces and five worked for them. This employment alone would not have earned their execution; scores of other ex-servicemen worked for the British authorities. Borgonovo thinks that the likely explanation is that 'the Volunteers believed their victims were guilty of spying'. Unlike Hart, he asserts that the IRA had the means to identify their civilian enemies and was not just acting without evidence. The IRA identified an 'anti Sinn Féin Society' in September 1920 and in the following months gathered evidence before retaliating against those they believed to be spies in February 1921. Borgonovo writes that given the strength of their well-organised intelligence network, the IRA were probably mostly right about who had informed.[15]

One of the reasons for these differing views is that Borgonovo, Leonard and Hart disagree with regard to the relationship between the ex-servicemen and both the general population and the IRA. Leonard writes that ex-soldiers were refused admission to technical colleges, hospitals, and asylums in local authorities controlled by Sinn Féin, while officials and clubrooms of the two main veteran organisations, the Comrades of the Great War and the Federation of Discharged and Demobilised Sailors and Soldiers, frequently came under attack from the IRA.[16] In contrast, Borgonovo claims there was no antagonism between the Irish Federation of Demobilised Soldiers and Sailors and the IRA in Cork, rather the opposite. The IRA did not interfere in displays of ex-servicemen's solidarity and the Federation condemned the death of two republican mayors, one shot, the other as a result of a hunger strike, and its members marched in both funeral processions. This is unsurprising given that according to Meehan, the secretary of the Federation was an IRA commander. Borgonovo claims in contrast that ill will existed between the ex-servicemen and the Crown Forces. When an ex-soldier named Burke was killed by an army patrol in July 1920, ex-servicemen brawled with off duty soldiers for two days and 5,000 ex-servicemen attended Burke's funeral.[17] Leonard writes, 'ex-servicemen, by virtue of long absence on military service and the altered cultural and political identities that years of foreign service with the British army tended to have forged, were no longer part of the communities to which they returned on demobilisation'. This, she argues, made them inefficient as spies; isolated, 'shunned in their

15 John Borgonovo, *Spies, Informers and the 'Anti-Sinn Féin Society': The Intelligence War in Cork City, 1920–1921* (Dublin, 1996), 75–83, 172–80; Niall Meehan, *Troubles in Irish History: A 10th Anniversary Critique of Peter Hart's The IRA and its Enemies* (Aubane Historical Society, 2008). Meehan also writes that Borgonovo's book, based on a 1997 MA dissertation for UCC, was gathering dust until the Aubane Historical Society suggested that it be published (6, 9, 16–18); John Regan, 'The "Bandon Valley Massacre" as a Historical Problem', *History*, 97/325 (2012), 70–2, quoting Brian Murphy. Hart also incurred the ire of republican historians by questioning Tom Barry's account of his ambush of British Forces at Kilmichael in November 1920, claiming Barry had carried out executions after they surrendered, see Niall Meehan, 'Distorting Irish History', *Spinwatch* (November 2010) and the response, Eve Morrison, 'Kilmichael Revisited', in David Fitzpatrick (ed.), *Terror in Ireland, 1916–1923* (Dublin, 2012), 158–80, defending Hart's work after his death in 2010.

16 Leonard, 'Survivors', 215. Both veteran associations became part of the British Legion upon its formation, which may have reflected its political orientation.

17 Borgonovo, *Spies, Informers*, 79–83. Borgonovo writes that even ex-soldiers were killed by British Forces in Cork in 1920–21, noting ironically that this did not imply a general campaign against all ex-soldiers. See also Meehan, *Troubles in Irish History*, 18.

localities or house-bound by virtue of their war injuries'.[18] Hart argues that the long-established stereotype of the ex-soldier as a corner boy and drunk counted against them, particularly as many were unemployed.[19] In contrast, Borgonovo writes there was 'little indication of open hostility in Cork City between Volunteers and ex-servicemen in 1920–1', and that they 'were engrained in the city's social fabric' and many ex-servicemen were intimate with local IRA Volunteers.[20] Boyce states that, although ex-servicemen on occasion suffered at the hands of both the Black and Tans and the IRA, they were not generally subjected to vendettas.[21]

Local historians with deep knowledge of their communities, some of whom were interviewed as part of this research, also provide a different perspective to those of Leonard and Hart. Donal Hall argues that in County Louth Great War volunteers were mostly urban, recruitment had been considerably lower in rural areas and therefore almost every town or village was touched by the war, generating sympathy for those who returned. He writes,

> it is now part of the historical canon that these soldiers were subjected to a campaign of victimisation and murder. In truth, there is not much evidence of this in County Louth and the overwhelming majority of soldiers returned quietly to their homes ... There is no evidence that veterans were intimidated or victimised in County Louth because of their services in the forces. There is no evidence of beatings or mutilations, or that veterans became a marginalised group in society.[22]

Henry said that in Galway there was no widespread condemnation of the returning soldiers; with the economy entering recession, the priority was to earn a living.[23] Similarly, in his study of East Galway McNamara writes, 'there was little hostility towards ex-servicemen in the towns and their sacrifice was acknowledged by both the local government and the community'. Galway Urban Council supported ex-servicemen in terms of employment opportunities and housing. McNamara argues that the IRA's

18 Leonard, 'Getting Them at Last', 127–9.
19 Hart, *The IRA and its Enemies*, 312.
20 Borgonovo, *Spies, Informers*, 81, 83, 91. Borgonovo does point out that some of the ex-servicemen victims were impoverished and of low social standing.
21 Boyce, 'Party Politics Should Divide our Tents', 201; Harrison, *Ireland and the British Empire*, 30.
22 Donal Hall, *The Unreturned Army: County Louth Dead in the Great War, 1914–1918* (Dundalk, 2005), 15, 24–5; Donal Hall, *World War One and Nationalists Politics in County Louth: 1914–1920* (Dublin, 2005), 48.
23 Interview with William Henry, Galway, 3 August 2008. Henry is the author of *Galway and the Great War* (Cork, 2007).

activities were almost exclusively rural but that even in the countryside, 'being an ex-serviceman did not single someone out as a target for the IRA – unless they were known to associate with the Crown Forces and believed to be passing information', but 'they were not disproportionately targeted as a group'.[24] O'Callaghan writes that Hart's assertion that most of those executed were innocent did not apply in Limerick, and that although a disproportionate number of ex-servicemen were killed as spies, five out of seven, the weight of evidence in the majority of cases supports IRA veterans' claims that they were informers. He also asserts that there was no link between executions of ex-servicemen and the periods when the Crown Forces were under pressure, as argued by Leonard.[25]

There are varying estimates of the number of ex-servicemen killed in the conflict by the IRA. Leonard estimates in 'Facing the Finger of Scorn' that upwards of 120 were killed between 1919 and 1924. In an earlier article she wrote that at least 82 ex-servicemen were murdered prior to the Truce of July 1921, but that these statistics only included men whose military service (in the Great War or the Boer War) was considered a major factor in their murder; ex-servicemen who joined or re-joined the RIC on demobilisation were excluded. She notes that of 150 ex-servicemen killed by the IRA between 1 January 1920 and 1 April 1921, 80 were regular RIC men and 30 were members of the Auxiliary Division. Only 40 of them were civilians. She writes that no ex-servicemen were killed in 1919 and only 9 in 1920.[26] The final stages of the War of Independence were the most vicious, with the majority of victims being killed in 1921 up to the period ending with the Truce. British Government figures state that 73 civilians were killed by the IRA between January and April 1921, of whom 21 were ex-service men.[27] Borgonovo considers Hart's figures for violence to be inflated. The latter estimates that there were 131 victims of IRA shootings in Cork City in the months following November 1920, whereas Borgonovo calculates that in 1920–1 the IRA attempted to kill 33 suspected informers, of whom 26 were civilian, and in terms of ex-servicemen 26 were shot as suspected spies, of whom 19 died.[28] O'Halpin, in the most comprehensive study of fatalities, writes that between 1919 and 1921, 420 ex-servicemen were killed in all Ireland, constituting 19.6% of all deaths. Of these, 227 (54%) were serving policemen, and as such O'Halpin notes that their fate cannot be

24 Conor McNamara, 'Politics and Society in East Galway, 1914–21' (St. Patrick's College, Dublin Ph.D. thesis, 2009), 193–6, 226, 228.

25 John O'Callaghan, *Revolutionary Limerick: The Republican Campaign for Independence in Limerick 1913–1921* (Dublin, 2010), 174, 182.

26 Leonard, 'Facing the Finger of Scorn', 95; Leonard, 'Getting Them at Last', 118–21.

27 *Hansard*, HC Deb 21 April 1921, Vol. 140 c2086W.

28 Borgonovo, *Spies, Informers*, 75, 83.

ascribed to previous military service. Of the remaining 193, 16 (4%) died as IRA men, leaving 177 who were civilians. Of these, the Crown forces killed 46 (26%) and the IRA 99 (56%) and in another 32 cases, including 13 in Antrim, Northern Ireland, it is impossible to determine responsibility. The figures include pre-Great War veterans.[29] Of the ex-servicemen killed by the IRA, 85 were shot as spies, all in the 26 counties that became the Free State, representing 46.4% of all executed 183 civilian spies. Spying was the predominant reason for IRA killing of civilians; out of 277 such casualties, 66% were spies.[30] Although a high percentage of O'Halpin's estimate of civilian spies were ex-servicemen, they may not have been perceived as such by the IRA in all cases. He refers to Godfrey Jasper, who was both an ex-serviceman and ex-policeman. The Irish Military Archives/Bureau of Military History (IMA/BMH) witness statements related to his execution only mention that he was a Black and Tan; there is no reference to his being an ex-serviceman.[31] In the absence of RIC reports (and due to the fact that the IMA/BMH witness statements only cover the period to July 1921), there are no comprehensive statistics for those ex-servicemen killed during the Civil War. Leonard writes that at least nine were killed in the five months after the Treaty and a further four kidnapped, believed to have perished.[32] Hart writes that IRA antagonism to certain 'types' continued into the Civil War; in Cork 20% of civilians shot by the rebels after July 1921 were ex-soldiers, while 44% were Protestant.[33]

The analysis of the secondary literature indicates a number of contradictions. Some researchers, including Leonard, Hart, and Fedorowich, conclude that ex-servicemen were specifically intimidated, while others, including Augusteijn, Meehan, and Borgonovo, argue that they were intimidated for reasons other than war service *per se*, the latter further asserting that the ex-servicemen readily re-integrated back into society.

---

29 Eunan O'Halpin, 'Counting Terror: Bloody Sunday and the Dead of the Irish Revolution', in David Fitzpatrick (ed.), *Terror in Ireland, 1916–1923* (Dublin, 2012), 152–5.

30 O'Halpin, 'Problematic Killings during the War of Independence and its Aftermath', in James Kelly and Mary Ann Lyons (eds), *Death and Dying in Ireland, Britain and Europe, Historical Perspectives* (Dublin, 2013), 328–9 (figures based on table, some other figures within the article vary slightly). O'Halpin refers once to the 85, including ex-policeman but elsewhere in the article and in the tables he only mentions ex-servicemen in relation to this figure; there are some minor changes to O'Halpin's figures from his earlier 'The Dead of the Irish Revolution' article. O'Halpin writes there is the possibility of total fatalities being higher, not all the dead may have been accounted for, 341–3.

31 O'Halpin, 'Problematic Killings', 322; IMA/BMH, WS1413, Kennedy, Kerry; IMA/BMH, WS1205 Mc Kenna, Kerry.

32 Leonard, 'Getting Them at Last', 121.

33 Hart, *The IRA and its Enemies*, 314.

Although these contradictions are partly explained by new sources, not available at the time to earlier researchers, such as the IMA/BMH files, they predominantly reflect different attitudes towards the ex-servicemen, their role in society and whether they can be considered a homogenous group, targeted by the IRA simply because of their war service.

Records of the Perpetrators

The Irish Military Archives, Bureau of Military History (IMA/BMH) files contain republicans' recollections of their experiences during the period from 1913 to July 1921 and represent the perspective of the perpetrators. The 1,773 witness statements contain many examples of non-ex-servicemen being victims of intimidation but refer to only 50 ex-servicemen in such a context (in comparison, the files contain the names of more than double that number of ex-servicemen who served in the IRA).[34] Of the 50 cases, 40 men were intimidated for suspected spying; 33 ex-servicemen were executed and seven others escaped or disappeared from view, some after being shot. Most of the executions took place in 1921 prior to the Truce in the period when the Tans and Auxiliaries were most active.

Table 4: Suspected spies targeted by the IRA

Executed

Name	Location	Date Killed
Halpin	Clontarf, Dublin	c. June 1921
Robert Pike	Drumcondra, Dublin	June 1921
'Chanters' Ryan	Dublin	Pre Truce 1921

34 The 50 ex-servicemen are referred to in around 65 witness statements, several of which refer to the same incident. The files are not a comprehensive record of all intimidation. RIC reports, for example in TNA, CO 904/114, contain further details on ex-servicemen targeted by the IRA. The extracts from the IMA/BMH Witness Statements used in this section represent the comments of the relevant IRA members whose names are contained in the related footnote. As illustrated in the Maher case, other sources may provide a different perspective. In addition to the case studies referred to here, there are some references in the files to unnamed ex-servicemen who were targeted but little substantive information is given. There were also some cases of ex-servicemen under suspicion of informing but not subject to violence due to lack of evidence; some details are provided in this section. The figures refer to victims who were identified as ex-servicemen e.g. David Walsh was an ex-serviceman killed as a spy. He is referred to in IMA/BMH, WS1009, and WS1065, but no mention is made of his war service and he is therefore excluded from this analysis. See O'Halpin, 'Problematic Killings', 326.

Executed Name	Location	Date Killed
Jack Straw (Hemstraw)	Fingal, Dublin	October 1920.
Martin Darmody	Kilmanagh, Callan, County Kilkenny	May 1921
Michael Keefe	Kilmanagh, Callan, County Kilkenny	May 1921
Kenny	Graiguenamanagh, County Kilkenny	August 1920
John Donaogue	Dunshaughlin, County Meath	Spring 1920 to pre Truce 1921
Blagriff,	Athlone, County Westmeath.	January/February 1921
Maher	Athlone, County Westmeath	Winter 1920/21 (estimated)
Jimmy Morrissey	Marshalstown, County Wexford	Summer 1920
John O'Reilly	Newmarket, County Clare	April 1921
Begley	Cork City, County Cork	June 1920 to pre Truce 1921
Denis Dwyer	Bandon, County Cork	January 1921
Crowley	County Cork	July 1920
O'Sullivan	Cork City, County Cork	c. September 1920
Major O'Connor	Cork City, County Cork	February 1921
Finbar O'Sullivan	Cork City, County Cork	February 1921
William O'Sullivan	Cork City, County Cork	February 1921
T. O'Sullivan	Cork City, County Cork	Early 1921
McPherson	Mallow, County Cork	July 1921
Lt Colonel Peacock	Innishannon, County Cork	June 1921 (shot, presumed dead)
Michael Walsh	Cork City, County Cork	February 1921
John Quinlisk	Cork City, County Cork	February 1920
John Fitzgerald	Tralee, County Kerry	June 1921
Paddy Foley	Castlegregory, County Kerry	Post summer 1920

Executed		
Name	Location	Date Killed
Denis O'Loughlin	Tralee, County Kerry	April 1921
John O'Mahony	Tralee, County Kerry	April 1921
Jack Maloney	Bruff, County Limerick.	Spring 1921
Thomas Kirby	Dundrum, County Tipperary	January 1921
James Maher	Thurles, County Tipperary	March 1921
Patrick Meara	Thurles, County Tipperary	March 1921
Unnamed	County Roscommon	Winter 1920

Not Executed		
Name	Location	Shot/escaped
Patrick Duke	Dunshaughlin, County Meath	Escaped but returned after conflict
S. Flynn	Cork City, County Cork	Escaped early 1921
Hamill	Cork City, County Cork	Shot June 1920/pre Truce 1921, recovered, left Ireland
Hawkins	Cork City, County Cork	Shot June 1920/pre Truce 1921, recovered, left Ireland
D. (Monkey) McDonnell	Cork City, County Cork	Thought to have left Ireland in 1921
Shiels	Kanturk, County Cork	Escaped c. March 1921
Thomas Hanly	Newcastlewest, County Limerick	Shot June 1921 but survived

Source: IMA/BMH, WS1-1773 (analysis of).

Of the 40 spying incidents, 27 took place in Munster and 17 in County Cork. In terms of population, Munster had more than 2.5 times the number of killings/ex-servicemen targeted per 10,000 than Leinster.

Table 5: Ex-servicemen killed/targeted as spies pro rata to population

County	Population	Incidents	Incidents per 10,000	% of Total
Carlow	34,476	0	0.00	0.0
Dublin	505,654	4	0.08	10.0
Kildare	58,028	0	0.00	0.0
Kilkenny	70,990	3	0.42	7.5
Longford	39,847	0	0.00	0.0
Louth	62,739	0	0.00	0.0
Meath	62,969	2	0.32	5.0
Kings	52,592	0	0.00	0.0
Queens	51,540	0	0.00	0.0
Westmeath	56,818	2	0.35	5.0
Wexford	95,848	1	0.10	2.5
Wicklow	57,591	0	0.00	0.0
Leinster	**1,149,092**	**12**	**0.10**	**30.0**
Clare	95,064	1	0.11	2.5
Cork	365,747	17	0.46	42.5
Kerry	149,171	4	0.27	10.0
Limerick	140,343	2	0.14	5.0
Tipperary	141,015	3	0.21	7.5
Waterford	78,562	0	0.00	0.0
Munster	**969,902**	**27**	**0.28**	**67.5**
Galway	169,366	0	0.00	0.0
Leitrim	55,907	0	0.00	0.0
Mayo	172,690	0	0.00	0.0
Roscommon	83,556	1	0.12	2.5
Sligo	71,388	0	0.00	0.0
Connaught	552,907	1	0.02	2.5
Cavan	82,452	0	0.00	0.0
Donegal	152,508	0	0.00	0.0
Monaghan	65,131	0	0.00	0.0
Ulster (3 counties)	**300,091**	**0**	**0.00**	**0.0**
Total	2,971,992	40	0.13	100.0

Source: IMA/BMH, WS1-1773 (analysis of); Population data from Central Statistics Office (Ireland), 1926 census.

If the number of ex-servicemen (based on recruitment figures) is taken into account, then there were 2.5 killings/ex-servicemen targeted for every 10,000 ex-servicemen in Leinster, and 15.43 in Munster.

Of the ten ex-servicemen involved in incidents not related to spying, seven were subject to firearm raids, one refused to resign as a Justice of the Peace (JP), one refused to make a contribution to a levy and one was executed for murder. In each case the victims were not specifically targeted because of their war service; with the exception of the incident related to murder, they were part of general campaigns by the IRA to collect much-needed arms and money, and to dismantle the British judiciary system and replace it with a republican alternative. They took place in the period 1919/20 before the escalation of the conflict with the arrival of the Tans. By July 1920 all British appointed JPs in Graiguenamanagh, County Kilkenny had resigned, except for Captain Howlett. He was arrested as he was 'likely to assist the enemy', and taken before a Sinn Féin court. Michael O'Carroll, a local IRA officer, wrote that Howlett defended himself in 'one of the finest speeches it has ever been my lot to listen to'. He was acquitted as the witnesses had failed to prove their case against him, but he agreed to resign as a JP.[35]

The IRA was desperately short of weapons. In autumn 1920 general headquarters ordered a raid across the country for arms; inevitably this included the big houses of the Ascendancy class and homes of RIC officers and retired British army officers, the latter proving a valuable source of revolvers.[36] One such raid was carried out on the property of Captain Clarke, who lived just outside Cork City and was holding a shooting party. Clarke proved threatening and was shot in the hand. Sean O'Connell, a quarter-master in Cork City who led the incursion, bandaged Clarke's arm and then left with a number of guns. He wrote that this was the only occasion it had been necessary to use a weapon on such a raid.[37] The incident does not evidence any general animosity towards ex-servicemen. In late 1919, a levy was made on property owners in County Westmeath to raise money for arms based on a valuation of their property. All paid 'willingly' except Colonel King-Harmon of Athlone. He was visited by two IRA members and paid under threat. As they left, the colonel told them, 'There is no hope of your beating the British Empire'.[38] In Bandon, County Cork in winter 1920/21,

35 IMA/BMH, WS966, Walsh, Kilkenny; WS1609, O'Carroll, Kilkenny.
36 IMA/BMH, WS1454, Leahy, Tipperary; WS1296, Costello, Westmeath; WS1708, Barry, Cork; WS1503, McCormack, Westmeath; WS894, Deignan, Sligo.
37 IMA/BMH, WS1706, O'Connell, City; The IRA witnesses for the other named victims were: Hope Nelson (WS742, Halpin, Tipperary); Colonel Hickey (WS996, Carmody, Kerry); Hope Wilson (WS1350, Davin, Tipperary); and Major Gubbins (WS1631, Meaney, Cork).
38 IMA/BMH, WS1500, McCormack, Westmeath.

cattle and other goods were seized from retired British officers and other loyalists who had refused to subscribe to the arms levy fund.[39]

Table 6: Other offences

Name	Location	Incident	Date
Captain Howlett	Graiguenamanagh, County Kilkenny	Forced to resign as JP	August 1920
Colonel King-Harmon	Athlone, County Westmeath	Refused to pay IRA levy	Late 1919
Captain Clarke	Cork City, County Cork	Raided/firearms stolen	Early 1919
Major Gubbins	County Cork	Raided/firearms stolen	1920
Hope Nelson	County Tipperary	Raided/firearms stolen	1919
Hope Wilson	County Tipperary	Raided/firearms stolen	Winter 1918
Colonel Hickey	County Kerry	Raided/firearms stolen	1919
Unnamed	County Galway	Raided/firearms stolen	1919
Unnamed	County Sligo	Raided/firearms stolen	1920
William Gordon	County Meath	Murder	June 1920

Source: IMA/BMH, WS1-1773 (analysis of).

The witness statements indicate there were two periods of the Anglo-Irish War, divided by the arrival of the Black and Tans. Michael McCormack, an officer from County Westmeath, wrote that police work was the principal occupation of the Volunteers during 1919 and the first half of 1920.[40] Thomas Costello, an IRA officer from Athlone, County Westmeath, wrote that from early 1920, when the RIC started to withdraw from their smaller stations, to the arrival of the Tans, the IRA took over the function of policing and the courts. He claimed that when the RIC initially withdrew, 'unruly elements' made capital out of the situation, but this was stopped as the republicans took control and sought, 'to demonstrate to people of all shades of political thought that we could maintain discipline and order'.[41] The republican courts started sitting in Kilkenny in June 1920. One of the first cases related to the theft of jewellery and other valuables from Major

39 IMA/BMH, WS1591, Russell, Cork.
40 IMA/BMH, WS1503, McCormack, Westmeath.
41 IMA/BMH, WS1296, Costello, Westmeath.

Humphrey and Major Joyce, two ex-British army officers. They reported their loss to the RIC without result. They then reported it to someone with a Sinn Féin connection and the republican police became involved, found the culprits, and returned the stolen property. Thomas Treacy, a brigade commander in Kilkenny, wrote that the majors, both of whom were Unionists, expressed their appreciation of the republican police, and one visited the RIC to castigate them for their hopelessness. Treacy used this to illustrate that republican justice was even handed.[42] Costello claimed that the country was law abiding up to the arrival of the Tans and the Auxiliaries, when it became impossible to maintain police work and deal with robbers and murderers, both official and unofficial.[43] One of the few examples of an execution for an offence other than spying involved an ex-serviceman, William Gordon, who was accused of murdering a young farmer named Clinton, a Volunteer, in a land dispute. Gordon received the sum of £2 for the shooting from William Rogers, a former South African policeman, who intended to seize the land. After a 'mock trial' by the British authorities, who had arrested him first, he was found not guilty and released. He was later arrested by the IRA, tried, sentenced to death, and executed in June 1920. The RIC concluded that Gordon's killing arose from an agrarian crime. It was unrelated to his war service.[44]

The arrival of the Tans from March 1920 resulted in a change in the activities of the IRA and a significant escalation in the violence. Unlike the RIC, the Tans were generally unfamiliar with the area in which they operated. John Walsh, a battalion commander in County Kilkenny, wrote that without local knowledge the British Crown Forces would be powerless.[45] Robert Ahern, an intelligence officer in Cork City, wrote, 'civilian spies were considered the most dangerous of all. They were well acquainted with the IRA men in the different localities in which they operated, being natives of the district in certain cases, and unless they were quickly and severely dealt with would create havoc in our organisation'.[46] The IRA believed that there were organised spying groups working against them. William Foley, an IRA officer from Bandon, County Cork, wrote that in 1918, 'the loyalist section of the population formed an organisation known as the anti-Sinn Féin League, and were active in organising intelligence for the British'.[47] William Barry, an IRA officer in Cork City, said an organisation run by

42 IMA/BMH, WS1093, Treacy, Kilkenny.
43 IMA/BMH, WS1296, Costello, Westmeath.
44 IMA/BMH, WS1625, Govern, Meath; WS 1715, Boylan, Meath; O'Halpin, 'Problematic Killings', 324–5.
45 IMA/BMH, WS966, Walsh, Kilkenny.
46 IMA/BMH, WS1676, Ahern, Cork.
47 IMA/BMH, WS1560, Foley, Cork.

the Freemasons and the YMCA had been established to spy on the IRA.[48] Michael Murphy, a commander from Cork City, wrote that the YMCA was a Protestant organisation that had within it two sections, senior and junior, who informed on the IRA.[49] The IRA was also aware of traitors within its own ranks. T. Crawley, an officer in the South Roscommon brigade, wrote, 'we were damned right from the start by having traitors and agents amongst us, even the intelligence officer worked for the British'.[50]

Many of the 40 ex-servicemen accused of informing were local men who knew who within the community were members of the IRA and where they lived. A number had close associations with the Crown Forces. Paddy Foley was related to most of the Volunteer officers in his neighbourhood and provided the RIC with a notebook of all their names. Under suspicion, he had been advised to leave but was arrested having failed to do so, tried and executed, the sentence passed outside the area because of his family connections.[51] In July 1920, a British regiment stationed in Graiguenamanagh, County Kilkenny, was aided by an ex-serviceman called Kenny, who resided with them and accompanied them on their raids, pointing out IRA members. In August 1920 the IRA arrested him at the railway station. He had money and a ticket to Canada, a reward from the British Government for his services. He was tried, found guilty, and executed by drowning because shots would have been heard by British soldiers. There was no more trouble from spies in the area.[52] John O'Mahony and John Fitzgerald were both from Tralee, County Kerry and were executed in the locality and labelled as spies. O'Mahony was reputed to be a 'tout' or informer and was known as a constant visitor to the RIC barracks in Tralee. He was arrested in a public house, tried, found guilty, sentenced to death and then executed in April 1921. Fitzgerald was suspected of spying and was under observation by the IRA (he had previously been prominent in Redmond's Volunteers). The suspicion was confirmed when an IRA man named George Nagle, in British custody, was identified for the Tans by Fitzgerald, who was later arrested by the IRA, tried and then executed in June 1921.[53] John Donogue from Dunshaughlin, County Meath gave information to the local police that resulted in the Tans arresting a Volunteer and beating him. He was shot and

48 IMA/BMH, WS1708, Barry, Cork.
49 IMA/BMH, WS1547, Murphy, Cork.
50 IMA/BMH, WS718, Crawley, Roscommon.
51 IMA/BMH, WS1413, Kennedy, Kerry. Another ex-serviceman, Michael Moriarty, was arrested at the same time but there is no mention of his being executed, the witness, Kennedy, was also related to the Moriarty family.
52 IMA/BMH, WS966, Walsh, Kilkenny.
53 IMA/BMH, WS1011, Garvey, Kerry; WS1117, O'Riordan, Kerry; T. Ryle Dwyer, *Tans, Terror and Troubles: Kerry's Real Fighting Story 1913–23* (Cork, 2001), 318.

a label, 'Spies and Informers Beware', put on the body. Others in the area were suspected but there was no concrete evidence against them.[54] Michael Keefe and Martin Darmody gave information on the positions of the IRA at Kilmanagh, County Kilkenny, from which the latter had planned an ambush in May 1921. Both were executed.[55] In June 1921, in Newcastlewest, County Limerick, the IRA shot ex-serviceman Thomas Hanly, suspected of spying. Nearby troops heard the shots and arrived in time to save his life.[56] Jack Maloney from County Limerick was executed in spring 1921 for providing information to the RIC on the whereabouts of IRA members.[57] Robert Pike was a member of the tinker class living in Drumcondra, Dublin. The IRA had evidence that he was a 'tout' working for the British Intelligence Service and had followed republicans before informing the British of their whereabouts. He was shot outside a pub in June 1921.[58] An ex-British military policeman, 'Chanters' Ryan, was shot near his home in Dublin after giving information on where Peadar Clancy, a senior IRA officer, was staying, leading to the latter's arrest and death at the hands of the Auxiliaries. Ryan was considered to have plenty of money although he did not work.[59] In an incident referred to as the 'Sack of Balbriggan', in September 1920 Black and Tans attacked the town in County Dublin in retaliation for the shooting of RIC officers. Afterwards according to Michael Rock, an IRA commander, 'an ex-British army soldier, who went by the name of Jack Straw, which was not his real name, guided the Tans around the town and pointed out to them the houses to burn. Straw was not a native of the area'. Intelligence officer Thomas Peppard called him Hemstraw and said he may have been a serving soldier. Both IRA officers said there were no spies in the area. Straw was executed for his alleged activities in this one incident. Police reports say he was wrongly accused. According to O'Mahony, while notable republicans were targeted, 'the majority of those attacked were victims innocent of any complicity'.[60] A case in County Roscommon indicates the diligence of the IRA in checking if suspects really were spies. In the winter of 1920 two men, an ex-RIC man and an ex-serviceman, were suspected of informing. A group of republicans dressed as British soldiers visited them and were given

54 IMA/BMH, WS1539, Hall, Meath.
55 IMA/BMH, WS1642, Halley, Kilkenny.
56 IMA/BMH, WS85, Kiely, Limerick.
57 IMA/BMH, WS1525, Maloney, Limerick.
58 IMA/BMH, WS43, Dalton, Dublin; WS818, Stafford, Dublin (Stafford indicates that Pike was shot in 1920).
59 IMA/BMH, WS818, Stafford, Dublin (Charles Dalton said Ryan was a serving military policeman, WS434).
60 IMA/BMH, WS1398, Rock, Dublin; IMA/BMH, WS1399 Peppard, Dublin; Ross O'Mahony, 'The Sack of Balbriggan', in David Fitzpatrick (ed.), *Terror in Ireland, 1916–1923* (Dublin, 2012), 58, 67, 70.

information on the IRA, confirming that both men were informers, after which they were shot.[61]

By far the greater number of reported incidents took place in County Cork, including Cork City. Laurence Neville, an IRA officer from Cork City, wrote that parts of the city had a strong loyalist element, particularly in the Douglas-Blackrock districts, where many 'big' businessmen and retired British army officers lived, almost all of whom were antagonistic to the republican cause.[62] Nevertheless, many of the ex-servicemen accused of spying were ordinary soldiers closely integrated into the same communities from which the IRA recruited. William O'Sullivan, a local Cork man who worked for Cork Corporation, was, according to IRA man William Barry, a paid spy of the Freemasons. He was followed for some time until it was established that he was an enemy agent and executed in February 1921; a note, 'Spies and Informers beware', was left on the body. O'Sullivan would most likely have had intimate knowledge on republican activities for his brother served in the local IRA. Given the family connection it seems unlikely he would have been shot without proof, or for merely being an ex-serviceman. D. (Monkey) McDonald, also from Cork, was shot in February 1921 but survived. He lived at Cork military barracks until the Truce in July 1921 and went out on patrol until then, identifying IRA members and their houses. He left Ireland after the Truce and was not heard of again.[63] Two men who lived in the same street in Cork City were suspected of informing: in early 1921 T. O'Sullivan was shot dead in a quarry, while several attempts to execute S. Flynn failed and he left the country.[64] Three ex-servicemen from the city, Hawkins, Hamill, and Begley were suspected of spying and taken outside the city and shot; the first two were found by the military, recovered, and left the country.[65] After the Sinn Féin courts started to function in Cork (c. 1919), one of the first actions was the eviction of ex-soldier Michael Walsh from a house owned by the father of P.J. Murphy, a company commander from Cork City. No reason was given for the eviction. After the trial Walsh gave the names of the court and the Volunteers to the police, for which he was rewarded with money. He was arrested by the IRA and sentenced to be deported. He returned and two attempts were made to arrest him without

61 IMA/BMH, WS1178, Keaveney, Roscommon; WS718, Crawley, Roscommon.
62 IMA/BMH, WS1639, Neville, Cork.
63 IMA/BMH, WS1676, Ahern, Cork; WS869, Murphy, Cork; WS1639, Neville, Cork; WS1547, Murphy, Cork; IMA/BMH, WS1708, Barry, Cork. According to Barry, McDonald survived his shooting because the ammunition stolen from the British was deliberately made defective by them.
64 IMA/BMH, WS869, Murphy, Cork.
65 IMA/BMH, WS1706, O'Connell, Cork. (No date given, but the incidents probably occurred around June 1920 to pre-Truce, 1921.)

success. On both occasions he went to military barracks, with the result that
the army visited the Volunteers in their homes. Walsh stayed in the barracks
but became ill and had to be transferred to the workhouse in February 1921.
He was shot by the IRA as he was brought out on a stretcher.[66]

Raids on the mail helped provide evidence. At the end of summer 1920
following such a raid the IRA came into possession of an incriminating letter
from an ex-RIC officer called Nagle to an ex-serviceman called O'Sullivan.
Nagle was arrested and gave information which led the IRA to travel to Cork
City, where the two had been planning to meet. The IRA located O'Sullivan
and shot him.[67] In July 1921 an ex-British sergeant major, McPherson, from
Mallow, was arrested for spying; suspicion was aroused by a letter captured
in a raid on the local mail and by cheques from the British that he had
cashed. He was executed. Details of his case were recorded in three of the
witness statements.[68] This case illustrates the problem posed by conflicting
information for academic studies. Daithi Ó'Corráin, who is part of a project
under the auspices of Trinity College Dublin to identify the dead of the Irish
Revolution, writes that McPherson (whom he refers to as Mac Pherson) 'had
no record of any political activity'. He suffered from an illness contracted
while serving in India, which made him unfit for anything but light work
and was unemployed.[69] This may have explained a need to inform for
payment. A number of informants were motivated by money; in July 1920
in West Cork an ex-soldier named Crowley was arrested and executed after
informing for a payment of £20 on an IRA party who had ambushed the
RIC.[70] Denis Dwyer incriminated himself when he met officers of an IRA
Flying Column on a road near Bandon, West Cork, and believing them to
be British Auxiliaries offered to give them information in return for money
on the movements of IRA officers and where they could most easily be
captured. His mistake led to him being court-martialled and executed in
January 1921, his body left with a label bearing the words 'Spies beware'.
He had already given considerable information to the British and after his
execution the British raids ceased whenever IRA officers were in the area.[71]

Some of the spies were 'professional'. John Quinlisk, an ex-serviceman
from Wexford, was a spy in the employ of the British. He arrived in Cork in

66 IMA/BMH, WS869, Murphy, Cork.
67 IMA/BMH, WS810, Herlihy, Cork.
68 IMA/BMH, WS978, O'Callaghan, Cork; WS1097, Morgan, Cork; WS1200, O'Regen,
    Cork.
69 Daithi Ó'Corráin, 'The Dead of the Irish Revolution 1921–25', *The Blue Cap*, 12 (2005),
    3.
70 IMA/BMH, WS443, Neville, Cork.
71 IMA/BMH, WS470, Lordon, Cork. Tom Barry refers to this incident in *Guerrilla
    Days in Ireland*, 101–2, noting the informer was Catholic.

February 1920 claiming he was from republican headquarters in Dublin and wanted to see Michael Collins. He gave information on a raid to establish his credentials but Michael Murphy, an IRA commander from Cork City, was suspicious of him. Quinlisk was shot and incriminating letters to the RIC proved his intention to capture Collins. His father, who had served in the RIC, came to collect the body.[72] Few senior British officers were named in the files. One such was Lieutenant Colonel Peacock, who had guided raiding parties while in disguise. His mask slipped on a raid in December 1920 and he was identified. From this time he stayed in Bandon barracks, only occasionally visiting his home in Innishannon, County Cork, and then with a Tan guard. He was shot on a visit in June 1921.[73] A one-legged ex-British officer named 'Slickfoot' Maher from Athlone, County Westmeath was long suspected of spying and, after incriminating evidence had been found in the mail, he was arrested, court-martialled, and shot, his body quietly buried to prevent reprisals.[74] In February 1921, Major O'Connor was shot, according to Michael Murphy, in the company of a member of the senior secret service of the YMCA, although it was unclear whether O'Connor was suspected of spying.[75]

It was local men who joined the Crown Forces, especially the Tans, who were of particular concern. At the beginning of 1921 an ex-serviceman called Blagriff was executed near Athlone. He was going to join the Tans and, under the influence of drink, had told his employer, who also found incriminating papers on him. He knew all the Volunteers and was a considerable risk to the IRA.[76] Finbar O'Sullivan was well acquainted with the IRA in the district where he lived in Cork City. He joined the Tans and was arrested returning to his home one evening, and executed in February 1921. O'Sullivan was well known from childhood to Laurence Neville, a local IRA officer, again emphasising the close community ties of many of the informers.[77] Denis O'Loughlin joined the Tans and was executed in April 1921 in Tralee, County Kerry.[78] Tadhg Dwyer, a battalion commander

72 IMA/BMH, WS1547, Murphy, Cork.
73 IMA/BMH, WS1591, Russell, Cork. Barry refers to this incident in *Guerrilla Days in Ireland*, 104.
74 IMA/BMH, WS1504, O'Meara, Westmeath; WS1336, Lennon, Westmeath.
75 IMA/BMH, WS1547, Murphy, Cork.
76 IMA/BMH, WS1308, O'Brien, Westmeath; WS1309, O'Connor, Westmeath; WS1500, McCormack, Westmeath; WS1503, McCormack, Westmeath.
77 IMA/BMH, WS1676, Ahern, Cork; WS1639, Neville, Cork; WS1547, Murphy, Cork. According to William Barry, an IRA officer in Cork, O'Sullivan was a member of the British army home on leave and about to join the Tans (IMA/BMH, WS1708).
78 IMA/BMH, WS1011, Garvey, Kerry; WS1189, O'Connor, Kerry, 1921. According to O'Connor, O'Loughlin (whom he calls Loughlin) was an associate of Major McKinnon, an RIC (Auxiliaries) officer executed by the IRA.

in County Tipperary, wrote that towards the end of 1920 it was clear that the British were getting information on the places used by IRA men on the run. Thomas Kirby, a local man, knew all the Volunteers and drank with the Tans. He was ordered to leave the area but re-joined the British Forces and was posted to Dundrum within the county. In disguise, he helped the British in their search for wanted republicans. He was captured in a public house and admitted he was a spy but pleaded 'insanity'. He was executed in January 1921.[79] Patrick Duke of Dunshaughlin, County Meath provided details of a wanted Volunteer to the police, paradoxically a friend of his. He was arrested by two Volunteers but escaped and joined the RIC in Dublin, but did not provide further information regarding IRA activities in County Meath. He returned home after the conflict and married a local girl. David Hall, a senior IRA officer in County Meath who provided the witness statement, said he had often spoken afterwards with Duke about the affair.[80] Ceasing to provide information appears to have saved Duke.

The IRA reserved their most extreme reaction to spies within their own ranks. An ex-serviceman called Shiels joined the Kanturk Battalion, County Cork in 1920 and had a reputation for being absent when an engagement was due. In March 1921 the brigade's headquarters in Nadd planned an attack on nearby Mourneabbey. Shiels went into Kanturk to draw his army pension and was seen calling into the RIC office and drinking with British soldiers. Next day a large concentration of British troops with Shiels accompanying them in a Tan uniform surrounded the IRA in Nadd. Shiels disappeared but the IRA pursued him; photographs were circulated in England and the USA but he was not found and was believed dead.[81]

On occasion the IRA gave warnings to suspects before taking action. Jimmy Morrissey, a postman from Marshalstown, County Wexford, was thought to be giving information to the police. He failed to heed a warning and was shot on his rounds in the summer of 1920, a sign, 'shot by the IRA', left on his body.[82] William Desmond, a Volunteer from West Cork, said two suspected spies were released on condition that they ceased associating with the enemy or they would be executed.[83] Sometimes, if there was insufficient evidence for an execution, the suspect was told to leave the area. Seumas O'Meara, senior officer from Athlone, County Westmeath, claimed he saved several people suspected of spying from being shot as there was no

79 IMA/BMH, WS1356, Dwyer, Tipperary; WS1450, Ryan, Tipperary; WS1348, Davern, Tipperary.
80 IMA/BMH, WS1539, Hall, Meath.
81 IMA/BMH, WS978, O'Callaghan, Cork; WS1097, Morgan, Cork; WS1200, O'Regen, Cork.
82 IMA/BMH, WS1373, Balfe, Wexford; WS1041, Doyle, Wexford.
83 IMA/BMH, WS832, Desmond, Cork.

proof, only suspicion; such people were sent a warning letter which, he said, had the desired effect.[84] John Walsh, a battalion commander in County Kilkenny, said the IRA was suspicious of anyone with close associations to the military. He cites an example of one person who spent time in the company of the RIC. There was no definite evidence but he was warned to leave the country.[85] Tim Herlihy, an officer from County Cork, stated that when the republican courts were initially convened in November 1919, some of the first offenders were accused of spying but not executed due to insufficient evidence, two were expelled from Ireland, a third just released.[86] McMahon and Anglis, who frequented the ex-servicemen's club in Merrion Square, Dublin, were suspected of spying but, although followed, were not shot.[87] Not even the IRA considered all executions to be justified. Two men, Brady and Halpin, were shot by the IRA in Dublin just before the Truce. Brady, a Tan, was the principal target. Frank Saurin, an intelligence officer in Dublin wrote, 'Halpin was ex-British Navy, and it is open to question whether he deserved to be shot'.[88] John O'Reilly was tried by an IRA court martial and executed in County Clare in April 1921. He was compromised by a letter from the RIC, the contents of which made it appear that he was a British spy. One IRA officer said he was known to mix with the Black and Tans. Another, Seamus Connelly, who was not present at either the trial or the execution, wrote, 'I believe the man was innocent and that he was the victim of an unscrupulous villain who was then employed as a postman in Newmarket and who was the actual spy himself. He used O'Reilly's name as a cover to shield his own identity'.[89]

It was inevitable that their military background would draw suspicion of ex-servicemen and this could help explain why a significant percentage of civilian spies killed by the IRA were ex-servicemen. They had volunteered to fight for the Crown, albeit not necessarily for reasons of loyalty; they were more likely to have social contact, supply to or work in ancillary roles for the British Forces, and they may have received official letters, perhaps

---

84 IMA/BMH, WS1504, O'Meara, Westmeath. An ex-soldier called O'Halloran was suspected of informing but with insufficient evidence available he was given 'the usual warning', see WS1729, Togher, Galway.
85 IMA/BMH, WS966, Walsh, Kilkenny.
86 IMA/BMH, WS810, Herlihy, Cork. In 1919 an ex-soldier named Collins was suspected of informing and likely deported to England. See WS1593, Reilly, Westmeath. In September 1920 another suspect, an ex-officer named McLean, was arrested and released on condition he left the country. See WS1324, Barrett, Clare.
87 IMA/BMH, WS434, Dalton, Dublin.
88 IMA/BMH, WS715, Saurin, Dublin.
89 IMA/BMH, WS976, Connelly, Clare; WS1073, Quinn (gives the date of execution as 19 April 1920); WS1112, Reidy, Claire. John Reilly is also referred to as O'Reilly in the witness statements.

in relation to pensions. Those who were unemployed may have been open to payment, others travelling and seeking work may have fallen into the category of suspicious stranger. In seeking information, the British Forces, and particularly the Black and Tans, may have approached them expecting co-operation due to shared experiences.

All these reasons would have brought ex-servicemen to the attention of the IRA. The question is whether they were executed simply because of their war service. Barry Egan, Deputy Lord Mayor of Cork and a leading republican, said, 'I believe that no executions are carried out by the IRA except after the most careful investigation, and when the accused has been found guilty of being a murderer or a spy'.[90] IRA GHQ instructed local commanders to 'convict' only on the basis of definite evidence.[91] Tom Barry, commander of the West Cork IRA, wrote there were cases when after investigation alleged informers were released due to lack of evidence.[92] Republican supporters would most likely argue that due process was followed. Inevitably though, in wartime conditions and with local commanders resenting the restrictions of the headquarters and imposing their own decisions, there were times when IRA justice was cursory and variable, or when victims suffered simply for their unwillingness to comply with republican authority. These circumstances may also have provided the opportunity to settle old scores. Some ex-servicemen were most likely wrongly shot, as the cases of Halpin and O'Reilly indicate. But there were also examples of non-ex-service men who were erroneously executed on unsubstantiated suspicions.[93] In witness statements and most of the cases involving ex-servicemen, the IRA claimed that executions only took place after it had gathered evidence and its hierarchy satisfied themselves that their suspicion was correct. In most cases the files support this, giving reasons as to why these men were suspected of spying, and appear to provide incriminating evidence. For example, James Maher, Seumas O'Meara, and John O'Mahony had close associations with the British Forces; Kenny, McDonald, Walsh and Peacock actually resided in their barracks and were seen on patrol with them; Blagriff, Finbar O'Sullivan, O'Loughlin, Kirby, and Shiels joined or planned to join the Tans (the latter while serving in the IRA), while incriminating evidence was found against Foley, 'Slickfoot' Maher, Fitzgerald, Pike, Quinlisk, William O'Sullivan, McPherson and Dwyer. The evidence supports Borgonovo's

90 Ewart, *A Journey in Ireland*, 39.
91 Charles Townsend, *The Republic: The Fight for Irish Independence 1918–1923* (London, 2013), 263. IRA GHQ was worried about escalating rates of conviction.
92 Barry, *Guerrilla Days in Ireland*, 100–1.
93 O'Halpin, 'Problematic Killings', 321–5, 332–4; Thomas Earls FitzGerald, 'The Execution of "Spies and Informers" in West Cork, 1921', in David Fitzpatrick (ed.), *Terror in Ireland, 1916–1923* (Dublin, 2012), 189–90.

contention that the IRA had a well-organised intelligence network to identify spies, and challenges Hart's argument that most of those who were punished never informed. That suspects were given warnings or told to leave, or in some cases left alone because of insufficient evidence, contradicts the proposition that ex-servicemen were executed simply for their war service.

The ex-servicemen who were suspected of informing were often low-ranking soldiers, members of the same community from which the IRA drew its volunteers. The witness statements provide significant evidence of the threat posed by such informers. Without this local intelligence the Tans would have been ineffective for, unlike the RIC, they generally had little knowledge, in terms of geography and people, of the areas in which they operated. Barry wrote that by 1920 the effectiveness of the locally recruited RIC had been reduced to such an extent that spies and informers were practically the only source of British intelligence; 'these were the bloodhounds who nosed out the victims for the British murder gangs. From June 1920 they were a menace to the very existence of the Army of the Republic'.[94] The majority (86%) of civilian spies were killed in the last seven months of the War of Independence. Although total fatalities also increased in this, the most violent period of the war, the deaths of civilian spies escalated faster. One explanation is that supposed civilians spies were being killed not because they posed a real threat or for what they had done but because they made a more convenient and attainable target than the increasingly effective Crown forces.[95] But Barry provides a more likely reason: with the demise of the RIC, civilian spies became essential to the effectiveness of the Black and Tans and therefore played an increasing role in the war. Given the devastating impact informers had on their ranks, the IRA's strong reaction to them was inevitable and, on occasion, it would err on the side of caution in executing suspect spies. There was no campaign specifically waged against veterans. In a vicious war the IRA targeted anyone they suspected of collaborating with the British. Barry wrote that they demanded the local population 'not commit any hostile act against us and that they should not actively aid the British troops or administration'.[96] According to an officer in the South Roscommon brigade, anyone who informed was punished, including women; their houses were burnt and they were compelled to leave.[97] The extent to which the IRA was prepared to exact revenge against informers was indicated in the case of six IRA men who were killed in March 1921 after being betrayed by one of their own

94 Barry, *Guerrilla Days in Ireland*, 99.
95 O'Halpin, 'Problematic Killings', 327, 343.
96 Barry, *Guerrilla Days in Ireland*, 107.
97 IMA/BMH, WS718, Crawley, Roscommon.

members. The informer was eventually traced to New York and shot, two Volunteers travelling there for the purpose.[98]

Records of the Victims

The files of the Irish Grants Committee (IGC), which was established by the British Government, represent the most comprehensive and detailed repository of claims for compensation arising out of violence and intimidation by the IRA against loyalists. Of the 3,439 incidents recorded only 262 (7.6%) involved claims by ex-servicemen, a particularly low figure as they were encouraged to apply by allowing war service as a proof of loyalty.[99] Claimants had to demonstrate that loyalty to the Crown was the cause of intimidation, and the IGC's terms of reference did not require it to have been given only in the period immediately preceding the Truce or on Irish soil, thereby allowing service in the Great War to be taken into account. The final report of the IGC in 1930 stated that 'the demobilised soldier or sailor, who was victimised within the post-truce period, while residing or carrying on business in the Free State, because he had served in the British army or Navy during the European War, was fully entitled to consideration', provided the nexus between loyalty and injury was clearly established.[100] Perhaps even more surprising was that of the 262 claims made by ex-servicemen, in only 73 was war service cited as a cause of intimidation, despite it being an obvious proof of loyalty.[101] In

---

98 IMA/BMH, WS1547, Murphy, Cork.
99 TNA, CO, 762/1-212, analysis of all claims. The number of incidents, 3,439 incidents, is lower than the total claims (around 4,000) in the IGC records. This analysis includes all applications, whether compensation was awarded or not, unless they were withdrawn. Cases in which there were multiple claims for the one incident, for example, a family making individual claims arising out of the burning of their home, are recorded as one incident. Also excluded are claims against Crown Forces and any claim related to Northern Ireland. The figures for ex-servicemen relate only to those who served in the War and returned home afterwards and therefore exclude pre-war veterans. Only claims from the ex-servicemen or from family members in cases in which an ex-serviceman was referred to as a victim, e.g. a widow claiming for a dead husband, are included in the ex-servicemen figures. Excluded from the figures for ex-servicemen are non-ex-servicemen who claim injury arising out of a member of the family having served but without referring to that family member having been a victim. The analysis is based on the location in which the incident took place. In a very limited number of cases incidents took place at two locations within one claim and both are included in the analysis.
100 TNA, CO, 762/212.
101 TNA, CO, 762/1-212, analysis of all claims.

contrast, applicants frequently cited their Protestant religion when asked for their loyalist credentials.[102]

Of the 262 incidents, 152 took place in the Province of Munster, 74 in Leinster, 20 in Connaught and 16 in Ulster (three counties). The discrepancy between Munster and Leinster is accentuated when taking into account the larger population of the latter; Leinster recorded 0.64 incidents involving ex-servicemen per 10,000 people, Munster 1.57 incidents per 10,000.

Table 7: Geographical analysis of ex-servicemen claims pro rata to population and enlistment

County	Incidents	Population	Claims per 10,000	Recruits	Claims per 10,000
Carlow	2	34,476	0.58		
Dublin	17	505,654	0.34		
Kildare	7	58,028	1.21		
Kilkenny	3	70,990	0.42		
Longford	2	39,847	0.50		
Louth	1	62,739	0.16		
Meath	8	62,969	1.27		
Kings	5	52,592	0.95		
Queens	13	51,540	2.52		
Westmeath	6	56,818	1.06		
Wexford	6	95,848	0.63		
Wicklow	4	57,591	0.69		
Leinster	74	1,149,092	0.64	48,000	15.42
Clare	30	95,064	3.16		
Cork	58	365,747	1.59		
Kerry	9	149,171	0.60		
Limerick	16	140,343	1.14		
Tipperary	35	141,015	2.48		
Waterford	4	78,562	0.51		

102 Leigh-Ann Coffey, 'Loyalism in Transition: Southern Loyalists and the Irish Free State, 1921–1937', in James W. McAuley and Graham Spencer (eds), *Ulster Loyalism after the Good Friday Agreement: History, Identity and Change* (Basingstoke, 2011), 29.

	Incidents	Population	Claims per 10,000	Recruits	Claims per 10,000
Munster	152	969,902	1.57	17,500	86.86
Galway	7	169,366	0.41		
Leitrim	0	55,907	0.00		
Mayo	7	172,690	0.41		
Roscommon	6	83,556	0.72		
Sligo	0	71,388	0.00		
Connaught	20	552,907	0.36	6,500	30.77
Cavan	5	82,452	0.61		
Donegal	8	152,508	0.52		
Monaghan	3	65,131	0.46		
Ulster (3 counties)	16	300,091	0.53	5,500	29.09
Total	262	2,971,992	0.88	77,500	33.81

Source: TNA, CO, 762/1-212 (analysis of all claims); TNA, PIN, 15/757;
Population data from Central Statistics Office (Ireland), 1926 census.

Perhaps surprising is that Connaught records only 0.36 incidents per 10,000 people. One reason is that the number of ex-servicemen in that area was significantly lower than in Leinster, both absolutely and relative to population. If the number of ex-servicemen is taken into account then there were 15.42 incidents for every 10,000 ex-servicemen in Leinster and around twice as many, 30.77, in Connaught. The discrepancy between Munster and Leinster is also accentuated further with the former reporting 86.86 incidents for every 10,000 servicemen, 5.6 times the figure for Leinster. There was significant variation between provinces. Cork and Cork County, which provided 10,106 recruits, had 57.39 incidents for every 10,000 ex-servicemen, while Clare, Limerick, and Kerry, which provided 5,745 recruits, had 95.74 incidents for every 10,000 ex-servicemen. Dublin and Dublin County, which provided 24,276 recruits, had 7.0 incidents for every 10,000 ex-servicemen.[103] In total, only 0.34% of ex-servicemen were involved in incidents leading to a claim; even in Munster the figure was less than 1% (0.87).[104]

103 TNA, PIN, 15/757. Recruitment figures by recruitment district/county are only available for the end of 1917 but as 1918 recruitment for all Ireland was only 10,617, the total would not vary significantly.
104 The number of ex-servicemen is based on recruitment figures, and is most likely an underestimate, making the percentage of incidents involving ex-servicemen even lower.

An analysis of the 262 cases involving ex-servicemen shows that the cause of any violence and intimidation was not war service *per se* but one or a combination of reasons that could be applicable to other members of the population and that fell into four main categories:[105]

- Membership of a particular category of people, including landowners, the gentry and Protestants, or of the judicial system.
- The result of a specific action on the part of the ex-serviceman, including spying or closely associating with or joining the Crown Forces, especially the RIC and the Black and Tans, or supplying to them in contravention of boycotts.
- Part of a general campaign by the republicans against all of the population, including the levy of financial dues and confiscating arms and equipment.
- Refusal to join the IRA.

The majority of claimants to the IGC fit these categories but did not serve in the Great War. There were some categories in which the ex-serviceman was more likely to feature, including suspicion of any association with the Crown Forces. Also, given their military experience, they were more likely to join the Crown Forces or be intimidated to join the IRA.

The targeting of landlords had a historic precedence. Agrarian agitators in rural Ireland in the Land Wars of the nineteenth century sought to remedy the perceived injustice of plantation settlements and ensure the redistribution of land to tenants, especially from absentee landlords. In the period of conflict after the War, Protestants were targeted for a variety of reasons, because they were loyalists, because they were suspected of co-operating with the British Forces, or as part of revenge attacks for anti-Catholic atrocities in Belfast. But the primary reason was land and ancestral grievances. Protestants suffered disproportionately because they held a disproportionate share of large holdings.[106] As Fitzpatrick writes, 'the revolution gave bite to the agrarian struggle and drew much of its vitality from it'.[107] Several reasons contributed to the outbreak of agrarian conflict from March 1920, including farmers with uneconomic holdings seeking to gain land as the ability to transfer land to small farmers was severely curtailed during the war; wartime and post-war prosperity making land a

---

105 The statements of the victims, all of whom were ex-servicemen, and their solicitors date from the time of the claims. Many of the files are extremely substantial and the enclosed documentation and statements often lengthy; relevant extracts used reflect the substance of the claim and the IGC's comments on them. As illustrated in the Maher case, other sources may provide a different perspective.

106 Terence Dooley, *The Land for the People: The Land Question in Independent Ireland* (Dublin, 2004), 43–5.

107 Fitzpatrick, *Politics and Irish Life*, 65.

more attractive prospect; and restrictions on wartime emigration causing a surplus of non-inheriting farmers' sons. Politics had become radicalised in the absence of the traditional valve of emigration, a situation exacerbated by the Dáil, which continued its prohibition on the basis that it was unpatriotic to leave the country in time of war. The resultant agitation for land redistribution was given impetus by reduced state authority.[108] This provided an opportunity for disputed claims and old scores to be settled by force. Army officers who were part of the landed gentry were often subject to such intimidation. Many were from the Protestant Ascendancy who had a record of military service and had volunteered in large numbers at the outset of the war. David Mullins of Queen's County claimed he had suffered from the 'hostility displayed to all old soldiers and Loyalists', when the Luggacurren Land Committee forced him from his land in March 1922. Luggacurren was the location of evictions in the 1880s of 40 Catholic families who were forced from their homes for failing to pay Lord Lansdowne's rent and were replaced by Protestant tenants from Ulster. Animosity inevitably endured between these Protestant 'colonists' and their Catholic neighbours.[109] Henry Blake inherited land in County Mayo and in early 1920 his stock was driven off and the lands were seized 'by certain Committees formed for taking over such places'.[110] Colonel Henry Sidney inherited property in County Tipperary in 1921 while serving in the British army. In September 1921 his land and house were forcibly seized and damaged. He wrote that 'the British and afterwards the Irish Government remained powerless to protect property'. The IGC noted:

> The injuries and loss complained of appear to have their foundation in agrarian troubles, and as it has been shown that the applicant has never been resident on the property it should hardly be contended that the injuries were directed against him on account of his support of the British Government.[111]

Epenetus Fitzgibbon had an estate in Dripsey, County Cork. Throughout 1921 he suffered intimidation with raids, property stolen and demands for money. The house was occupied and in October 1922 burnt down. He wrote

---

108 Fergus Campbell and Kevin O'Shiel, '"The Last Land War?" Kevin O'Shiel's Memoir of the Irish Revolution (1916–21)', *Archivium Hibernicum*, 57 (2003), 161–2; Tomás Kenny, *Galway: Politics and Society 1910–23* (Dublin, 2011), 8, 18, 27–8; Diarmaid Ferriter, *The Transformation of Ireland, 1900–2000* (London, 2005), 211.

109 TNA, CO, 762/71/3; http://athyeyeonthepast.blogspot.com/1999/06/luggacurran-evictions.html; Dooley, *The Land for the People*, 43.

110 TNA, CO, 762/165/1.

111 TNA, CO, 762/32/1.

that 'if those in authority in England only went through some of sufferings of loyal people in Southern Ireland, they might cease to think that they had done so splendidly for Irish Loyalists'.[112] From 1919 George Davidge suffered attacks on his family, servants and estate in Listowel, Kerry. Fisheries were poisoned, fences smashed, and trees damaged. He wrote:

> so persistent were the outrages that we had to leave and go to England. Any hope of returning to reside was destroyed in June 1920 when the house was burnt down. The IRA took possession of the land. They were driven out by Free State Troops, leaving the land completely derelict.[113]

William Roe owned a large farm in Rathmore, County Kerry. He claimed a conspiracy was organised to drive him out and on eleven occasions between March and June 1920 all his cattle were driven off and gates and fences were broken down. The local people became so hostile that Roe had to leave towards the end of 1920. He never recovered his lands.[114] Robert Otway-Ruthven claimed that from March to September 1922 he suffered 'malicious damage and destruction by fire' at his property, Castle Otway in Templederry, County Tipperary.[115] James Bryne owned a farm in Rathvilly, County Carlow and was subject to persecution and boycotting and was unable to continue farming. He was threatened with being shot on several occasions for denouncing the Sinn Féin movement.[116] Major J.R. North Bomford's mansion house in County Meath was destroyed by armed men in April 1923.[117]

Many of the landowners, particularly Protestants, held privileged positions in the Ascendancy class, often in a position of authority. Captain Richard Winter Bayley from Ballinderry, Moate, County Westmeath was a Protestant and had been a JP for Roscommon and High Sheriff for Westmeath in 1902, and owned 952 acres of land where he bred horses. In January 1920 the stables were subject to a 'malicious burning', and he suffered threats and raids until January 1923.[118] Major E.J.M. Briscoe of Tullamore, King's County owned Screggan Manor and 850 acres of farmland. His house was raided several times from May 1921 to October 1922 and was finally burnt down. He was a JP and Grand Juror, and said his family had been noted

112 TNA, CO, 762/114/23.
113 TNA, CO, 762/147/6.
114 TNA, CO, 762/101/1714.
115 TNA, CO, 762/78/12.
116 TNA, CO, 762/128/3.
117 TNA, CO, 762/12/1.
118 TNA, CO, 762/77/7.

loyalists since 1580.[119] Henry Edwyn, Earl of Kingston, owned Kilronan
Castle in Boyle, County Roscommon, which was occupied by the anti-Treaty
IRA from November 1921 until January 1922 with considerable loss and
damage.[120]

Several of the landowners complained of a lack of support from the
authorities. After the war, Captain Pim Goodbody returned to Ballytore,
County Kildare, where he had three farms. He wrote that after the RIC
withdrew from the area, he was continuously raided and threatened by
rebels. After receiving information from the police that he was to be shot, he
left for London in May 1921 where he remained for three months. He then
returned but was again raided and threatened. He complained to the police,
who told him they had instructions not to interfere with the rebels. He had
'refused to assist the IRA or to give them money or supplies but gave all the
assistance I could to the RIC'. He sold his lands for £4,000, although they
had been valued at £12,000.[121] Captain Butler-Stoney, a Protestant, owned
property in King's County. In February 1921, he was visited by two members
of the IRA who demanded money for their cause. After he refused the house
was ransacked. In 1922, the IRA demanded that he give up his land from
which they had driven his tenants' cattle, replacing them with their own. He
said he was forced to leave and that he received little support, complaining
that an RIC sergeant was in league with the IRA.[122]

A number of landowning complainants mentioned their army service
as a specific cause for their intimidation, but there was little to distinguish
them from any other case. Colonel Raleigh Chichester Constable owned
tenanted land in County Roscommon. He wrote that from 'sometime prior
to July 1921 a campaign of cattle driving and intimidation was in progress'.
In July 1922 his mansion house was set on fire by anti-Treaty IRA forces
who had been illegally occupying it for 'a considerable time'. The lands
continued to be occupied by the raiders until 1923. He wrote, 'I claim that
the loss and injury described was occasioned because I was a retired Colonel
in the British Army and because it was known I was in favour of British
Administration in Ireland and was a loyal subject of His Majesty the King'.[123]
Edward Kenelm, Baron Digby, was an absentee landowner of a large estate
in King's County. He wrote that 'prior to 1920 a conspiracy was organised
to drive all Loyalists out of Ireland', and as his loyalist sympathies were 'well

119 TNA, CO, 762/53/13.
120 TNA, CO, 762/132/1.
121 TNA, CO, 762/85/1.
122 TNA, CO, 762/113/12. The house referred to is Portland Park, which other records
     show as being in the neighbouring county of Tipperary. The family appear to have
     owned lands in both counties.
123 TNA, CO, 762/63/23.

known and his family had been identified for years with the British Army',
he was prevented from grazing the lands, timber was looted and in August
1922 Geashill Castle was burnt down by the anti-Treaty IRA.[124] Colonel
Cyril Cary-Barnard endured a boycott, looting, and destruction of his estate
in Galway, stating that service in the army and loyalty had aroused considerable hostility. He had remained in the army until August 1922 and served
in Dublin from October 1919 to September 1920.[125] All three were absentee
landlords and so would have been particularly vulnerable. In addition, the
first two appeared to be prominent loyalists while Cary-Barnard's service
in Ireland may have counted against him. Major Arthur Blennerhassett
owned a large house near Tralee, County Kerry. In 1920 and 1921 he was the
victim of 'several malicious injuries', and in February 1922 was kidnapped
and beaten before being returned to his home. Intimidation against his
family continued and they left. He said the kidnappers 'taunted me with
having been in the British service'.[126] Charles Hachett was the son of a JP
and owned land on the border of counties Tipperary and King's County. He
wrote that he found country people extremely hostile and that 'all British
soldiers were subjected to the same treatment'. Owing to the local pressure
and boycotting, he agreed in February 1921 to sell his lands at much less
than their true value.[127] Captain James McLean of Borrisokane, Tipperary,
who owned 56 acres of farming land, wrote that due to 'the fact that I was
an ex-British Officer my house was raided by armed men between 1921
and 1923'. In January 1923 he was threatened with being shot if he did not
leave. He departed, returning in January 1924.[128] Captain Martin Daly from
County Mayo claimed that on account of war service and refusing to join the
IRA after demobilising, his cattle were driven off and his house burnt down
between February and April 1922. His solicitor wrote to the IGC stating that
'Mr Daly served through the War with distinction; this in itself would render
him extremely unpopular and make his property a likely subject of outrage in
the country'. His unpopularity did not prevent him in May 1922 from taking
up the position of Superintendent for Shell Mex, residing in Galway.[129] Many
landowners had served in the war but it was not the primary reason for their
intimidation. Certainly there were many claimants to the IGC of a similar
profile but with no war service who were nevertheless persecuted.

The emotive issue of land affected another very different category of

124 TNA, CO, 762/73/4.
125 TNA, CO, 762/25/3.
126 TNA, CO, 762/55/18. In March 1923 republicans were executed by the IFS Army at
      Ballyseedy.
127 TNA, CO, 762/129/4.
128 TNA, CO, 762/86/14.
129 TNA, CO, 762/29/2.

owners, who were accused of being part of a new 'plantation' campaign by the British Government: ordinary soldiers who applied for and received small grants of land, usually around 30 acres, under the provision of the Soldiers' and Sailors' Re-settlement Act. Aalen comments that 'any attempt by a British Government to interfere with Irish Land inevitably aroused deep, almost paranoid, responses'.[130] The ex-servicemen received the land in appreciation of war service but it was their acceptance of it that caused offence. Seven soldiers in Knocklong, County Limerick were forced from land allocated them under the scheme between March and July 1921. Joseph Wheeler claimed the IRA broke fences and threatened him. He reported the matter to the police, but they were 'not doing ordinary duty only just keeping in power and guarding themselves', and that the Irish Land Commission also did nothing but continued to demand rent. He received a notice from the IRA to quit the land and wrote, 'all the ex-soldiers got the same order'.[131] The IGC wrote of Edmund Harty that 'in July 1921 owing to local hostilities and threats he was driven from the land and kept out of possession until February 1923'. He wrote that the IRA told me that 'if I wanted land I should go to England and get it from the Government I acknowledge. My case was that of all or at least most of the British ex-soldiers in the Free State – Nobody's Children'.[132] The solicitor of Robert Coll wrote that:

> on account of his being an ex-serviceman and it being implied that he was therefore a supporter of the British Government, [he] suffered damage to his property, ... he was deprived of the use of his farm for a period of 18 months, during which time the land was grazed and used by parties antagonistic to him.[133]

Edmund Davern's cattle were driven from his land in March 1921 after his fences, gates and crops were destroyed. He was a member of the Australian Imperial Forces having enlisted in Australia, and when demobilised in 1919 he had returned to his native country. His case suggests that intimidation was not restricted to locally recruited volunteers. On his return to Ireland he was appointed Postmaster at nearby Elton, a position he still held at the time of application, indicating the antagonism against him arose out of the allocation

130 F.H.A., Aalen, 'Homes for Irish Heroes: Housing under the Irish Land (Provision for Soldiers and Sailors) Act 1919, and the Irish Sailors' and Soldiers' Land Trust', *Town Planning Review*, 59/3 (July 1988), 307.
131 TNA, CO, 762/31/8. Some of the ex-servicemen were from the area in which they were allocated land and therefore may have known those who dispossessed them.
132 TNA, CO, 762/40/3
133 TNA, CO, 762/40/2.

of land.[134] Timothy Ryan wrote, 'I drew upon myself the hostility of the local people in general and the Republican Army in particular. My allegiance was well known and I received threatening communications'. His crops and fences were destroyed and he was forced off by the IRA, 'in consequence of having been an ex-soldier'.[135] Similarly, Gerald Harris[136] and William Fitzgerald[137] were forced off their land. The IGC noted that Limerick was 'especially disturbed during the troubles in Ireland and the ex-service men who had been given lands were subjected to considerable interference'.[138] Patrick Corrigan, ex RIC, wrote to the IGC in November 1926 in support of Ryan's claim, 'I know that he and all the other loyal subjects that got the lands were subjected to a deal of trouble and annoyance'.[139] A solicitor writing in support of Fitzgerald's application wrote that 'he was in common with other ex-British soldiers who were allotted land in this district very badly treated and suffered considerable financial consequences'.[140] The time of dispossession was comparatively limited; most of the above claimants were back in possession by May 1923 at the latest, following the reassertion of authority by the Free State, the latter willing to enforce the rights of the ex-servicemen against the republicans. Ex-servicemen allocated land elsewhere also experienced problems, usually in areas in which the IRA was most active. Twenty-five former soldiers who had been offered land in County Cork received letters from the IRA stating they would be shot if they accepted.[141] James Cleary was allocated land near Cloyne, County Cork. He wrote that 'I received a warning from the Churchtown Sinn Féin Club not to take up the land and if I did I would be immediately dealt with. I had to leave at once with my wife and family. In March 1924 I was given back possession of my land'.[142] Richard Walsh was allocated land in the same area but republicans took possession and damaged buildings and fences. He wrote that during the troubled period 1920–2 other farms were unmolested, 'but ex-servicemen's property was specially selected for wanton destruction and we were threatened not to dare attempt to occupy it'. The IGC noted that he found alternative employment from March 1921, indicating his problem was related to his allocation of land.[143] Walsh was incorrect in saying that other

134 TNA, CO, 762/49/12.
135 TNA, CO, 762/43/8.
136 TNA, CO, 762/53/21.
137 TNA, CO, 762/79/ 6.
138 TNA, CO, 762/53/21.
139 TNA, CO, 762/43/8.
140 TNA, CO, 762/79/ 6.
141 *IT*, 19 February 1921.
142 TNA, CO, 762/199/10.
143 TNA, CO, 762/47/13.

farms were unmolested; during the War of Independence, the IRA took forcible possession of 11 farms in Cork purported to be owned by 'loyalist spies'.[144] James Belfory was granted a smallholding in County Kildare in 1920. He was also employed with the military at Curragh Camp. He wrote:

> As the result of threats and intimidation, the military authorities made me leave the house and come to the barracks with my family for safety about June 1921. I had to leave my home in a hurry and it was looted a very short time later. On withdrawal of the Crown Forces from Ireland it was considered I was still in danger, and I decided to come to England, which I did in March 1922.[145]

Belfory drew antagonism both for his allocation of a smallholding and for working for the military; unlike others he did not return, remaining in England.

The IRA was determined to undermine the structure of British rule. All tiers of the British judicial system were targeted, including JPs, solicitors and court officials, as the IRA sought to establish a republican alternative. Walter Butler farmed in Queen's County and Kildare. He wrote:

> In the early summer of 1921 the RIC were ambushed in the neighbourhood, two of the Rebels being shot dead. I being the only Justice of the Peace in the district signed some 40 summaries which were served by the police on the rebels. I was boycotted and neither allowed to till or let my lands.[146]

Captain C.R. Barton of Tipperary, a JP, was forced out of his house and land in May 1922 by the IRA.[147] Upon his return, Captain Robert Thomas of County Cork served as a staff officer in Dublin until 1920, when on leaving service he took up an appointment in the Ministry of Labour, Cork and continued as a magistrate, which he had been since 1907. He wrote, 'when the troubles in Ireland became acute during the year 1921, Fermoy (County Cork) where I resided was a centre for disaffection'. He said he was continually threatened because he was a soldier and magistrate and transferred together with his family to England.[148] Laurence Roche from Limerick, a JP, claimed damage to his property and theft and seizure of land

144 Dooley, *The Land for the People*, 44.
145 TNA, CO, 762/84/8.
146 TNA, CO, 762/203/3679.
147 TNA, CO, 762/16/12.
148 TNA, CO, 762/47/3.

by republicans between 1919 and August 1922. He wrote, 'I was a marked man and was several times threatened and revolvers pushed into my ribs'. He had a high profile; he had helped to recruit 2,000 men with whom he served in France and was employed by the British Ministry of Labour as the manager of a disabled soldiers' centre in Tipperary.[149] Major Hugh Jones was appointed Crown Solicitor for Wexford in July 1920 but was dismissed in January 1922. He had to go into hiding, sleeping in a barricaded room with a gun after he received several anonymous letters warning there were plans to kidnap him. He left for England in August 1922. At the time of his claim in 1926 he lived in Waterford, where his situation was improving as he was 'living down' his former connection to the government. He attributed the harassment to his 'dual capacity' as an officer and Crown Solicitor.[150] Norris Goddard from Rathmines, County Dublin was also a Crown Solicitor. He received threatening letters from the IRA imposing the death sentence, which broke his health. His business was boycotted and collapsed.[151]

Intimidation was also motivated by sectarianism. Colonel John Purvis of Innishannon, West Cork wrote that in May 1922 'several Protestants were murdered within a mile of my house'. His next-door neighbour, another Colonel, was shot in his garage and 'all the Loyalist houses were burnt down'. He received warnings and threats telling him to leave, and so he left for England, not returning.[152] Arthur Travers of Clonakilty, West Cork wrote that:

In April 1922 there were a number of Protestants shot around this part of the country. At the same period three armed men came to my residence, but I left through a back way. In August, as the trouble and conflict was getting more and more acute, I left for England and stayed there until the end of September. I then returned home.[153]

Henry Newton Kevin returned to Youghal, County Cork to set up a private medical practice. He wrote:

I found that owing to my well-known loyal views, and also because I was a Protestant Loyalist, it was useless to start a practice while the Rebellion was in progress. I have been told that policemen in Youghal

149 TNA, CO, 762/14/8.
150 TNA, CO, 762/77/11.
151 TNA, CO, 762/152/13.
152 TNA, CO, 762/89/13.
153 TNA, CO, 762/121/4.

have openly said that they could not have me for a doctor owing to my support of the British Crown. I lost many cases owing to this form of boycott. People have been told in their chapels by their priest that they must have doctors of their own faith.[154]

William McKenna, of Tyrellspass, County Westmeath, was a Protestant ex-serviceman whose wife's father was in the RIC. According to the IGC report he claimed for destruction of his house and crops and being forced to leave Ireland for a period of six months. In April 1922 he was turned out of his home and beaten during a raid by 50 republicans who told him to remember Belfast. His crops were destroyed and his land taken away as was that of his brothers (also ex-servicemen) and father. His solicitor wrote 'particular animosity was shown to him as his wife's father was a sergeant in the old RIC'. He wrote in his application, 'Thank God times are better and quieter, but a Protestant in Southern Ireland remains more or less in anxiety, because only a Protestant will admit themselves to be loyalist'. The actions against McKenna were related to his wife's father being in the RIC, his being a Protestant and revenge attacks for Belfast, not specifically because he was an ex-soldier.[155] Protestant clergy were also targeted. Richard Madden, a Church of England chaplain in the war, wrote that due to not supporting the republicans in the period to 1923, he suffered raids and harassment at his rectory in Tipperary from 1920–3, and at a farm in Galway from 1919.[156] Canon Charles Atkinson of Kilpeacan Rectory, County Limerick wrote that in March 1922

a party of about 20 armed men entered my house, turned me out with my wife and daughter and set fire to it. We were sent away under armed guard to a house nearby and released after the fire had been in progress for an hour.[157]

IRA officers admitted that houses of prominent Protestant loyalists were burnt in retaliation for the destruction of property of republican sympathisers by the British.[158] The evidence supports Hart's argument that Protestants were specifically targeted.

Those whose loyalism was well known were also threatened. Benjamin Rose of Limerick owned Boswell House, which he described as a 'gentleman's

154 TNA, CO, 762/199/9.
155 TNA, CO, 762/42/2.
156 TNA, CO, 762/44/5.
157 TNA, CO, 762/184 3.
158 IMA/BMH, WS443, Neville, Cork; WS1296, Costello, Westmeath; WS1547, Murphy, Cork.

residence and as one of the County family seats in Ireland'. He took up residence again in 1919 but wrote, 'I was known to be a Loyalist and hostile to the aims of the rebels, I found that people could only live by compromising with them'. He claimed that owing to threats from armed men and constant raids, and because he was without protection, he left the country in 1920.[159] Jeremiah Connolly wrote, 'before joining the forces I was employed under the Cork Corporation and I got my job back in 1920. After the election in that year it became republican. Anyone who was loyal was marked down for dismissal. I was Chairman of BLSI, Cork branch'.[160] Francis Wallen from Dublin said he first became unpopular with the Sinn Féiners after enlisting and was 'always outspoken in his views, and was recognised as one of the leading Loyalists'. After the withdrawal of British troops, many of his old customers were afraid to do business with him and went elsewhere.[161] Edward Ryan was a veterinary surgeon who prior to the war had worked for Roscommon Council. Despite a promise that the position would be kept open, he lost his appointment. He wrote that as 'a result of my unpopularity as an ex-British soldier and supporter of his Majesty's Government and with the council supporting the Republican movement', he found it futile to try and recover his practice. He was raided several times and threatened and 'my life was made intolerable in my own country and I had to leave it'. He acknowledged that a contributory factor was 'my open attitude of resentful disgust to the then popular movement of disloyalty and terrorism'.[162] Captain John Tighe's dental practice in Clonmel, County Tipperary was boycotted. He wrote, 'I was well known for loyalty, and when the trouble began I was a marked man and in a short time my practice consisted of local Loyalists'.[163] Thomas Good from County Cork claimed that he was forced to sell his farm because of intimidation by republicans and that his father, also a farmer in Cork County and a loyalist, was killed by rebels in March 1921. He writes, 'my brother, William Good, an ex-Army Captain in the Great War, came home to attend my father's funeral, he was taken out of his trap and killed, without any reason being given'. Another brother who had been living with the father escaped to England the night his brother was killed and after the farm was attacked by rebels. It is the type of story that may well have appeared in the press, as the execution of an ex-serviceman by the IRA, but it is clear the family were targeted as loyalists, not because one brother served in the army. Indeed, Thomas Good writes in his claim, 'the losses were due

---

159   TNA, CO, 762/41/2.
160   TNA, CO, 762/204/3686.
161   TNA, CO, 762/77/5.
162   TNA, CO, 762/62/23.
163   TNA, CO, 762/117/4.

entirely to my allegiance to the King and the British Government. I was a
Loyalist living in a neighbourhood of rebels'. There is no mention of the
father or his two brothers having been in the army.[164] The house of Colonel
Charles Davis Guinness at Clermont Park, Dundalk, County Louth was
burned down in February 1923 by armed men and he had to leave Ireland.
He was county representative of the Irish Unionist Alliance.[165] In February
1922 armed men failed in an attempt to kidnap Robert Lyon Moore from
his house in County Donegal. From May to June 1922 they took possession
of his house, looted the contents, and did 'considerable damage'. Moore
was unable to return home unless under military protection and had to live
in hotels in Northern Ireland for a year. There were several likely reasons
other than wartime service for the antagonism. Moore was a commandant
in the Special Constabulary, a Deputy Lieutenant of the County, a member
of the Irish Unionist Alliance and on the Standing Committee of the
Ulster Unionist Alliance.[166] Army service was not necessarily an indicator
of exceptional loyalty, although in the above cases it was almost certainly a
manifestation of such. Yet army service was only one aspect; all were in other
regards high-profile loyalists and this was the main cause of their problems.

Specific actions or behaviour on the part of the ex-serviceman, including
spying or associating closely with or joining the Crown Forces, especially the
RIC and the Black and Tans, or supplying to them, could cause intimidation.
Those who supplied to or worked in administrative and support capacities
for the Crown Forces could be subject to intimidation, but this generally
stopped short of killing, unless it was associated with informing. The Dáil
Éireann passed a decree of social ostracism against members of the RIC to
undermine their morale, while a boycott of them caused the IRA to seek to
prevent traders from supplying them with goods.[167] Similar steps were taken
against the army and, upon their arrival, the Tans and Auxiliaries. But it
was civilian spies, who often had local knowledge and were of considerable
danger to the IRA, who could expect the most severe retribution. James
Foran returned home to Milltown-Mal-Bay, County Clare in May 1919.
He wrote, 'I remained a loyal supporter of the British Government and
at once became a marked man. Armed men visited my home and accused
me of being an English spy. Certainly I did do all in my power to help the
British soldiers in their search for the IRA'. He claimed he was subjected to a

---

164 TNA, CO, 762/32/18.
165 TNA, CO, 762/104/1784.
166 TNA, CO, 762/57/9.
167 IMA/BMH, WS718, Crawley, Roscommon; Walsh, *News from Ireland*, 69; Charles
     Townshend, 'Policing Insurgency in Ireland' in Anderson and Killingray (eds), *Policing
     and Decolonisation: Politics, Nationalism and the Police 1917–65* (Manchester, 1992), 36.

'severe beating'. It was surprising he was not executed.[168] Thomas Fitzsimons purchased a small farm in County Westmeath in May 1920. He wrote, 'my neighbours became cool towards me and threatening letters began to reach me because I had been a British Officer, and also I was friendly with the police'. Throughout 1921 he suffered continual harassment and damage to his property. The reason for the intimidation was not that he was an ex-serviceman but an informer. He wrote, 'I reported information given to me by a girl, about an ambush, to the police. I was challenged for my action and taken by a party of men who fired shots across my face'.[169] In both these cases the claimants admitted informing. In other cases the situation was unclear. James Donovan of Kinsale, County Cork was killed in July 1922 as a suspected spy.[170] Kate O'Donovan from Bandon, County Cork wrote that her husband, a navy pensioner, was shot dead in front of her at their home in March 1921 because he was suspected of assisting the authorities.[171] Robert Norman worked as a post office official in Cork City. In September 1922 a bomb was thrown through the kitchen window of his house. The bomb did not explode but a note was left in his backyard with the words, 'Convicted spy. Traitors beware'. He left for England.[172] George Thomson of Bandon, County Cork claimed he was kidnapped by the IRA in October 1920 because he was 'suspected of thwarting republicans who were planning to attack the Military', and was charged with treason and sentenced to be shot. He was released on condition that he left the country. He did so and did not return.[173] Shortly after starting a course at a college in Dublin in January 1921 with a guarantee of a job in the British Excise, James Fitzpatrick was 'singled out as a spy' and given 48 hours to leave the city. He reported this to the authorities. In May 1921 he was kidnapped by armed men and taken to Kingstown, where he was told to leave on a night boat or be shot dead.[174] Paul Goodwin of Athy, County Kildare wrote that he was 'regarded as a spy and informer. My movements were watched', and in June 1921 he was held up by armed men and told he was next to be shot for giving information. He left the country.[175] George Hall, a farmer from County Wicklow, received information in June 1921 that he was going to be shot. He went to Wexford

---

168   TNA, CO, 762/107/9.
169   TNA, CO, 762/192/6.
170   TNA, CO, 762/46/14. The claim was made by his father, based on financial dependency.
171   TNA, CO, 762/78/13.
172   TNA, CO, 762/119/4.
173   TNA, CO, 762/90/8.
174   TNA, CO, 762/61/17.
175   TNA, CO, 762/193/7.

for safety but was followed, beaten and told he was an English spy and a traitor. They let him go but warned him to leave the country.[176]

In all these cases the claimants stated that the violence was a response to suspected spying. Their guilt is unclear from the files but, according to Borgonovo, the IRA had a well-organised intelligence network with the means to correctly identify informers. In the case of Hall, it seems unlikely that they would follow him to another county unless they had evidence. In many of the cases, the IRA had opportunities to kill the suspect but did not. If their objective was simply to kill ex-servicemen, they would have not have gone to the trouble of warning them to leave. The following case illustrates the conflicting information that can be found in different sources. Margaret Maher of Thurles, County Tipperary wrote that in December 1920 her son, John Maher, received information that the IRA had sentenced him to death for giving information to the RIC. In March 1921 he and another ex-soldier, Patrick Meara, were kidnapped and murdered by the IRA, who put notices on the bodies warning spies and informers to beware. In October 1922 her husband, Patrick Maher, also an ex-serviceman, was dismissed from his bank job after the manager told him he had received a letter from the IRA ordering him to do this. He was unable to get other employment. In October 1922 the IRA smashed the windows of their home with stones.[177] The IMA/BMH witness statements contain the republican perspective. James Leahy, an IRA officer, wrote that Maher (the son) and Meara were known to be close to the RIC and the Tans and were suspected of giving information on wanted republicans; a number of raids in the town were attributed to information supplied by them. He confirms the date of execution, March 1921 and the warning notices. In reprisal, republicans' homes were raided and they were shot. RIC reports state that this was carried out by friends of the ex-servicemen but dispute the accusation that Maher and Meara were spies, claiming that they were 'absolutely useless' to them. According to Leahy, the raiders were masked and armed policemen, and one of their leaders, Sergeant Enright, gave him a detailed account of the shooting during the Truce.[178] Much research has been based on the RIC police files. The IRA witness statements, not surprisingly, provide a different perspective of events. What is interesting is the specific reference to the RIC officer involved. Martin Donohue's case illustrates the stance often taken by SILRA in claiming that intimidation was only due to war service. They wrote of Donahue that, as he had been an ex-serviceman, he would probably have been discriminated against had he remained in Ireland. In reality, Donohue, who worked as

176 TNA, CO, 762/59/5.
177 TNA, CO, 762/67/9.
178 IMA/BMH, WS1454. Leahy refers to the son as James: TNA, CO, 904/114,860.

a librarian in an internment prison for Sinn Féiners, was 'a marked man' because he got the inmates into trouble by 'snitching'.[179] Due to their shared military background, ex-servicemen may have been more susceptible to friendly relationships with the Crown Forces. In January 1921 a number of Tans were drafted into Arva County Cavan. Most were, like Richard Kemp, ex-soldiers and members of the Protestant Church. He noted, 'they used to visit my house and chat. This brought me under the notice of the IRA, who warned me to cease all communication and threatened to shoot me'.[180] There is no evidence that Kemp was an informer, but it was inevitable that the IRA would be suspicious.

Those who supplied to the British Forces could be subjected to intimidation. Thomas Deignan, an IRA battalion commander in County Sligo, wrote, 'the police were boycotted. No one would supply them with food. No one would hire them cars or associate or speak to them and anyone doing so incurred the immediate displeasure of the IRA'.[181] The republicans were concerned that not only goods and services would be supplied, but also that those with close connections to the Crown Forces would provide sensitive information. That they had cause to be suspicious was demonstrated by the case of Benjamin Stone, a Protestant from Cork with a family history of army and RIC service. He wrote that while with the RIC 'in the nineties I suffered great hardship through the Land War, protecting landlords from agrarian outrage'. Upon his return from the War, he opened a shop that supplied the British Forces. He was also an informer. 'I gave them a great deal of help as to localities, individuals and happenings and prevented, at least, two ambushes of military'. His shop windows were broken by republicans, his donkey taken away and the delivery cart smashed and he received threatening letters. After an incident in which an ex-service man was shot returning from a dance, soldiers retaliated by breaking windows, all except for his, making him a marked man; his shop was boycotted by civilians. He was treasurer of the Comrades of the Great War. Their building was burnt down and he was warned his house would also be torched if he found new premises. His shop takings dwindled and in April 1923 he had to sell his house and business, but the IGC noted that the major part of his income came from the Crown Forces and so declined when they withdrew.[182]

Edward Delany of Newport, County Tipperary, supplied the Crown Forces with food and acted as a guide for them in unfamiliar areas. Two of his friends, an ex-soldier called Patrick Galligan and an ex-RIC sergeant

179   TNA, CO, 762/53/8.
180   TNA, CO, 762/187/10.
181   IMA/BMH, WS894.
182   TNA, CO, 762/14/19.

were murdered in May 1922, and he 'got word' he would be next, so he immediately left Ireland.[183] If acting as a 'guide' included providing information on the local IRA, it was inevitable that Delaney would receive retribution. Galligan's wife Bridget wrote that her husband was murdered by the anti-Treaty IRA in front of her and that 'there was no other reason except that he had served many years in the British Army'.[184] As he was friends with Delany he may also have been an informer. Patrick Lynass from Cork was fired at by the IRA in May 1921 whilst coming home from a military dance where he had performed as a musician. Although Lynass sought to blame his problems on being an ex-serviceman, he wrote that others 'received threatening letters warning them not to attend the dance', and that 'while the trouble was on in Ireland I gave my moral support to the British Government and gave every assistance I could to members of the Crown'.[185] Simon Cartwright and his wife ran a boarding house in Bundoran, County Donegal. In May 1922 they were raided by republican forces and accused of 'keeping two special policemen the previous night'. They received the following notice, 'we want your house for the people your gang is putting out of the Six Counties. Go back and live with your brother Specials there. If you do not go within the week you will be shot'. They left, eventually settling in Londonderry.[186]

Patrick McGrath of County Carlow and his father, also an ex-serviceman, refused to support the IRA. His father gave evidence against them after the local police barrack was burned down, and provided laundry services for the military when others refused. An apprenticeship in motor engineering was organised for McGrath by the Civil Liabilities Department in 1921, following which he was approached by the IRA and told to join or leave the district. He refused and was arrested and told to depart or he would be shot as a spy. He re-joined the armed forces in August 1921 and was stationed in County Wicklow. His father obtained a pass to sell the troops fruit and confectionaries but was told by the IRA to stay out of the camp. They killed his pony, broke his cart, and sent him threatening letters. McGrath wrote that he felt 'everyone was against us'.[187] George Kelly was a partner in a general merchant business in Cahir, County Tipperary. He was threatened against supplying goods to the Crown Forces. He wrote, 'my association with H.M. Forces brought me into ill favour with the Republicans'.[188] The father of Richard Broderick from Youghal, Cork owned a pub frequented by British

183   TNA, CO, 762/83/12.
184   TNA, CO, 762/19/9.
185   TNA, CO, 762/73/9.
186   TNA, CO, 762/98/20.
187   TNA, CO, 762/60/7.
188   TNA, CO, 762/178/9.

soldiers. At the end of 1920 the IRA tried to close it; his father refused, after which there was a boycott and civilians ceased using the pub. After the British Forces left all trade was therefore lost.[189] James McLoughlin, also of Youghal, County Cork, worked at the local barracks as a harness repairer for the British army. He claimed he had been boycotted but the IGC attributed part of his loss to a diminution in trade, following the departure of the Crown Forces.[190] Some shop owners on friendly relations with the Crown Forces suffered. Henry Alcock from Cork claimed he was waylaid and beaten by the IRA in September 1921, after which his haberdashery shop was boycotted. He helped recruit locally before volunteering and on his return organised annual poppy day functions and was friendly with military. Alcock's solicitor wrote that his business suffered 'on account of his connection and association with the Crown Forces'.[191] In January 1921 John Browlow opened a garage in Nenagh, County Tipperary. He wrote that from August 1921 he was boycotted because of his friendliness with the RIC and military. After receiving a threatening letter he left in December 1921. He returned in May 1922 but after more threats left for London, returning in March 1924.[192] On returning to Tipperary, Vincent O'Riordan started a motor hire business. He was friendly with the Crown Forces and had driven them on numerous occasions, and as a result lost business because customers knew 'that owing to his unpopularity with Sinn Féin his car was liable to be stopped and taken away when on a journey'. After the military left Ireland, armed men seized his car in July 1922.[193] In 1919 Charles Nyhan returned to his medical practice in Clonakilty, County Cork. He was appointed doctor to the British military and was on friendly terms with them. He gave evidence in a number of cases where members of the RIC had been injured performing their duties. In November 1921 his motor car was seized by the IRA. In April 1922 he was held up by the anti-Treaty IRA on a public road. In August 1922 his house was raided by armed men. He went to England for six weeks, returning after hearing that Clonakilty had been occupied by government troops. He claimed his practice suffered but the IGC concluded that this was due to the Crown Forces withdrawing and the expulsion of many of the landowning classes.[194] In a number of cases the IGC considered the problems of those who supplied to the Crown Forces to be caused not

189 TNA, CO, 762/35/15.
190 TNA, CO, 762/143/16. McLoughlin had previously received assistance from the Irish Loyalists' Relief Association and the Army Benevolent Funds.
191 TNA, CO, 762/10/3.
192 TNA, CO, 762/3714.
193 TNA, CO, 762/66/1.
194 TNA, CO, 762/120/2.

by boycotts but due to the withdrawal of British Forces, leading to a loss of business for which no compensation was due.

Some of those employed by the Crown Forces or their agencies in administrative and support roles claimed they were intimidated. Charles Kelly wrote that he was attacked twice, in 1920 and 1921, by republicans 'due to my services to the British Government as a Dublin Castle official during the reign of terror in Ireland', and because his son was Chief Intelligence Officer on the staff of General Strickland in Cork.[195] John Kavanagh from Dublin was employed as a clerk at the Royal Army Service Corp until June 1922. He claimed that there was a 'relentless murder campaign by Republicans against loyal Government employees', citing another ex-soldier clerk named Denis Lenehan, who was badly wounded on his way home from work in 1921.[196] While the IRA did sometimes target non-military personnel who worked for the Crown Forces (their employment released soldiers for active duty), according to Borgonovo most were left alone unless they were also informing. The majority of IGC claims relate not to intimidation while the claimant was working for the Crown Forces but to problems after their departure. Frank Redman worked as a clerk at Curragh Camp, County Kildare. After the British vacated, he sought employment but received threats that drove him to leave with his family for England.[197] Matthew Forsyth was employed as a canteen manager at the Fermoy Military Barracks in Cork. He lost the job when the troops withdrew in March 1922. Following warnings from the IRA, he left Ireland in July 1922 with his family.[198] William Chilcott worked as an auditor in the RIC office in Dublin Castle until July 1922, after which he was intimidated into leaving the country.[199] David Kelley was employed as a civilian foreman mechanic with the army in the Royal Barracks, Dublin until December 1922. He claimed after the government changed he received threats and with no prospects of employment in Ireland went to England in January 1923.[200] Although working in administration functions for the Crown Forces may in some cases have caused intimidation or impeded future employment opportunities, as with those who supplied the Crown Forces and suffered loss of business, the IGC concluded that Kelley's complaint was primarily based on economic problems arising from the departure of British Forces, that is loss of employment, which was not a basis for compensation. The economic impact was significant: in Kildare, where an average of 10,000 troops had been based in camps such as Curragh

195 TNA, CO, 762/16/10.
196 TNA, CO, 762/14/14.
197 TNA, CO, 762/13/11.
198 TNA, CO, 762/96/16.
199 TNA, CO, 762/120/14.
200 TNA, CO, 762/94/12.

and Naas, the withdrawal of the military led to the redundancy of 4,000 garrison workers.[201] In any case the problem was not caused by the claimant being an ex-serviceman except to the extent that this was more likely to have led to his employment in the first instance.

The IRA considered the RIC to be 'the chief weapon by which the British Government maintained such a hold on the country'.[202] Ex-servicemen who planned to join, particularly the Black and Tans or Auxiliaries, were threatened. Those that did were considered part of the enemy forces, and even had problems after returning home following their disbandment. Michael O'Brien from Callan, Kilkenny joined the RIC/Black and Tans. After being disbanded in January 1922, a group of armed men broke into his house, took him to the old RIC barracks, and imprisoned him. He escaped and fled to England.[203] Michael St. Legier of Durrow, Queen's County returned to the RIC after the War. He wrote, 'In 1922 I was disbanded from the RIC and [was] obliged to leave this county'. He returned and in 1923 purchased two cottages and land. Notices were posted that a planter, spy and an enemy of the country was present. He was obliged to leave again, as 'I was subjected to every annoyance and intimidation'.[204] Dennis Roche of Dublin joined the RIC. He claimed that his elderly father, a retired RIC officer, was shunned after refusing to influence him to resign. In 1921 he went to live with his father. In March 1923 he claimed, 'the front door was battered down and a band of disguised ruffians rushed in and shouted for the dog that did England's dirty work'. He was accused of being involved in the shooting of the Lord Mayor of Cork, Sinn Féin's Tomás Mac Curtain, who was shot in March 1920 by, according to the inquest, the RIC. He was allowed to go but was told he would be immediately shot if he returned.[205] John Lavelle was employed with the Auxiliaries in Galway as an officer's mess servant. He lost his job with the disbandment of the RIC in 1922. He wrote, 'I was looked upon as a Tan, no one in the neighbourhood would employ me. I succeeded in getting employment but when I turned up the 50 men employed on the works downed tools'.[206] Captain John Rogers joined the Auxiliaries and served in Cork. When they disbanded in January 1922 he claimed he had to leave Ireland for England to find work.[207]

Edward O'Callaghan returned to Cork in 1919 and claimed he refused a

---

201 Michael Murphy, 'Revolution and Terror in Kildare, 1919–1923', in David Fitzpatrick (ed.), *Terror in Ireland, 1916–1923* (Dublin, 2012), 195–6, 201.
202 IMA/BMH, WS1296, Costello, Westmeath.
203 TNA, CO, 762/93/25.
204 TNA, CO, 762/186/6.
205 TNA, CO, 762/192/18.
206 TNA, CO, 762/194/27.
207 TNA, CO, 762/9/10.

'high command' in the IRA, joining instead the Auxiliaries. He wrote, 'I was compelled to leave my home in May 1922. I am looked upon as a traitor as I fought in the British Crown Forces, during what they termed the Anglo-Irish War'. The IGC recognised the difficulties faced by those who had served in the RIC, concluding in O'Callaghan's case that 'in consequence of his connection with the Constabulary he found it impossible to get employment and was eventually obliged to seek refuge in Great Britain'.[208] The intimidation in these cases was a response to the fact that they had fought Irishmen on Irish soil. Likewise army service in Ireland during the conflict was a cause for retribution; a distinction was made for service overseas. Patrick McCormack enlisted in 1916 and served with the British army in Ireland from April 1920 until February 1922. He said that when he returned home to Ennistymon, County Clare he was 'considered an enemy of the country by everyone', beaten and called a Black and Tan'. In contrast, he claimed, 'other discharged British soldiers were set up in various businesses who never served against the IRA'.[209] Martin Conway wrote, 'when it became known in Limerick that I was serving in the British Army during the trouble here I was unable to find any employment'. If he obtained work it was only until 'it was found out I was serving under the British flag when the fight was on in Ireland'.[210] William Wilson wrote that he lost his job in 1923 at the Office of Public Works and had to leave Ireland on account of threats due to his army service against the rebels in 1916.[211] Cecil Burchett from County Tipperary served in Limerick during the Rising and was part of raiding parties that brought him within a few miles of his home. After returning home he received warnings to leave Ireland. He also wrote that his recruiting activities during the War were an additional reason for intimidation.[212] Recruitment activities in Ireland during the War increased the likelihood of retribution. Captain Daniel Sheehan was an MP for Cork, a barrister and journalist. He claimed to have helped recruit 5,000 volunteers before enlisting himself. He wrote, 'as a consequence of my war service and especially because of my successful recruitment activities it was impossible for me to return to Ireland and resume my career'.[213] Major Hamilton Johnstone of Glenties,

208 TNA, CO, 762/32/4.
209 TNA, CO, 762/63/7. The IGC questioned the validity of claims from this area, see below.
210 TNA, CO, 762/36/2.
211 TNA, CO, 762/24/5.
212 TNA, CO, 762/57/4. Burchett's case needs qualifying. He was able to run his business until 1924, when it was sold. He writes that most of his customers were loyalists who had been driven out of the country; this was likely a significant reason for the sale of the business.
213 TNA, CO, 762/24/14.

County Donegal re-joined his old regiment but due to his age remained in Ireland, taking a very active part in the recruiting campaign. He was also a Magistrate for the County of Donegal. In August 1922, armed men entered his house and shot him dead; the house was later burned down.[214] Prior to enlistment, Francis Costello from Nenagh, County Tipperary had raised a troop of local yeomanry. He wrote that from 1919 to 1922 he owned three properties, but was forced to leave after he was raided.[215] Martin Bennett returned to Mountrath in 1922 after the Leinster Regiment was disbanded. He claimed he met with a good deal of opposition as he had recruited in the area from 1916 to 1918.[216]

The IRA launched general campaigns to obtain arms, equipment, supplies, and finance in order to sustain their activities. Some of the claims from those subject to these campaigns were particularly trivial. Thomas Browning of County Tipperary said in 1922 that his house was raided by Irish republican forces who took two field glasses. He claimed 'as a British Officer I was always under suspicion'.[217] It seems likely that if the IRA were antagonistic to him for being an ex-British officer, the sanction would have been more severe. The house of Sir Arthur Hance in Bantry, County Cork was raided several times by the IRA in 1921 and items, including two bicycles and binoculars, were taken.[218] In Joseph Corcullion's case the threat was more serious. He opened a bicycle shop in Castlefin, County Donegal and in March 1921 and May 1922 armed men raided his premises, looting equipment. He was told he would not be allowed to carry on business in the Free State and was finally forced to vacate his shop, owing to threats to shoot him.[219] Between July and November 1922, armed men stole the motorcar and horse of Major Richard Philips from County Tipperary. In a time of turmoil, as the IGC noted, it may have been a simple robbery.[220] The difficulty of distinguishing politically motivated intimidation and simple theft is illustrated in the case of Robert Browne from Rathkenny, County Cavan, who was a member of the Loyal Orange Institution in his district. In 1920/21 his shop was raided because, he claimed, he had been purchasing goods from Northern Ireland at the time of the Belfast boycott. In April 1924 masked men came into his shop and attempted to extort money. In December 1925 he was again robbed.[221] It seems unlikely that these latter

214   TNA, CO, 762/123/3.
215   TNA, CO, 762/174/1.
216   TNA, CO, 762/148/6.
217   TNA, CO, 762/62/17.
218   TNA, CO, 762/84/9.
219   TNA, CO, 762/109/11.
220   TNA, CO, 762/67/10.
221   TNA, CO, 762/95/20.

incidents were politically motivated, considering when they occurred and particularly since in 1924 Browne's wife identified one of the men, who was then arrested by the authorities and sentenced to a year's imprisonment. Others were punished for refusing to pay levies. George Bradley owned a farm in Mountrath, Queen's County and because he refused to subscribe to IRA funds, he was boycotted from 1920 to 1924 and his pigs were poisoned.[222] James Bannon resumed his tailor's business in Thurles, Tipperary. He wrote he was getting back his customers when boycotted in 1921, having refused to subscribe to IRA funds.[223] Owen Gill of Nenagh, County Tipperary wrote that he refused to subscribe to IRA funds and his house was raided.[224]

Those who refused to join the IRA suffered retribution. Given their military skills it ex-servicemen were more likely to be particularly targeted. David Mullins of Queen's County wrote, 'there was the greatest hostility displayed to all old soldiers and Loyalists unless they joined the rebellion against the Crown'.[225] Simon O'Flaherty from Doolin, County Clare claimed that in March 1920 he refused to join the IRA and consequently suffered severe threats and insults.[226] William Caldbeck from Mountrath, Queen's County claimed that because he refused to join the IRA, or subscribe to their funds, he was 'marked out for bad treatment', and could not get work between 1921 and 1922.[227] Wilfred Trey was refused his old job back in County Limerick unless he joined the IRA.[228] In other cases there were additional circumstances that caused intimidation. William Leahy of Cork City wrote that, as he was an ex-soldier and loyalist, he refused to join the IRA and consequently his house was raided in June 1920. In February 1921 a friend of his from the British army was shot dead on leaving his house in the company of his sister, suggesting the real problem may have been friendliness with British soldiers. Leahy lived in the barracks for fourteen months for safety, a protection normally offered informers, after which he left for England.[229] Patrick Baker from Liscannor, County Clare was asked to join the IRA in 1920 but refused. Later that year, when the Royal Marines came to Liscannor, he volunteered to cart foodstuffs for them. In December 1921, he was kidnapped and court-martialled as a British spy and was sentenced to leave Clare or be executed. He remained and was 'severely beaten' in July

222 TNA, CO, 762/148/10.
223 TNA, CO, 762/196/18.
224 TNA, CO, 762/193/19.
225 TNA, CO, 762/71/3.
226 TNA, CO, 762/94/21.
227 TNA, CO, 762/146/1.
228 TNA, CO, 762/167/7.
229 TNA, CO, 762/155/4.

1922.[230] Michael Martin of Wexford refused to join the republicans in 1920 and had his motor lorry taken in 1922. That he made a living with it in the intervening period does not indicate significant intimidation. Additionally, he said that he had made many enemies through helping to recruit for the British army before enlisting.[231]

The IGC described parts of County Cork as 'very bad'.[232] Many of the claims were from West Cork but the majority did not attribute any intimidation to war service.[233] Some did including Richard Jermyn who worked as a driver. In August 1921 his employers dismissed him as 'they did not want a British ex-soldier in their employment'.[234] George Grogan worked for the railway until August 1921, when he 'received a letter warning me under penalty of death to leave my employment owing to being an ex-serviceman'. He remained in the locality and lived on his army pension.[235] County Tipperary was another area of significant IRA activity and again most claimants did not attribute the cause of their intimidation to army service.[236] Patrick Maloney was an exception. He was employed as a postman before enlisting and was promised his job back on return, but was told that he 'had no further claims on the post office as promises made to ex-British Soldiers were withdrawn'.[237] The case of Michael Dillon from Clonmel, County Tipperary is interesting as it illustrates how support for the Free State caused intimidation from the anti-Treaty IRA. His father's home was attacked in July 1921 and his sister was murdered; he was fired at, but escaped. His younger brother was also killed. Dillon was subject to further intimidation until October 1922, when he gave up his position in the post office and left for England. Newspapers articles under the headlines, 'Life under the Irish Rebels', and 'Clonmel Savagery', gave more details of the intimidation suffered by the family. They refer to 'the callousness which has marked the operations of the Irregulars (the anti-Treaty IRA) in Southern Ireland', and report that the republicans tortured the younger brother and executed him. Whatever caused the murder of his younger siblings, it was likely more than Michael Dillon's army service. The paper states that the younger brother was a 'Free Stater', and that 'this act has done more against the Republicans, even

230 TNA, CO, 762/158/1.
231 TNA, CO, 762/41/16.
232 TNA, CO, 762/89/13.
233 TNA, CO, 762/187/17, John Harley; TNA, CO, 762/129/11, Richard Bright; TNA, CO, 762/105/10, Henry Synan.
234 TNA, CO, 762/192/23.
235 TNA, CO, 762/21/13.
236 TNA, CO, 762/147/15, Patrick Rourke; TNA, CO, 762/193/18, Samuel Dann; TNA, CO, 762/132/7, John Savage; TNA, CO, 762/88/19, Mary/George Brophy; TNA, CO, 762/196/5, George Holland.
237 TNA, CO, 762/36/10.

their own people are horrified'.[238] Perhaps surprisingly, many complaints
emanated from Queen's County, as comparatively it was not an area of
significant IRA activity. A number of the claims indicated comparatively low
levels of intimidation. Robert Milne of Mountrath had turf stolen and his
pig poisoned.[239] More seriously, Henry Nagle of Mountmellick was ordered
to leave but remained until in April 1922 his brother Robert was murdered
in Clonakilty, West Cork, and Henry decided it was too dangerous to stay
and left for England.[240]

Not all violence had a political cause. The IGC believed that the
breakdown of law and order, particularly in the period after the withdrawal
of the British and the enforcement of authority at a local level by the new
Irish state, may have been the reason for some intimidation. As an example,
in one case the IGC concluded that it was hard to determine whether the
injuries claimed for were the result of a specific vendetta arising out of
loyalty to the British or just an example of 'the lawless element', taking
advantage of anarchic conditions prevalent in parts of Ireland.[241]

A review of the 73 claimants who stated that war service was a contributory
factor of the violence experienced indicates that in a number of cases the
IGC concluded that such claims were at the least questionable. Robert Tobin
returned to Cork and worked for Cork City Pensions Office. In September
1922 he joined the Free State army. In January 1923 he returned home and
was shot by three men. His wife wrote that:

> He joined the Free State Army, and this fact, coupled with his
> being an ex-British soldier was the cause of his assassination, several
> other ex-soldiers of the British Army were murdered previous to and
> subsequent to the murder of my husband, many others received notices
> of death and had to leave the City of Cork.

The IGC noted that he might not have been a loyalist as 'he had joined
the Free State Army at a time when they were not anxious to admit any
Loyalists', and that his death could have resulted from an action in the
Free State army.[242] The case is interesting insofar as Tobin worked for the
local council, implying he was not subject to prejudice due to his having
served in the British army and that his death was caused by National army
service not, despite the protestation of his wife, his having been a British

238 TNA, CO, 762/119/11.
239 TNA, CO, 762/192/15.
240 TNA, CO, 762/147/7.
241 TNA, CO, 762/78/2.
242 TNA, CO, 762/23/12.

soldier. In November 1922 Liam Lynch, the commanding officer of the anti-Treaty Forces, ordered the assassination of British army veterans who had joined the Free State army.[243] Daniel Cretin was employed by Southern Railway in Mallow, County Cork in July 1921. He claimed he had to leave the country because he was a navy pensioner. The IGC report stated, 'it does not appear from the evidence submitted that the claimant was obliged through threats or intimidation to leave'.[244] William Brereton from Roscrea, County Tipperary bought a threshing mill in November 1920 for £800 paid for using a £750 bank loan. He wrote, 'on account of me being an ex-soldier of the British Army there was an agitation started against me and people who were inclined to employ me got threatening letters not to do so'. He claimed that the boycott was also a punishment for his brother joining the RIC when he came out of the army. The IGC reported that he had reduced his loan to £200 by 1926, which 'does not suggest a rigorous boycott but rather a successful venture'.[245] His having been given a bank loan of around £40,000 in today's money does not suggest victimisation. Captain Timothy Collins returned to run his grocery business in Cork City and claimed, 'as a result of my service in H.M. Forces I have been practically boycotted in 1921 and 1922', and that from January 1922 threats were made on his life and he was warned to leave the country. Canon Hodges replied to a query from the IGC stating that Collins was 'a prosperous man and if he does not make the income he made in previous days it would be due to the present business depression and certainly not a boycott'.[246] Matthew Steele wrote that:

In February 1921 I commenced grocery business in Clonmel, County Tipperary and did a good trade until August 1921 when trouble between the Irregulars [the anti-Treaty IRA] and Free State Troops began. A great portion of my stock was commandeered and my business suffered. Owing to being an ex-British Officer I was boycotted. Finally, in May 1923, I had to sell my business.

It seems unlikely that Steele's problems were caused by his being an ex-British Officer or they would have been apparent earlier. Clonmel was a British army base and more likely his business declined with their departure, which is perhaps why the IGC rejected his claim.[247] Thomas Glynne of County Longford complained that the anti-Treaty IRA shot many ex-army

243 Karsten, 'Irish Soldiers in the British Army', 54.
244 TNA, CO, 762/47/5.
245 TNA, CO, 762/50/20.
246 TNA, CO, 762/120/12.
247 TNA, CO, 762/194/24.

officers on sight. Yet his punishment for refusing to join the IRA in October 1921 was the theft of his bicycle. The IGC did not find this explanation satisfactory and he was not awarded any money.[248] Patrick Collins of County Cork wrote that 'ex-servicemen are victimised and prevented from obtaining employment'. The IGC asked for evidence, but none was forthcoming so no compensation was paid.[249] In two other cases in which the applicant cited army service as a cause for their problems, local newspapers provide a different perspective. Patrick Clarke wrote:

> I was a Rate Collector to the Wicklow Urban Council from which I got permission to join the British Army, the then Council passed a resolution congratulating me and promising to keep my position open for me on my return. The Council during my absence had changed to Republican and when I made an application for my old position they refused to reinstate me because I had served in H.M. Forces.

He had not applied for reinstatement until 1922. According to the local newspaper, the Council argued that he did not ask for his job in the time of Troubles but 'now he comes when everything is over', and that the current incumbent 'had been a most efficient officer'.[250] On demobilisation, John Dart returned to work in his father's business in Roscrea, County Tipperary. He wrote, 'during the troubled times in which we had the protection of the RIC, feeling was not so extreme against us although I received several threatening letters. But when the RIC were withdrawn and the Free State republicans were left in charge, things were made unpleasant for me as an ex-officer of the British Army'. He wrote that on account of an incident in which he was accused of removing a republican flag that the IRA had hoisted in Roscrea, following which he was tried by a republican court but acquitted, his father's business was boycotted, the premises damaged and he was threatened, after which he left the country. The IGC report noted that 'the claimant on account of being an ex-British Officer, and he and his father being known as Loyalists, suffered a considerable amount of abuse subsequent to the withdrawal of the Constabulary'. An article in the *Midland Tribune* in March 1922 provides a different perspective, stating that Dart had attended a hearing held by IRA officers in March 1922 for being disrespectful to the flag of the Irish. The charge was withdrawn. In relation to the boycott and the damage to the business, the senior IRA officer stated that it was the action of 'irresponsibles' and it was the responsibility of himself and his

248 TNA, CO, 762/74/5.
249 TNA, CO, 762/45/3.
250 TNA, CO, 762/45/7; *Wicklow Newsletter*, 11 March 1922.

officers 'to see firms are accorded protection from unlawful interference'. The newspaper also condemned such actions, writing that 'irresponsible people should not take the law into their own hands', and noted that the clergy at local masses had also criticised the damaging of the company's premises. The Darts had the support of the press, clergy, and the authorities. Dart remained in England for two years and at the time of his claim was working as a commercial traveller and living in Dublin.[251]

An unusually high number of claimants from Ennistymon, County Clare stated that intimidation was caused by their army service. Joseph O'Brien wrote that employers were threatened not to give him a job as he was a British ex-serviceman.[252] Michael Shannon wrote, 'I cannot get work since I was an ex-soldier and am not wanted anywhere'.[253] Austin O'Connor attributed his lack of work to being a soldier.[254] John Ronan stated, 'My loss of trade is attributable to service in the Great War'.[255] Thomas O'Brien claimed, 'The reason I give for not getting work is on account of my father, three brothers and myself serving with the British Forces. Nobody seemed to want to have anything to do with the family'.[256] George Roberts said that after demobilisation he 'considerably suffered in consequence of my loyalty'.[257] Michael Halloran and his two sons John and Michael made similar claims that they had suffered threats 'in consequence of ... family loyalty to the British Empire', but after an investigation the IGC concluded that 'the statements that they were boycotted and unpopular in the district and assaulted by the IRA are perfect nonsense', and that they had 'a thoroughly bad reputation'.[258] None of the above received compensation. Such cases may have been used by loyalist lobbying groups keen to illustrate the plight of ex-servicemen and they often received extensive press coverage. Unlike perhaps newspapers, the IGC had a duty to investigate thoroughly as they had to make a decision on whether to recommend compensation; also, they did not have the political motivations of the lobbying groups. Under closer examination the above claims were proved false. It would be ironic if those most likely to directly attribute the cause of their intimidation to army service were fraudulent republican claimants.

The IGC files demonstrate that intimidation of ex-servicemen was predominantly motivated by reasons other than just war service; of the

251 TNA, CO, 762/40/1; *Midland Tribune*, 11 March 1922.
252 TNA, CO, 762/96/2.
253 TNA, CO, 762/96/6.
254 TNA, CO, 762/91/3.
255 TNA, CO, 762/94/19.
256 TNA, CO. 762/108/5.
257 TNA, CO, 762/86/5.
258 TNA, CO, 762/51/1; 762/63/9; 762/68/3.

comparatively small number of ex-servicemen who made claims, the majority did not consider war service to be a cause of intimidation. The reasons they gave were equally applicable to other segments of the population who had not served in the War. The final report of the IGC identified illustrative cases of those who submitted claims as follows: mansion/estate owners and their employees, small farmers, merchants and shopkeepers (who, the report noted, could be boycotted if they sold to the Crown Forces) and professional classes (including solicitors, doctors, dentists, and schoolmasters). Ex-servicemen received no special mention. Great War volunteers were representative of a wide spectrum of Irish society and many from the categories mentioned above could have served in that conflict. The report noted that the type of injury for which claims were considered found its victims among all classes of the loyalist community.[259]

259 TNA, CO, 762/212.

2

Were Ex-Servicemen Targeted?

Patterns of Violence

During the period of conflict the intensity of violence and intimidation experienced by returning soldiers varied considerably depending on locality. The question is whether they were specifically targeted or did their experience simply reflect the patterns of violence experienced by other sectors of the population in different locations? An analysis of IRA violence (1917–23), members of the RIC killed on duty (1916–22), total fatalities (1917–21), and incidents recorded in complaints to the IGC demonstrates a consistency in the geographical distribution of violence and intimidation. The first three metrics focus on those killed and, in the case of IRA violence as measured by Hart, those wounded. O'Halpin's analysis covers total fatalities arising from Irish political violence from January 1917 to December 1921. Hart excludes lesser intimidation such as raids, vandalism, assaults, and robberies because of the difficulty in obtaining accurate information. They are recorded in the IGC files and the four metrics together demonstrate that the range of violence and intimidation from simple robberies to killings was uniform in its geographical variation. Of the two largest provinces in all of the metrics, Munster and Leinster, in both absolute terms and pro rata to the population, the former had around double or more incidents of violence than the latter. Although there are county anomalies (Queen's had comparatively few killings and shootings but records large instances of 'low level' intimidation), the main areas of violence were Cork, Tipperary, Clare, Kerry, and Limerick. Incidents of violence in Dublin were high in terms of absolute numbers; pro rata to the population it ranked lower than the national average on all metrics with the exception of all fatalities, in which it was approximately the same.[1] Taking into account population levels, Connaught and Ulster in particular (three counties) had lower levels of violence than the national average on all four metrics. On two of the metrics, RIC killings and IGC incidents, Connaught had a higher ratio of incidents than Leinster pro rata to the population.

Table 8: Analysis of violence and intimidation: general population/RIC pro rata to population

County	Population	IRA Violence		RIC Killed		All Fatalities		IGC Total	
		Incidents	per 10,000	Incidents	per 10,000	Incidents	per 10,000	Incidents	per 10,000
Carlow	34,476	15	4.4	3	0.9	13	3.8	72	20.9
Dublin	505,654	460	9.1	32	0.6	309	6.1	203	4.0
Kildare	58,028	20	3.4	1	0.2	12	2.1	43	7.4
Kilkenny	70,990	35	5.0	4	0.6	19	2.7	40	5.6
Longford	39,847	55	13.7	12	3.0	26	6.5	43	10.8
Louth	62,739	37	5.8	6	1.0	26	4.1	17	2.7
Meath	62,969	24	3.8	10	1.6	17	2.7	62	9.8
Kings	52,592	22	4.2	5	1.0	21	4.0	91	17.3
Queens	51,540	34	6.6	1	0.2	10	1.9	292	56.7
Westmeath	56,818	37	6.5	4	0.7	18	3.2	35	6.2
Wexford	95,848	50	5.2	3	0.3	23	2.4	52	5.4
Wicklow	57,591	5	0.8	7	1.2	7	1.2	41	7.1
Leinster	1,149,092	794	6.9	88	0.8	501	4.4	991	8.6
Clare	95,064	113	11.9	35	3.7	95	10.0	315	33.1
Cork	365,747	876	24.0	96	2.6	495	13.5	780	21.3
Kerry	149,171	262	17.6	35	2.3	136	9.1	175	11.7
Limerick	140,343	196	14.0	38	2.7	121	8.6	123	8.8
Tipperary	141,015	217	15.5	43	3.0	152	10.8	280	19.9
Waterford	78,562	47	5.9	7	0.9	35	4.5	43	5.5

1 Metrics are for Dublin County. The city represented around two-thirds of the county population. The city was more violent than the rest of the county; extrapolating Hart's figures for IRA violence there were 13.1 incidents per 10,000 people in the city compared to 2.4 in the countryside.

County	Population	IRA Violence		RIC Killed		All Fatalities		IGC Total	
		Incidents	per 10,000	Incidents	per 10,000	Incidents	per 10,000	Incidents	per 10,000
Munster	969,902	1,711	17.7	254	2.6	1,034	10.7	1,716	17.7
Galway	169,366	83	4.9	14	0.8	58	3.4	126	7.4
Leitrim	55,907	20	3.5	1	0.2	15	2.7	83	14.8
Mayo	172,690	103	6.0	21	1.2	43	2.5	139	8.0
Roscommon	83,556	66	7.8	14	1.7	58	6.9	75	9.0
Sligo	71,388	48	6.8	14	2.0	18	2.5	82	11.5
Connaught	552,907	320	5.8	64	1.2	192	3.5	505	9.1
Cavan	82,452	21	2.6	3	0.4	9	1.1	93	11.3
Donegal	152,508	41	2.7	7	0.5	20	1.3	112	7.3
Monaghan	65,131	53	8.1	5	0.8	25	3.8	22	3.4
Ulster (3 counties)	300,091	115	3.8	15	0.5	54	1.8	227	7.6
Total	2,971,992	2,940	9.9	421	1.4	1,781	6.0	3,439	11.6

Source: Herlihy, Hart, O'Halpin, TNA, CO, 762/1-212 (analysis of all claims); Population data from Central Statistics Office (Ireland), 1926 census. Ulster refers to three Free State counties.[2]

Analysing the same metrics, but this time in each case as a percentage of their total, and comparing each with the equivalent figures for violence and intimidation against ex-servicemen as recorded in the IGC files, demonstrates that the pattern of violence and intimidation against ex-servicemen correlates closely with that of other sectors of the population, indicating that ex-servicemen were not singled out. Of the number of incidents involving ex-servicemen, 28.2% are recorded in Leinster. The equivalent figures for IRA violence are 27%, for RIC killings 20.9%, for all fatalities 28.1%, and for total incidents recorded by the IGC 28.8%. The comparable figures for Munster are 58% for incidents involving ex-servicemen, 58.2% for IRA

2 Jim Herlihy, *The Royal Irish Constabulary: A Short History and Genealogical Guide with a Select List of Medal Awards and Casualties* (Dublin, 1997), 152; Hart, *The IRA at War*, 36. The number of incidents of IRA violence for 1917–23 is derived from an extrapolation of Hart's data based on the 1926 census, except for the population of Dublin City, which is from *Dáil Éireann*, Vol. 239, 15 April 1969; O'Halpin, 'The Dead of the Irish Revolution', 152.

violence, 60.3% for RIC killings, 58.1% for all fatalities, and 49.9% for total incidents recorded by the IGC.[3] Although Cork had the highest percentage of incidents for all metrics, the percentage of incidents involving ex-servicemen was lower than the other metrics, indicating that they were not specifically targeted even in an area of high republican activity.

Table 9: Analysis of violence and intimidation: general population/RIC v ex-servicemen

County	IRA Violence		RIC Killed		All Fatalities		IGC Total		IGC Ex-Service-men	
	Incidents	% of Total	Incidents	% of Total	Incidents	% of Total	Incidents	% of Total	Incidents	% of Total
Carlow	15	0.5	3	0.7	13	0.7	72	2.1	2	0.8
Dublin	460	15.6	32	7.6	309	17.3	203	5.9	17	6.5
Kildare	20	0.7	1	0.2	12	0.7	43	1.3	7	2.7
Kilkenny	35	1.2	4	1.0	19	1.1	40	1.2	3	1.1
Queens	34	1.2	1	0.2	10	0.6	292	8.5	13	5.0
Longford	55	1.9	12	2.9	26	1.5	43	1.3	2	0.8
Louth	37	1.3	6	1.4	26	1.5	17	0.5	1	0.4
Meath	24	0.8	10	2.4	17	1.0	62	1.8	8	3.1
Kings	22	0.7	5	1.2	21	1.2	91	2.6	5	1.9
Westmeath	37	1.3	4	1.0	18	1.0	35	1.0	6	2.3
Wexford	50	1.7	3	0.7	23	1.3	52	1.5	6	2.3
Wicklow	5	0.2	7	1.7	7	0.4	41	1.2	4	1.5
Leinster	**794**	**27.0**	**88**	**20.9**	**501**	**28.1**	**991**	**28.8**	**74**	**28.2**
Clare	113	3.8	35	8.3	95	5.3	315	9.2	30	11.5
Cork	876	29.8	96	22.8	495	27.8	780	22.7	58	22.1
Kerry	262	8.9	35	8.3	136	7.6	175	5.1	9	3.4
Limerick	196	6.7	38	9.0	121	6.8	123	3.6	16	6.1
Tipperary	217	7.4	43	10.2	152	8.5	280	8.1	35	13.4

3　RIC reports for 1916–19 show a similar pattern: of 1,293 'outrages' committed by the IRA, 29% were recorded in Leinster and 48% in Munster, illustrating that returning ex-servicemen did not alter existing patterns. See TNA, CO, 904/225.

County	IRA Violence		RIC Killed		All Fatalities		IGC Total		IGC Ex-Servicemen	
	Incidents	% of Total	Incidents	% of Total	Incidents	% of Total	Incidents	% of Total	Incidents	% of Total
Waterford	47	1.6	7	1.7	35	2.0	43	1.3	4	1.5
Munster	1,711	58.2	254	60.3	1,034	58.1	1,716	49.9	152	58.0
Galway	83	2.8	14	3.3	58	3.3	126	3.7	7	2.7
Leitrim	20	0.7	1	0.2	15	0.8	83	2.4	0	0.0
Mayo	103	3.5	21	5.0	43	2.4	139	4.0	7	2.7
Roscommon	66	2.2	14	3.3	58	3.3	75	2.2	6	2.3
Sligo	48	1.6	14	3.3	18	1.0	82	2.4	0	0.0
Connaught	320	10.9	64	15.2	192	10.8	505	14.7	20	7.6
Cavan	21	0.7	3	0.7	9	0.5	93	2.7	5	1.9
Donegal	41	1.4	7	1.7	20	1.1	112	3.3	8	3.1
Monaghan	53	1.8	5	1.2	25	1.4	22	0.6	3	1.1
Ulster (3 counties)	115	3.9	15	3.6	54	3.0	227	6.6	16	6.1
Total	2,940	100.0	421	100.0	1,781	100.0	3,439	100.0	262	100.0

Source: Herlihy, Hart, O'Halpin, TNA, CO, 762, Analysis of IGC boxes 1-212; Ulster refers to three Free State counties.

IRA killing or attempted shooting of ex-servicemen spies, as recorded in the IMA/BMH witness statements, show a similar geographical pattern with 67.5% of incidents occurring in Munster and 30% in Leinster.[4] The violence towards ex-servicemen varied in intensity in correlation to the level of violence experienced by other segments of the population, indicating they were not disproportionately targeted as a group. Based on all metrics, IRA violence, RIC officers killed, total fatalities, IGC general and ex-servicemen specific complaints, Munster had around twice as many incidents as Leinster.

4 O'Halpin estimates that the IRA killed 14 ex-servicemen in Dublin and 32 in Cork. See O'Halpin, 'The Dead of the Irish Revolution', 154–5.

Loyalists and Republicans

The argument that ex-servicemen suffered widespread intimidation presupposes that Ireland was radicalised and republican with a resultant animosity to all that was British, including ex-servicemen, who were guilty by association. The analysis of the geography of violence demonstrates that significant swathes of the country were relatively peaceful, indicating that support for extreme nationalism was limited. This is partly explained by two competing concepts of national identity, both defined in relation to Britain. Constitutional nationalists such as Thomas Kettle believed that 'the maintenance of the Anglo-Irish relationship [was] central to a vision for a free and sovereign Ireland'. Irish independence would be achieved within Great Britain, a self-governing state with the benefits of empire.[5] In contrast, Eoin MacNeill, the 'father' of modern Irish historiography, perceived a Gaelic Ireland emerging from centuries of foreign domination through the heroism of its leaders to rediscover the Gaelic civilisation that had been suppressed by the invader.[6] Augusteijn argues that the widespread support for extreme nationalism in the west of the country was due to a lesser acceptance of British rule. He writes,

> the mental distance between the British Government and its Irish subjects was considerably greater in rural and western areas than in urban and eastern areas. Economic independence, a high number of Irish speakers, few Protestants and poor recruitment figures for the British Army are the main indicators of this.

The urban-rural divide was particularly important: urbanised Tipperary was conservative, the countryside radical.[7] Fitzpatrick argues that

> wherever the economic interests of a community were closely linked to England, one might expect widespread opposition to the pursuit of separation; wherever violence was not a generally accepted means of achieving nationalist ends, one might expect a lack of willing helpers in the violent pursuit of separation.

These factors largely explain the relative quietness of Leinster in the War

---

5 Pašeta, 'Thomas Kettle', 12–13; Pennell, *A Kingdom United*, 183.
6 John Hutchinson, 'Irish Nationalism', in D.G. Boyce and Alan O'Day (eds), *The Making of Modern Irish History: Revisionism and the Revisionist Controversy* (London, 1996), 100–4.
7 Augusteijn, *From Public Defiance to Guerrilla Warfare*, 347.

of Independence. Leinster's economy, dominated by farmers fattening stock for export to British slaughterhouses, was far more closely tied to the British economy than Munster's, which was dominated by dairy farming for the home market.[8]

The geographical variation in attitude to Britain was evidenced by, for example, army recruitment, Gaelic activities, and election results. During the war the level of enlistment in Leinster was significantly higher than in Munster, both absolutely and as a percentage of population. Gaelic language, literature, and sports flourished more in the south and west, and their events were used to raise money for the IRA.[9] The local elections of January 1920 highlighted the variation in support for Sinn Féin: excluding the four counties of north-east Ulster, they secured only 572 seats in comparison to 872 won by other parties. In Meath less than 20% of the electorate supported them,[10] and in Birr the Unionists won. In Leinster 19.7% of the vote was Unionist in comparison to 9.3% in Munster and 4.7% in Connaught.[11] Sinn Féin was significantly less successful in towns than in rural areas. Augusteijn notes that 'in all provinces, Sinn Féin received less than half the level of support in the elections for the urban districts voted for in January 1920 than in their rural counterparts in June 1920'.[12]

These consequences of regional variations were accentuated with the collapse of central authority. The Dáil Éireann had successfully undermined British authority yet at the same time its own remit in the provinces was varied and often limited. In this power vacuum local influence prevailed, the level of violence varying significantly by region as a result. Hugh Martin, a correspondent for the *Daily News* who had toured Ireland in 1919, wrote that 'a central gathering of well-meaning idealists such as the Dáil Éireann is utterly unable to control the physical force of men in the provinces. These men from Sligo hold Dublin meetings of mere talkers about moral force in the utmost contempt'. Martin concluded that the real power, as

---

8 David Fitzpatrick refers to Rumpf in 'The Geography of Irish Nationalism 1910–1921', *Past & Present*, 78 (1978), 118.

9 IRA officers in West Cork acknowledged the importance of the Gaelic revival. Patrick O'Brien wrote that 'a further awakening of the national feeling was fostered' through the Gaelic League (an organisation to propagate the Irish language). See IMA/BMH, WS764, O'Brien, Cork. Similarly, Denis Lordon stated that in 1917 in West Cork many Gaelic classes were started. At these gatherings support was solicited for Sinn Féin and the Voluntary Movement; many participated in Gaelic sports and used the events to raise money for the cause. There was, Lordon concluded, perfect cooperation between all the organisations – Volunteers, Sinn Féin, Gaelic League and GAA. See IMA/BMH, WS470, Lordon, Cork.

10 R.F. Foster, *Modern Ireland: 1600–1972* (London, 1989), 497.

11 Fitzpatrick, 'The Geography of Irish Nationalism', 124.

12 Augusteijn, *From Public Defiance to Guerrilla Warfare*, 261–4.

with earlier Fenian revolts, lay in the hands of gunmen in the countryside and provincial towns.[13] The extreme Fenian element in the new Sinn Féin movement gained domination over the political non-revolutionary element for which people had voted. By the spring of 1920, the country found itself committed to a violent rebellion against British rule for which it had given no sanction.[14] Although the British had already conceded Home Rule for the 26 counties and by 1920 the Labour Party and many Liberals were supportive of Dominion status, republican extremists sought through confrontational practices 'to propel affairs to a point of no return', and 'the campaign of killing policemen was a deliberate assertion against the political wing, as well as evidence of the continuing effort of a minority to enforce their own alternative reality'.[15] That by 1920 Ireland was a people in arms in support of the IRA became the dominant nationalist story of the independent struggle. The republican movement considered itself the expression of the national will of a 'united, homogenous self-identifying nation' seeking national freedom from a foreign invader. But that commitment was not universal; Republican military operations ran against the grain of local feeling in many cases.[16] Support for complete independence was precarious. The Irish revolutionary movement derived its energies from grievances, including those related to land, which were slowly being resolved through constitutional nationalism.[17]

This reality was recorded by contemporary journalists and writers. Carl Ackerman, an American journalist wrote from Cork in April 1920, 'everywhere I go, I meet Sinn Féiners, determined, defiant, confident' and 'I met the same group of eight, ten or twelve members of the RIC, huddled together in a corner, from outward appearance, terrified, while across the street crowds passed, avoiding the police as if they were contaminated'.[18] In contrast Wilfrid Ewart, an English writer and ex-British army officer who toured Ireland in spring 1921, wrote of Birr, King's County that

a noticeable characteristic of this placid oasis in the heart of stormy Ireland was its normal daily social life, the apparently well-to-do contentment of its inhabitants. Black and Tans played football with the

---

13 *Daily News*, 24 January 1919.
14 Robert Kee, *The Green Flag: A History of Irish Nationalism* (London, 1972), 698.
15 Foster, *Modern Ireland*, 492, 506, 494.
16 Charles Townsend, *The Republic*, 259; Hart, *The IRA at War*, 4–5.
17 William Sheehan, *A Hard Local War: The British Army and the Guerrilla War in Cork, 1919–1921* (Dublin, 2011), 15; Tom Garvin, *Nationalist Revolutionaries in Ireland 1858–1928* (Oxford, 1987), 1.
18 Carl Ackerman, *Philadelphia Public Ledger*, 5 April 1920, quoted in Walsh, *News from Ireland*, 137.

local youths. Nowhere in the district did the landed gentry appear to be disturbed in their normal habits by local conditions.

Local inhabitants told Ewart that the town had contributed a higher proportion of volunteers to the army than any other town in Ireland and 'Birr and the district around it have always been loyal, chiefly I suppose, because it's been a garrison town. At the local election out of twenty one elected candidates, only four were Sinn Féiners'.[19] The Unionist *King's County Chronicle* wrote of the celebrations on the return of the local Leinster Regiment in 1919 that 'There was an immense gathering of enthusiastic spectators and the ex-servicemen were warmly cheered. Three cheers were given for the King.'[20] Contemporary reporters found people had become more radicalised but not to an extreme, just one step more than their original positions, and that the policies of the British Government had caused this change, both through the introduction of the Tans and the perceived faithlessness of its political leaders. Nevertheless many, including republicans, found a continued association with Britain acceptable, albeit with local autonomy, and were prepared to compromise to gain peace. Liam de Róiste, a Sinn Féin politician from Cork City, claimed, 'we feel no hostility to the English people or to the army; only to the Irregular Forces of the Crown'. He accepted the possibility of Dominion Home Rule as 'all our economic interests, all our future, are bound up with yours'.[21] A Cork unionist told Ewart, 'Everybody's taken a step to the left. Your old Nationalists have joined pacifist Sinn Féin; pacifist Sinn Féin has become active Republican. We Unionists take our stand on the old Nationalism'. A director of the Munster and Leinster Bank claimed that 'the only thing the country wants is peace – peace under a liberalised form of self-government'. Another Cork man said:

the bulk of the country longs for peace under a decent measure of Home Rule. A constitution which would leave naval and military control and foreign affairs as at present, whilst giving the right to levy our own taxes, customs, and excise, would meet the views of all parties, providing a free vote could be obtained.

19 Ewart, *A Journey in Ireland*, 112, 118.
20 *King's County Chronicle*, July 24 1919. In contrast, in reporting the same parade, the Nationalist *Midland Tribune* wrote, 'the people were not impressed with Saturday's "Peace" celebrations which in the main were confined to the garrison and its supporters. The day passed quietly, businesses stayed open. There were few flags. The Leinsters marched through the street. There was some booing of ex-servicemen later in the evening. A similar reaction was reported in surrounding towns'. *Midland Tribune*, 26 July 1919.
21 Ewart, *A Journey in Ireland*, 40–3. Ewart referred to him as Liamon de Roiste.

An elderly man, a known loyalist whose son had fought in the British army, complained of the Tans who had harassed him, 'It's incidents like this that turn people into extremists'.[22] A local resident of Mallow, West Cork told Ewart,

> people want a change, but they would be content with Dominion Home Rule or indeed any generous measure of self-Government, providing it brought peace. We don't want an Irish army or navy, and we don't want separation from the Empire.[23]

S. O'Mara, the Sinn Féin ex-mayor of Limerick (whose son, the mayor in 1921, had just been arrested and given a one-year prison sentence) complained of 'the bad faith and methods of the British Government' but said that 'the majority in Ireland would accept a liberal measure of Home Rule for the sake of peace'. Similarly John Dooley, a nationalist member of the King's County Council said there was 'no personal hostility to English people', but the problem is 'the present policy of the Crown, all moderate people are being alienated by it'. O'Mara and Dooley both agreed that nationalists had become Sinn Féiners and Unionists had become constitutionalist nationalists.[24] Ewart visited Kilmallock, County Limerick, childhood home of de Valera. A local brewer said:

> The people only want to settle down. You cannot gauge the real state of feeling by the actions of the IRA. They only represent a section of the people. People would be content with a fair measure of Home Rule – yes, dominion Home Rule. We have no quarrel with England.[25]

Sinn Féin's inability to preserve unity within the movement over the Treaty with Britain in 1921 was to some extent due to a resurfacing of the differences between constitutional and revolutionary nationalists.[26] In the general election of June 1922, the pro-Treaty party won 58 seats out of 128, the republicans 36, and the minority parties and independents, most of whom backed the Treaty, 34.[27] By early 1923 Ireland was ready for peace even in republican strongholds. Pritchett, a journalist who visited Cork in February 1923, wrote, 'the men who are causing the present troubles in the

22 Ewart, *A Journey in Ireland*, 47–53.
23 Ewart, *A Journey in Ireland*, 61–2.
24 Ewart, *A Journey in Ireland*, 110–22.
25 Ewart, *A Journey in Ireland*, 73–4.
26 Augusteijn, *From Public Defiance to Guerrilla Warfare*, 339.
27 Dorothy Macardle, *The Irish Republic: A Documented Chronicle of the Anglo-Irish Conflict and the Partitioning of Ireland, with a Detailed Account of the Period 1916–1923* (Dublin, 1951), 982.

country are a noisy minority. People have only a theoretical sympathy, if any at all, with republican ideas, and no sympathy whatever with their methods', and that most had, 'realized that constructive economics are the better part of patriotic idealism'.[28]

Support for extreme republicanism was generational. The Civil War and the War of Independence were largely instigated and fought by young men.[29] Ewart writes, 'one was repeatedly reassured in Cork that militant Sinn Féin was a Young Man's Movement exclusively – that the parents disapproved, indeed begged their sons not to participate in political activity'.[30] Pritchett referred to the Irregulars (the anti-Treaty IRA) as 'mostly young men and the dupes of their leaders'.[31] Frank Neville, an IRA officer from West Cork, wrote that small farmers were at least passive supporters of the IRA, although many of their sons were active participants.[32] Hopkinson writes that IRA membership was 'overwhelmingly youthful'.[33] Foster makes a similar point that 'IRA activists came from the youth of small towns, and the rural lower middle classes'. This demographic was also evident in the War; the West Cork branch of the Irish Volunteers was profiled by a police inspector in 1915 as 'entirely composed of farmer's sons of military age' who were 'active propagandists, bitterly disloyal'.[34]

Several often-interrelated factors, including perspectives of Irish identity and economic independence, as evidenced by political affiliation, and military and cultural links, influenced the propensity of a particular region to violence and intimidation, and its attitudes to Britain and its ex-servicemen. Support for extreme nationalism was not only limited by geography but also generation, and decreased over time.

The Case against Ex-Servicemen being Targeted

With the country in armed struggle for independence, followed by a bitter Civil War, it is understandable that the needs of those returning from a distantly fought war had little purchase on a population with other concerns. They could not expect the homecoming celebrations evident in Britain and

---

28 V.S. Pritchett, 'A Glimpse at a Southern Irish Town', *Christian Science Monitor*, 6 March 1923, 18, referring to a visit to Cork on 24 February 1923.
29 Ferriter, *The Transformation of Ireland*, 257.
30 Ewart, *A Journey in Ireland*, 32.
31 Pritchett, 'A Glimpse at a Southern Irish Town', 18, referring to a visit to Cork on 24 February 1923.
32 IMA/BMH, WS443.
33 Michael Hopkinson, *Irish War of Independence* (Dublin, 2002), 200.
34 Foster, *Modern Ireland*, 500, 473.

north of the border. But it is difficult to support Leonard's argument that ex-servicemen often experienced hostility and rejection, or that the vast majority of killings were simply retrospective punishments for their service in the Great War. The records of both the perpetrators and the victims show that comparatively few ex-servicemen suffered from intimidation, and where it occurred it was not due to war service but for reasons that were applicable to other segments of the population, although their military background made veterans more likely to associate with or join the Crown Forces.

Where the cause of intimidation was suspected spying, the evidence from both files, and particularly the witness statements, indicates that there was incriminating evidence against those accused. Of those ex-servicemen who made claims to the IGC, the majority did not consider war service to be the cause of intimidation despite it being an obvious proof of loyalty, and where they did the IGC concluded that in many cases the claims were at the least questionable. Due to the concentration of violence in parts of Munster and Dublin, there were significant swathes of the country that were relatively peaceful. The violence experienced by ex-servicemen varied in intensity in correlation to the level of violence experienced by other segments of the population, indicating that they were not disproportionately targeted as a group.

There are several reasons to question the proposition that ex-servicemen were specifically and extensively victimised. As a group they could not be defined as 'loyalist' any more than the general population could be defined as 'republican'. Volunteering for the Great War did not imply exceptional behaviour or loyalty to the Crown; large numbers did so with the support of their communities, and the motives for Catholics volunteering were often expressed as less to do with support of the imperial power and more the rights of small countries and the fight for Home Rule. In this regard the soldiers may have returned home disillusioned; veteran organisations condemned British 'political treachery'. Many ex-servicemen joined the IRA; some 109 are mentioned as doing so in the witness statements, more than double the number referred to as victims of intimidation.[35] It would be ironic if they persecuted fellow ex-servicemen merely for serving in the same army they had. There were often close familial or social connections between IRA members and those who served in the British army during the war; many recruits to both had been pre-war Volunteers. John Sheehy, the IRA commanding officer who gave the order for John O'Mahony's execution, had a brother who died on the Somme. It seems likely he would have based his decision on the evidence that O'Mahony was a spy, rather than that he had fought in the British army.[36]

---

35 Later evidence indicates that a majority of ex-servicemen became Fianna Fáil supporters.
36 Dwyer, *Tans, Terror and Troubles*, 299–300; IMA/BMH, WS1117, O'Riordan, Kerry.

Borgonovo argues that ex-servicemen were an integrated part of the social fabric. Hart's view of the negative stereotype of Irish soldiers as corner boys and drunks may have had currency among those serving in the ranks of the pre-1914 regular British army, but the Great War volunteers were from different backgrounds, more representative of society. In numbers they were not an isolated small minority. Borgonovo writes in 1918, when Cork City had a male population of 38,000, over 5,500 were serving overseas with British Forces. To this number must be added the large number of discharged and retired ex-servicemen already in the city.[37] In a survey of 14 towns, the BLSI estimated that ex-servicemen made up on average 12.4% of the population, around 25% of the male population; in Cork's case, over 40%. While the Legion may have overestimated the number of ex-servicemen, it is clear they made up a sizable portion of the population. If the IRA wished to make a statement that they were targeting ex-servicemen, it would have sought to assassinate higher-profile ex-officers. Most of those executed were of low status and the resultant publicity minimal. The number of ex-servicemen killed by the IRA, 99 (in all Ireland), represented an extremely small percentage of all ex-servicemen, less than 0.066%, making it difficult to argue that there was a widespread campaign against them. Around half that number, 46, were killed by the Crown Forces.[38] Borgonovo points out that there was antagonism between the Crown Forces and ex-servicemen.

Support for extreme nationalism was limited by geography, generation, and time, increasing in rural areas in the south and west of the country, particularly amongst the young. Based on the observations of contemporary writers, Ireland was by no means radicalised and republican, and thus inherently hostile to all that was British, ex-servicemen included. Intimidation was also limited by time. Of the claimants to the IGC who were forced to leave, almost all, including those soldiers driven from their allocated smallholdings by the IRA, returned after the Anglo-Irish War, often under the protection of the Free State army. Even when a group was deliberately targeted, such as the RIC, who were described by one IRA officer 'as the number one enemy of the people', there was much variance in their treatment depending on the degree of threat they posed.[39] Solicitor Herbert Deane wrote to the IGC in January 1927 on behalf of 40 policemen who were expelled from Ireland:

such men were driven out because they were especially loyal to the British Crown. Those policeman who were not operating in troubled

---

37 Borgonovo, *Spies, Informers*, 79.
38 O'Halpin, 'The Dead of the Irish Revolution', 154–5. The figure of 0.066 is based on an assumption that 150,000 ex-servicemen returned to all Ireland.
39 IMA/BMH, WS1296, Costello, Westmeath.

districts and who were regarded as innocuous and doing no special services for the Crown against the then rebels, were allowed to remain in Ireland.[40]

In 1922, 160 ex-RIC members joined the newly formed Garda Síochína.[41]

Persecution was not such as to stop British army recruitment, 20,000 enlisting throughout Ireland between 1919 and 1921. Dublin recruited more than Belfast. The most successful recruitment office in Ireland in 1919–20 was Clonmel, County Tipperary. Some were re-enlisting, perhaps escaping intimidation; many were not. Recruitment rates in the south for 17 year olds were twice the pre-war rate.[42] If not to intimidate, there may have been reasons to resent ex-servicemen with their preferential treatment in employment and training schemes, allocation of land and housing, and generous pensions. According to Fitzpatrick, the economic expectations of labourers, enhanced by wartime labour shortages, were threatened with the arrival of hordes of soldiers seeking jobs.[43]

The view that ex-servicemen were persecuted and marginalised became persuasive. One reason was that high-profile conflict in areas such as West Cork was widely publicised at the time, and obscured the reality that in much of Ireland intimidation was minimal. These were also the areas that later became the focus of academic research. Loyalist lobbying groups, such as SILRA, found that perceived discrimination against those who had fought for Britain brought a sympathetic and well-publicised response from both the press and politicians and aided their cause. War service was highlighted even if it was not the cause of the violence; SILRA did not have the same motivation to investigate cases as the IGC. In reality, incidents of violence and intimidation were highly focussed both geographically and chrono-logically, and with regard to ex-servicemen usually occurred for a cause, and one that was also applicable to the general population.

40 TNA, CO, 762/21/18, Letter from Herbert Deane, London solicitor, to IGC, 31 January 1927.
41 Herlihy, *The Royal Irish Constabulary*, 153.
42 Karsten, 'Irish Soldiers in the British Army', 49; Keith Jeffery, 'The Irish Military Tradition and the British Empire' in Jeffery (ed.), *An Irish Empire? Aspects of Ireland and the British Empire* (Manchester, 1996), 101. These figures demonstrate that historical recruitment patterns were not affected by the conflict. In the First World War, Dublin provided more recruits as a percentage of male population than Belfast, 16.4% to 11.9%, while Clonmel, outside the large urban centres of Belfast, Dublin, and Cork, was the most successful recruitment centre in Ireland both in absolute terms and as a percentage of male population. See TNA, PIN, 15/757. In the interwar years recruitment carried on with the tacit support of the Irish authorities.
43 Fitzpatrick, *Politics and Irish Life*, 233.

PART II
BRITAIN: LEGACY OF OBLIGATION, 1919–39

3

An Imperial Obligation

The scale of destruction and loss of life arising from the Great War was unprecedented and even the victors questioned the value of the carnage. In total, 20 million were severely wounded and 8 million permanently disabled, all seeking reintegration into much-changed societies.[1] In the United Kingdom 6.1 million were mobilised; 722,785 lost their lives, 1.7 million were wounded, 755,000 permanently disabled. With the collapse of empires, many of the countries for which they had fought had ceased to exist. All the countries involved were impoverished by the cost of an industrial scale war but, to varying degrees, there was recognition of the obligation of both state and society to the returning soldiers, particularly to those who were disabled. In Britain following previous wars, after-care of disabled ex-servicemen and disability pensions was managed by the War Office and the army, specifically through The Royal Hospital Chelsea. Conscription and the scale of enlistment established the precedent that the state was directly responsible for pension gratuities, disabled rehabilitation and all facets of recovery and maintenance, and the establishment of the necessary agencies to provide such support. The Ministry of Pensions was formed in 1916 and took over pension administration from Chelsea Hospital the following year.[2]

Cohen contrasts the experiences of ex-servicemen in two of the major combatants, Britain and Germany, arguing that although the German state provided Europe's most comprehensive support for disabled veterans with far

---

1 J.M. Winter, *The Great War and the British People* (London, 1985), 71; Deborah Cohen, *The War Come Home: Disabled Veterans in Britain and Germany* (London, 2001), 1, 193; Hew Strachan, *The First World War* (London, 2003), 329.

2 Stephen R. Ward, 'Intelligence Surveillance of British Ex-Servicemen, 1918–1920', *The Historical Journal*, 16/1 (1973), 180–1; Meaghan Kowalsky, 'Enabling the Great War: Ex-Servicemen, the Mixed Economy of Welfare and the Social Construction of Disability, 1899–1930' (University of Leeds Ph.D. thesis, 2007), 131–2. The Royal Hospital Kilmainham, Dublin performed a similar function to Chelsea and remained an old soldiers' home until 1927. See http://www.rhk.ie/history.aspx.

more generous benefits than those available within Great Britain, German ex-serviceman became alienated from it, contributing to the collapse of the Weimar Republic. The British state assumed only the bare minimum of responsibility for its disabled veterans. Between 1925 and 1933, Germany spent around 20% of its national budget on war pensions, some three times that of Britain, although it had only double the number of disabled. British ministries sought to limit the state's liability for wounded soldiers by pleading fiscal stringency. According to Cohen there was little difference between the political parties in their attitude to ex-servicemen: 'in its first-ever government, Labour had, like the Conservative government that followed, done little to assist these men'. The comparative paucity of British Government support was compensated for by philanthropy, community initiatives, and private business; the gratitude of society reconciled the disabled with those for whom they had suffered, and shielded the state from hostility. In contrast, German bureaucratic regulations limited the functioning of charities, causing in the veterans a perception of public ingratitude that alienated them from society and resulted in a profound antagonism towards the state.[3] The King's National Roll Scheme (KNRS), an employment programme for disabled ex-servicemen, illustrated the co-operation of the state and community in Britain. Previously the government had attempted to train disabled men in government-run instructional factories as part of the Industrial Training Scheme, but the programme was judged to be a failure, predominantly due to the difficulty of ensuring jobs upon completion of training.[4] In contrast, as part of the KNRS, companies were encouraged to employ disabled ex-servicemen in return for which they were listed on a national Roll of Honour and awarded the King's Seal for use in correspondence. The state led by example, increasing the number of disabled ex-servicemen in government offices, encouraging local authorities to employ them, reserving lucrative contracts for companies on the Roll and instructing employment exchanges to give preference to disabled ex-servicemen. But it was the co-operation of private enterprise that was essential. Although the KNRS was voluntary, it achieved remarkable success. As many as 30,000 companies were on the Roll at any given time, employing an average of 341,000 men per year throughout the 1920s. The scheme helped reduce unemployment among disabled ex-servicemen: approximately 80% of all disabled men in receipt of a pension were employed through the KNRS between 1921 and 1938. Unemployment figures for disabled ex-servicemen hovered between 8% and 11% during the interwar years, significantly lower than for the able-bodied population. Local King's Roll committees co-operated with

3   Cohen, *The War Come Home*, 4, 46, 188–94.
4   Kowalsky, 'Enabling the Great War', 98–102.

employment exchanges, local war pensions' committees, and hospitals. The formation of the KNRS was the most important piece of legislation put in place for disabled veterans in interwar Britain. It was significant not simply in providing employment but also because it invoked substantial changes in both governmental policy and societal attitudes towards the disabled, increasing awareness and tolerance and integrating them into industry and the community.[5]

The British Legion played a significant role in reconciling ex-serviceman to the community. It tempered hostility towards the state within a non-political ideology that brought them closer to society; a central tenet of the Legion was an acknowledgement of the public support for the ex-servicemen both in terms of voluntary activities and in pressurising the British Government. The latter was criticised for inadequate provision but usually with a narrow focus directed towards the pension bureaucracy and the Treasury. This lack of confrontation led to accusations that the Legion was a 'sell out', its privileged relationship with the establishment at odds with rank-and-file opinion.[6] The Legion assisted Britain in reaching a new consensus, whereas in France the political culture was far too divided and ex-servicemen's organisations mirrored societal extremes.[7]

The mentally disabled had particular difficulties. According to Joanna Bourke, the emotional stress of such men was exacerbated by the realisation that their actions in wartime were not appreciated, their loyalty was derided, and they were considered 'too lazy to find employment', 'weak and degenerate', or 'childish and infantile', their masculinity in doubt. Mental illness arising from battle was little understood by the public, who suspected that the cause was cowardice. Pension officers sought to prove that mentally ill men were liars and malingerers. Although work was widely regarded as the best remedy for psychiatric patients, it was in short supply in the interwar years. An investigation of Scottish neurasthenics noted the high level of relapse caused by 'secondary economic neurasthenia', arising from

5 Kowalsky, 'Enabling the Great War', 98–102; Meaghan Kowalsky, 'This Honourable Obligation: The King's National Roll Scheme for Disabled Ex-Servicemen 1915–1944', *European Review of History*, 14/4 (2007), 567–84. Cohen disagrees with Kowalsky arguing, 'Government departments baulked at joining the King's Roll'. See Cohen, *The War Come Home*, 47.

6 Cohen, *The War Come Home*, 49–51. By contrast, the short-lived National Union of Ex-Servicemen was socialist and confrontational. See David Englander, 'The National Union of Ex-Servicemen and the Labour Movement, 1918–1920', *History*, 76/246 (1991).

7 Graham Wootton, *The Politics of Influence: British Ex-Servicemen, Cabinet Decisions and Cultural Change (1917–57)* (London, 1963), 260.

unemployment and economic stress.[8] The treatment meted out to mentally distressed ex-servicemen in asylums was often one of prolonged misery.[9]

British dominions (excepting the Free State, which had the same status) initiated significant governmental and societal programmes to support their ex-servicemen. In 1917 the Australian Parliament passed the Australian Soldiers' Repatriation Act, which provided the framework for a federally co-ordinated rehabilitation programme for disabled soldiers, including medical care, housing, education, and training and reflected the strong public feeling that the 'wounded heroes of the Great War' must be looked after by the state. Again, non-government organisations such as the Red Cross were a vital part of the national rehabilitation infrastructure, generating funds, managing convalescent facilities, and providing a formidable volunteer workforce. The return of battle-scarred and wounded men became the 'emotive core of national mobilisation', with the intent of making the men feel 'valued and not forgotten'.[10] Australia, Canada, and New Zealand instigated large-scale programmes, significantly more ambitious than those envisaged in the United Kingdom, to provide farming land for ex-servicemen. In Australia conscription for military service never became law, and the principal motive for embarking upon so ambitious a scheme of land settlement was the desire to redeem promises made to ex-soldiers that every man who returned should have a farm of his own, if he wanted it.[11]

Britain retained the same legal obligation for Irish ex-servicemen even after the formation of the Free State. The Transfer of Function Order, 1922, transferred to the Provisional Government the whole body of public officials, excluding Crown Forces. Clause nine of the Order specifically stated that the Crown Forces would not be transferred to the Free State Government, and nor would duties regarding pensions and allowances and provision for the training, education, and assistance for the re-instatement in civil life of ex-servicemen.[12] The obligation to Irish ex-servicemen had several motivations in addition to the general obligation to all ex-servicemen. It included a perceived debt to those whose service to the Crown had caused them hardship in the conflict in Ireland after the transition of

---

8 Joanna Bourke, 'Effeminacy, Ethnicity and the End of Trauma: The Sufferings of "Shell-Shocked" Men in Great Britain and Ireland, 1914–1939', *Journal of Contemporary History*, 35/1 (2000), 57–69.

9 Peter Barham, *Forgotten Lunatics of the Great War* (New Haven, CT, 2004), 358.

10 Marina Larsson, 'Restoring the Spirit: The Rehabilitation of Disabled Soldiers in Australia after the Great War', *Health and History*, 6/2 (2004), 45–59.

11 A. J. Hannan, 'Land Settlement of Ex-Service Men in Australia, Canada, and the United States', *Journal of Comparative Legislation and International Law*, Third Series, 2/3 (1920), 225–37.

12 TNA, AP, 1/143, Leggett Case, 10 March 1932.

government. More pragmatically, during the Anglo-Irish War the British Government was concerned that disaffected ex-servicemen would use their skills on behalf of the republicans, knowing that the combination of a hostile homecoming and unemployment would make them susceptible to Sinn Féin propaganda. A conference of British ministers meeting in February 1919 to discuss help for Irish ex-servicemen acknowledged both points, concluding 'that ex-servicemen were being excluded from employment and for this reason and general propaganda were forced into the ranks of the disaffected', and that this was not a state of affairs that could continue, 'having regard for the duty the Government owed these men'.[13] The Ministries of Labour and Transport were responsible for helping ex-servicemen find employment. In 1919 an official of the former noted, 'I should be glad if authority could be given us to place fit demobilised men in training. There are a large number of these in the country being driven into disloyalty through not being able to find work, and the unrest is very considerable in consequence'.[14] The following year a Ministry of Transport official in Dublin wrote that in view of the state of the country, special steps should be taken to initiate essential projects on which the ex-servicemen could be employed, 'while ex-soldiers are unemployed they are liable to be influenced in other directions, making the position in Ireland worse than it is'.[15] Veteran organisations warned that these conditions created 'the possibility of thousands of these once loyal men being won over to the side of the extremists'.[16]

Some claimed that specific promises were made to Irishmen as an inducement to volunteer. Conscription was not enforced in Ireland, unlike in Britain after 1916; other incentives were needed. The need for fresh troops following the disasters of the 1916 campaigns led to suggestions that a post-war social housing programme might prove useful in recruitment.[17] In order to encourage volunteers, Lord French, the new Viceroy of Ireland, announced in June 1918 that 'land shall be available for men who have fought for their country'.[18] The Irish Land (Provision for Sailors and Soldiers) Act 1919 (hereafter referred to as the Land Act 1919) reflected both a desire to make good these recruitment promises and a pragmatic need to be seen to be doing something for ex-servicemen, particularly as there was a concern that they might be excluded from social housing because the republicans dominated

13 TNA, LAB, 2/492, Conference of Ministers, 13 February 1919.
14 TNA, LAB, 2/628, MoL, note, 29 Aug 1919
15 TNA, MT, 47/6, MoT, note, 12 January 1920.
16 TNA, LAB, 2/855, IFDDSS to the Prime Minister, 17 February 1920.
17 Joseph Brady and Patrick Lynch, 'The Irish Sailors' and Soldiers' Trust and its Killester Nemesis', *Irish Geography*, 42/3 (2009), 264.
18 Aalen, 'Homes for Irish Heroes', 307.

local authorities.[19] There was a well-orchestrated lobbying campaign by veterans' associations, particularly the British Legion, and general loyalist organisations such as SILRA, aimed at both the government and the British public reminding them of the obligation towards those who had served the Crown. While allegiance to Britain may not have been their reason for volunteering, service in its armed forces gave the ex-servicemen the right to claim the same debt as loyalists. SILRA's primary objective was 'to keep before the Public the great hardships endured by Loyalists and ex-service men under conditions in Southern Ireland'.[20] In 1925 its chairman, the Duke of Northumberland, wrote to the *Daily Mail* to describe the condition of ex-servicemen in Ireland as 'heartbreaking'. An editorial endorsed the letter, stating that 'almost all of them are in extreme poverty and distress'.[21] There remained a significant number of advocates for the loyalists in Parliament, particularly the House of Lords. Veteran organisations ensured that questions were often raised on the grievances of the ex-servicemen, the *Irish Times* reporting that the secretary of the British Legion said that he was 'instrumental in having questions raised in the House on the slow progress of house building for ex-servicemen'.[22] Ex-servicemen organisations made emotional appeals arguing that 'the promises and pledges given by the Government' should be honoured; the Irish Federation of Discharged and Demobilised Sailors and Soldiers (IFDDSS) wrote to the Prime Minister in February 1920, complaining that ex-servicemen had lost everything through their duty to the British Empire and were 'forced to line up in queues and accept charity', and now 'regard prison as a haven of refuge from the horrors of starvation in the streets'. They complained of the failure of government schemes to provide employment and to train disabled men, of inadequate out-of-work donations, and inefficient pension administration. The letter concluded, 'that the case of the ex-servicemen in Ireland is one of special urgency', and 'the Irish ex-serviceman has no friends capable of helping him in his own country, and he looks to the Government for that assistance which he justly considers his right'.[23] The Ministry of Labour considered that the comments of the Federation 'did not greatly exaggerate the general conditions of the ex-servicemen in Ireland', although they advised the Prime Minister's office not to reply to it.[24] The lobbying resulted in extensive

19 Murray Fraser, *John Bull's Other Homes: State Housing and British Policy in Ireland, 1883–1922* (Liverpool, 1996), 240.
20 PRONI, D/989/B/5/6.
21 *Daily Mail*, 2 February 1925.
22 TNA, AP, 1/98, Statement by Colonel Heath, Secretary of BL; *IT*, 7 July 1926. Duckworth wrote to Haig complaining about the Legion's lobbying, 14 June 1926,
23 TNA, LAB, 2/855, IFDDSS to Prime Minister, 17 February 1920.
24 TNA, LAB, 2/855, MoL, note, 12 March 1920; IFDDSS to Prime Minister' Office, 17

and generally sympathetic coverage in the mainstream British and Irish newspapers. Politicians of all persuasions found it necessary to respond; in the British general election of 1922 over 300 candidates pledged their support for the claims of disadvantaged Irish loyalists.[25] Brennan writes, 'it was the point from which no party in Britain could escape; the debt of honour had been acknowledged by all parties in 1922'.[26]

The grievances expressed by the ex-servicemen were such that in November 1927 the Free State Government established a 'Committee on Claims of British Ex-Servicemen' (hereafter referred to as the Lavery Committee after its chairman) specifically to determine:

- The nature and extent of the claims made by ex-servicemen against the British Government in respect of rights to have arisen out of past services.
- The nature and extent of their claims, if any, against the government of the Irish Free State in respect of alleged discrimination against them in regard to employment or otherwise.

The Committee examined complaints against the British Government in relation to pensions and healthcare provision, housing, land, and emigration. With the exception of transitional arrangements for temporary government clerks, it did not address British obligations with regard to employment, as this was then a Free State responsibility. Ex-servicemen were encouraged to write through veteran associations such as the BLSI but there were also several hundred individual submissions. There was no precedent for a dominion government to sanction a report into the failure or otherwise of the British Government to fulfil its obligations. The Committee presented its report in November 1928 (hereafter referred to as the Lavery Report). Most of the grievances were directed at the British Government and its findings received extensive press coverage, forcing the British Government to justify its record in seeking to meet its obligations to the ex-servicemen.[27]

Legal, pragmatic, moral, and political pressures therefore combined to ensure that the British Government was forced to face the need to fulfil a special obligation to Irish ex-servicemen in the south. This obligation was reflected in schemes to encourage employment, pensions, and health care for the physically and mentally disabled, support for emigration, compensation, and the provision of land and houses. Some obligations, such as those related to employment and land, were only relevant up until the formation

February 1920; MoL to Prime Minister's office, 24 March 1920.

25 TNA, DO, 35/343/3.

26 Niamh Brennan, 'A Political Minefield: Southern Loyalists, the Irish Grants Committee and the British Government, 1922–31', *Irish Historical Studies*, 30/119 (May 1997), 406–19.

27 TNA, PIN, 15/757-8.

of the Free State. The British were faced with discharging this obligation in a time of conflict and thereafter in a country in which they had limited and decreasing jurisdiction.

Employment – The Able Bodied

In its efforts to remedy the high unemployment of ex-servicemen and the possibility of their disaffection to Sinn Féin, the British Government was faced with significant problems: lack of co-operation from companies and local authorities, diminishing British control, and the collapse of commerce due to the conflict. The methods used in Great Britain, particularly through the co-operation of private industry, were much less appropriate in Ireland. This did not stop British Government departments, specifically the Ministries of Labour and Transport, making significant efforts to help the ex-servicemen. Such preferential treatment generated considerable resentment from a wider population also suffering hardship, an antagonism of which the republicans sought to take advantage. British ministers did not expect the armistice to create the same economic difficulties in Ireland as in Britain; the economy remained predominantly agricultural and less dependent on war work, particularly in the south.[28] Nevertheless, Irish recruitment was primarily urban and a significant number of the ex-servicemen returning to Ireland faced unemployment, a higher percentage than in Great Britain. By October 1919, 35,000 ex-servicemen were receiving the out-of-work donations in Ireland, accounting for an unemployment rate of 46%, compared with only 10% in Britain.[29] According to the British Ministry of Labour, the number of demobilised men to February 1920 in Britain was 3,365,000 and in Ireland 83,500. The number of unemployed (on donation) ex-servicemen in Britain was 311,646 and in Ireland 27,648. This gives a percentage of 9.3% unemployment among demobilised men in Great Britain and 33.1% in Ireland, the figure 3.6 times greater in Ireland.[30] The Ministry of Transport estimated that there were 40,000 unemployed ex-servicemen in Ireland in February 1920.[31] Irrespective of the exact figures, the problem was serious and the Ministry of Labour noted that 'one of the most urgent of the outstanding problems is that of finding employment for the ex-service

28 TNA, LAB, 2/492, MoL, note, 11 February 1919; TNA, LAB, 2/492, Conference of Ministers, 13 February 1919.
29 Ferriter, *The Transformation of Ireland*, 399.
30 TNA, LAB, 2/855, MoL, note, 23 Feb 1920.
31 TNA, MT, 47/6, MoT, note, 2 February 1920.

men in Ireland'.[32] A briefing note to Bonar Law MP in April 1920 from the Ministry of Labour outlined the severity of the problem:

> there is no doubt that the position of ex-servicemen in Ireland at present is very difficult indeed, in view of the unsympathetic attitude of the great majority of employers ... there is political antagonism to the employment of ex-soldiers in the south and west. Local Authorities and employers holding public positions are afraid to run counter to this feeling.

The note outlined several other factors that accentuated the problem: before the war 30,000 emigrated every year but emigration was prohibited in the war, increasing the labour market; civilians had taken the place of those who enlisted and, with the growth in trade unions, could not be easily replaced without trouble; the ex-servicemen were prejudiced against the unions, making their absorption into industry more difficult; and finally, the conflict restricted economic development and the establishment of new enterprises, and consequentially caused considerable unemployment among all civilians.[33] The Ministry of Labour reported that:

> it will be practically impossible to place fit men in training or employment under ordinary conditions anywhere except in the North, and that the only hope was Lord French's scheme of providing factories where ex-service men could be employed together. Training in Ireland will have to be highly centralised[34] ... due to the political situation it has not been possible to apply the methods used in Britain for obtaining employment for ex-servicemen,[35] ... in the present political state of Ireland, the ex-service man is a God-send to those who want a concrete political bone to pick.[36]

Following interviews with veteran organisations such as the Irish branches of the Comrades of the Great War and the Discharged Sailors' and Soldiers' Federation, the ministry concluded that the position of ex-servicemen in Ireland was so serious and pitiful that they should be treated as disabled men were in Great Britain, that is, as disability made it impossible for a man to

---

32 TNA, LAB, 2/747, MoL, note, 8 April 1920.
33 TNA, LAB, 2/747. Briefing note to Bonar Law, MP, 28 April 1920 from MoL in relation to a question expected to be raised by Captain Coote in the House of Commons.
34 TNA, LAB, 2/522, MoL, note, 6 June 1919.
35 TNA, LAB, 2/747, MoL to Foreign Office, early 1920.
36 TNA, LAB, 2/747, MoL, note, 9 Feb 1920.

resume his old employment, so military service in Ireland disqualified a man from employment.[37]

Lord French was eager to help returning Irish veterans; in November 1918 he proposed to the British cabinet that the Dublin Castle administration be given £2 million for industrial and agricultural development; his idea was declined.[38] A conference of ministers in February 1919 provided an interim grant of £250,000 for employment programmes, with further sums to follow;[39] £175,000 had been allocated by July 1919.[40] The expenditure was supervised by an Inter Departmental Committee and the division of responsibility made it difficult to use the money effectively.[41] Lord French was not satisfied. In January 1920 he invited 15 to 20 representatives from each province to ask them to give more work to ex-soldiers, influence other employers to do likewise, and form local committees to achieve this; meetings were arranged the same month. At the same time a further grant was sought from the Treasury to build roads, harbours, etc., to provide work for the ex-servicemen.[42] The Ministry of Transport took over responsibility for the execution of public works and a sum of £100,000 (which would provide 1,500 with employment for five months) was allocated as a first instalment – only the amounts related to ex-servicemen would be charged against the sum. The Irish Office of the Ministry of Labour was responsible to Parliament for the expenditure and decided where the work should be carried out. The Ministry of Transport submitted proposals to the Chief Secretary for Ireland in London for approval, the latter to the exclusion of Dublin Castle.[43] It was considered that submitting the schemes to Dublin Castle after negotiations with the local authorities would excite political opposition.[44] Numerous local bodies, harbour boards, local councils, and highway authorities, made applications for harbour, rail, and road improvements.[45] Lord French thought only ex-servicemen should be employed on such schemes, but the Ministry of Labour disagreed, noting 'it would be clearly impossible in the present state of Ireland to engage ex-service men

37 TNA, LAB, 2/855, MoL, note, 4 May 1920.
38 Fedorowich, 'Reconstruction and Resettlement', 1154; *Dáil Éireann*, Vol. 21, 16 November 1927.
39 TNA, LAB, 2/492, Conference of Ministers, 13 February 1919.
40 TNA, MT, 47/6, MoT, note, 19 Jan 1920.
41 TNA, LAB, 2/747, MoL, note, April 1920.
42 TNA, MT, 47/6, MoT, note, 12 January 1920.
43 TNA, LAB, 2/747, Meeting of Ministries of Labour/Transport 4 May 1920 (the exclusion of Dublin Castle was omitted from the official minutes); MoL, note, April 1920.
44 TNA, Lab, 2/747/10, MoL, note, 19 April 1920.
45 TNA, MT, 47/6, MoT, note, 12 January 1920.

exclusively'.[46] The Ministry of Transport concurred, arguing that grants to provide employment for only ex-servicemen would 'aggravate the unfortunate feeling in Ireland' towards them[47] and that it was not politic to 'inaugurate works where ex-soldiers only would be employed, because such a course would only mean that the men would be boycotted and made uncomfortable in other ways. General employment should be given on the works, care being taken to give preference to the ex-soldiers',[48] and 'that any public reference to the arrangements made to provide work for them on schemes under the Ministry of Transport would seriously mitigate against the success of those scheme'.[49] They also argued that investing money in infrastructure was better than paying unemployment benefits.[50] In any event, the prevailing political climate, and the impossibility of aiding ex-servicemen specifically, significantly reduced the effectiveness of these schemes.

Training was also organised in growth industries, including the training of wireless operators. By March 1920, 136 men were in training or had just completed training; the Treasury even paid for their uniforms upon completion.[51] According to Leonard, training courses at universities and technical colleges and placements on farms and in workshops were provided for veterans.[52] But little progress was made, as evidenced by a report in March 1921, following a visit to Ireland by Dr P.L. Forward, who had responsibility for pensions in Ireland. Although his primary focus was disabled soldiers, he commented on the general problems of providing employment for ex-servicemen and that work was difficult to obtain 'owing to the present hostile attitude against men who served in the Great War. Even those employers who are sympathetically disposed towards the ex-soldier are prevented from offering employment to these men, owing to threats and other methods of intimidation'. Forward proposed a 'work colony', a proposal similar to that of Lord French, to build factories where ex-service men could be trained and employed together. He believed that even after the country became settled, the ex-soldier would remain 'an outcast and an undesirable by his fellow men'. Forward did not think that such a colony would be subject to molestation as in his opinion it was individuals not communities that were subject to such treatment. He cited the building of homes for ex-servicemen at Clondorf near Dublin, where veterans were employed in

46 TNA, Lab, 2/747/10, MoL, note, 19 April 1920.
47 TNA, MT, 47/6, MoT, note, 2 February 1920.
48 TNA, MT, 47/6, MoT, note, 12 January 1920.
49 TNA, LAB, 2/747, briefing note to Bonar Law MP 28 April 1920 from MoL.
50 TNA, MT, 47/6, MoT, note, 12 January 1920.
51 TNA, LAB, 2/628, MoL, note, 29 August 1919; Treasury note, 31 March 1920, sent to MoL 14 April 1920.
52 Leonard, 'Survivors', 215.

construction.[53] Work at Killester, the Trust's largest development, was also carried out by demobilised soldiers and tenants;[54] some 800 veterans were employed on the scheme.[55]

The government also committed to intervene in cases where soldiers found their jobs no longer available when they returned home. John O'Brien was employed before the War by Limerick Corporation as a night watchman and on joining the British army in 1915 claimed he was promised re-employment upon his return. When this was not offered he sued the Corporation for breach of agreement and was awarded £25 compensation. In the House of Commons on 11 November 1919, Sir Maurice Dockrell asked the Chief Secretary for Ireland if the Irish Government would afford legal assistance to others in a similar position. Mr Macpherson in reply said the government would intervene, 'in all cases where the demobilised soldier or sailor is penalised because of his loyalty to Ireland'.[56]

Efforts were made to employ ex-servicemen in government offices, although they generally represented a smaller percentage of the workforce than in Great Britain, partly due to the political climate. The Substitution Scheme, introduced into Britain in 1919 to facilitate the employment of ex-servicemen in British ministries, was not enforced in Ireland. Notwithstanding this, from October 1919 to March 1920, the Ministry of Labour secured 350 appointments for ex-servicemen in 60 different government offices in Ireland. In March 1920, 50.8% of the total male staff and 32.9% of the total staff within the Irish offices of the Ministry of Labour were ex-servicemen, and measures were in place to increase the latter figure to 38.9%. The corresponding figures for the whole ministry were 80% and 44.7% respectively. The percentage of the temporary male staff in Ireland represented by ex-servicemen was 63% compared to 83% in the United Kingdom.[57]

53 TNA, PIN, 15/899, Forward 'Provision of Employment for Ex-serviceman in Ireland', 11 March 1921; TNA, LAB 2/522, MoL, note, 6 June 1919.
54 *IT*, 5 August 1933.
55 Leonard, 'Survivors', 217; Fraser, *John Bull's Other Homes*, 240, 271.
56 *Cork Examiner*, 13 November 1919, 5; *Hansard*, HC Deb, 121, 11 November 1919.
57 TNA, LAB, 2/855, MoL to PM's office, 16 and 24 March 1920, give slightly different figures, the latter stating there were 315 ex-servicemen employed in its Irish offices out of a total male staff of 534.

Table 10: Ministry of Labour, Ireland, staffing

Category	Total Staff Employed			Ex-Servicemen Employed		
	Men	Women	Total	Disabled	Others	Total
Permanent	155	40	195	1	24	25
Temporary	443	285	728	99	180	279
Total	598	325	923	100	204	304

Source: TNA, LAB, 2/855.

The IFDDSS presented a contrasting perspective, stating that:

> a considerable number of ex-officers, suitable for clerical positions, are unable to find employment and the efforts of the Ministry of Labour on their behalf do not appear to be successful. The enormous outlay of public money by the Appointments and Training Branch of the Ministry of Labour is not justified by the results achieved.[58]

Other methods of obtaining employment were limited. The Ministry of Labour noted that since the Armistice there had been considerable difficulty in finding employment for ex-servicemen through the Irish employment exchanges. Only 9,256 ex-servicemen were placed by them between the Armistice and 5 March 1920; 2,086 had been placed during the three months preceding 5 March 1920, and 22,884 were on the registers of employment exchanges in Ireland in March 1920.[59] Irish employers did not use employment exchanges to the same extent as those in Britain, and Irish exchanges were therefore less successful in obtaining jobs.[60] Another factor distorting employment in Ireland was the out-of-work donation scheme that allowed unemployed ex-servicemen 26 weeks' donation at 24/ per week, within a period of 12 months from the end of their four-week furlough.[61] Many were willing to remain on donation, as outside Dublin and Belfast the low cost of living made it an adequate substitute for wages. Wages seldom exceeded the donation,[62] and in most cases the

---

58 TNA, LAB, 2/855, IFDDSS to PM, 17 February 1920.
59 TNA, LAB, 2/747, MoL, note. Recorded number of discharged men exceeding 100,000, April 1920.
60 TNA, LAB, 2/855, MoL, note, 23 Feb 1920.
61 TNA, LAB, 2/492.
62 TNA, LAB, 2/855, MoL, note, 23 Feb 1920.

latter was higher than the average wage[63] as it was designed for the higher living costs in Britain. It was referred to as the stop work donation, an 'inexplicable phenomenon' that made work economically unattractive for a large segment of the population.[64] The problem was quickly recognised and partly remedied when in February 1919 ministers restricted the donation in Ireland to insured trades, trades designated by the Lord Lieutenant of Ireland, and demobilised soldiers. Ex-servicemen continued to be eligible and therefore to have an incentive not to work, at least until the donation period ended. The number of ex-servicemen on out-of-work donation fell from 301,588 to 199,871 in Great Britain and 34,979 to 19,001 in Ireland between November 1919 and May 1920, declining consistently each month as entitlement ended.[65]

Employment – The Disabled

The problem of training ex-servicemen and then helping them to find employment was accentuated in the case of the disabled. It proved challenging in Britain, and even more so in Ireland. The designation as to who was entitled to such support was well defined and reasonably inclusive. Any man disabled at the time of discharge whose disability was attributable or aggravated by war service, or whose disability existed at the time of discharge, even if the cause was not attributable to war service, was entitled to training if it was medically certified that due to their disability they could not resume their job or profession, or could not do so without a reduction of earnings.[66] A Ministry of Labour report in April 1919 summarised the challenges providing employment for disabled ex-servicemen, noting that there were 100,000 unemployed in Ireland and 100,000 soldiers waiting to be demobilised and that such a surplus of labour made it difficult to find employment for the 4–5,000 disabled men. The Ministry of Pensions had arranged training for only 180 men. Training was also only the first step; employment then had to be found, and the report concluded that given political considerations and the economic environment, this would only be achieved if the government put together a scheme to provide permanent employment. Special officers had been allocated only to a few of the larger

---

63 TNA, LAB, 2/492 Conference of Ministers, 13 February 1919.
64 TNA, LAB, 2/492, MoL, note, 11 February 1919.
65 TNA, LAB, 2/492, Note, 21 Feb 1919, arising out of the Conference of Ministers, 13 February 1919; TNA, LAB, 2/222.
66 TNA, LAB, 2/522, MoL, note, 30 April 1919 and 6 June 1919.

employment exchanges to help disabled men but there were 152 other exchanges that did not benefit.[67]

The British Government was not prepared for the task of training and finding work for the disabled. It was unclear which department would have responsibility and the resources in Ireland were inadequate. Initially the Ministry of Pensions was responsible and admitted that 'few facilities exist for disabled soldiers in Ireland such that exist in England and many of the men are really badly off'.[68] In terms of training and employment, the Ministry of Labour was the more appropriate agency. It was intended to take over these functions in June 1919 while the War Pension Committee was restricted to determining whether the applicant was eligible for training.[69] A disabled man undergoing training, unless he required curative treatment as well, would fall within the responsibility of the Ministry of Labour.[70] The Ministry of Labour did not initially have the necessary resources; in June 1919 it established an Irish Department in Dublin with an Appointments and Training Branch, but did not have the necessary staff.[71] It was recognised that the new Irish Department should not be 'a mere outpost of the departments in London, but that it should have ample authority and full powers as industrial and labour conditions in Ireland are fundamentally different to Britain'.[72]

The Ministry of Labour was disdainful of its inheritance from the Ministry of Pensions, claiming that the latter's organisation was in a 'hopelessly chaotic condition', that only 300 men had been trained without any assessment of their suitability for the trade in which they were trained. According to the Ministry of Labour, the men 'were seething with discontent at nothing having been done for them, were mocked for having served in the British army and were forced to join the Sinn Féin through discontent, and as the only chance to get employment'.[73] By November 1919 the Ministry of Labour had assumed full responsibility for training[74] and over 447 ex-servicemen had been trained and 2,085 registered for training.[75] This ministry too found it difficult to make sufficient progress, writing to the Prime Minister's office in March 1920 that the training of

67 TNA, LAB, 2/522, MoL, note, 5 April 1919
68 TNA, LAB, 2/528, MoP, note, 18 May 1919.
69 TNA, LAB, 2/522, MoL, note, 30 May 1919.
70 TNA, AB, 2/522, MoL, note, 10 May 1919.
71 TNA, LAB, 2/522, MoL, note, 30 May 1919; TNA, LAB, 2/522. MoL, note, 28 June 1919.
72 TNA, LAB, 2/522, MoP, note, 10 April 1919.
73 TNA, LAB, 2/522, MoL, notes, 5 May and 18 November 1919.
74 TNA, LAB, 2/628, MoL, note, 21 November 1919.
75 TNA, LAB, 2/522, MoL, note, 18 November 1919.

disabled men was in a very unsatisfactory state due to insufficient premises and staff and a lack of vacancies.[76] It claimed the delay 'is entirely on the Treasury's part', as it had been in correspondence with that department since October 1919 and their long delay in approving additional staff has 'hindered very seriously the work of the Appointments and Training branch in Ireland', and prejudiced the success of the Industrial Training Scheme.[77]

Progress was hindered not only by bureaucratic infighting, but also an increasingly adverse political climate. In May 1919 the Ministry of Labour had proposed setting up an Irish Industrial Conference with employers and trade unions to persuade them to establish joint trade committees, but eventually realised such co-operation was unforthcoming.[78] By December 1919 an internal report stated that the political unrest had increased the hostile attitude of employers and their employees and, as long as the political attitude remained unchanged, it was almost hopeless to find employment for disabled ex-servicemen. The employers wanted fees and wages to be paid by the Ministry of Labour. The report advocated government factories for disabled ex-servicemen paid at union rates and sale of the goods produced in the open market.[79] Irish employers would generally only accept ex-servicemen for training if they were paid for it.[80] No steps were taken to apply the King's National Roll Scheme; it was feared that republican and trade union opposition would make the scheme unworkable. The Ministry of Labour had written to the Comrades of the Great War that as there were no local employment committees in Ireland, it had not been possible to apply the Scheme, though employers who desired to co-operate in the Scheme were entitled to do so.[81] In 1920 the Ministry of Labour believed that there would also be difficulty in implementing the Scheme in the north of Ireland.[82] Even Dublin Castle informed the Ministry of Labour that there would be problems in giving preference to firms employing disabled ex-servicemen in the contracts it awarded, as their contracts (e.g. for the RIC and the Prisons Board) were too small or specialised to have a far-reaching effect, and that there was no comprehensive list of approved companies. The Office of Public Works

76 TNA, LAB, 2/855, MoL to PM's office 24 March 1920.
77 TNA, LAB, 2/855, MoL to PM's office 16 March 1920.
78 TNA, LAB, 2/522, MoL note, 5 May 1919.
79 TNA, LAB, 2/522, MoL note, undated but around December 1919.
80 TNA, LAB, 2/522, MoL note, 20 February 1920.
81 TNA, LAB, 2/220; Reply to question in House of Commons as to why no names of Irish Employers on King's National Roll, 29 March 1920; MoL to Comrades of the Great War, 11 May 1920; Leonard, 'Survivors', 216.
82 TNA, LAB, 2/222, MoL, note, 31 March 1920.

wrote that 'no general condition with regard to the employment of disabled men could be laid down without seriously increasing the difficulty of obtaining tenders for works and enhancing their costs', but by negotiation a certain number of such men could be employed. They also stated that larger building firms employed a number of ex-servicemen but would not be prepared to give a specific undertaking.[83]

The Ministry of Labour persisted in its efforts to provide training for the disabled, despite the difficulties caused by continued conflict. As post offices and employment exchanges could not be used to publicise training courses, the BLSI and the Ministry of Pensions were used as alternative means of communication.[84] A Ministry of Labour report to the Treasury in July 1923 noted that the Industrial Training Scheme to train all disabled men was late in starting in Ireland, and that communication with trainees and training centres outside Dublin was uncertain and staff worked in conditions of extreme difficulty and danger. The Government Instructional Factory (GIF) in Tipperary, which provided training for 182 men, was the only building of size in the locality not to be destroyed, although threatened by the British army, the Tans, the Sinn Féiners, the IRA, and the Free State army. It had been preserved by the manager, Major Roche, with help from the local training committee, chaired by the parish priest. The report noted that owing to the difficulty of establishing the Ministry's own centres due to the disturbed nature of the country, a larger proportion of training than in England was carried out with private employers, which was 'not a satisfactory arrangement given the Irishman's attitude to the Government'. There was also difficulty getting reliable medical help to review claims for training. Some men on the waiting list had served in the Free State army, and as it was disbanded they renewed their application for disability training, perhaps having accentuated injuries. It was also noted that even after training, until trade revived, there were limited opportunities for employment. It also contained details of the men trained, the infrastructure in place, and the many still awaiting training.[85]

83 TNA, LAB, 2/222, Dublin Castle to MoL, London, 4 Oct 1920; Office of Public Works to Dublin Castle, 15 October 1920.
84 TNA, LAB, 2/528, MoL, note, 16 May 1922.
85 TNA, LAB, 2/528, MoL, report, 6 July 1923, sent to Treasury, 27 July 1923.

Table 11: Numbers trained/awaiting training

	May 1922	November 1922	May 1923
Waiting List	3,101	3,914	2,289
GIF	181	163	163
Other Centres	104	124	109
Employers' Workshops	517	568	345

Source: TNA, LAB, 2/528, Report from Ministry of Labour
6 July 1923, sent to the Treasury 27 July 1923.

Table 12: Activities of training centres

Name	Courses
Tipperary GIF	Boot and Shoe, Harness Making, Basket Making, Commercial, Estate Carpentry
Clonmel Tech School	Blacksmithing, Estate Carpentry
Dublin, Hume Street	Watch and Clock
Dublin, Kearney and Co	Marine Motors
Dublin Training Centre	Boot and Shoe

Source: TNA, LAB, 2/528, Report from Ministry of Labour
6 July 1923, sent to the Treasury 27 July 1923.

The same report also commented on the implications of the formation of the Irish Free State. From a legal position under the Government of Ireland Act 1920, confirmed under the Order in Council of 1 April 1922, training was a reserved service. In subsequent legislation with regard to the establishment of the Free State, training was not mentioned, with the effect that this service remained an Imperial obligation for which the Free State Government was not in any way responsible. The Ministry of Labour therefore continued with both responsibility and resources in the Free State. There were local training committees composed of persons of standing who were supportive of the ministry's training scheme. The Free State Government accepted the British Government investing money in Ireland and did not display hostility towards the scheme. It was careful though to avoid any open connection and did not wish to be regarded as in any way responsible for the scheme's activities. The Ministry of Labour's report noted it was anomalous to have a department of the British Ministry of Labour functioning in the Irish Free State. There was an arrangement that the Secretary of the Free State's

Minister of Labour, Gordon Campbell, would exercise general supervision, but in practical terms this did not happen.[86] The British Ministry of Labour concluded therefore that 'the right course for us is to carry on quietly as may be with the scheme on present lines'.[87] The Treasury concurred, stating, 'the view now held in this Department is that transfer of administrative responsibility for training to either of the local Governments is not practicable'.[88] Despite considerable efforts, 'owing to the disturbed state of affairs in many parts of Ireland', it had been impossible for the Ministry of Labour 'to make arrangements to afford training to all the men who are entitled to it'. In December 1923 there were still 1,865 men on the waiting list with a further 560 in training; 182 were at the GIF in Tipperary, but the majority (258) were in employers' workshops. Although discussions took place with the Board of Works in Dublin to open a large, centralised training facility at Gormanston Camp on a three-year lease from 1924,[89] the training programme for 1924/25 estimated that of 1,230 men, 790 would be trained in employers' workshops and only 190 in GIFs, with an estimated budget of £198,328.[90]

In addition to the physically disabled, the need to make training and employment provision for the mentally disabled was also recognised. Employment was a critical factor in the recovery and self-esteem of soldiers suffering mental illness. Dr P.L. Forward from the Ministry of Pensions wrote in March 1921 that

> these patients, in addition to their nervous disabilities resulting from the stress of the War, all have the super-added anxiety states occasioned by the hopeless outlook for the future in respect to their obtaining employment, and earning the means wherewith to maintain themselves and their dependents. No amount of psychotherapy can relieve this super-imposed anxiety condition,

and that the only solution to enable them to leave hospital was

> to provide an occupational outlet through which a man on discharge from treatment may be placed in a suitable position to allow of his earning a living, and by his own efforts to become self-supporting ... in many instances men are kept on treatment allowances and in hospital because they have no prospect of employment.

---

86 TNA, LAB, 2/528, MoL, report, 6 July 1923, sent to Treasury 27 July 1923.
87 TNA, LAB, 2/528, MoL, note, 9 July 1923.
88 TNA, LAB, 2/528, Treasury to MoL, 16 Aug 1923.
89 TNA, LAB, 2/528, MoL, note, around December 1923.
90 TNA, LAB, 2/528, MoL, note, 22 Aug 1923.

As has been noted, to counter the hostility to ex-servicemen, he advocated 'work colonies', where they could be trained and employed with a section set aside for the mentally ill. He concluded that without such employment there would be no decrease in the number of men listed for treatment for neurasthenia but rather, because of the stress the men were subject to, the numbers were likely to increase.[91] The therapeutic need for men suffering neurasthenia to have remunerative occupations was also acknowledged by the Ministry of Pensions, Medical Services in Ulster, who highlighted the 'great lack' of such opportunities even in the north.[92] The problem was accentuated in the south with little real possibility of remedying it; mentally ill ex-soldiers were the most disadvantaged of those seeking employment.

Employment – Transitional Arrangements and Post-1922

With the formation of the Free State, Britain ceased to have any meaningful influence in terms of ability to provide employment schemes for ex-servicemen, nor indeed did it any longer have responsibility for unemployment benefit. Yet problems persisted. The Ministry of Labour wrote to the Treasury in July 1923 that as the country became more settled, Civil Liability Grants, available in Britain from 1919 to help returning soldiers, could be used to provide assistance.[93] There were also some concerns that British Government entities continuing to operate in Ireland did not give preference to ex-servicemen; the BLSI complained that the Trust employed civilians despite there being 'an appalling state of unemployment existing amongst ex-servicemen'.[94] The complaint appeared unjustified: of the 53 males employed by the Trust, 45 were ex-servicemen.[95] The reality that the British Government had little influence with regard to employment was acknowledged in the mandate given to the Lavery Committee; with regard to employment it was tasked with examining any claims against the Irish Government in respect of alleged discrimination in regard to employment. A primary grievance against the British Government was that it did not ensure, through Treaty provisions at the time of the transfer of power, security of employment or adequate compensation upon dismissal for British ex-servicemen who had become

---

91 TNA, PIN, 15/899, Forward 'Provision of Employment for Ex-serviceman in Ireland', 11 March 1921.
92 TNA, PIN, 15/899, MoP, Medical Services, Ulster Region, Memorandum, 21 March 1921.
93 TNA, LAB, 2/528, MoL, report, 6 July 1923, sent to Treasury, 27 July 1923.
94 TNA, AP, 1/98, BLSI, Council to Secretary of State, 3 February 1926, copy sent Duckworth, 4 Feb 1926.
95 TNA, AP, 1/84, Duckworth to Haig, 13 November 1925.

civil servants, specifically for those employed on a non-permanent basis, or a reasonable opportunity for them to obtain a permanent post. They could therefore be dismissed without compensation and in reapplying considered themselves to be disadvantaged against ex-National army servicemen.[96] This was particularly important as most ex-servicemen were usually only eligible for temporary appointments.[97] This criticism was valid. In the United Kingdom, irrespective of any contractual conditions, the government could not dismiss ex-servicemen without public protest, but there were no such moral safeguards in the Free State. The Lavery Report acknowledged the problem but proposed no solution. An additional complaint of ex-servicemen civil servants was that they were no longer considered for posts in the United Kingdom.[98] A further claim of those who continued in employment with the Free State Government was that those who had been Lytton entrants (a scheme for ex-servicemen to gain employment in the civil service) did not benefit from subsequent improvements to the conditions of service in the United Kingdom.[99] The Lavery Report noted that the British Government might wish to remedy these problems. The Civil Service Clerical Association made a representation to the British Government to provide compensation to Irish Lytton entrants or allow them to re-enter the British civil service. The British Government responded that it could not see any reason to become involved in the concerns of Irish civil servants about improvement in the employment conditions of United Kingdom civil servants after the date of transfer.[100] In both the latter cases the reason for the complaints was an unwillingness to accept that Ireland was a separate state, and that pay rises in Britain were no longer applicable in Ireland, or that civil service transfers between the two countries were no longer appropriate.

Pensions and Health – The Physically Disabled

The Ministry of Pensions was formed in 1916 to deal with war pensions. Its administrative structure and processes in Ireland, and later the Irish Free State, were similar to Britain, and pensioners benefited from the same entitlements. It was established in Ireland under hostile circumstances. The staff and premises of local war pension committees frequently came under

96 TNA, PIN, 15/758, Lavery Report.
97 TNA, LAB, 2/855, MoL to PM's office, 24 March 1920.
98 Haughton, Branch General Secretary of the Association of Ex-Service Civil Servants, letter, *Dublin Evening Mail*, 28 November 1927.
99 TNA, PIN, 15/758, Lavery Report.
100 TNA, PIN, 15/758, Lavery Report; IFS Government Memorandum on Lavery Report; TNA, AP, 1/121, DO to BL, 17 March 1930.

attack from republicans.[101] There were early charges that the Ministry was ineffective. In 1920 the IFDDSS complained of the deplorable conditions under which pensioners had to attend the offices of the Local Pensions Committee; the premises were inadequate; the staff unable to cope; men, women, and children were herded together in a stifling and insanitary atmosphere for as many as seven hours in the day; and there were long delays in the issuing of documentation by the ministry in London.[102] Leonard writes that the problems with the Ministry of Pensions were such that in 1920 none of the responsible authorities could estimate the number of disabled men in Ireland, and a civil servant visiting Cork that year was horrified to find that nothing had been done with thousands of applications for financial assistance from Munster veterans.[103] The Ministry of Labour on several occasions criticised the performance of the Ministry of Pensions in Ireland, noting in a report to the Treasury that its organisation was 'unreliable'.[104]

By 1927 P.W. Shaw, TD for Longford-Westmeath and Chairman of Mullingar and district area pension advisory committee, presented a contrasting picture. In a debate in the Dáil Éireann in November 1927 on the grievances of ex-servicemen, he noted that the British Ministry of Pensions had a comprehensive structure in the Free State for the administration of benefits. There were five war pension advisory committees with a membership of 62 supported by 524 voluntary workers. In addition, there were area offices in Dublin and Cork, with 36 sub-offices throughout the country employing 164 people. Shaw described the workload at these offices for a typical month: in September 1927 there were 3,602 direct interviews, 456 applications dealt with, and 1,711 disabled men examined. The average monthly expenditure on pensions alone (excluding administration or special allowances) was £85,500 to disabled men, £25,300 to widows, and £13,300 to dependents. The role of the advisory committees was to see that every claimant received the maximum pension, treatment allowance, sickness benefit, and educational grant, as well as grants from voluntary funds. Shaw explained that his local pension advisory committee had arranged for the education of 60 children, the ministry paying for their maintenance, education, and clothing.[105] The Ministry of Pensions could not have succeeded without local infrastructure, and this could not have been established without the support of the Irish Government. This was forthcoming. The ministry's comparative ease of operation after the transition may have been due to it being the most

---

101 Leonard, 'Survivors', 215.
102 TNA, LAB, 2/855, IFDDSS to PM, 17 February 1920.
103 Leonard, 'Survivors', 215.
104 TNA, LAB, 2/528, MoL report, 6 July 1923, sent to Treasury, 27 July 1923.
105 *Dáil Éireann*, Vol. 21, 16 November 1927; 1927; *IT*, 23 November 1927 (reporting the debate).

substantial source of finance to the Free State from the British Exchequer, and benefiting from the support of influential people such as Shaw, who in turn gained politically from the distribution of such largesse.[106] A High Court judge described this comprehensive infrastructure as 'an elaborate scheme of pensions and gratuities and free medical and surgical treatment'.[107]

Pensions were the major source of grievance raised with the Lavery Committee. One complaint from the British Legion related to ex-servicemen and their dependents who were in receipt of a need pension, paid by the Ministry of Pensions. A person in receipt of such a pension in Great Britain suffered no reduction of income when becoming eligible for the old age pension, whereas a resident in the Free State lost up to 4/ per week. This was caused by the difference in the 'standard income' (or minimum income) between the two countries: 20/ a week in the United Kingdom, 16/ in the Free State. The maximum pension payable in both counties was 10/ (the pension in the Free State was increased from 9/ in April 1928). Upon becoming eligible for an old age pension, a United Kingdom recipient of a need pension of 20/ was subject to a reduction of 10/, the amount was then made up by the 10/ pension. In the Free State a similar deduction was made but the amount of pension paid was only 6/ due to the lower 'standard income', leading to a financial loss. The Committee acknowledged the problem but no remedy was suggested.[108]

The complaint illustrates the problems faced by ex-servicemen in dealing with two governments. The Irish Government Memorandum on the Lavery Report noted that the number of cases was small and it would be unjust for the Irish Government to alleviate them without also helping the other more numerous classes with equal claims for relief. The Irish Government suggested proposing to the British Government that in the case of Irish recipients of need pensions exceeding 16/, they should continue to pay them in full and not reduce them by 10/ when the recipient reached pensionable age.[109] In a debate on the Report in the House of Lords in June 1930, Lord Danesfort noted with reference to this proposal, 'according to the usual fashion of communications from the Free State, it appears to me that they want to throw an additional burden upon the British Government'. Lord Passfield explained that since the Irish standard income was fixed at 16/ it was impossible to resolve the issue of a decline in income without the British Government paying the entire amount, adding:

106 TNA, PIN, 15/757, MoP to Major General Lovat, 28 November 1927.
107 TNA, AP, 1/143, Justice Johnston, Leggett Case, 10 March 1932.
108 TNA, PIN, 15/758, Lavery Report.
109 TNA, PIN, 15/758, IFS Government Memorandum on Lavery Report.

It is not true that the beneficiary always suffers a reduction in the need pension when he or she obtains an old age pension. In the vast majority of cases it so works out that the beneficiary receives an increased income. It is only in the cases in which the need pension is 16/ or more per week that there is in the Irish Free State an automatic reduction in the need pension. It is a theoretical case that has been discovered.[110]

The British Legion raised the issue with the Ministry of Pensions after the publication of the report. The latter reiterated the British Government's position and concluded that the 'standard income' adopted by the Irish Free State was fixed with reference to a standard of living appropriate to the whole class of pensioners in the Free State, and that a special exception should not be made for persons eligible for a need pension from the British Government.[111] In reality the anomaly arose in the first instance because war pensioners resident in the Free State benefited from higher pensions and allowances set in the context of the higher cost of living in the United Kingdom. The problem of pensions impacting on benefits received by ex-servicemen from the Irish State persisted. The annual meeting of the BLSI in February 1935 passed a resolution protesting against the Irish Government taking into account disability pensions when means testing individuals in accordance with the Public Assistance Act, which contradicted assurances given by the government in April 1934.[112] A BLSI conference in February 1938 complained that British ex-servicemen with pensions remained subject to means testing.[113]

The Lavery Report did recognise some disadvantages suffered by Irish pensioners, noting that 'ex-servicemen in the Irish Free State form a small proportion of the population and that a large number do not belong to any veteran organisation, owing to being scattered over wide geographical areas', and because of their geographical dispersal Irish veterans were 'less well acquainted with their rights and were less liable to have pension regulations brought to their attention'. Additionally the Report continued, 'ex-servicemen in the Irish Free State were at a disadvantage owing to the disturbed state of the country in the years 1918–1923 … normal postal services were not available resulting in loss of letters dealing with their pensions', including those related to the right of appeal.[114] The Report indicated that in contrast, as British ex-servicemen were a larger portion of the population,

110 *Hansard*, HL Deb 25 June 1930, vol. 78.
111 TNA, PIN, 15/758, BLSI to the MoP, 9 August 1929; MoP to BLSI, 24 October 1929; TNA, PIN, 15/757, MoP report (and earlier draft) to DO, 3 May 1929.
112 TNA, AP, 1/145, *IT*, 4 February 1935.
113 TNA, AP, 1/148, *IT*, reporting BLSI meeting, 21 February 1938.
114 TNA, PIN, 15/758, Lavery Report.

concentrated in industrial centres, they were better able to know their rights. The Ministry of Pensions disagreed that Irish ex-servicemen were at a disadvantage, noting:

That having regard for the smaller number of men from the Free State mobilised in relation to the male population, the number of pensioners is on average similar to the UK and most were mobilised in the towns and those in the countryside were in a similar position to those in Scotland and Wales. Pension administration was not through ex-servicemen associations but local offices of the Ministry with which the Free State is well served and which provided information even during the times of disturbances.

The Ministry also argued that if an applicant had been prejudiced by the disturbances, then upon appeal special consideration would have been given but a 'general plea could not be considered as to the state of the country 6 years ago, and where a final award was seriously inadequate then a system to rectify it already existed but in many cases appeals were made arising out of hardship wholly unconnected to war service'.[115] The latter point echoes the Committee's overall finding: that the hardship of many of the ex-servicemen was typical of the labouring class in Ireland. It was not caused by a failure of the British Government to fulfil its obligations.

Of over 500 letters of complaint sent to the Lavery Committee from individuals, the majority, 337, related to pensions, mostly to do with them not being awarded or deemed insufficient or later reduced or stopped, that is, the same complaints as British ex-servicemen. There were no grievances specific to Ireland.[116] The Lavery Report noted that with regard to dealing with complaints, 'the existing machinery seems adequate', and that 'nothing was brought to our attention that as regards War Pensions, ex-servicemen in the Irish Free State are treated in any way differently from such men in Great Britain'; it concluded that with the administration of such an elaborate code, cases of hardship would occur but 'they are in no sense peculiar to ex-servicemen in the Irish Free State'.[117] The British Treasury observed that 'on the whole it seems that the Committee give quite a handsome testimonial to the Ministry of Pensions'.[118]

The bureaucratic 'buck passing' following the publication of the Report was

115 TNA, PIN, 15/757, MoP report (and earlier draft) to DO, 3 May 1929.
116 TNA, PIN, 15/758, IFS to DO, with attached details of pension complaints, 31 December 1929.
117 TNA, PIN, 15/758, Lavery Report.
118 TNA, PIN, 15/757, Treasury to MoP, 19 February 1929.

perhaps indicative of some more of the challenges faced by the ex-servicemen in dealing with two states. The Lavery Committee recommended that individual complaints should be sent to the Ministry of Pensions in London. Consequently, in December 1929, the Free State Government sent the list of pension-related complaints to the Dominions Office, which in April 1930 forwarded it to the Ministry of Pensions. The ministry in an internal memorandum noted that the only means of identifying the complainants were the addresses, which after two years they could not be relied upon, and that therefore the labour of identifying the claimants would be too great. The ministry decided that the complaints were in any event expressed in vague terms and therefore mostly 'without definite basis' and that, given the lapse in time, 'if there was good ground for application to the Ministry, some further action will have been taken in the interval'. The memorandum concluded that 'we should not be justified in making any attempt to investigate these cases but, if the Free State considers any action should be taken, they should advise the complainant to apply to the relevant British Government department'. The Dominions Office was informed accordingly in May 1930 that the Ministry of Pensions would take no further action.[119]

In responding to the Lavery Report, the Ministry of Pensions conducted an analysis that demonstrated that war pensioners in Ireland were extremely favourably treated in comparison to their counterparts in the United Kingdom.[120] A larger proportion of men who enlisted in what became the Irish Free State were pensioned than elsewhere; the percentage being 31.6% as against 16% in Northern Ireland and 9.8% in Great Britain (England, Wales and Scotland).

Table 13: Percentage of enlisted men pensioned

	Great Britain	Northern Ireland	Irish Free State
Enlisted	4,836,700	62,104	72,104
Men Pensioners	471,805	9,947	22,767
% of Enlisted	9.8	16.0	31.6

Source: TNA, PIN, 15/757. Number of pensioners as at financial year 1926/27. Enlistments in Ireland exclude Irish recruitment in Great Britain.[121]

119 TNA, PIN, 15/758, IFS to DO, with attached details of pension complaints, 31 December 1929; DO to MoP, 11 April 1930; MoP, note, 23 April 1930; MoP to DO, 13 May 1930.
120 TNA, PIN, 15/757, MoP report, February 1928. Tables 16–23 are based on this report.
121 The MoP based their analysis on recruitment figures, not the estimated number of

The pension costs per enlistment in relation to men, widows, or dependents were in all cases significantly higher in the Free State; in the case of men, over three times as much as Great Britain, using 1926/27 as the comparable year, although previous years showed similar disparities. The costs for Northern Ireland were significantly higher than the rest of the UK, but still considerably lower than those of the Free State.

Table 14: Cost of pensions related to the number of enlistments

	Great Britain			Northern Ireland			Irish Free State		
Enlisted	4,836,700			62,104			72,104		
	Amount	Cost per man		Amount	Cost per man		Amount	Cost per man	
	£	£ s d		£	£ s d		£	£ s d	
Men	24,321	5 0 7		619	9 19 8		1,251	17 7 6	
Widows	15,709	3 5 0		249	4 0 4		339	4 14 2	
Dependents	6,938	1 8 7		122	1 19 4		178	2 9 5	

Source: TNA, PIN, 15/757. Costs of pensions for financial year 1926/27.
Pensions include treatment allowances.
Amount of pensions rounded and in thousands.

ex-servicemen, and appear to have excluded regular soldiers serving in 1914. Recruitment figures (around 5,500) for the three Ulster counties that became part of the IFS seem to have been included as part of Northern Ireland. Conversely, Irish ex-servicemen may have left the IFS after the war; it was the only part of what had been the UK to experience a reduction in population, which would have decreased the number of pensioners.

In the period between the financial years 1922/23 and 1926/27, the total disbursements on pensions and treatment allowances fell significantly more in England/Wales and Scotland than in both parts of Ireland:

Table 15: Decrease in pension-related costs

Country	Percentage Decrease
England/Wales	17.4
Scotland	18.6
Northern Ireland	6.0
Irish Free State	7.2

Source: TNA, PIN, 15/757.

In terms of pensions, the amount expended in the Free State actually increased:

Table 16: Pensions and treatment allowances paid

Financial Year	Great Britain			Northern Ireland			Irish Free State		
	P	T/A	Total	P	T/A	Total	P	T/A	Total
1922/23	51,566	5,386	56,952	907	148	1,055	1,607	297	1,904
1923/24	48,141	4,041	52,182	874	106	980	1,615	177	1,792
1924/25	47,157	3,266	50,423	909	74	983	1,591	196	1,787
1925/26	46,404	2,693	49,097	946	56	1,002	1,636	155	1,791
1926/27	44,751	2,217	46,968	943	48	991	1,632	136	1,768

Source: TNA, PIN, 15/757. Pensions include men, widows,
and dependents. Costs rounded and in thousands.
P: Pensions. T/A: Treatment Allowances.

In the period between the financial years 1923/24 and 1926/27, the total disbursements on pensions and treatment allowances per pensioner (including pensions paid to men, widows, and dependents) fell in England, from £51 11s 11d to £50 8s 6d, but increased in the Free State, from £49 15s 7d to £52 7d.

The percentage of pensioners drawing treatment allowance in the Irish Free State was much higher than in Great Britain and Northern Ireland. In December 1927 the number of pensioners drawing allowances outside the Irish Free State was 228 in every 10,000, while in the Free State the comparative figure was 365.

Table 17: Percentage of pensioners drawing treatment allowances

	Great Britain	Northern Ireland	Irish Free State
Pensioners	427,359	11,483	22,366
Men on Treatment Allowances	9,714	274	817
Percentage on Treatment Allowances	2.27	2.39	3.65

Source: TNA, PIN, 15/757. Number of pensioners as at December 1927, excluding cases of insanity.

The amount paid in treatment allowances related to the number of enlistments shows that the cost per enlisted man in the Irish Free State was far in excess of that elsewhere; the cost in 1926/27 was roughly four times that of Great Britain.

Table 18: Cost of treatment allowances per enlisted man

	Great Britain				Northern Ireland				Irish Free State			
Enlisted	4,279,082				62,104				72,104			
Financial Year	T/A	Per man			T/A	Per man			T/A	Per man		
	£	£	s	d	£	£	s	d	£	£	s	d
1922/23	5,386	1	2	2	148	2	7	9	297	4	2	6
1923/24	4,041		16	10	106	1	14	2	177	2	9	2
1924/25	3,266		13	8	74	1	3	10	196	2	14	5
1925/26	2,693		11	2	56		18	1	155	2	3	1
1926/27	2,217		9	5	48		15	6	136	1	17	9

Source: TNA, PIN, 15/757. Amount of allowances rounded
and in thousands. T/A: Total Allowances.

The amount paid in treatment allowances in the Free State related to the number of pensioners was also higher but less so due to the higher pro rata number of pensioners than in Great Britain.

Table 19: Cost of treatment allowances per pensioner

	Great Britain					Northern Ireland					Irish Free State				
Financial Year	Total Pens. 000s	T/A £000s	Cost per Pen.			Total Pens. 000s	T/A £000s	Cost per Pen.			Total Pens. 000s	T/A £000s	Cost per Pen.		
			£	s	d			£	s	d			£	s	d
1923/24	519	3,799	7	6	5	10	106	10	14	7	25	177	7	2	7
1924/25	507	3,060	6	0	10	10	74	7	10	1	23	196	8	10	11
1925/26	484	2,532	5	4	7	10	56	5	11	7	23	155	6	14	11
1926/27	472	2,082	4	8	2	10	48	4	16	7	23	136	5	19	8

Source: TNA, PIN, 15/757. Number of pensioners in thousands. Total
of allowances rounded and in thousands. T/A: Total Allowances.

The cost of administration was significantly higher in the Free State than in Northern Ireland. The figures in Table 20 are for the financial year 1926/27; previous years show similar discrepancies:

Table 20: Cost of administration

Northern Ireland			Irish Free State		
General Admin- istration	Medical Services Administration	Total	General Admin- istration	Medical Services Administration	Total
15,836	8,258	24,094	39,424	18,380	57,804

Source: TNA, PIN, 15/757. Costs are for financial year 1926/7 and in pounds.

Information that indicated that Free State pensioners were disadvantaged was suppressed. An internal document noted that there were five pension committees in the Free State, which resulted in a lower ratio of committees to both population and area covered in the Free State in comparison to the United Kingdom. The document recommended excluding this information from any circulated comments.[122] Notwithstanding this point, the evidence indicates that compared to their counterparts in the United Kingdom, the Free State's ex-servicemen were very favourably treated. The percentage of enlisted men receiving pensions, and the costs per enlisted man in terms of pensions and treatment allowances were greater in Northern Ireland than in the UK, but the figures for the Free State were higher again. Nor were they reduced to take account of the lower cost of living in Ireland.

Although they seem insufficient to explain the extent of the discrepancy, there were several possible reasons for the higher cost of pensions in Ireland. Most surviving Irish soldiers would have served longer than their British counterparts: some 68% of recruitment for all Ireland took place before February 1916, over half volunteered in the first year of the War.[123] The percentage for southern Ireland was likely even higher given the dearth of recruits after 1916, as a result of both increased radicalism and opposition to conscription. The Irish divisions fought in many of the main battle areas including Ypres, the Somme, and Gallipoli. In the latter, and in Salonika and

---

122 TNA, PIN, 15/757, MoP, note, 25 April 1929.
123 According to some pension authorities, Irish recruits may also have been in poorer health on enlistment than recruits from the rest of the UK. See Bourke, 'Effeminacy, Ethnicity and the End of Trauma', 61.

Palestine, the troops may have been exposed to malaria, a disease that often recurred. Injuries may have been accentuated during the post-Great War conflict, particularly with the large numbers who joined the Free State army. The Irish Government admitted that it had accepted for active service men who would not normally be regarded as medically suitable for enlistment but could not provide the British Government with any medical records after they were discharged.[124] One other possibility is that knowing the disabled had little benefit from civil society, the Ministry of Pensions may have responded more favourably to the Irish pension advisory committees; P.W. Shaw noted that 'the British Ministry of Pensions are very sympathetic, and if there is any possibility of falling in with the claims we put before them they do so'.[125] Or, as Lord Danesfort implied, the Irish may have been more adept at extracting money from the British Treasury.

Pensions and Health – The Mentally Disabled

The Ministry of Pensions was responsible for the payment of treatment for ex-servicemen designated as mentally ill. For the payment to be made they had to be classified as 'service patients' – disabled by reason of mental illness attributable or aggravated by war service. The designation included military personnel whose mental illness was not due to or aggravated by military service, provided that the arrangement did not extend beyond one year. Service patients were to be placed on the same footing as a paying patient.[126] The problem was that asylums received a higher grant for men designated criminal lunatics. Hence the Medical Superintendent of Waterford District Lunatic Asylum wrote to the Ministry of Pensions, complaining that they had classified three inmates as 'service patients' but that 'these men are Criminal Lunatics by Act of Parliament and the Committee of this Asylum will not accept any other classification which means a loss in the cost of maintenance'.[127] The problems extended to the process of admissions, particularly in the case of those considered 'dangerous'. The 1838 Dangerous Lunatic Act (with its 1867 amendments) was introduced to 'protect' society from individuals whose 'derangement of mind' was considered a threat to the community. The process started with the police, usually acting at

---

124 TNA, PIN, 15/663, TM Healy, Governor-General, IFS, to the Secretary of State for the Colonies, 1 September 1923.
125 *Dáil Éireann*, Vol. 21, 16 November 1927; *IT*, 23 November 1927.
126 TNA, PIN, 15/898; Dublin Castle note, 6 Aug 1919; TNA, PIN, 15/899, Dublin Castle circulars, 28 Aug 1919.
127 TNA, PIN, 15/899, Medical Superintendent of Waterford District Lunatic Asylum to MoP, 22 October 1919.

the behest of the family, and certification required the signature of two magistrates and a medical officer.[128] Applications to asylums for discharged men suffering from insanity had to be signed by a relative (or the secretary of a war pensions committee or the head of the receiving asylum), a medical practitioner, and a magistrate and, if dangerous, the police called. This created a problem if, either due to the breakdown of law and order, or the political bias of officials, signatures were not forthcoming. In terms of non-violent cases, the medical expenses incurred in certification were only repaid by the ministry if the man was subsequently designated a service patient. Medical practitioners and families were reluctant to assume the risk of non-payment.[129] If a man was considered dangerous to the community, the police were responsible to bring him before a magistrate and for the payment of fees to doctors to certify him. In certain regions, though, the police force was ineffective, Ministry of Pension officials recording that 'the arresting of lunatics is in abeyance, owing to other difficulties', and that 'lunatics have been admitted through the police of the Irish Republic, but this was not a process to be relied on for ex-soldiers'. In some districts the magistrates were Sinn Féiners.[130] The Dublin office of the Ministry of Pensions reported to London that, in certain areas in particular, 'owing to the local political difficulties there is not much tendency to assist the ex-soldier'.[131] An attempt to alleviate this problem was made through the Commissioner of Medical Services of the Ministry of Pensions, assembling a board to include medical expertise and asylum management to make a decision on commitment.[132]

Asylums were subsidised by government grants and as the ministry noted, 'a great majority of the local authorities have declined to recognise the government and to submit their accounts for audit, so there are no government grants available. Asylums are carrying on in a very reduced condition, and not admitting any patients if it is possible to avoid doing so'. Ex-servicemen in particular were excluded. At the same time, the Ministry of Pensions wished to delay the discharge of the mentally disabled because of 'the possibility of action being taken by their neighbours on their return home, which may make them in a worse condition than they were when they were admitted to hospital'. Dr P.L. Forward believed that work had a

128 Catherine Cox, *Negotiating Insanity in the Southeast of Ireland, 1820–1900* (Manchester, 2012), 77–9, 85.
129 TNA, PIN, 15/899, MoP, note, 30 Dec 1920; MoP to Departmental Committee of Enquiry, London, 15 March 1921.
130 TNA, PIN, 15/899, MoP, note, Dublin to London based on interview with Dr Dawson, Inspector of Lunatics, 20 September 1920; MoP note, 24 March 1921.
131 TNA, PIN, 15/899, MoP, note, Dublin to London, 26 May 1920.
132 TNA, PIN, 15/899, Circular from Office of Lunatic Asylums, Dublin Castle, October 1920.

therapeutic value essential for recovery, but this was not easily provided given the hostile attitude to ex-servicemen.[133] The absence of suitable employment meant that many patients were detained in hospital, as given the political climate the alternative was to 'allow the men to drift and starve'. In some republican areas their discharge could not be prevented as local authorities were saving expenses by discharging inmates, except those certified by Sinn Féin magistrates. The political situation was forcing the ministry to put patients into private clinics.[134] Richmond District Asylum in Dublin is an example of an asylum that proved unco-operative. Its governors had already written to the ministry in September 1919, complaining with regard to the lower payment for service patients and stating that, while a portion of the building had been set aside as a war hospital, it had not been anticipated that the institution would become a central mental hospital for discharged soldiers from every part of Ireland.[135] In October 1920, the ministry noted that

> it is not the desire of the committee of this asylum at present instituted to have anything to do with service patients, and however the Ministry may meet them on this occasion, until there is some resettlement of a lasting nature of the present position in Ireland, there will be perpetual friction with this committee.

A patient from Clonmel was refused a transfer to the asylum, even though he was born and had lived in Dublin.[136] In the following month the ministry identified alternative accommodation in a private asylum at Farnham House, Finglas, County Dublin.[137]

Southern Ireland had a high proportion of ex-servicemen receiving pensions for neurasthenia and awaiting treatment. Various reasons were postulated for this by British medical experts: it was a legacy of mental weakness dating from the sufferings of the famine years and Irishmen were 'childlike'. Even the pension authorities attributed negative reasons. The District Commissioner of Medical Services for 'Ireland (South)', Dr Boldie, argued that it was not only due to the 'special political conditions', but also to 'a definite neurasthenic temperament which is

---

133 Work was considered fundamental to therapeutic regimes and concepts of respectability see Cox, *Negotiating Insanity*, 212.
134 TNA, PIN, 15/899, MoP, note, Dublin to London, 26 Nov 1920; MoP note, 24 March 1921; Forward, 'Provision of Employment for Ex-Serviceman in Ireland', 11 March 1921.
135 TNA, PIN, 15/899, Richmond District Asylum, Dublin to MoP 18 September 1919.
136 TNA, PIN, 15/899, MoP, note Dublin to London, 27 October 1920.
137 TNA, PIN, 15/899. MoP, note, 4 November 1920.

prevalent amongst the South Irish'. Dr Wallace claimed that recruitment practice in Ireland was more lax and therefore some of those recruited were physically unfit, mentally defective, and subject to a wide range of nervous disorders.[138] More realistically, the prevalence of Irish soldiers requiring treatment for neurasthenia may have mirrored some of the reasons for the larger proportion of physically disabled veterans as outlined in the previous section. There is some evidence that Irish troops may have been more susceptible to mental trauma during the war, perhaps again due to their long service. They were four times more likely to be condemned to death by a British court martial than troops from the rest of the United Kingdom.[139] Despite the assumption that Irishmen were predisposed to lunacy, there were inadequate means for treatment. In 1921, the percentage of patients awaiting treatment in southern Ireland was significantly higher than both the north and all regions of Great Britain.

Table 21: Mental health patients awaiting in-patient or out-patient treatment, 1921

Area	% Awaiting In/ Out-Patient Treatment	% Awaiting In-Patient Treatment	% Awaiting Out-Patient Treatment
Scotland	2.5	21.0	0
North	7.5	0	13.5
North-west	37.1	22.5	56.3
Yorkshire	20.9	7.3	24.5
Wales	4.5	5.3	7.6
North Midlands	40.9	22.2	53.1
Midlands	58.6	39.2	64.8
South-west	7.6	8.7	7.3
London	7.2	32.8	5.9
Northern Ireland	22.2	42.1	4.3
Southern Ireland	69.0	87.9	48.2

Source: Bourke from TNA, PIN, 15/56.[140]

138 Bourke, 'Effeminacy, Ethnicity and the End of Trauma', 57–69.
139 Gerard Oram, *Worthless Men: Race, Eugenics and the Death Penalty in the British Army during the First World War* (London, 1998), 69. The death sentence could be imposed for offences other than those potentially related to mental trauma.
140 Bourke, 'Effeminacy, Ethnicity and the End of Trauma', 69.

In 1917, the first Irish hospital for shell-shocked soldiers was opened in Lucan, west of Dublin and later another at Leopardstown Park, south of Dublin. The latter expanded to provide general treatment for veterans in the 1920s. Leopardstown and its counterpart in Ulster, Craigavon Hospital, were constantly short of resources and even under threat of closure.[141] According to reports from March 1921, there was a lack of facilities to deal with specialist mental illnesses attributable to war. There was no epileptic colony in Ireland and it was not even possible to ascertain how many cases there were; 142 men were under treatment and almost all were out-patients due to limited facilities. An estimate of the actual number of cases put the figure at 247. There were 120 officers and 1,200 men awaiting hospital treatment for neurasthenia, the majority of whom were on home treatment allowances, costing the ministry £2,000 per week. The payments were expected to continue indefinitely due to insufficient clinics and an inadequate supply of trained staff. The inability to provide services was not just an economic problem but very much influenced by the 'present situation in Ireland'.[142]

The mentally disabled in Ireland suffered from the lack of understanding and scarcity of resources prevalent in Britain, but the political conditions in Ireland meant that perhaps the most vulnerable group of returning soldiers were also denied the therapeutic benefits of employment and in many cases support from the community.

Pensions and Health – Ex-Servicemen in the Free State Army

As the Free State army rapidly grew to 60,000 men, it was inevitable that a source of manpower would be Great War veterans and the Ministry of Pensions was concerned that British ex-servicemen on disability pensions would join the new army and aggravate their injuries, which could lead to further claims on the British Government. The ministry proposed that the Free State army should require recruits to provide any regimental details related to Great War service and whether they were in receipt of a pension, and that the Free State Government should then check these details with the ministry, and on demobilisation provide a précis of service and medical history, if the man was a British army pensioner.[143] The ministry also wished for the Free State army to keep the recruitment of disabled men to a minimum

141 Leonard, 'Survivors', 212.
142 TNA, PIN, 15/899, MoP, note, 15 March 1921; TNA, PIN, 15/899, Forward, 'Provision of Employment for Ex-serviceman in Ireland', 11 March 1921.
143 TNA, PIN, 15/663, MoP, note, 31 October 1922.

and intended to scrutinise more carefully any application for treatment on the part of ex-soldiers who had served in it.[144] Although by January 1923 the Free State had ceased enlisting men considered more than 20% disabled and was in fact discharging the same, prior to this date, according to the ministry, astonishingly, a considerable number of pensioners with disabilities of up to 100% were enlisted and an estimated 2,000 had been discharged by that point.[145] Equally, the Irish Government was concerned that ex-soldiers would not declare a pensionable disability when enlisting and might then seek a second pension from the Free State. Colonel Commandant Hackett of the Free State army wrote to the ministry asking whether information could in such suspected cases be provided in confidence. The ministry was prepared to co-operate subject to reciprocal information regarding the Free State army service of all British ex-servicemen, including when they were discharged and a précis of their medical history and military service.[146] This information was not forthcoming. T.M. Healy, Governor-General of the Irish Free State wrote to the British Government that during the national emergency men were accepted for active service who would not normally be regarded as medically suitable for enlistment, and no information was sought as to receipt or otherwise of disability pensions in respect of service with the Imperial Forces, and that due to the exceptional circumstances under which the Free State Force served, medical reports were not available for many of the discharged.[147]

Perhaps even more controversially, ex-servicemen in receipt of pensions may also have fought for the republicans during the War of Independence and thereafter for the anti-Treaty forces in the Civil War. A disabled former member of the Royal Munster Fusiliers wrote to the British Government complaining that there are 'dozens of men who are drawing pensions from the British and are traitors to King and Country', due to service in the

---

144 TNA, PIN, 15/663, MoP, note, 22 November 1922.
145 TNA, PIN, 15/663, MoP, note, 31 January 1923. Given that up to 25–30,000 ex-servicemen were recruited into the National army, and that of an estimated 100,000 ex-servicemen in the Free State, some 23,000 qualified for a pension, it was inevitable that some recruits may have had disabilities, particularly as entry standards were lax. But to receive a 100% pension a man would have to have lost both legs, eyes, or arms, or to be suffering from TB (see Niall Barr, *The Lion and the Poppy: British Veterans, Politics and Society, 1921–1939* (Westport, CT, 2005), 121). The Ministry of Pensions' note states that the disabilities were 'up to' 100% disabilities; it can only be assumed that most were less.
146 TNA, PIN, 15/663, Colonel Commandant Hackett, IFS army to MoP, October 1922 and attached MoP note.
147 TNA, PIN, 15/663, TM Healy, Governor-General, IFS, to the Secretary of State for the Colonies, 1 September 1923.

Republican army. Service in the Free State army or indeed the rebel forces did not preclude the payment of pensions.[148]

Claims and Compensation

In the aftermath of the conflict many claimed that their allegiance to the British Crown had caused injuries and/or financial loss due to the activities of the IRA. Ex-servicemen could argue that war service, particularly as theirs was voluntary, constituted a demonstration of allegiance to the Crown and entitled them to be considered alongside other loyalists. A well-organised campaign was mounted by loyalist organisations, supported by influential politicians, which received extensive and often sympathetic press coverage highlighting perceived atrocities and demanded compensation for the victims. In a House of Lords debate in July 1922, Lord Carson referred to the 'outrages' committed against 'those who have been loyal to this country', and were 'absolutely helpless' due to the 'utter want of protection'. He claimed that he received many hundreds of letters from such victims and asked the government to set up a commission to help and advise them. The Marquis of Salisbury noted that upon the withdrawal of the British, Ireland was left with 'no proper provision of courts, or of law, recognised by the Provisional Government, or of armed forces or of police forces'.[149] Such pressure on the British Government to help loyalists, who had suffered during the War of Independence and after the British withdrawal, resulted in the establishment of an extensive system of compensation. The Anglo-Irish Treaty stated that 'fair compensation should be paid for criminal injuries inflicted during the conflict'. As a consequence the Compensation (Ireland) Commission was established jointly by the British and Free State Governments in 1922. It sat in Ireland, initially under the presidency of Lord Shaw of Dunfermline, and subsequently Sir Alexander Wood-Renton. The Commission's terms of reference were confined to the consideration of claims in respect of damage or injury incurred between 21 January 1919 and 11 July 1921. They dealt with 41,000 claims and an outlay of around £7 million.[150] The expenditure was apportioned between the two governments; each compensated their own

---

148 TNA, PIN, 15/663, Gerald McDonnell, disabled ex-member of the Royal Munster Fusiliers, born in Tralee but residing in Liverpool, to DO, 13 July 1935; TNA, PIN, 15/248, ex-servicemen serving in rebel forces under internment as defined by the Civil Authorities (Special Powers) Act (Northern Ireland) 1922 also remain entitled to their pension.

149 *Hansard*, HL Deb 3 July 1922, Vol. 51 cc 196–202.

150 TNA, CO, 762/212, Final Report; TNA, CO, 905, File Introduction. The Commissions files provide limited details on claimants.

supporters and split the cost where the injured person was a neutral in the Anglo-Irish conflict. In contrast, in the case of property each government paid for the damage caused by their own supporters.[151]

While the two governments were jointly responsible for the pre-truce settlement, the Free State Government was solely responsible for the settlement of post-truce compensation.[152] Claimants were frustrated with the slow speed of the Irish judicial process. The British Government remained involved. The Irish Distress Committee was established in May 1922 with the objective of helping Irish loyalist refugees settle in Great Britain. It was re-constituted as the original Irish Grants Committee in March 1923, its brief extended to cover advances for well-founded claims made under Irish compensation legislation. It made grants totalling £64,000.[153]

The problems with the compensation were more fundamental than a delay in receipt however. Lobbying groups such as SILRA argued that the recompense sought and deserved by loyalists was not forthcoming from Free State judges or ministers, and it was the responsibility of the British Government to compensate its supporters for what the Free State had neither the power nor the inclination to grant.[154] As an example, many of the ex-servicemen provided land through the Irish Land (Provision for Sailors and Soldiers) Act were forced to leave during the period of conflict. Compensation procedures allowed for damage to property but not the consequential loss arising out of an inability to work the land. A committee was constituted in 1925 under Lord Dunedin to assess any further action that the British Government should take in terms of injuries to person or property in Ireland since 11 July 1921. The report concluded that while no legal obligation existed it was desirable, given past pledges of successive ministers, to assess which other grants should be made.[155] The British Government was under pressure to accept a special obligation towards those who had supported the Crown. Brennan writes that Dunedin acknowledged the loyalists' need of better compensation than they may have got from the Free State and that:

The report was a turning-point in the compensation saga because it finally forced the British authorities to acknowledge their debt to

---

151 Gemma Clark, 'A Study of Three Munster Counties during the Irish Civil War' (University of Oxford D.Phil. thesis, 2011), 31; David Fitzpatrick, 'The Price of Balbriggan', in David Fitzpatrick (ed.), *Terror in Ireland, 1916–1923* (Dublin, 2012), 76–7.
152 *Hansard*, HL Deb 2 July 1925, Vol. 61 cc 977–8.
153 TNA, CO, 762/212, IGC Final Report.
154 Brennan, 'A Political Minefield', 406–19.
155 TNA, CO, 762/212, IGC Final Report.

southern Irish Loyalists. It was the qualified confession of neglect, even guilt, which Carson, Northumberland and others in the House of Lords had spent years trying to extract from the highest levels of government. For however much their criticisms of the Irish authorities were inspired by a sense of righteous indignation, Loyalists had always reserved their greatest bitterness for their grievances at the failures – as they perceived them – of His Majesty's Government.[156]

The new Irish Grants Committee (IGC) was therefore established in October 1926 to consider

claims from British subjects now or formerly residing or carrying on business in the area of the Irish Free State who on account of their support of His Majesty's Government prior to 11 July 1921 sustained hardship and loss by personal injuries or by the malicious destruction of or injuries to their property in the area of the Irish Free State between 11th July 1921 and 12th May 1923.

The IGC considered compensation related to: forcible dispossession of property or lands, expulsion from the Free State by threat or intimidation, loss arising from boycotts, the theft or destruction of property, and fines imposed by the anti-Treaty IRA. The IGC dealt with 4,032 claims (originally 3,036, but the time limit to apply was extended); 895 were ruled outside the scope of the Committee's terms of reference, often because the incident upon which the claim was based predated the Truce. Compensation was refused in 900 cases and recommended in 2,237, with grants totalling almost £2.2 million awarded.[157] The IGC considered service in the Great War a suitable demonstration of loyalty but comparatively few ex-servicemen applied for compensation. An attempt was made by the Irish Loyalist Association (not the more established SILRA), through a petition to the British Government in May 1931, to have a new committee established on the basis that some 500 people had failed to submit claims. They were a new association and not regarded by the Dominions Office as credible, not least because they were charging people a guinea to take details of their claims. The government decided that it had met its obligations and was not prepared to open up another enquiry.[158]

156 Brennan, 'A Political Minefield', 406–19.
157 TNA, CO, 762/212.
158 TNA, DO, 35/343/3.

Emigration

Ex-servicemen resident in the newly created Free State Dominion were excluded from the benefits of assisted passage available, under the Empire Settlement Act 1922, to veterans in the United Kingdom who wished to migrate to other parts of the empire.[159] In the Dáil Éireann debate on the claims of ex-servicemen in November 1927, Bryan Cooper refuted Redmond's assertion that there had been a promise of assisted emigration at the outset of the war, rather what was promised was 'a land fit for heroes', but when it became clear that it was beyond the power of the British Government to achieve this, emigration was suggested as a substitute.[160] The issue was raised as a grievance to the Lavery Committee, whose report suggested that a means should be found to extend such benefits to the Free State. It noted that there was no evidence of 'anything like a widespread demand for the application of the Empire Settlement Act to British ex-servicemen resident in the Free State', and that 'there was no desire for any scheme calculated to bring pressure upon British ex-servicemen in the Free State to leave the country'; only should they wish to, ex-servicemen in the Free State should have the same assistance to emigrate as ex-servicemen in the United Kingdom.[161] The British Government also believed that there would be few requests from Irish veterans for subsidised passages as any animosity there may have been towards them had disappeared. It also thought demand would come primarily from unemployed veterans residing in urban centres, who would be unwanted in the dominions since immigrants with agricultural experience were preferred, a point with which Cooper agreed.[162]

It was not the intention of the British Government to actively promote emigration from Ireland during the conflict. The Ministry of Labour declared in 1920 that 'any steps to encourage the emigration of ex-servicemen from Ireland ought to be regarded as a measure of despair and should not be entertained at this stage'.[163] Indeed, there was reason to encourage them to stay. According to Fedorowich, 'it was clear in some departments of Whitehall that Irish veterans, if properly handled and rewarded, could act as a leaven in the nationalist lump'. Perhaps for the same reason, nationalists were prepared for the imperial authorities to subsidise free passage for those ex-servicemen, former RIC, and southern unionists who had remained loyal to

159 TNA, PIN, 15/758, Lavery Report.
160 *Dáil Éireann Debates*, Vol. 21, 16 November 1927, Motion by Deputy Redmond – Disabilities of British Ex-servicemen.
161 TNA, PIN, 15/758, Lavery Report.
162 Fedorowich, 'Reconstruction and Resettlement', 1172: *Dáil Éireann Debates*, Vol. 21, 16 November 1927, Motion by Deputy Redmond – Disabilities of British Ex-servicemen.
163 TNA, LAB, 2/747, Ministries of Labour and Transport meetings, 4 May 1920.

London. However, many ex-servicemen were not loyalists, and nationalists and republicans did not want to encourage general emigration. Cathal Brugha, the Minister for Defence for the Revolutionary Government, stated in June 1920:

> The enemy has declared that there are too many young men in Ireland, and he is anxious to clear them out. It suited his purpose to refuse them passports during the War, but he will now give them every facility to emigrate. Those facilities must not be availed of, Ireland wants all her young men. Their presence in the country is more necessary now than ever.[164]

Within Whitehall there were conflicting views regarding assisted migration, with the Colonial Office advocating a liberal interpretation of the existing legislation because, it argued, the British Government was duty-bound to help ex-servicemen and loyalist refugees, and the Treasury objecting on financial and jurisdictional grounds. Even up to 1929, the Dominions Office advocated schemes to help ex-servicemen emigrate but was opposed by the Treasury, and as there seemed little requirement the idea was dropped.[165] The debate was in any event theoretical. Irish ex-servicemen were sponsored for emigration if they had lived in England for six months.[166] According to Fedorowich, the conditions were not even that onerous:

> Despite the exclusion of the Irish Free State Empire Settlement Act after 1922, residency requirements were often waived and privileges extended to southern Irish citizens, provided that they embarked from ports in Northern Ireland or Britain. 'In effect', carped one cynical Treasury official, 'they have only to set foot on these [United Kingdom] shores in order to take their passage to the Dominions'.[167]

In fact, before the Act was passed and the Free State established, the British Government did provide assistance to officers and men who had served in the War, including free passage for them and their dependents provided they were accepted by the territory to which they intended to emigrate. By May 1920, 326 free passages from Ireland to the 'Empire Overseas' had been granted to ex-servicemen. Applications were approved for more than 3,000 men, women, and children.[168] William Greene of County Wexford,

---

164 Fedorowich, 'Reconstruction and Resettlement', 1162, 1176.
165 Fedorowich, 'Reconstruction and Resettlement', 1160
166 Captain F.C. Hitchcock, 'Plight of ex-servicemen in the IFS', *Morning Post*, 19 Dec. 1927.
167 Fedorowich, 'Reconstruction and Resettlement', 1999.
168 TNA, LAB, 2/855, MoL, note, 3 May 1920.

a claimant to the IGC, wrote that his shipping agency was 'doing a lot in preparing ex-British service men for Canada'.[169]

Migration from Ireland had declined by 90% between 1913 and 1919, down to 4,300, due in part to war restrictions.[170] It increased again after the War and Ireland's population declined by over 5% between 1911 and 1926. There is little evidence though of a more than proportional demand from ex-soldiers wishing to leave the country and making demands of the British Government to assist them. Permanent migration was, in general, not undertaken due to threats of violence or intimidation; most of the ex-servicemen who lodged complaints to the IGC remained in the area where the incident took place or if they left, they returned home after 1923, including those who had been allocated land. Irish emigration to Britain increased in the late 1930s due to lack of work at home and the additional employment opportunities as Britain prepared for the Second World War. That many of these migrants were ex-servicemen is evidenced by the number of Trust property tenants who left to find work in the Britain.

The complaints regarding the exclusion of southern Irish ex-servicemen from the Empire Settlement Act 1922 seem unjustified from a pragmatic perspective: prior to the Act, schemes existed for subsidised passage and were taken advantage of, and in practice the theoretical limits of the Act were ignored as Irishmen who reached British shores qualified for assistance; and in any event by 1926 the demand seemed to be limited.

Allocation of Land

The Land Act 1919 allowed for the provision of land and housing to ex-servicemen. The Land Commission had responsibility to provide holdings to ex-servicemen who had served in the war and 'who satisfied the Land Commission as to their fitness and suitability to work land, amongst the classes of people as defined by the Irish Land Act, 1909'. The transaction was carried out as a sale under the Land Purchase Acts with the soldier-purchaser paying the purchase price for his farm by means of an annuity paid back over a prescribed number of years, allowing him to become the absolute owner of the land. In total, 360 ex-servicemen in the Irish Free State received 10,106 acres, the land worth £249,944. Some £130,417 was expended on the provision of buildings, roads, and fences to make the land workable. Of this amount, £30,527 was included in the price at which land was sold to the purchasers. The balance of £99,890 constituted a free gift by the

169 TNA, CO, 762/8/1.
170 TNA, LAB, 2/855, MoL, note, 3 May 1920.

British Government; otherwise the ex-servicemen acquired their holdings on conditions identical to other tenant purchasers. The Lavery Committee received complaints relating to land from ex-servicemen tenants falling into three categories. The first was that insufficient holdings were available.[171] In practice the award of holdings by the Land Commission was limited to areas in which land had been acquired, or was in the process of being acquired at the time of the Anglo-Irish Treaty. It was the change of government that precluded the British Government from making any long-term plans to continue the scheme. Land ownership remained a sensitive issue within Ireland and the award of land to soldiers was depicted by republicans as a new form of 'plantation'. The *Cork Examiner* in 1919 described the scheme as an attempt to create 'soldiers' colonies' in Ireland, and predicted that it would rekindle the devastating fires of land wars. The article continued that the colonies were being justified by the ex-servicemen's need for self-protection, but argued instead that 'the project aims at stereotyping them as a separate class by planting colonies in different localities in what is regarded as a reversion to the Cromwellian plan'.[172] Even an ex-serviceman wrote, 'the Land is still there, but the same old landlord still has it, not the "landless" who fought for it'.[173] Fedorowich writes that

> the revolutionary government was adamant that the compulsory taking of land by the British Government for ex-servicemen was completely unacceptable. This 'new Plantation' had to be resisted declared Robert Barton TD. To undermine British policy further, while at the same time reinforcing its own legitimacy, the Dáil Éireann announced its own land acquisition scheme.[174]

The second cause for complaint related to excessive purchase annuities. The Lavery Report noted that evidence was heard that the purchase annuities payable in respect of holdings occupied by ex-servicemen were excessive and consequentially uneconomical, and the British Government should be approached with a view to reducing them. It also acknowledged that land prices were high immediately following the War, which impacted all who purchased at this time. The report concluded 'that on present values the annuities payable in respect of many of the holdings occupied by ex-servicemen are uneconomical'. The final issue related to the inadequacy of improvement

171 TNA, PIN, 15/758, Lavery Report. By 1923, 16,800 ex-servicemen had settled on smallholdings in England and Wales. See Aalen, 'Homes for Irish Heroes', 307.
172 *Cork Examiner*, 22 November 1919, 5.
173 Article by anonymous ex-serviceman, *Honesty*, 2 November 1929.
174 Fedorowich, 'Reconstruction and Resettlement', 1159.

works. The report recorded the complaints but stated that the policy of the Land Commission was the same as for holdings provided for other persons under the Land Purchase Act. The Irish Government memorandum on the report concurred with this point, noting that there was no evidence that improvement works carried out by the Land Commission were inadequate, and that holdings for ex-servicemen were dealt with by the Land Commission in exactly the same way as holdings for other persons. The memorandum also stated that in the majority of cases the holdings were not uneconomical and moreover any difficulty was not confined to ex-servicemen.[175]

Some of the complaints related to an inability to use the land due to republican activity. William Callan of Mullingar, County Westmeath secured land under the scheme but was prevented from working it, 'owing to the hostile activities of the IRA in the year 1921, that is to say the first year we had the land, it was rendered useless'.[176] Although the British Government was unable to enforce the law and prevent evictions by the republicans, and was aware that after its departure an absence of civil authority persisted, it continued to insist that the annuities be paid even though the farms could not generate income. In doing so the government showed remarkable insensitivity. Edmund Davern was allocated land in Knocklong, County Limerick and, although deprived of the use of the land from March 1921 until May 1923, he was obliged to continue to pay annuities to the Irish Land Commission and other outgoings, including poor rates. According to the IGC report, 'owing to the Truce at that time existing and the non-enforcement of the law, either during that period or the period during which Civil War raged in Ireland from 1922 to May 1923, no protection could be afforded him by the Civil Authorities'.[177] Irrespective of the complaints to the Committee regarding the working of the land being uneconomical, most of the ex-soldiers who were forced to leave by republicans returned after the conflict ended and the Free State Government enforced its authority. The IGC recorded complaints from seven soldiers awarded land in Knocklong and evicted by republicans, all of whom had returned by May 1923.

The provision of land differed from that of housing in one key respect. The capital cost of the land was paid for by a purchase annuity; in the case of housing the tenants only paid the cost of maintenance and after 1933 not even that, although the advantage with regard to land was that the purchaser assumed ownership. Housing was a significant capital outlay for the British Government and, as such, it was making a real contribution to the Irish economy in terms of building works and the provision of much-needed

175 TNA, PIN, 15/758, Lavery Report; Irish Government Memorandum.
176 TNA, NAI, Lavery Committee, Individual Claims.
177 TNA, CO, 762/49/12.

housing stock. Under the scheme to provide land the British Government was effectively a mortgage provider. With little added value from the British, and given the sensitivity of the land issue, it was inevitable that the Irish Government would assume control as to whom it allocated holdings. The Free State Government passed the enabling legislation to allow a Trust, established by the British Government, to acquire and hold land upon which to build houses. No such legislation was enacted with regard to land for farming. The ability of the British Government to provide land to ex-servicemen was terminated by legislation passed by the new government shortly after the establishment of the Free State. The Land Act, 1923, abolished all classes of person for whom land might have been provided under the Land Purchase Acts, establishing a new series of classes of persons without specific mention of British ex-servicemen, who henceforth could only receive land under the general articles of the act to provide land 'to any person or body to whom in the opinion of the Land Commission an advance ought to be made', thus ending any preferential treatment for ex-servicemen.[178] Irrespective of the opposition of the IRA and the Irish Government, the impact of the British Government's scheme to allocate land to Irish ex-servicemen was always going to be limited, because it lacked the financial resources and ambition of equivalent schemes in Australia and Canada. The British Government was under significant pressure in 1919 to be seen to be doing something for Irish ex-servicemen and, although inadequately funded, the announcement of the Irish Land Act helped it achieve that objective.

178   TNA, PIN, 15/758, Lavery Report, November 1928.

4

Homes for Heroes

A scheme unique to Ireland in which the British Government initiated a programme to build cottages for ex-servicemen, including garden city developments not emulated by Free State housing projects for many years, perhaps best epitomised the fulfilment of an obligation to the ex-servicemen. The building programme continued after the formation of the Free State, which resulted in an imperial body being dependent on the Irish Government to meet its objectives. Ironically, this was not the only challenge. Antagonism from those who were to benefit resulted in the British Government agency responsible spending much energy and time in litigation with the ex-servicemen tenants. The genesis of the trouble was the ambiguity of the original legislation, the Irish Land (Provision for Soldiers and Sailors) Act, 1919. It did not specify how many houses would be built or how much money would be allocated. Ex-servicemen understood that they had been given a promise of housing at low or no rents as a recompense for war service; the British Government was of the view that the promise was never as comprehensive as that. It was going to provide a limited number of houses and charge rent for it.[1]

Under the Land Act 1919, the Irish Local Government Board (LGB) had responsibility for the administration of the provision of housing for ex-servicemen.[2] As this remained an imperial responsibility, a new structure was required after the formation of the Free State. In January 1924 the Irish Sailors' and Soldiers' Land Trust was established under the provision of Section Three of the Irish Free State (Consequential Provisions) Act passed in December 1922 by the British Parliament. The Irish Government passed the Land Trust Powers Act 1923, allowing for the transfer of the relevant assets of the LGB to the Trust and for it to acquire and hold land in the conduct of its responsibilities. The Trust had five trustees, including two

---

1 Brady and Lynch, 'The Irish Sailors' and Soldiers' Trust and its Killester Nemesis', 266–7.
2 TNA, PIN, 15/758, Lavery Report, November 1928; *IT*, 5 August 1933.

responsible for southern Ireland, one of whom was appointed by the Free State President.[3]

Table 22: Trust personnel

Trustees	
Chairman	George Duckworth, Chairman, replaced upon his retirement in 1927 by Sir James Brunyate
Southern Trustee (nominated by the President of the Free State)	General the Rt. Hon. Sir Bryan Mahon, replaced upon his death in 1930 by Major General Sir George Franks
Southern Trustee	Major Harry Lefroy, replaced upon his termination in December 1925 by Brigadier General the Earl of Meath
Northern Trustee/Deputy Chairman	Brigadier General Ross
Northern Trustee	Lord Dufferin
Permanent Staff	
Secretary	G.F. Alexander, replaced upon his death in 1937 by A.A. Phillips
Director, Dublin Office	Cyril Browne
Deputy Director, Dublin Office	Richard Grubb

The Trust was a microcosm of the imperial relationship between Britain and Ireland with the London Head Office acting within the guidelines of the Dominions Office and the Treasury, and often in conflict with the Irish trustees, who sought greater independence. George Duckworth, the first chairman, would not consent to the headquarters being in Ireland.[4] The director of the Dublin office, Cyril Browne, initiated schemes for the approval of the local trustees before submission to London for final sanction.[5] This inevitably made decision making slow and ponderous. There was sometimes a condescending tone towards the Irish, Duckworth writing, 'It is bewildering to the English mind to have to listen to such continuous

3   TNA, PIN, 15/758, Lavery Report, November 1928.
4   TNA, AP, 3/19.
5   TNA, AP, 1/39.

complaints and to find that the Irishman when the power lies wholly in his own hands takes so few active steps to see that the work is carried out'.[6] Duckworth terminated the appointment of Major Harry Lefroy, a southern trustee, because he refused to sign eviction orders, and failed in Duckworth's view to realise that, in addition to the ex-servicemen, he also represented the British Exchequer, a responsibility 'the Irishman is apt to regard as somewhat immaterial'.[7] The BLSI wrote to the British Government that Lefroy's removal had 'created a feeling of hostility and suspicion amongst ex-servicemen', and advocated that the London office should be abolished.[8] Field Marshal Earl Haig, President of the British Legion, was insistent on co-operation between the Trust and the Legion but this reflected attitudes in London rather than Dublin.[9] The BLSI, particularly under W. P. Walker, its first chairman (until his death in September 1925), was antagonistic and confrontational towards the Trust. It worked closely with the militant Killester Tenants' Association, many of its members including its leader, William D. McLean, were members of the BLSI. The latter passed a resolution stating that 'the whole workings of the Housing Trust is most unsatisfactory'. Walker wrote in March 1925 that

> Mr Duckworth's lack of knowledge of Ireland, the Irish people and the psychology of the Irish ex-servicemen is leading him to think more of the British tax payers pocket than the payment to Irish ex-servicemen of part of the price that was agreed upon by the British Government when our men went voluntarily to the Great War.[10]

The Trust was aware of the difficulties caused by this antagonism, particularly given the problems of administering a scheme scattered throughout the Free State. A Trust report stated, 'there are signs of a determined propaganda which belittles the work of the Trust. In the remote districts where the tenants are hardly ever visited there can be no counter propaganda', resulting in 'a curious ignorance of the purpose and policy of the Trust, and a want of that sympathy as between landlord and tenant which is essential to good relations'.[11] Ironically, it was the largest estate at Killester, where tenants could most readily combine together, which proved the main source

6 TNA, AP, 1/98, Duckworth to Haig's representative, 9 July 1926.
7 TNA, AP, Duckworth to DO, 10 September 1925; TNA, AP, 3/7, Duckworth to Lord Cavan, 22 October 1925.
8 TNA, AP, 1/98, BLSI to British Secretary of State, 3 February 1926.
9 TNA, AP, 1/84, Duckworth to Ross, 21 November 1925.
10 TNA, AP, 1/54, Walker to Alexander (referring to BLSI meeting, 4 February 1924), 6 March 1925.
11 TNA, PIN, 15/758, Lavery Report; First report of Trust, January 1924–March 1926.

of friction. The replacement of Lefroy by Brigadier General, the Earl of Meath improved matters considerably. The second trustee was General Sir Bryan Mahon, who was replaced upon his death in 1930 by Major General Sir George Franks. These three senior officers had the respect of the ex-servicemen and the Irish Government and contributed effectively as southern trustees for some two decades.

The 1919 Act did not specify the number of houses to be built as the amount expended was to be decided annually by Parliament. With the transfer of power the Treasury allocated £1.5 million as a final settlement. By the end of 1923, £1.9 million (including expenditures prior to the transfer of power and a portion of the final settlement) had been spent, leaving the Trust upon its formation in January 1924 with £1.3 million to complete 2,626 cottages in the Free State and 1,046 cottages in Northern Ireland.[12] As an estimated 55% of all Irish volunteers were from what became the Free State it appears that veterans returning to the south were more favourably treated in terms of cottages per numbers enlisted than those in the north. By March 1928, 1,927 houses had been built in the Free State. This figure comprises 1,508 taken over from the LGB, 157 houses which were either under construction when the Trust took over or subsequently bought, and 262 houses that the Trust built. The distribution of the 1,927 houses by province was: 1,122 in Leinster, (526 in County Dublin); 644 in Munster (268 in County Cork); 144 in Connaught; and 17 in Ulster (three counties).[13] The majority of the houses were in large urban areas or near towns.[14] Based on recruitment figures, there was one cottage per 42.8 soldiers in Leinster and one per 27.2 soldiers in Munster. As many of the cottages were built or planned during the conflict there is therefore some indication that the British sought to pacify the ex-servicemen by providing benefits in areas of greatest republican activity.[15]

Walker was extremely critical of the speed of building after the Trust assumed responsibility and of the quality of the housing, writing, 'I have lost count of the number of occasions that Cork was visited in the past by

12 TNA, PIN, 15/758, Lavery Report, The £1.3 million included an additional £150,000, allocated in March 1925; TNA, AP, 1/209 British Government to Jack Jones, MP, 29 October 1932.

13 TNA, PIN, 15/758, Lavery Report.

14 TNA, AP, 1/10, Browne to Duckworth, 16 May 1924.

15 According to recruitment figures to the end of 1917, there was one cottage per 46.1 soldiers in County Dublin and one cottage per 37.7 soldiers in County Cork. The majority of the cottages in County Dublin were in the vicinity of Dublin City, the Killester estate alone constituted 247 cottages, whereas the cottages in County Cork were more geographically dispersed, with only 72 in Cork City. As Dublin City was a focus of republican activity this could again explain the desire to focus housing projects in that area to seek to placate large numbers of ex-servicemen.

Figure 2   Trust Cottages, Killester, Dublin
Source: Paul Taylor, 2014; William McLean, the Killester
tenants' strike leader lived in number 47.

highly paid officials, and not a single house built yet'.[16] Walker claimed that
delays in the building programme were caused by the Trust demanding a
guarantee of excessively high rents before proceeding. Writing with regard
to planned schemes, he claimed that Duckworth 'has cancelled the lot, as he
insists on a guarantee by the local trustees of a minimum rental of 8/ per
week. This is absurd enough to be ridiculous, and is only another proof that
there is no real intention of carrying out the work of the Trust'.[17] Walker's
comments seemed justified to some extent. The LGB built 1,508 houses
during the conflict; the Trust only 262 houses in the four years to March
1928. The BLSI believed that many of the initial houses were of poor quality
and located out of town with no services.[18] Commenting on a scheme outside
Dublin, Walker said 'the sanitary accommodation is similar to what existed
in the wilds of Connemara fifty years ago'.[19] He wrote in the *Irish Truth* that
the Trust houses were 'dog kennels' and that the Treasury was saving money
at the expense of the Irish ex-serviceman.[20] An ex-serviceman wrote, 'despite
having capital free of all charge the Trust was far slower in providing houses
than the majority of public bodies', and 'what would be said of a modern
society building a thousand houses without making any provision for a water
supply?'[21] The Lavery Committee expressed concerns at the speed of the

16 TNA, AP, 1/39, Walker to Lefroy, 8 July 1924.
17 TNA, AP, 1/84, Heath to Duckworth, containing comments from Walker, 18 May
    1925.
18 TNA, AP, 1/84, Trust/BLSI meeting, 12 May 1924.
19 TNA, AP, 1/39, Walker to Lefroy, dated 8 July 1924.
20 TNA, AP, 1/84, Duckworth, note, 29 October 1925.
21 Article by anonymous ex-serviceman, *Honesty*, 2 November 1929.

Trust's building programme, comparing it to the 4,128 houses completed by municipal authorities between 1922 and 1928. The Trust argued that the delays were the result of inherited problems, rent strikes and, until March 1925, an unrealistic restriction of £500 per house imposed by the Treasury. The Trust also blamed legacy problems for the lack of local infrastructure and the condition of some of the houses, stating that half the houses they had taken over required expenditure to bring them up to the Trust's standards. The Committee noted that the Trust's property was in general maintained in good condition. It also concluded that the monies allocated by the British Government were inadequate; some 18,000 applications had been received for housing and a minimum of 10,000 houses were required.[22] The Trust acknowledged that demand exceeded their resources. Practically every town of any size asked for a scheme and when a scheme proceeded, financial constraints meant that the number of houses was always fewer than needed.[23] One thousand applications were received for the 150 cottages built in the city of Cork.[24] The Trust had accepted a final grant from the Treasury that limited the number of houses to be built, leaving it open to criticism that it had surrendered the rights of the ex-servicemen.[25] Walker claimed that the intention had been to build 40,000 houses.[26] There was also criticism that the Trust built houses that were too large. The BLSI and the local trustees were advocates of smaller, cheaper houses,[27] and in 1930 the Trust eventually agreed to build more two-bedroom cottages.[28] The Trust did not agree with the Committee's criticisms; Browne wrote that

> apart from the Ministry of Pensions, the work of the Trust is the only concrete effort to benefit the ex-serviceman in the Free State. I think that the practical results already attained by the Trust are widely admitted to be highly successful; the character and quality of their housing schemes are acknowledged to be of the highest class. All this is ignored by the Committee, who have thought fit to adopt the arguments of the Legion.[29]

22 TNA, PIN, 15/758, First Report of the Trust for period January 1924–March 1926, quoted in Lavery Report; TNA, AP, 1/121, Browne to Alexander, 22 February 1929.
23 TNA, AP, 1/10, Browne to Duckworth, 16 May 1924.
24 *IT*, 24 January 1928.
25 TNA, AP, 1/121, Alexander to DO, 8 August 1930.
26 TNA, AP, 1/84, Trust/BLSI meeting, 12 May 1924.
27 TNA, AP, 1/84, Trust/BLSI meeting, 14 May 1924; TNA, AP, 1/10, Browne to Duckworth, 16 May 1924.
28 TNA, PIN, 15/758, DO to BL, 17 March 1930.
29 TNA, AP, 1/121, Browne to Alexander, 22 February 1929.

The *Irish Times* agreed, writing in 1933 that Killester, the Trust's largest development with 247 houses, was Dublin's first garden suburb and still the 'biggest and best', a notable advance in town planning and, 'its creation under the disturbed conditions of 11 years ago a unique kind of achievement'.[30] Wide-scale town planning and state intervention by the Irish Government were needed to remedy an acute housing problem, and Aalen's comments that 'the ex-servicemen's houses helped to improved standards for Irish working-class housing generally' is indicative of the Trust's achievement.[31]

Rental Policy and Rent Strikes

The Trust's policy on rent and the basis on which it was calculated were the subject of considerable controversy. Central to the argument was whether the rents should cover the costs of maintenance and basic services, or include a component to provide additional capital for the building of more cottages; and whether they should be comparable to the rent level of similar social housing. Rental policy also impacted on the selection of tenants. Were the houses to be allocated to those who could afford the highest rent or to those most in need? Duckworth said a 'minimum rent' would cover the costs of administration, insurance, repairs and maintenance, and empties while a 'full economic rent' would include interest on the money invested.[32]

The BLSI argued that paying the full economic rent would imply repaying the British Government and that was not the intent of the enabling legislation.[33] Duckworth presented the argument for the inclusion of a capital component as meeting the needs of the majority on the waiting lists against those fortunate to have already been allocated a cottage. He believed that if the Trust responded to pressure to reduce rents once the original capital had been expended, 'the unhoused ex-serviceman would say too little rent was asked and the sitting tenant had been favoured at the expense of the unhoused'. He wished to allow a margin for additional houses through creating a contingency, arguing that it was important not to 'unduly favour sitting tenants at the expense of the unhoused'.[34]

A Trust report stated that even with lower rents they hoped 'a small

---

30 *IT*, 5 August 1935.

31 Ruth McManus, *Dublin, 1910–1940: Shaping the City and Suburbs* (Dublin, 2006), 95, 443–5; Aalen, 'Homes for Irish Heroes', 321.

32 TNA, AP, 1/84, Trust/Ulster ex-servicemen's association meeting, 15 July 1924.

33 TNA, AP, 1/84, Trust/BLSI meeting, 14 May 1924; Reply from Walker in letter from BL to Duckworth, 28 April 1925.

34 TNA, AP, 1/84, Duckworth/Haig's representative meeting, 16 November 1925; TNA, AP 1/84, Duckworth to Ross, 21 Nov 1925.

annual surplus will be made available which will eventually be used for additional building' as, although no interest was calculated on capital, a 'liberal calculation' was made regarding costs.[35] The BLSI objected, 'You want the Irish ex-services man to do something which the British Government promised to do; apart from paying their own rents they are paying for other men's houses'.[36] The Trust also argued that the rents were 25% lower than comparable social housing and that the accommodation was superior to that in which the tenants had previously lived with lower rent.[37] As an example, the tenants' leader William McLean paid a small amount more for twice the accommodation.[38] The Trust contended that at the outset of the tenancies, the rents had been agreed and the applicants had declared their ability to pay. According to the Trust, the Killester tenants had previously paid high prices for rooms and that the salaries they showed when they were originally accepted as tenants indicated an ability to pay the Trust rents.[39] The BLSI argued that economic conditions had changed, 'many had signed agreements that are now not affordable as the average workman had suffered at least a 20% reduction in wages and many were unemployed or had suffered a reduction in pensions'.[40]

The Trust was under escalating pressure to decrease rents. In response to strikes by Dublin tenants in May 1924 it reduced Killester rents by up to 30% with a promise from the BLSI that arrears would be paid and future rent paid punctually.[41] This agreement was not kept. In February 1925 tenants started to pay 'provisional rents' at a rate they fixed and asked for further rent reductions.[42] In July 1925 the Trust set up an internal committee to review rents, which concluded that while rents were low in comparison to the open market, as the Trust did not have to take into account a provision for interest, capital outlay, or profit, average rents for all properties could be reduced to 6/ per week and the Killester rents reduced

35 TNA, PIN, 15/758, First Report of Trust for period January 1924–March 1926, quoted in Lavery Report.
36 TNA, AP, 1/84, Trust/BLSI meeting, 12 May 1924.
37 TNA, AP, 1/84, Alexander (on behalf of Duckworth) to Heath, BLSI, referring to earlier correspondence with Walker, 16 March 1925; TNA, AP, 1/84, Trust/BLSI meeting, 18 December 1924; TNA, AP, 1/8, internal report.
38 TNA, AP, 3/32, Duckworth to Mahon, 13 May 1926; TNA, AP, 1/130, 1929-30 ejections; TNA, AP, 3/32, Browne to Duckworth, 20 April 1926.
39 TNA, AP, 1/84, Duckworth, note, 29 October 1925.
40 TNA, AP, 1/84, Trust/BLSI meeting, 14 May 1924.
41 TNA, AP, 3/32, Duckworth to Mahon, 13 May 1926.
42 TNA, AP, 3/32, Browne to Alexander, 19 November 1926; TNA, AP, 1/84, Internal report, 29 October 1925.

further (Killester rents were higher than average for the IFS).[43] The new rents were implemented from January 1926.[44]

Table 23: Killester rent reductions (per week rents)

House Category	Large			Medium			Small		
	£	s	d	£	s	d	£	s	d
Pre May 1924	1	0	0		16	0		12	6
May 1924		16	0		12	0		8	6
January 1926		12	6		10	6		8	6

Source: TNA, AP, 3/32, Duckworth to Mahon, 13 May 1926.

The Lavery Committee noted that the Trust sought to generate capital for building out of the rents and concluded,

we consider that the policy of providing capital for building out of the rents of tenants is out of accord with the spirit of the provision made by the British Government in the Acts of 1919. The capital provided by the British Government is admittedly insufficient to provide adequate accommodation for ex-servicemen, but it appears a sorry expedient to try and make good this insufficiency by raising capital out of the pockets of ex-servicemen.[45]

The report stated that the costs that the Trust sought to recover through rents were not just 'fairly liberal' but 'extremely liberal' and as such 'the basis upon which the average rent of 6/ per house was arrived at in 1925 should be reviewed by the Trust', and the rents reduced.[46] Average weekly rents were reduced to 5/6 in 1933, then 4/9 after eliminating an allocation to reserve, then 4/3 if the tenants did internal repairs.[47] Average rent at the time the Trust was constituted was 7/9 per cottage, indicating that the Trust was overcharging at its inception.[48]

The question of rental policy was also linked to the selection of tenants.

43 TNA, PIN, 15/758, Lavery Report; TNA, AP, 3/32, Duckworth to Mahon, 13 May 1926.
44 TNA, AP, 3/32, Trust meeting, 6 January 1926.
45 TNA, PIN, 15/758, Lavery Report.
46 TNA, PIN, 15/758, Lavery Report.
47 TNA, AP, 1/148, Browne note, 28 January 1938. Figures vary in files; TNA, PIN, 15/758, DO to BLSI, 17 March 1930, records average rent of 5/2 per cottage by 1930.
48 TNA, PIN, 15/758, DO to BL, 17 March 1930.

Rents were initially excessive, certainly higher than necessary to maintain the estate, and led to the houses being allocated not to those most in need but to those who could afford them, which was not the original intention. The Land Act 1919 was the basis for the provision of housing for any man who served in the Great War.[49] In his summary in the Callan/Duggan case, the judge said that the LGB 'passed over the needy and deserving and selected the tenants better able to pay the substantial rents demanded'.[50] The judge in the Leggett case (see below) determined under the Land Act 1919 it was not intended that rents should be paid and that the intention to charge had led to the houses being rented on the ability to pay rather than those most in need as the legislation intended.[51] The British Legion said the spirit of the Act was that the houses should be let as 'state subsidised houses' and the rents affordable for those most in need.[52] Tenants were required to provide information on income and existing rents on their tenancy application forms.[53] The Trust would admit in 1940 that an inability to pay had excluded applicants and that the houses were previously given to those who could afford the rent.[54]

The agitation to reduce the rent became a power struggle between the Trust and both the BLSI and the Killester Tenants' Association. A rent strike commenced in May 1924 and the Trust responded by reducing the Killester rents on an undertaking by Walker that rents and arrears would be paid.[55] The BSLI considered the reduction an interim measure, pending the defining of a 'minimum rent' for all tenants.[56] Both sides were disappointed; the Killester tenants rejected the agreement and the Trust made little progress in a general rent reduction. In November 1924, the BLSI called a meeting of all tenants in County Dublin at which a rent strike was called.[57] Browne believed that a general strike was being deliberately engineered by the BLSI and the purpose of the meeting was to 'influence the tenants against the Trust'.[58] He wrote that 'a large number of tenants are intimidated into striking', afraid of incurring the hostility of the Legion's executive.[59] BLSI canvassers followed rent collectors

49 TNA, AP, 1/165.
50 TNA, AP, 4/11, Trust meeting, 15 April 1937, summary of Judge J. Murnaghan in Callan case (Duggan, Casey, and Caprani were other applicants).
51 *IT*, 5 March 1937.
52 TNA, AP, 1/84, Trust/BL Ulster ex-servicemen's association meeting, 29 July 1924.
53 TNA, AP, 1/84, Duckworth, note, 29 October 1925.
54 TNA, AP, 1/150, Browne evidence to Shannon Committee, April 1940.
55 TNA, AP, 3/32, Browne to Alexander, 19 November 1926.
56 TNA, AP, 1/54, Walker to Alexander, 6 December 1924.
57 TNA, AP, 1/84, Trust/BLSI meeting, 18 December 1924.
58 TNA, AP, 1/39, Walker to Duckworth, 27 Oct 1924 and Duckworth to Walker, 30 October 1924: Browne to Alexander and Duckworth, 30 October 1924.
59 TNA, AP, 1/54, Browne to Alexander, 31 December 1924; TNA, AP, 1/84, Dublin to

to induce the tenants to join the strike.[60] The Ministry of Pensions complained that their 'staff were unwilling partisans in this action and that they had been subject to threats of violence unless they fell into line'.[61] Guinness employees, many of whom were tenants of the Trust, had got into trouble with their employers for joining the strike.[62] The Legion told the press that they were 'fighting with the Trust and gradually compelling them to fulfil the duties entrusted of them'.[63] Likewise, the Trust considered the rent strike 'a trial of strength', and issued eviction notices, including to the strike leaders, which resulted by March 1925 in many tenants paying rent albeit often at a reduced rate.[64] The southern trustees, after meeting in June 1925 with Legion representatives from London and Dublin, halted eviction proceedings and offered reduced rents, which were accepted by the Killester tenants. Hickie, the BLSI President, informed the tenants that the southern trustees were on 'our side'. Lacking Duckworth's approval, the actions of the southern trustees had no validity.[65] Walker thought that all individual members of the Trust acknowledged that the rents were too high but Duckworth prevented any readjustment.[66] Duckworth was to resign in 1927 citing concerns with the southern trustees.[67]

In January 1926 the Trust introduced new lower rents, the Dublin office reporting, 'we have quite a number of tenants thanking us', only Killester anticipated to be a source of continued trouble.[68] But there was a demand that the reduction should be retrospective as the previous rents had been too high. The Lavery Committee concluded that 'some limited retrospective adjustment' was warranted.[69] Total arrears were £14,000 in March 1926. The British Legion recommended that the reduction be backdated to April 1924 at a total cost of £5,500, including credit for those who had paid.[70] The Trust were against making rent reductions retrospective as this would be 'fatal

London, 8 May 1925.

60 TNA, AP, 1/54, Trust meeting, 2 December 1924.

61 TNA, AP, 1/54, MoP to Colonial Office, 9 February 1925.

62 TNA, AP, 1/98, Trust meeting, 30 March 1926.

63 TNA, AP, 1/84, *IT*, 25 September 1925.

64 TNA, AP, 1/54, Duckworth to Treasury, 27 November 1924; TNA, AP, 1/54, Trust Meeting report, 17 December 1924; TNA, AP, 1/54, Grubb to Alexander, 7 March 1925.

65 TNA, AP, 1/84, Trust/BLSI meeting, 22 June 1925; Browne and Grubb to Alexander, 23 June 1925; Duckworth to BL, 24 June 1925; Tenants' meeting, 26 June 1925.

66 TNA, AP, 1/84, Reply from Walker contained in letter from BL to Duckworth, 28 April 1925.

67 TNA, AP, 3/19.

68 TNA, AP, 3/32, Browne to Alexander, 25 January 1926.

69 TNA, PIN, 15/758, Lavery Report.

70 TNA, AP, 3/32, Browne to Alexander, 19 November 1926; TNA, AP, 3/32, BL to Duckworth, 20 May 1927.

to rent stability, encouraging slackness of payment and persistent agitation for further reductions', and would make future rent decreases impossible.[71] They were also concerned at the precedent of giving credit to those who had paid.[72] Browne argued against compromise, claiming that the agitation was led by the Legion in Dublin and a small group at Killester directed by McLean, against whom eviction proceedings were taking place, and that most tenants were paying well, and to compromise would demoralise the majority of tenants and increase bad debt.[73] Duckworth said that individual cases of hardship could be considered in light of individuals' efforts to repay any arrears.[74] In September 1926, although Browne claimed that 'the agitation engineered by the Legion has died a natural death', the Legion and the Killester strike leaders continued to lobby for the rent reduction to be made retrospective.[75]

Between 1925 and 1933 there were 98 evictions, all for rent arrears.[76] The number of evictions was comparatively small, even during the rent strike, with many paying at least some arrears upon a legal threat.

Table 24: Evictions by year

Year	Number of Evictions
1925	16
1926	30
1927	14
1928	12
1929	8
1930	2
1931	4
1932	9
1933	3
Total	98

Source: TNA, AP, 1/155, Report on evictions, 1933.

71 TNA, AP, 3/32, Duckworth to Mahon, 13 May 1926; TNA, AP, 1/121, Alexander to DO, 8 August 1930; TNA, AP, 3/32, Browne to Alexander, 15 June 1927.
72 TNA, AP, 3/32, Grubb to Alexander, 12 March 1926.
73 TNA, AP, 3/32, Browne to Duckworth, 15 March 1926; TNA, AP, 1/98, Trust Meeting, 30 March 1926.
74 TNA, AP, 3/32, Trust meeting, 30 May 1927.
75 TNA, AP, 3/32, Browne to Duckworth, 1 September 1926; TNA, AP, 3/32, McLean to Browne, 18 Sept 1926; TNA, AP, 3/32, BLSI to Trust, 6 Oct 1926.
76 TNA, AP, 1/155, Report on evictions, 1933.

Many of the tenants in arrears were employed in skilled or regular jobs such as tailors, civil servants, and commercial travellers, or had army or RIC pensions.[77] John Molloy was a butcher earning 70/ per week. His rent was 3/6 per week and his arrears around £7. A decree for ejection was obtained in September 1932.[78] Patrick Carroll was employed as a labourer at 30/ per week and had a pension of 19/1 per week. He had arrears of almost £16 and a decree was obtained on 15 June 1927.[79] In some cases, although the Trust acknowledged an inability to pay, it still sought eviction. Thomas Hibbitts was unemployed and, according to the Trust, 'appears to be entirely without means', but still it concluded that 'there is no reason why proceedings should not be taken against him'.[80] John McMahon was a casual labourer with little chance of employment and only a small pension and arrears of £23. A decree for possession was obtained in October 1925.[81] Two tenants described as 'decent' but badly off were evicted in 1927–28; one went to live in a damp, unhealthy cellar and suffered ill health, the other a council house.[82] Duggan lived in a cottage for 2/10 rent and though old it provided shelter. The Trust's predecessor then bought the land and erected new houses, one of which was rented to Duggan at 5/ per week. His pension, initially adequate to pay the rent, was reduced, and he was ejected and lived with his family in a primitive dug out.[83]

Disability did not prevent eviction. Patrick Moreland of Balbriggan was unemployed with rent of 4/6 per week and arrears of £3 9s. The Trust obtained a decree against him in June 1933 together with costs of £5. He had a disability pension of 46/ per week due to vascular disease of the heart.[84] William Riggs received a pension of 28/ per week due to the loss of a leg;[85] he had a rent of 4/6 per week with arrears of £8 8s, but a decree for possession was obtained in January 1926. In the above cases the disability pensions were of a sufficient size that there was little excuse not to pay the rent. In other cases, tenants with disabilities could not afford to pay but were still evicted. Francis Mohill had a disability pension of £1 per week for deafness and gastritis and was unemployed with arrears of over £18, which the Trust could not see any hope of his paying; a decree was obtained in

---

77 TNA, AP, 1/138, Report on evictions, 1931; TNA, AP, 1/155, Report on evictions 1933.
78 TNA, AP, 1/153, Alexander, note, 3 October 1932.
79 TNA, AP, 1/117, Alexander, note, 5 July 1927.
80 TNA, AP, 1/117, Alexander, note, 4 February 1927.
81 TNA, AP, 1/108.
82 TNA, AP, 1/155, Report on evictions, 1933.
83 TNA, AP, 4/11, Meeting 15 April 1937, summary of Judge J. Murnaghan in Callan case (Duggan, Casey and Caprani are other applicants).
84 TNA, AP, 1/155, Alexander, note, 31 July 1933.
85 TNA, AP, 1/108.

December 1925.[86] In some cases the tenants suffered mental illness, most likely related to war service, but eviction was still sought. James Monaghan was employed as a labourer and had a pension of 12/ per week on account of a gunshot wound. His arrears were £18 and a decree was obtained in February 1927, although the Trust noted he was described as 'a half-wit, and it is possible that his mental condition may have been caused by his war service'.[87] John Appleby was unemployed and 'entirely without means', and described as a 'half-wit' who begged from house to house. He had arrears of over £11 and a decree was obtained in April 1927. Duckworth noted 'one cannot but feel very sorry for him. Probably he should never have been selected as a tenant'.[88] Evictions were sought even when young children were involved. Frank Smith had five children between the ages of ten months and 11 years; James Palmer was unemployed, disabled, and had four young children; and Hugh Callan of Killester was serving a five-year prison sentence while his wife and four children aged under 7 lived in the house. In the latter case the Trust wished to evict them, provided they had friends to live with.[89] Noting, 'it is much better to take an action against a tenant when he owes £2 or £3 rather than when he owes £20 or £30',[90] the Trust also sought eviction for comparatively small amounts of arrears: John Collins's £4 7s, William Boshell's £2 18s, and Patrick Dwyer's £2 18s.

In some cases the tenants were unsuitable for reasons other than rent arrears: houses in a deplorable state, lodgers kept, and families deserted. A Trust report described some of the tenants as 'bad characters' with 12 of the 98 evicted addicted to drink.[91] The Trust's agent at Killester wrote that E.G. Roberts was 'a most undesirable tenant, he spends his money on drink and boasts to other tenants that he does not pay his rent', and 'P. Kett's conduct ever since he has been a tenant has been very bad, he has been prosecuted for insulting the local stationmaster, other tenants complain of his conduct, and if he is not evicted the moral effect on them will be ruinous'.[92] C. Dineen and his family from Cork were described by the local agent as 'blackguards, unfit to live among human beings'. Other tenants were withholding rent because of Dineen's behaviour; he had a 'terrible fight' that left three members of the

---

86   TNA, AP, 1/108.
87   TNA, AP, 1/117, Alexander, note, 24 February 1927.
88   TNA, AP, 1/117, Alexander, note, 20 April 1927.
89   TNA, AP, 1/117, Alexander, note, 28 February 1927; TNA, AP, 1/130, TNA, AP, 1/108.
90   TNA, AP, 1/153, Alexander, note, 19 April 1932 and 14 June 1932; TNA, AP, 1/130, Alexander, note, 4 March 1929.
91   TNA, AP, 1/155, Report on evictions, 1933.
92   TNA, AP, 1/69, Grubb to Alexander, 7 February 1925.

Corcoran family in hospital.[93] Some tenants refused to leave and the Trust required the assistance of the authorities to ensure their physical removal. H. J. Hayden of Clontarf owed £67 as of June 1925. He had vacated the house in May 1924, leaving his family in occupation. They were evicted on 10 August 1925, their goods stacked on the kerbside. Lt. Colonel Robinson, a Trust inspector, wrote that he attended with the sheriff and a police sergeant with four constables, and on entering found the house in a 'filthy condition'. The occupants re-entered the house and on the 12 August 1925, again with the presence of the sheriff and police, were evicted once again, but not before they were warned by the police sergeant of the consequences of seeking to re-enter the house.[94]

The policy of the Trust in terms of the amount of arrears owing before legal redress was pursued was inconsistent. Although the Trust argued that cases of individual hardship were considered, in many instances little regard was given to the tenants' circumstances or ability to pay. Some were in arrears because they had been charged rents which the Trust later acknowledged to be excessive. There were no evictions for other causes of tenancy abuse alone, indicating that the Trust was predominately focussed on non-payment of rent. The Trust was also extremely inconsistent in its rental policy and the principle upon which it was based. It claimed that the rental income only covered essential costs of maintenance and repair when they actually sought to include a capital component to fund new housing, which contradicted both the legal basis and spirit of the establishing legislation. Although they implemented significant reductions, it was under the duress of rent strikes. The scale of the reductions indicated that the initial rents were too high and resulted in demands that new rental levels be retrospective. The problem of rent arrears persisted and the animosity created was to result in a legal challenge as to whether any rent should be levied.

Supreme Court Rulings and the Struggle
to Reassert Authority

Even when rents were reduced, the continued adversarial tactics of the Killester Tenants' Association and the BLSI eventually halted the building programme. In what became known as the Leggett case, nine tenants from Killester, with the support of the Killester Tenants' Association, proved in the Irish Supreme Court in July 1933 that the Trust had no right to charge

93 TNA, AP, 1/153, Alexander, note, 31 Aug 1932.
94 TNA, AP, 1/69, Grubb to Alexander, 27 April 1925; Grubb to Alexander, 7 May 1925;
    Colonel Robinson, Trust Inspector, to Grubb, 10 and 12 August 1925.

rent. The case undermined the authority of the Trust and caused considerable confusion as to the responsibilities of both the Trust and its tenants,
and the rights of the latter. For over a decade the Trust sought a resolution
through further court actions, requests to the Irish Government to enact
corrective legislation, and finally through attempts to reach a settlement with
the occupiers.

The judge in the Leggett case declared that the Irish Free State
(Consequential Provisions) 1922 created a Trust with funds from the British
Treasury for the purpose of providing accommodation to men who served
in the Great War but made no mention of intent that rents should be levied.
He dismissed a claim that the houses were absolute gifts, or that widows or
dependents could live in them after the death of the ex-serviceman tenant.
The Trust could have recourse to the courts to remove ex-serviceman
tenants who were guilty of waste and destruction.[95]

The judgement created considerable ambiguity as to the exact status
of the tenants and who had liability for maintenance, central services,
and the payment of rates. Browne argued that the ruling was not in
the tenants' interests, 'it is now admitted that the sole practical benefit
derived from the Leggett judgement is immunity from the admittedly
uneconomic rents hitherto paid. Against this they find themselves burdened
with new obligations and new disabilities'.[96] Due to the uncertainty of their
legal position and future liabilities, and without income, the Trust halted
the building programme and ceased repairs, the payment of rates, and
evictions.[97]

The Trust was potentially liable for the return of the £275,000 of rent
collected prior to the ruling.[98] The liability of tenants previously evicted for
non-payment of rents was in question. The Killester Tenants' Association
hoped to compel the Trust to refund all 'back rent'.[99] In Callan and Others
versus the Trust, the Supreme Court in March 1937 found in favour of the
Trust and that the tenants could not recover rents as they had been paid
under a 'mistake of law'. The judge concluded that the tenants were 'tenants
at will' (a weakening of their position from the Leggett ruling) and that

---

95 TNA, AP, 1/150, Note (reviewing previous seven years), 15 January 1940; TNA, AP,
    4/9, Trust meeting, 30 October 1934; TNA, AP, 1/142, *IT*, 31 July 1933.
96 TNA, AP, 4/9, Trust meeting, 30 October 1934; TNA, AP, 1/144, Browne, report, 16
    October 1934.
97 TNA, AP, 4/8, Trust meeting, 9 Aug 1933; TNA, AP, 4/9, Trust meeting, 30 October
    1934.
98 TNA, AP, 4/8, Trust meeting, 9 Aug 1933 (the judge in Callan case put the sum at
    £294,000).
99 TNA, AP, 4/9, Trust meeting, 26 March 1935.

existing letting agreements were void.[100] The result according to the Trust's legal counsel was that the occupiers could only be evicted if they were 'no longer fit and suitable objects of the Trust but not related to any formal rental agreement'. It remained unclear whether the Trust was liable for repairs but in any case such liability would be limited to the money available and, as the use of the reserve was subject to Treasury sanction, the Trust could refuse to do any remedial work.[101] The Trust sought clarification through a judicial ruling but without success and therefore ceased to carry out repairs, resulting in the 'progressive deterioration' of the properties.[102]

Killester tenant Patrick Bray and others formed an association, the Ex-Servicemen's Defence League, with the intention of securing a legal ruling against the tenants' liability for rates. Following the Leggett ruling, local authorities in many cases had obtained decrees for rates against tenants. The tenants had responsibility for rates but, under the Rates on Small Dwellings Act of 1928, the Trust as landlords were liable in the first instance on their cottages with a Poor Law Valuation of £6 or under, although in such cases the landlord normally recovered the amount through the rent. The Supreme Court in Cork County Council versus Tuohy in July 1939 found that tenants covered by the 1928 Act were not liable for rates. The position of the tenants not within that definition was the subject of a High Court action, Beattie versus Dublin Corporation, in July 1939, in which no decision was given. None of the Dublin schemes came under the 1928 Act and the tenants were directly liable for the rates, except the Clontarf estate of 38 cottages, which was in the Corporation area, and came under a local Act of 1849 in which the landlord was liable but would again in normal circumstances recover the rates from the tenant. Forty-five Killester tenants argued that their properties were Crown land and therefore rates were not due to the Dublin Corporation. Bray's case, in which he was one of four plaintiffs seeking to prove that the Trust was liable for rates, was dismissed for want of prosecution. The Trust remained not liable for rates but the situation was confusing.[103] The Irish Government passed legislation in 1941 imposing liability on the tenant, showing a willingness when it was in its interest to take legislative action to correct inconsistencies arising from court rulings that failed to resolve the problems encountered by the Trust.[104]

In addition to litigation, the Trust sought to resolve the issues arising out

---

100 TNA, AP, 1/147.
101 TNA, AP, 4/11, Trust meeting, 15 April 1937.
102 TNA, AP, 1/150, note, 15 January 1940; *IT*, 3 March 1939; TNA, AP, 1/151, Brunyate to Treasury, 24 April 1945.
103 TNA, AP, 1/150, note, 15 January 1940; TNA, AP, 1/164, notes, 8 and 20 July 1937; TNA, AP, 1/144; TNA, AP, 4/11, Trust meeting, 15 April 1937.
104 TNA, AP, 1/162.

of the Leggett ruling through both seeking accommodation with the tenants and in persuading the Irish Government to enact corrective legislation. The Trust canvassed tenants and concluded that a majority, including those at Killester, would 'welcome a reasonable settlement', the exception being the Killester Tenants' Association.[105] Cork tenant James Hornibrook wrote that he would 'prefer to be paying rent so that my wife and family would be left the house'.[106]

Those without houses also wished for a settlement as the building programme had been halted. The Trust recognised that 'there is a strong feeling among those who have not yet been fortunate to obtain houses that they have been badly let down'.[107] In August 1934, the Trust submitted a proposal for a settlement to the Free State Government, including tenancy for life, rights for widows, a charge for maintenance and rates, and a purchase scheme.[108] The Killester representatives also put their own proposals to the Irish Government, which were more onerous on the Trust.[109] The Free State Government took no action but suggested that if all parties could agree, it would be prepared to introduce legislation.[110]

A meeting took place in Dublin in June 1936 attended by Father T.J. Traynor and P. Griffen from Killester, representing the tenants, the BLSI representing the 'unhoused', and the Trust. The meeting concluded with 'Agreed Proposals', that the Trust believed were 'with no serious variation' to those submitted to the Free State Government in August 1934.[111] In September 1936 Traynor and Griffen wrote to the Trust that that they were unable to secure support for the 'Agreed Proposals' from the occupiers. The two circulated 'bogus proposals', claiming the houses would be given free and that any Trust funds remaining distributed to the tenants.[112]

At a meeting of Dublin tenants in April 1937, Traynor claimed that they only had the meeting with the Trust to play for time, as the Tenants' Association had no funds for litigation. He announced a new organisation, the Ex-Servicemen's Tenants Association, to cover all the country but

105 TNA, AP, 1/144, Clonmel Tenants' Association to Trust, 5 January 1934; Browne, report, 16 October 1934.
106 TNA, AP, 1/162, Hornibrook to British Government, 26 April 1935.
107 TNA, AP, 1/144, Browne, meeting, 16 October 1934.
108 TNA, AP, 1/144, Trust/Treasury/DO, meeting, 5 June 1934; DO to John Dulanty, IFS High Commissioner, 20 August 1934.
109 TNA, AP, 1/145; Killester representatives/Irish Attorney General, meeting, 17 December 1935.
110 TNA, AP, 1/146, Browne to Brunyate, 21 February 1936.
111 TNA, AP, 1/143, Meeting 4/5 June 1936; TNA, AP1/146, Alexander to Brunyate, June 1936.
112 TNA, AP, 1/146, Traynor/Griffin to Trust, 9 Sept 1936; Browne to Alexander, 26 September 1936.

admitted that the Cork tenants were not supportive of Killester.[113] The Trust saw little point meeting with Traynor and Griffen again, but without an agreement the Irish Government refused to introduce legislation.[114]

In January 1937 the Trust circulated a copy of the Agreed Proposals to all occupiers and claimed positive feedback, particularly from tenants in County Cork but made the error of not asking for a formal response.[115] They circulated the proposals again in December 1938 with similar terms, this time asking for a reply. Out of 2,492 tenants (excluding 227 widows) around 25% responded, 70% in favour of the Trust's proposals, despite the intensive lobbying of the Ex-Serviceman's Association. Almost no replies were received from the Dublin estates but a tenants' association in Cork wrote in favour of the Trust's proposal. In February 1939, the Trust wrote to de Valera's office with the results, asking for legislative action to allow their implementation.[116] The Irish Government's response was to set up the Shannon committee to make recommendations. Its findings were never published.[117]

Given the lack of maintenance of the estates and the uncertainty caused to families of deceased tenants, it is perhaps unsurprising that a seemingly significant number of tenants supported an agreement. The opposition of a group of tenants, mainly from Killester, and the ultimate disinterest of the Irish Government, precluded a resolution despite the persistent efforts of the Trust.

After the Leggett case the Trust ceased evictions. It no longer had a legal basis to proceed with outstanding cases of rent arrears, and was under pressure from the Irish Government to halt legal proceedings for other offences, supposedly to ensure a better atmosphere for the negotiations with the tenants, although the latter continued legal action against the Trust.[118] Most importantly, the Trust was uncertain of its authority. The Killester Tenants' Association encouraged occupiers to assume 'ownership': to sell or sublet houses or hand them over to relatives.[119] Browne wrote, 'there is a deliberate propaganda to persuade the tenants to refuse to recognise the

113 TNA, AP, 1/147, Dublin tenants, meeting, 4 April 1937.
114 TNA, AP, 1/148; TNA, AP, 1/143, de Valera's secretary to Alexander, 3 February 1937.
115 TNA, AP, 1/172, Browne to Phillips, 5 February 1937; Patrick Potter of Cork to Trust, 26 May 1937; TNA, AP, 1/143; TNA, AP, 1/172, Browne to Phillips, 5 February 1937.
116 TNA, AP, 1/148, Browne to London, 29 December 1938; Circular from The Ex-Servicemen's Tenants' Rights Association to the tenants, 15 December 1938; *IT*, 23 December 1938; TNA, AP, 1/149, Ross (as acting chairman) to President's office, 10 February 1939.
117 *IT*, 6 March 1940; TNA, AP, 1/151.
118 TNA, AP, 1/155, Report, 5 January 1933; TNA, AP, 1/146, Browne to Alexander, 30 January 1936; Browne to Alexander, 16 September 1936.
119 TNA, AP, 1/150, Note (reviewing previous seven years), 15 January 1940.

Trust's authority'.[120] Tenants made alterations to the houses and opened them as commercial premises in the belief that the Trust had little power.[121] A Trust meeting in March 1935 noted, 'The question of trafficking in houses was becoming more urgent, breaches of agreement becoming more frequent and the Trust risked resigning all authority over their property'.[122] Browne wrote in September 1936 that the Trust should have its 'legal powers defined to put an end to an undignified situation'.[123]

The Trust referred to the period following the Leggett judgement as one of 'appeasement'.[124] From 1937 it considered itself free to tackle the question of irregular tenancies and seek evictions.[125] Three factors led to this change of policy: the unwillingness of the Irish Government to enact legislation clarifying the Trust's legal position; the failure of negotiations with the tenants' representatives; and finally the Supreme Court ruling in the Callan case in March 1937. The latter stated that the occupiers were objects of charity with the status of tenants-at-will or tenants-on-sufferance, a ruling that increased the legal powers of the Trust to stop the widespread misuses of the properties.[126]

After the Callan case, in seeking evictions the Trust made a formal declaration that the tenant was no longer a proper object of the Trust. This applied only to those who had signed tenancy agreements, others had not even the status of tenants-at-will but were trespassers or occupiers with no legal title and therefore no declaration was necessary.[127] James Brunyate, Chairman of the Trust since 1927, advocated 'systematic litigation' to ascertain the Trust's power.[128] The Trust was successful in seeking evictions against a number of tenants for a range of offences, including using the premises for industrial purposes, selling the 'key' (to the cottage), otherwise unauthorised transfers such as reassigning the house to other family members, subletting, absence, and alterations to the house. Eviction was also sought due to the death of both parents. In July 1937 the Trust took action 78 times, of which 18 cases involved tenants leaving the country, 17 to England and one to the USA. From July 1937 to August 1938, 36 tenants left Ireland, 34 for England and two for the USA. In some cases the tenant was absent for several years while his family remained in possession. Once the Trust became aware of

120 TNA, AP, 1/144, Browne, report, 16 October 1934.
121 TNA, AP, 1/144, Alexander to Treasury, 12 July 1934.
122 TNA, AP, 4/9, Trust meeting, 20 March 1935.
123 TNA, AP, 1/146, Browne to Alexander, 16 September 1936.
124 TNA, AP, 1/150, Brunyate to Browne, 25 January 1941.
125 TNA, AP, 1/151, Browne to Phillips, 15 March 1944.
126 TNA, AP, 1/150, note, 15 January 1940.
127 TNA, AP, 1/167, Browne to Alexander, 19 April 1937.
128 TNA, AP, 1/147, Brunyate to Ross 14 February 1937.

an absence, it set a deadline for the tenant's return and when they did not the house was surrendered.[129] Andrew McLaughlin and Thomas Downey of Cork claimed that they could not find employment in Ireland and were working on a temporary basis in Dagenham, leaving their wives and children (all 18 or under) in possession of their cottages. Both were interviewed by Franks and Meath. McLaughlin wrote afterwards that he had secured work in Ireland and would return home. These were borderline cases; other tenants were long-term absentees and had left relatives other than wives and children in possession of their property.[130]

There was considerable 'trafficking' in houses and even in more deserving cases the Trust sought evictions. William Coffey of Galway had 'bought the key' from a tenant for £25, although he was warned by a Trust representative not to do so. He pleaded in a letter to the Trust in February 1938 that he had served four years in France and Mesopotamia, after which he joined the RIC and served for two years, for which service he had had to leave Ireland, and when he was able to return there were no houses available. Although the trustees recognised that he qualified, they would not countenance trafficking or give him priority over the many deserving applicants on the waiting list, and took out a decree for repossession. After the judge's order for eviction Coffey refused to leave until forced by the sheriff.[131] W. Leckie obtained a cottage in Limerick by an unauthorised transfer in November 1936 and was given notice to quit, despite a recommendation from the Commanding Officer of the Irish Guards with whom he had won the Distinguished Conduct Medal. He was not a Limerick man and local applicants who had been on a waiting list for years were deemed to have priority.[132]

Other cases involved marital problems. Edward Adair, a Killester tenant since 1923, left his wife and the property deteriorated to 'the worst features of a slum dwelling'. The Inspector of Cruelty to Children made Adair take his children away. Adair said he would only return if the Trust removed his wife. The Trust was successful in reclaiming the property after a court hearing in July 1937.[133] Some tenants used their properties for commercial purposes. Henry O'Neill from Bluebell, Dublin used his entire plot for the manufacture of cement blocks, erecting a large shed and employing six men. Meath interviewed O'Neill and reported that he was defiant and insolent.[134]

The Trust was both diligent in investigating cases and prepared to show patience. Henry McMullin of Westport, County Mayo had sublet his cottage

129 TNA, AP, 1/167, Reports including one submitted to Trust Meeting, 2 July 1937.
130 TNA, AP, 1/167, McLaughlin to Trust, 2 November 1938.
131 TNA, AP, 1/167, Coffey to Trust, 7 February 1938; Browne to Phillips, 5 April 1938.
132 TNA, AP, 1/167.
133 TNA, AP, 1/167, Browne to Phillips, 10 May 1937; *IT* 28 July 1937.
134 TNA, AP, 1/167.

and no longer resided there. Franks ruled that a notice to quit be served but only after giving McMullin the chance to get rid of the lodgers and go back into residence. Thomas Muldoon of Ballymote, County Sligo lived in England for two years and was allowed two months to resume residence, though he failed to return.[135] In March 1938, Browne reported that:

> since we were instructed to institute proceedings, in April last, we have recovered possession of 60 houses, not including those voluntarily handed over. In addition, no fewer than 132 cases have been struck off the black list – bona fide occupation having been resumed, lodgers got rid of, badly kept houses put in order and inspections allowed. In seven cases decrees have been obtained, but not yet executed. There are 65 cases still on the list today.[136]

Between May 1937 and October 1939, 118 houses were recovered, again excluding a considerable number of cases where houses were surrendered without having to institute proceedings. From 1937 to 1944, 49 cottages were recovered in cases where both parents were dead.[137] Some tenants claimed the Trust's rules were too harsh and that, for example, in contrast to council house tenants, they were prevented from keeping lodgers, fowl, etc. to supplement their income.[138] Brunyate noted that this 'shows how imperatively necessary it had become to resume control'.[139] In 1939, cottages were still being sold illegally, but in general the Trust had succeeded in reasserting its authority.[140]

The advent of war brought new issues for the Trust as tenants, and/or their families, joined the armed forces or secured jobs in industries deemed critical to the war effort. P. Ryan, Secretary of the Ex-Servicemen's Tenants' Rights Association, wrote to the Trust in September 1939, asking that evictions of dependents be halted as some had joined HM Forces, claiming the Trust's policy was a 'victimisation of widows and orphans'. Referring to Ryan's letters, Browne wrote to Phillips, 'the suggestion that we should stop legal action against occupants during the period of the War is tantamount to a plea that, because there is a state of war, the Trust should countenance all manner of irregularities. Every case must be considered on its merits'. The

---

135 TNA, AP, 1/167, Grubb to Phillips, 19 May 1938.
136 TNA, AP, 1/167, Browne, Report, 14 March 1938.
137 TNA, AP, 1/151, Browne to Phillips, 15 March 1944.
138 TNA, AP, 3/34, Letter from Galway tenant in the *Connacht Tribune*, 29 September 1928.
139 TNA, AP, 1/168, Browne to Philips, 6 October 1939; Philips to Brown, 19 October 1939.
140 TNA, AP, 1/149, Grubb to Phillips, 20 May 1939.

Trust replied to Ryan that it could not enter into general discussion against unauthorised or otherwise unsuitable occupants of its cottages, but 'there is no question whatever of harassing the dependents of authorised occupants absent on approved National Service'.[141]

One such case involved an ex-serviceman from Killester who died in October 1938 leaving a son, Nicholas Flanagan, who was in the British army, two daughters aged 20 and 18, and a younger son of 14. Reverend James Kenny of Killester wrote to Nicholas's commanding officer to ask his support in having the Trust reassign the house to the son. The commanding officer sent the request to the War Office, who forwarded it to the Dominions Office, who sent it to the Trust. The plea was to no avail, by January 1940 a decree for eviction was obtained and the cottage re-let. This was a particularly harsh decision; a less deserving case was John Mulcahy of Killester, who had an unsatisfactory history as a tenant. He departed for England stating that he was going to join the Labour Corps. He left the house empty and sold the furniture, which he had bought on credit and not paid for. His wife and child were said to be in Dublin. The Trust took possession of the property and re-let it.[142]

During the 1930s, the Trust sought, through court action and negotiations with tenants and the Irish Government, to resolve the uncertainty caused by the inconsistencies arising out of the Leggett judgement, which precluded it from charging any rent. The negotiations proved fruitless; the more militant tenant representatives reneged on agreements and the de Valera Government took no substantive action to resolve the problem. Although the Trust was unable to charge rent or indeed any levy to maintain and repair the houses and the surrounding estates, it was successful in court actions seeking evictions for the more extreme forms of tenancy abuse and in reasserting its authority. As a landlord and an imperial body in an independent Ireland, the Trust was always going to face challenges. These were at times accentuated by bureaucratic intransigence and tenant militancy. For a charitable body, the Trust spent much of its time in litigation against the people it was serving.[143]

---

141 TNA, AP, 1/168, Ryan to Trust, 13 September 1939, 29 September 1939, 21 October 1939; Browne to Phillips 15 September 1939; Trust to Ryan, 4 November 1939.
142 TNA, AP, 1/168, Browne to Phillips, 27 November 1939.
143 Brady and Lynch, 'The Irish Sailors' and Soldiers' Trust and its Killester Nemesis', 288.

Treatment of Widows and the Disabled

The issue of widows and whether to allow them to continue occupancy after their husband's death was sensitive and became increasingly so with the rapid rise in their numbers; by December 1938 there were 227.[144] The Trust did not wish to make a widow and possibly a family of young children homeless but she was depriving other ex-servicemen, some of whom had been on waiting lists for a number of years and who themselves often had families, of the much needed house. The situation was yet more complex if the widow remarried, especially to a non-ex-serviceman. Without her husband's income or full pension, widows were more likely to be unable to pay the rent (before 1933) and often took in a lodger, which was contrary to Trust rules; in either case, she faced eviction. In general, the Trust's policy was to allow the widow to remain in occupation although, aside from the needs of the unhoused ex-servicemen, the Trust also operated under legal constraints. The legislation establishing the Trust made no provision for widows, but in 1929 the Trust obtained authority from the Treasury by statutory order to permit widows to continue occupation, subject to the needs of unhoused ex-servicemen.[145] The Supreme Court's judgements in the Leggett and Callan cases weakened the position of the widow, the former giving a life's interest, personal to the ex-serviceman tenant, and therefore no protection to his widow, and the latter allowed her eviction if the cottage was demanded by an unhoused ex-serviceman.[146]

The case of Mrs Slowey illustrates the problem faced by the Trust with regard to its treatment of widows. After her husband died in 1931 she took in two lodgers. An ex-serviceman who had been on the waiting list for five years applied for the cottage. Court proceedings commenced and by November 1935 she had been evicted. There was widespread criticism. In August 1931 the chairman of Palmerstown Ex-Servicemen's Tenants' Association wrote to protest at the contemplated eviction of 'the widow of one of our deceased comrades'. Later protests were received from the Lord Mayor of Dublin, William Cosgrave and the Private Secretary of the President of the Executive Council. A Catholic priest from Tipperary wrote that the public would expect 'an ex-serviceman to be spared the anticipation on his death bed of his wife and dependents going to the workhouse after his funeral'. The Trust was consistent in its replies, referring to the original legislation and to the

---

144   TNA, AP, 1/148, Browne to London, 29 December 1938.
145   TNA, AP, 1/30, Franks to Private Secretary of President, 21 November 1935; Alexander to Chairman of Palmerstown Tenants' Association, 11 August 1931.
146   TNA, AP, 1/144, Browne, report, 16 October 1934; TNA, AP, 4/11, Trust meeting 15 April 1937.

subsequent impact of the Supreme Court rulings, which limited its ability to show discretion as it would 'have preferred to leave the widow undisturbed, a course that would have been in consonance with Irish opinion'.[147]

While sitting tenants generally supported the rights of widows to security of tenure, motivated by the possibility that their own wives could find themselves in a similar position, the ex-servicemen on the waiting list had a different view and formed an association to lobby for their interests. The British Ex-Service Men's Non-Tenant Protective Association of Cork wrote to the Trust in November 1936 proposing 11 ex-service men to replace widows currently in occupation.[148] Despite such pressure, when from 1937 the Trust started evicting undesirable tenants, they generally allowed widows to remain provided they did not re-marry; although they sometimes used the threat of eviction to illustrate the legal limitations of their position to the Irish Government.[149]

Initially even total disability did not give preference in the allocation of cottages, although the Trust accepted that in rejecting such a man there was a 'burden of proof' to specify the reasons. From July 1928 it decided to offer overt preferential treatment in terms of a 20% reduction in rent to all tenants with 100% disability and, at the discretion of the Irish trustees, a similar reduction for those in urgent need of relief whose war disablement resulted in a practical total loss of earning. In both cases, again at the discretion of the Irish trustees, if the circumstances of the above men required it then existing arrears could be remitted up to a maximum of 20% of the total rent demanded from the commencement of the tenancy. If the disablement was not permanent, or if the ability to work improved, then the concession could be withdrawn. Not all trustees agreed; Ross argued against 'differential treatment of tenants who have already been compensated by the state in exact proportion to their disabilities'. Sixty-eight pensioners in the Free State were 100% disabled, of whom 62 were permanent and six subject to quarterly review. The estimated annual cost for the concession was £240. The reaction from some other tenants was not positive. A Galway tenant wrote to the *Connacht Tribune* that 'the reason for this reduction is beyond my powers of reasoning as someone with no pension and no work is worse off than a 100% pensioner'. Timothy Hyde of County Cork wrote to the Dominions Office in October 1928, claiming that those 'without a disability pension, and who

147 TNA, AP, 1/30, Browne to Alexander, 6 August 1931; McCabe, Chairman of Palmerstown's (Co. Dublin) Ex-Servicemen's Tenants' Association to Brunyate, 1 August 1931; Alexander to DO, 28 August 1931; Alexander to Ross, 15 November 1935; Canon Dunne to DO, 7 November 1935, and subsequent letters.
148 TNA, AP, 4/11, Trust meeting, 8 December 1936; The British Ex-Service Men's Non-Tenant Protective Association of Cork to Trust 12 November 1936.
149 TNA, AP, 1/167, Trust meeting report, 2 July 1937.

gave the full term on active service, as in my case, should also have the same consideration'. The Dominions Office replied that every tenant of the Trust was privileged in comparison to the general body of ex-servicemen and there was no 'ground of complaint if a small additional benefit is conferred on those of their comrades who have suffered the exceptional calamity of total disablement'.[150]

Begrudging Gratitude

The British Government had the responsibility to help the reintegration into society of large numbers of returning soldiers, many with physical and mental disabilities, and to support them in terms of pensions, medical care, training, and employment programmes. New administrative machinery had to be established and the difficulties of doing so were accentuated in Ireland, initially due to conflict and thereafter the transfer of power. For the first four years after the Armistice, the breakdown of British, or indeed any, central authority impeded the ability to support the ex-servicemen. Political circumstances, economic stagnation, and the attitude of employers meant that many returned to a position of unemployment.

The risk of disaffected ex-servicemen joining the IRA was recognised but Treasury parsimony, co-ordination problems and bureaucratic infighting hindered substantial progress, although British efforts were persistent. The Local Government Board, the Trust's predecessor, built 1,508 houses during the conflict, even though there were shortages of materials and opposition to establishing 'colonies' for ex-servicemen. The Ministries of Labour and Transport provided employment schemes for ex-servicemen; government training centres for the disabled such as that in Tipperary remained in operation, despite threats to staff. When it was not able to open its own training facilities, the Ministry of Labour funded the more expensive option of paying Irish employers, who unlike British firms, were reluctant to make any financial contribution to training schemes for disabled ex-servicemen. But the political climate precluded the success of any large-scale schemes to provide employment for ex-servicemen.

The grievances of the ex-servicemen in southern Ireland were not unique. Protestant veterans occupied the Lord Mayor's office in 'loyalist' Belfast in 1919 and ex-servicemen in Britain disrupted peace celebrations; the town hall in Luton was burnt down. The protests were about pensions,

---

150 TNA, AP, 3/34, Trust meeting, 30 March 1928, 4 June 1928; *Connacht Tribune*, 29 September 1928; Hyde, County Cork, to DO, 26 October 1928; Reply, 23 November 1928.

employment, and housing.[151] Inadequate disability awards and inept administration aggravated the growing sense of injustice amongst ex-servicemen.[152]
Of 1,250,000 unemployed men in the United Kingdom in 1922, the British
Legion estimated that up to 600,000 were ex-servicemen.[153] The continuing
complaints of Irish ex-servicemen led the Free State Government in 1927
to establish the Lavery Committee to examine their grievances with regard
to the obligations of the British Government. Given the unusualness of
a Dominion Government investigating the performance of the Imperial
Government, it is likely that the Committee did not want to be over critical.
The Ministry of Pensions noted that it was a 'departure in Imperial relations
which may easily become an awkward precedent'. Despite the sensitivities
related to their mandate, and some criticism of the process, the Committee
was diligent in its task, adding validity to its conclusions. In its report of
November 1928, the Committee's concluding remarks put the complaints
into context, noting that the ex-servicemen were distributed through all
classes of the community, and that:

> Nothing was brought to our notice to suggest that such ex-servicemen
> form a class with grievances or disabilities common to them as a class.
> Much of the evidence tendered related to grievances and disabilities
> common to all members of the community being dealt with e.g. bad
> housing conditions amongst the labouring classes, unemployment,
> unsatisfactory working conditions of employment in the Civil Service
> or amongst ex-temporary Civil Servants. Again many of the disabilities
> complained of were in no way peculiar to British ex-servicemen but
> were the result of the setting up of the Free State as a distinct entity.
> Generally speaking, all the grievances and disabilities complained of
> were grounded on claims to special treatment by reasons of promises
> given or of war service generally, or were the result of the severance of
> the Free State Government from that of the United Kingdom.[154]

Writing on behalf of the BLSI, Mahon expressed similar views: 'many
ex-servicemen are in need, but as a class they are not alone, nor are
ex-servicemen in any other country, free from distress'.[155] An internal
memorandum of the Trust commented on the report:

---

151 Ward, 'Intelligence Surveillance of British Ex-Servicemen', 187; *Irish News*, 5 July 1919,
     5; *Belfast News Letter*, 21 July 1919.
152 David, Englander, 'The National Union of Ex-Servicemen', 28.
153 Graham Wootton, *The Official History of the British Legion* (London, 1956), 46.
154 TNA, PIN, 15/758, Lavery Report.
155 *IT*, 3 February 1925.

Out of 56 pages, no fewer than 27 relate to the work of the Trust. I think the explanation is that the Committee found that the 'claims' against both governments were so thin, and there was so little in the way of claims or grievances to enquire into, that they were glad to seize the opportunity of swelling their report by a detailed analysis of the Trust's work.[156]

Some 500 individual complaints were submitted, which generally reflected the same issues put forward by ex-servicemen organisations. Of these, 337 related to pensions and 67 to land and housing.[157] The pension complaints were little different to those of British veterans, indeed the Irish ex-serviceman was far more generously treated than his British counterpart. Although at times suffering from tenant militancy, government disinterest, and its own bureaucratic intransigence, in a scheme unique to Ireland, the Trust was responsible for over 2,600 cottages for ex-servicemen. Its first chairman, George Duckworth, commented, 'how much more generously in the matter of the provision of houses and land the ex-serviceman in Ireland is being treated by the British Government than his comrades in England'. Winston Churchill, as Chancellor of the Exchequer, said the same in 1926 when refusing additional funds.[158]

British motives in fulfilling an obligation to the ex-servicemen were varied. There was a legal duty as pensions, health, and the responsibilities of the Trust remained imperial responsibilities. The efforts to ensure the loyalty of ex-servicemen during the Anglo-Irish conflict was partly based on pragmatism, but the comment from an ex-serviceman that the Land Act 1919 was 'only a "sop" to help stop the ex-servicemen from joining the Republican forces, to keep him out of harm for the time being', was an exaggeration; the "sop" lasted the rest of the century and far beyond any political benefits for the British Government.[159]

The persistent efforts made by the British Government, despite the difficulties presented by the conflict and afterwards operating in a country that was no longer part of the United Kingdom, sometimes with the seeming ingratitude of the recipients, and in a period of financial retrenchment in Britain, indicated a motive for obligation beyond legal requirements, republican threats, and lobbyists. The moral obligation that was reflected in the British attitude to all loyalists applied also to the ex-servicemen. The

---

156 TNA, AP, 1/121, Browne to Alexander, 22 February 1929.
157 TNA, PIN, 15/758, Lavery Report.
158 TNA, AP, 1/54, Duckworth to Lefroy, 25 February 1925; TNA, AP, 1/84, Alexander, on behalf of Duckworth, to BLSI, 16 March 1925; Fraser, *John Bull's Other Homes*, 265.
159 Article by ex-serviceman, *Honesty*, 2 November 1929.

British Legion contributed a portion of the money received from poppy sales in Great Britain to the Free State ex-servicemen. In the context of compensation schemes, particularly the IGC, for those whose service to the Crown had disadvantaged them in an independent Ireland, the *Irish Times* wrote, 'no other Government would have gone nearly so far as the British Government has gone in the honouring of a moral responsibility', while Sir William Davison, Conservative MP for Kensington, commented that it was 'a debt of honour recognised by successive governments of all parties in this country for years past'.[160]

The files recording the correspondence and minutes of the meetings of the ministries and the Trust are, as befits British Government organisations, extremely comprehensive. What is apparent throughout, despite the inevitable bureaucracy, politics, and the desire of the Treasury to limit financial commitments, was the commitment of many individuals, some of them over a long period, to fulfil the perceived obligations towards the ex-servicemen. Cyril Browne was the director of the Dublin office of the Trust from 1924 to his retirement in October 1949 (at which point he was awarded the OBE).[161] The unpaid southern trustees, Mahon, Franks, and Meath were diligent in their administration of the Trust, and in their representation of the interests of the ex-servicemen. Meath's predecessor, Major Lefroy, too much so, as he refused to sanction evictions or condemn strikes, and was removed from his responsibilities. Despite his antagonistic relationship with the BLSI, Duckworth still considered the Trust's houses 'an expressive memorial of the gratitude felt by the British public to the Irish soldiers who fought in the Great War'.[162] The report by Dr P.L. Forward from the Ministry of Pensions on disabled soldiers was that of a man with an acute sense of the wider problems related to returning soldiers.

The complaints of the ex-servicemen were those of their counterparts in the United Kingdom and of their own class in the Free State, although with regard to both pensions and housing they received benefits in excess of veterans in Britain, and such benefits as gave them an advantage over their fellow countrymen. That the British Government was still severely criticised for failing to fulfil its obligations was due to five main reasons: a lack of recognition that southern Ireland was no longer part of the United Kingdom, false expectations based on wartime promises and ambiguous legislation, the antagonism of the BLSI and loyalist lobbyists, the fact that most ex-servicemen were not in receipt of pensions or housing, and most importantly the lack of a societal contribution to complement government

160 *IT*, 21 February 1928 quoted in Brennan, 'A Political Minefield', 417–18.
161 TNA, AP, 4/19, Trust meeting, minutes, October 1949,
162 TNA, AP, 1/84, Duckworth to Haig, 12 November 1926.

efforts. The complaints that improved employment conditions for civil servants in Great Britain were not reflected in that for ex-servicemen civil servants in Ireland, or that it was no longer possible to be considered for civil servant positions in Britain, represented a failure to accept the inevitable consequences of Ireland's new status as a separate state. The Lavery Report highlighted that many grievances were based on promises claimed to have been made during the war to encourage recruitment. The British Government refuted such obligations stating, for example, that it had 'never accepted responsibility for providing the total cost of housing all ex-service men in the Irish Free State', and that there was a general housing problem which was the responsibility of the Free State Government.[163] The Report noted that promises were made to provide cottages to returning servicemen, but 'we have not received any evidence that such promises were made in any formal manner or with the sanction of the British Government'.[164] There may have been no legal commitment, but Sir Henry McLaughlin wrote in 1925,

> shortly after Lord Kitchener appointed me as Director General of Recruitment for Ireland, the British Government gave me authority to say publicly from the platforms that everything would be done for the ex-service man on his return, and particularly in the way of housing. Time and again men have come to me and informed me that the British Government is not upholding the promises made through me.[165]

In a Dáil Éireann debate on the grievances of British ex-servicemen in November 1927, William Redmond said, 'they were told that if they survived the war they would get special, preferential treatment from the Government'.[166]

The ambiguity of the Land Act (1919) on the number of houses to be built and their financing encouraged false expectations. The absence of an authority to charge rent, in both the original Act and the legislation establishing the Trust, provided an opportunity for legal challenges. In Great Britain, the British Legion sought consensus; in southern Ireland, partly because of its different antecedents, it was highly confrontational.

---

163 TNA, AP, 1/209, British Government to Jack Jones, MP for Silvertown, 29 October 1932; TNA, AP, 1/121, DO to BLSI, 6 October 1930.

164 TNA, PIN, 15/758, Lavery Report.

165 *IT*, 12 December 1927, reporting on a BL meeting in December 1927 in which Major G. Studdert quoted a letter from the late Sir Henry McLaughlin in 1925 to L.S. Amery, Secretary of State for the Colonies; TNA, AP, 1/209, it was also quoted in a letter from Jack Jones MP to the British Minister of Health, 20 September 1932.

166 *Dáil Éireann*, Vol. 21, 16 November 1927.

According to the Trust, the BLSI's antagonism was an attempt to increase its minimal membership. It publicly criticised the British Government and sought the help of the Free State Government in lobbying against it. In BLSI meetings any indication of support provided by the Irish Government was gratefully recognised, with almost all opprobrium directed at the British Government and its agencies. Lord Danesfort was representative of the powerful lobby that spoke on behalf of loyalists in general and of the ex-servicemen in particular. Loyalist lobbying groups found it useful to use ex-servicemen as examples of distressed loyalists; they were more likely to engender sympathy with the public than absentee landowners. The appeals were emotional, exaggerated, and intended to convince a British audience that the British Government needed to be pressurised to meet unfulfilled obligations to ex-servicemen, Lord Danesfort stating in Parliament:

> It is no exaggeration to say that they and their families are living under conditions of great poverty and in many cases of destitution, that they live in unsanitary tenements and are wholly unable to get any relief. So far the British Government, I regret to say, has not made itself responsible for relieving the sufferings of these men ... I do hope the time has come when the British Government will be responsible for the grave hardship under which these men labour, and will do something to relieve their sufferings, having regard to the fact that their sufferings are, in a very large measure, though not entirely, due to the action of the British Government at the time of the Treaty.[167]

The complaints of the veteran and loyalist organisations were played out in a generally sympathetic press, as was the report of the Lavery Committee. Such coverage of ex-servicemen, particularly at the time of Armistice Day, drew a cynical response from one ex-serviceman: 'the sad plight of the ex-serviceman in Ireland are [sic] obsessing the minds of the English Press but the time has come when the ex-servicemen must state his own case, when he must get rid of those patronising articles, and those people who have used him as a political lever'.[168]

Although many ex-servicemen benefited from comparatively generous benefits, most were not in receipt of a cottage (97%) and did not receive a pension (80%). The judge in the Leggett case said that in addition to pensioners, for whom there was 'an elaborate scheme' of support, 'there was a large body of men who had lost their place in the social economy and who required help which ought not be regarded as charity but more in

167 *Hansard*, HL Deb 25 June 1930, vol. 78.
168 Article by ex-serviceman, *Honesty*, 2 November 1929.

nature of a right'.[169] The British Government had limited means to support such men. Whether they received benefits or not, Irish ex-servicemen were disadvantaged insofar as the British Government's treatment of all its veterans was inadequate, but in Britain this deficiency was compensated for by a societal effort that was missing in Ireland. For example, government efforts to train disabled servicemen in state-run workshops ultimately failed in both countries. The King's National Roll Scheme was a success in Britain, but unworkable in Ireland; the commitment of Irish business and society in general was lacking. To an extent, the British Government compensated with additional benefits but the lack of support from the community and private enterprise meant not just the absence of practical assistance, but also the loss of reconciliation with those who had sent them to war. In this respect the experiences of Irish ex-servicemen mirrored those of veterans in Germany, where despite favourable levels of benefits, the dearth of societal support caused hostility towards the state. In Ireland, veterans directed their antagonism towards the British Government and its representatives.

169 TNA, AP, 1/143, Leggett Case, 10 March 1932.

PART III
Ireland: State and Community, 1922–39

5

Equal Citizens of the State

Attitude of the Government – Relationship with the Trust

From a legal perspective, under the Transfer of Function Order 1922, the Free State Government was excluded from all liability in respect of the re-instatement into civil life of the ex-servicemen and their dependents and any future support.[1] Although not responsible for ex-servicemen, the Free State Government took measures to ensure that supporters of the Crown were not penalised. Under an agreement on the implementation of the Anglo-Irish Treaty, the Irish Government undertook 'to protect from molestation or victimization the persons, property and interests of all who are thought to have sided or sympathised with the Forces of the Crown'.[2] As a consequence the Dáil Éireann enacted legislation which provided an amnesty for all members of the naval, military, police, or civil services of the British and all other persons 'by whom acts of hostility against the Irish people were committed, aided or abetted during the past six years'.[3] This may have not been relevant to the British Forces withdrawing from Ireland but it was important for many Irish ex-servicemen who had been part of or aided the Crown Forces and remained in Ireland.

The Irish Government took the unusual step of allowing a British Government agency, the Trust, to operate in the Free State and continue the programme to build cottages for ex-servicemen after the transfer of power, passing the necessary legislation, the Land Trust Powers Act in 1923, to enable it to function. This went against the views of the revolutionary government; Michael Collins resolved in 1920 to thwart British reconstruction policies

---

1 TNA, AP, 1/143, Leggett Case, 10 March 1932.
2 TNA, CO, 905/18.
3 Sheila Lawler, *Britain and Ireland 1914–23* (Dublin, 1983), 215; *Dáil Éireann*, Vol. 2, 20 December 1922; *Dáil Éireann*, Vol. 2, 11 January 1923.

aimed at helping returning veterans to find employment, purchase land, or establish a business, as he believed benefits should accrue to nationalist supporters not to enemies of the republican state, and that the British Government intended through suitable rewards to ensure the ex-servicemen were a bulwark against nationalism.[4]

The Free State Government recognised the severity of the housing crisis, with many thousands of Dublin citizens living in rat-infested slum properties. State intervention was needed but the government had inadequate resources.[5] Minister for Local Government, Ernest Blythe, in a Seanad Éireann debate in 1923 on the enabling of the Trust to function in the Free State said, 'That there should be money made available for the proper housing of any section of the citizens of the Saorstát is extremely desirable having regard to the great need for houses that exists'.[6] Therefore, although the more controversial land allocation scheme was halted, the financially constrained administration was prepared to let the construction of housing for ex-servicemen carry on if the British Government funded it; money from the British exchequer to help with an acute housing problem outweighing the anomaly of the continuation of an imperial scheme. It was politically impossible for the Irish Government to accede to the British Government's request to contribute financially as it had no intended similar scheme of its own for ex-National army servicemen, even less IRA veterans.[7]

The attitude to the ex-servicemen and how it changed over time is illustrated by the willingness or otherwise of the Irish Governments under Cosgrave and de Valera to intercede in the various conflicts between the Trust and its tenants. The period until 1932, in which the Free State was governed by Cumann na nGaedheal with Cosgrave as president, was characterised by his active involvement and support for the tenants and his close relationship with two ex-British army generals, Mahon and Hickie, in their respective roles as a southern Irish trustee and chairman of the BLSI. Mahon and his successor Franks were nominated by the president. After Fianna Fáil came to power in 1932, Franks publicly expressed an appreciation of the de Valera Government but in reality the Trust was not its priority; it did little to help resolve the impasse between the Trust and its tenants. Cosgrave supported the southern trustees in their conflict with the Trust's head office in London. When it became apparent that Lefroy's appointment as one of the southern trustees was to be terminated, Duckworth, the Trust chairman, believing he was putting the interests of the ex-servicemen before that of

---

4 Fedorowich, 'Reconstruction and Resettlement', 1176.
5 McManus, *Dublin, 1910–1940*, 99, 76–7, 443–5.
6 *Seanad Éireann*, Vol. 1, 4 July 1923.
7 Fraser, *John Bull's Other Homes*, 262.

the British Treasury, the Free State Government became involved. Lefroy's termination highlighted many of the concerns in Dublin with the way the Trust was run. Mahon and Lefroy wrote to Cosgrave requesting support, after which the Governor General, T.M. Healy, complained to L.S. Amery, the Secretary of State for the Dominions. Healy raised the disadvantages of having the Trust headquarters in London in terms of cost and remoteness and the restrictions on the southern trustees in performing their duties. He concluded that 'the delay in providing houses has given rise to great discontent among ex-servicemen, and, this is bound to lead to a serious situation'. Amery rejected the criticism and confirmed the termination of Lefroy's appointment.[8]

From 1924, the Trust was under pressure to reduce rents and deal with tenants withholding payment. Both the Trust and the Killester Tenants' Association and their allies, the BLSI, sought the help of the Irish Government. The tenants were supported by Bryan Cooper, a member of the Dáil Éireann, who claimed that issues related to ex-servicemen's housing took up 25% of his correspondence.[9] The Anglo-Irish perspective made the rent strike and the resultant evictions highly political. Cooper argued that it would be injudicious for the Dáil Éireann to involve itself in the affairs of the Trust, and that it would be even less appropriate for forces of the state to assist in evictions. He claimed that he could not raise the matter of the Trust in the Dáil Éireann, as the Trust was financed by the British Government and any reference to it would be ruled out of order. Cooper said, 'if the forces of the Free State were employed at the instances of the British Treasury' to evict tenants then a very difficult political situation would arise, as de Valera's party would represent the situation 'to show that the Free State Government does not act independently, but is merely a mask to conceal the fact that the British Government still controls Ireland'.[10]

Cooper's remarks were somewhat disingenuous; the courts and police supported the Trust in effecting evictions, and the affairs of the Trust were often raised in the Dáil, extensively so during the debates related to the committee established to examine the complaints of British ex-servicemen. Indeed, Cooper himself met Cosgrave and lobbied for his involvement. He said Cosgrave, who had been a member of the Dublin Housing Corporation, thought the rents too high and at Cooper's urging contacted the Colonial Office. He claimed he had approached Cosgrave because the rent strike 'will

8 TNA, AP, 3/7, Healy to Amery, DO, 26 August 1925; Amery to Healy, 31 December 1925.
9 TNA, AP, 1/54, Cooper to Duckworth, 2 January 1925; TNA, AP, 1/84, Trust/BLSI meeting, 18 December 1924.
10 TNA, AP, 1/54, Cooper to Duckworth, 2 January 1925.

raise a political issue of a very serious nature', and the ex-servicemen 'begin to talk revolutionary nonsense, and it is very difficult to deal with all these outcries unless we can put something tangible to them, there is an enormous amount of feeling among ex-servicemen scattered all over Ireland'.[11] The BLSI also lobbied Cosgrave; in a meeting with the Trust in May 1924, Walker, its chairman, said that Cosgrave had written to the Colonial Secretary stating, 'the houses, particularly at Killester, are not worth the money and that the rents are excessive'. Duckworth said a telegram would be sent to Cosgrave informing him that the rents would be sympathetically reviewed in comparison to local rates and requesting Cosgrave's help in calling off the rent strike.[12] The Trust was slow in reviewing rents and discontent continued. In May 1925, Mahon wrote to Duckworth:

> All our rents will have to be reduced soon as I hear the North have refused to have any rents above 5/ and are supported by their Government; if true we will have to follow suit. The Legion is working to get the Free State Government to interfere and sent a deputation to the President. He told them he would do nothing without consulting me but I have not heard from him since. Will try and see him this week.[13]

Cosgrave wrote a draft letter to Mahon responding to a deputation from the BLSI and the Killester Tenants' Association, including Hickie and Walker, who asked that he request the British Government instigate an inquiry into the working of the Trust, and in the meantime to halt evictions. Cosgrave's letter demonstrated his significant involvement with its references to the building programme, the costs of the houses, and the impact of the strike. He expressed concerns at the high rents and the Trust's delay in reviewing them. Cosgrave argued that rents for the houses built under the Housing of the Working Classes (Ireland) Acts were lower, even taking into account capital costs, which were excluded from the Trust's calculation. He concluded, 'this matter which is at present at such a dangerous turn causes me a great concern. The ex-servicemen form a large section of the community in this country and any unrest must react on the entire state'.[14] Cosgrave's detailed letter was six pages in length and reflected almost exactly the arguments of the BLSI, illustrating both the extent of his involvement and his sympathies.

---

11 TNA, AP, 1/84, Trust/BLSI meeting, 18 December 1924.
12 TNA, AP, 1/84, Trust/BLSI meeting, 12 May 1924.
13 TNA, AP, 1/84, Mahon to Duckworth, 16 May 1925.
14 TNA, AP, 1/84, Private draft of a letter from Cosgrave to Mahon, 19 May 1925, attached to a note from Grubb to Alexander, 20 May 1925.

It also showed the importance he attributed to the ex-servicemen and to the risk of unrest arising out of their dissatisfaction. Duckworth replied to Cosgrave, 'I must ask you not to rely wholly on the statements of the Executive of the Irish Branch of the British Legion'. He also noted that the evictions of tenants had the approval of Irish courts, despite the opposition of the Legion.[15]

Cosgrave remained concerned that evictions for non-payment of rent continued, writing to Mahon that he understood from Cooper that the Trust were proceeding with the evictions whereas he thought it had been Mahon's intention to halt them pending a revision of the high rents. He warned the Trust that 'in a conflict with the Killester tenants, sympathy would be entirely with them'.[16]

The conflict between the Trust and its tenants continued even after the introduction of new, lower rents in January 1926, as the tenants argued the reductions should be retrospective and rent arrears remained unpaid. Cosgrave again supported them, writing to Mahon in March 1926 that arrears should be calculated on the basis of the revised rents. Mahon concurred, arguing to his colleagues that a concession would ensure that 'the Government of Southern Ireland is on the Trust's side'. Hickie asked the President to again meet a deputation from the BLSI. Cosgrave wanted Mahon involved and arranged a meeting with him and Hickie, during which both informed Cosgrave that discontent still prevailed among the Trust's tenants, and Hickie warned him there would be resistance to evictions and that it would be undesirable to have Free State soldiers assisting in their enforcement.[17] Given the degree of antagonism between the Trust and its more extreme tenants it was inevitable that differences would remain, but Cosgrave sought to play a constructive role in seeking to resolve them. In a letter to the *Irish Times* Lefroy acknowledged the support given by Cosgrave, writing that he had seen several allusions (presumably negative) made regarding the attitude of the president to ex-soldiers but that regarding the work of the Trust, the president had written to the Colonial Office urging that more houses should be built, rents lowered, and evictions delayed pending an inquiry.[18]

The progress of the houses' construction was also discussed in the Dáil Éireann; the Trust's work was important in helping to alleviate the chronic housing shortage in the Free State. Speaking on behalf of the government in

15 TNA, AP, 1/84, Duckworth to Cosgrave in reply to his letter to Mahon, 27 May 1925.
16 TNA, AP, 1/84, Cosgrave to Mahon, 18 June 1925.
17 TNA, AP, 3/32, Trust meeting, 30 March 1926; Cosgrave to Mahon, 6 March 1926;
    TNA, AP, 1/98, Trust meeting notes, 30 March 1926.
18 *IT*, 12 September 1927.

the Dáil in July 1924, Kevin O'Higgins said, 'in view of the housing shortage, the delay as regards these schemes has been giving me much concern'.[19] The Free State made no contribution to the Trust for the building of cottages for the ex-servicemen.[20] The Trust was not eligible for housing subsidies provided to encourage the building of public housing, including those provided under both the 1924 Housing Act, which granted £100 for each newly built house, and the 1925 Act; in the latter the Trust was excluded by name.[21] The Irish Government Memorandum commenting on the Lavery Report noted that the Trust's complaint that it was excluded from subsidies under the Housing Acts overlooked the fact that the latter were never intended to subsidise a scheme for a particular class, and that the benefits of the various housing schemes were available to British ex-servicemen 'in their capacity as individuals, and that no discrimination in this regard has been made between them and their fellow citizens'. The Irish Government argued that the Trust already had funds allocated and must build anyway. In addition, only a prescribed number of houses were to be built, the Irish Government intimating that it would reconsider the position if more houses resulted.[22] In 1930 it relented, the Dominions Office writing to the Legion, 'Under the Irish Free State Housing Act of 1930, the Trust will in future be entitled to a subsidy for all cottages begun after 15 July 1930, amounting to £45 per cottage, and it is hoped that this will enable the Trust to build a further small number of cottages'.[23]

The Trust's relationship with the de Valera Government was dominated by the impasse caused by the Leggett ruling and by its attempts to resolve it through persuading the Irish Government to enact corrective legislation and asking for its support in discussions with the tenants. In October 1933, Franks met with de Valera and the Attorney General and afterwards wrote optimistically, 'de Valera's general attitude was helpful and indicated a very definite interest in the problem and a wish to find a solution to the difficulties'. He noted that de Valera was interested in the status of widows, the possibility of a purchase scheme, and particularly the continuation of the building programme. De Valera acknowledged that the Trust was in an impossible situation that needed to be rectified. Franks gave him a table of

19 *Dáil Éireann*, Vol. 8, 9 July 1924; *IT*, 10 July 1924.
20 TNA, AP, 1/39, Browne to Alexander, 22 October 1924.
21 Anthony O'Brien, 'The Soldiers' Houses in Limerick: The Story of the Irish Sailors' and Soldiers' Land Trust', *The Old Limerick Journal*, 35 (1998), 4.
22 TNA, PIN, 15/758, Lavery Report; TNA, AP, 1/2, Ardee to Brunyate, 21 November 1927; Browne to Brunyate, 11 March 1930.
23 TNA, AP, 1/121, DO to BLSI, 6 October 1930.

proposed reduced rents. De Valera said his 'Government is most willing to be helpful'.[24]

The optimism was premature; in December 1933 de Valera's office wrote to Franks that the Trust's affairs were under consideration but there would be no early statement.[25] The deteriorating relationship between Ireland and Britain, including trade sanctions, affected the Trust. In December 1933 Franks informed Alexander that the effect of the latest embargo on Irish cattle made it inopportune for him to again approach the President.[26] In January 1934, the Treasury, Dominions Office, and the Trust requested meetings with the finance and legal representatives of the Free State Government, taking the view that if a settlement was not reached the Trust would cease to operate in the Free State. De Valera responded by suggesting that the Trust and its beneficiaries come together to reach an agreement which would help Irish Government departments make a recommendation to the Executive.[27] In August 1934, the Trust submitted to the Free State High Commissioner through the Dominions Office, what in its opinion were generous terms most likely to meet the approval of the general body of tenants, with the request that they should be enshrined in new legislation; these included tenancy for life, rights for widows, a charge for maintenance and rates, and a purchase scheme.[28] Franks met de Valera in December 1934, commenting afterwards that he 'found his attitude was everything that could be desired. He was courteous and willing to help'. De Valera said the proposals were 'very reasonable', and requested that the Attorney General join the meeting, suggesting to him that early legislation should be enacted to give them legal enforcement. The Attorney General brought a report from the Local Government Board that indicated a general desire on the part of the tenants to settle.[29] De Valera asked Franks if the Irish Government representatives could disclose the proposals and the Trust replied that it had no objection.[30]

The Trust was frustrated by the lack of initiative thereafter displayed by the Free State Government. In May 1935, Alexander and Browne met E.P. McCarron, secretary in the Irish Ministry of Local Government and Public

24 TNA, AP, 1/142, Franks to Brunyate, 1 November 1933.
25 TNA, AP, 1/142, De Valera's office to Franks, 16 December 1933.
26 TNA, AP, 1/142, Franks to Alexander, 22 December 1933.
27 TNA, AP, 1/144, Treasury/DO/Trust meeting, 23 January 1934; HMG to John Dulanty, the Irish High Commissioner, 1 February 1934; Office of the President to Franks, 7 February 1934.
28 TNA, AP, 1/144, Trust/Treasury/DO meeting, 5 June 1934; DO to Dulanty, 20 August 1934.
29 TNA, AP, 1/144, Franks to Brunyate, 19 December 1934; TNA, AP, 1/150, note, 15 January 1940.
30 TNA, AP, 1/145, De Valera to Franks, 3 January 1935.

Health, who said 'it was quite incorrect to suggest that the matter had been lost sight of or pigeon-holed; that his Government looked sympathetically upon the proposals, and were anxious to have the matter satisfactorily settled', and as the tenants had not agreed a 'working arrangement' with the Trust, the government could not move. Alexander pointed out that, as the matter had been under consideration since August 1933, the delay was unreasonable.[31] The Trust believed it futile for it to ascertain the opinion of the tenants and considered that the Free State Government should satisfy itself.[32] At a meeting in July 1935 with the High Commissioner for the Free State, attended by the Dominions Office and the Treasury, Brunyate said the Trust had been deprived of all practical powers to maintain the estate and the remedy could be further litigation, which could take years to settle, or legislation, and that a proposal had been submitted to the Irish Government.[33] Brunyate's lobbying was to little purpose; in August 1935 the Free State informed the British Government of its decision to postpone discussions. At the same time and in contradiction, McCarron approached Browne to discuss informally the memorandum sent to the Irish High Commissioner in August 1934.[34]

When it became obvious that the Free State was not going to legislate to give force to its proposals or canvas the opinion of the tenants, the Trust through Franks wrote again to de Valera in December 1935, referring to the memorandum given to the High Commissioner in August 1934 and to de Valera in December 1934, confirming that the terms had the approval of the British ministries involved and suggesting a round table discussion to include one delegate each from Killester and Cork, and one non-tenant to represent the unhoused men, together with representatives of the Trust and the President.[35] De Valera replied that the suggestion was under consideration.[36] At the same time the Killester representatives, Father Traynor and Mr P. Griffen, were also lobbying, holding meetings with their legal advisers, the Free State Attorney General, and McCarron. They proposed a right to buy at a low market value, taking into account rent previously paid and a charge for maintenance but not administration or central services. The Attorney General said the matter would be referred to the President and the appropriate government departments.[37]

31 TNA, AP, 1/145, Alexander, note, 27 May 1935.
32 TNA, AP, 1/145, Trust meeting, 25 June 1935.
33 TNA, AP, 1/145, High Commissioner for the IFS, DO, Treasury and Trust meeting, 4 July 1935.
34 TNA, AP, 1/145; DO to Brunyate, 23 August 1935.
35 TNA, AP, 1/145, Franks to de Valera, 7 December 1935.
36 TNA, AP, 1/150, note, 15 January 1940; De Valera to Trust, 1 February 1936.
37 TNA, AP, 1/145; Killester representatives /IFS, 17 December 1935.

In January 1936, Browne wrote to Alexander that de Valera was 'engaged in considering the affairs of the Trust and hoped to arrange a conference in the next week', and had asked that pending evictions be postponed to ensure a better atmosphere. The Trust agreed. De Valera did not, however, put the same pressures on the Killester Tenants' Association to halt its legal actions against the Trust.[38] In February 1936, Browne wrote to Brunyate informing him that de Valera's office had contacted him to ask for a meeting with Franks and Major Tynan of the British Legion to discuss representatives for a planned meeting between the Trust and the tenants. Browne reported that de Valera had seen the Attorney General and the atmosphere was ready for an agreed solution, but that 'the President wished to hold aloof, to regard the conference with interested benevolence', and if all parties could agree he would be prepared to introduce legislation.[39] At the British Legion conference in February 1936 Franks said:

I should like to pay tribute to the President of the Executive Council, to the Attorney General and to the Government of the Free State, for the way in which they have tried to help us mutually, both the Trust and the tenants to come to a solution of our difficulties (applause). I have had two personal interviews with the President on this matter, and far from receiving me with any form of hostility as a Major General of the British Army, I received nothing but the greatest courtesy and I found in him every desire to help us to find a way out of our difficulties (loud applause).[40]

In February 1936 Franks met the Attorney General, confirming afterwards that the Trust was ready for a conference. The Office of the President reiterated that the government's role was limited to issuing formal invitations and the sympathetic examination of any agreed recommendations with a view to introducing the necessary legislation. It was also suggested to Franks that as the Trust's nominee of the Free State President, his formal participation could be viewed as committing the government to acceptance of recommendations arising from the meeting and that as the President might find 'it desirable to seek your advice', it would be best if he was not directly associated. Franks attended but not as a delegate. In June 1936, de Valera wrote to the delegates convening the meeting.[41] The meeting took

38 TNA, AP, 1/146; Browne to Alexander, 30 January 1936; Browne to Alexander, 16 September 1936.
39 TNA, AP, 1/146 Browne to Brunyate, 21 February 1936.
40 Report on BLSI Annual Meeting; *IT*, 24 February 1936.
41 TNA, AP, 1/143; Franks/IFS Attorney General meeting, 17 February 1936; TNA, AP,

place that month and concluded with the 'Agreed Proposals' similar to the Trust's original proposals.[42] The Trust wrote to de Valera in December 1936, stating that it did not believe the proposals had been given to the tenants by the Killester representatives, and that it saw little point in meeting again with them to be asked for further concessions. The Trust asked the Irish Government to initiate legislation to give effect to the proposals.[43] In February 1937, de Valera's secretary replied that as the tenants' represent-atives had been unable to secure the approval of the occupiers, there was no agreement and the Government was therefore unable to introduce legislation.[44] Brunyate wrote to the Treasury in February 1938, stating that the Trust saw little point in a plebiscite of tenants' opinions as the Irish Government's view was that 'the Trust's difficulties are not a matter of public interest, they are a private matter between the Trust and the tenants, and it is only in the event of these two parties coming to an agreement that the Irish Government can undertake legislation'. Brunyate continued that it had been the Trust's understanding that it was

> an institution of general public importance in which both governments must presumably be interested, that the two governments are also interested in fair treatment of ex-servicemen of all classes, and that they might be expected to come together to correct by a just settlement a situation which has only arisen from legislative error.[45]

The Irish Government claimed an 'impartial attitude' but its position was inconsistent. It said that it would be open to a referendum to ascertain the tenants' views but did not wish to be seen to endorse it; conversely, it wanted to see any circular in advance should one be sent. In February 1938, junior officials in the Irish Government indicated to the Trust that they would consider a settlement possible in the absence of the evidence they had previously sought from them (i.e. the tenants' views).[46] The Trust had hoped its affairs would be discussed in the Anglo-Irish discussions of March 1938, but this did not happen.[47] In July 1938, the Trust suggested to the Treasury that its assets be handed over to the Éire and Northern

1/146, Franks to the Attorney General, 6 March 1936; Office of President to Franks, 30 March 1936; de Valera to delegates, 4 June 1936.
42 TNA, AP, 1/143, Tenants' representatives/Trust meeting.
43 TNA, AP, 1/143, Trust to de Valera, 30 December 1936
44 TNA, AP, 1/143, de Valera's secretary to Alexander, 3 February 1937.
45 TNA, AP, 1/148, Brunyate to the Treasury, 3 February 1938.
46 TNA, AP, 1/148, IFS Department of Finance, to Grubb, 2 February 1938; IFC Department of Finance/Browne meeting, 10 February 1938.
47 TNA, AP, 1/148; IT, 2 July 1938.

Ireland Governments.[48] In October 1938, Irish Ministry of Finance officials informed the Trust that they wished for a settlement, but once more requested that the Trust provide proof of acceptance from the tenants. They were concerned about the possible expulsion of widows, to which Browne responded that the Trust was 'coerced by their legal obligations'.[49] Seeking again to meet the requirements of the Irish Government and expecting a positive response, the Trust circulated a letter to the tenants in December 1938 with similar terms to the 'Agreed Proposals', this time asking for a reply as to whether the tenants found them agreeable. A ratio in excess of two to one was in favour, but little more than a quarter replied.[50] In February 1939, Ross, the Deputy Chairman of the Trust, wrote to the President's office informing him of the result and asking for legislative action to allow for the implementation of the 'Agreed Proposals'.[51] In May 1939, Irish Government officials intimated to Browne that the government was considering the Trust's legal position but that any solution would be jeopardised if the Trust continued with the eviction of the Cork widows and a postponement was requested to avoid embarrassment. Browne noted that 'the imminence of the evictions has had some influence in taking the Trust's dossier out of the Government's pigeon holes'. At a Trust meeting in June 1939 it was agreed to halt evictions.[52]

In September 1939 the Irish Government wrote to the British Government, stating with regard to the Trust that they had established a committee to 'make recommendations as to the remedial action calculated to remove such difficulties as exist'.[53] By November 1939 the Trust had received no word from the Irish Government and concluded that 'the appointment of a committee at some time in the future means that the whole business will be prolonged indefinitely'.[54] The committee was eventually appointed in March 1940, though, and included General Hickie and Senator David Robinson under the chairmanship of Judge Shannon. It was asked to consider the issues of repairs, public services, house purchases, and widows.[55] The Shannon Report was presented to the Irish Government on 9 May 1940 but a year of inactivity later, the Trust concluded that they 'are shirking from the task of implementing the recommendations of the Shannon Committee and

48 TNA, AP, 1/148, Brunyate to Treasury, 29 July 1938
49 TNA, AP, 1/148, Browne to London, 21 October 1938.
50 TNA, AP, 1/148, Browne to London 29 December 1938.
51 TNA, AP, 1/149, Ross (as acting chairman) to President's office, 10 February 1939.
52 TNA, AP, 1/149, Browne to Phillips, 11 May 1939; TNA, AP, 1/168, Meeting, 9 June 1939.
53 TNA, AP, 1/149, High Commissioner for Ireland to DO, 25 September 1939.
54 TNA, AP, 1/149, Browne to Phillips, 24 November 1939.
55 *IT*, 6 March 1940.

have not even published the report and are to take no action but to shelve the whole question of the Trust's affairs'. Neither de Valera nor the Minister of Local Government was prepared to meet the Trust.[56] Browne commented that that 'the last thing the Irish Government want is to have anything to do with the administration of an activity which is British in its inception, its purpose and its function'.

By October 1941, although the Trust had not received a copy of the Shannon Report, it understood that it was 'substantially in accordance with the case presented to the committee by the Trust'.[57] The Trust suspected that the tenants' leaders had influenced the suppression of the Report.[58] It remained unpublished and in June 1947 the Irish Ministry of Local Government responded to a British Legion request for a meeting that 'no purpose would be served by receiving the proposed deputation at present'. In the previous six years the issue was raised at least six times in the Dáil Éireann to no effect.[59] In 1947 Franks informed the BLSI 'that the attitude of the Irish Government made further negotiations impossible'.[60]

The Shannon Report was never published.[61] A copy of the report is now in the NAI. Its recommendations were similar to the Trust proposals of August 1934, specifically with regard to the rights of widows, the introduction of a purchase scheme, and most importantly the allowance for the Trust to charge rent to cover the cost of maintenance, repairs, administration, and other outgoings, and the request that the Irish Government pass enabling legislation.[62] The suppression of the report is unsurprising. De Valera had provided no substantive support for similar proposals in the previous six years and would have found it difficult to reject the findings of a committee that he had established. Even more than before, the priorities of de Valera, and indeed the British Government, lay elsewhere.

De Valera's intermittent involvement seemed only to seek to dissuade the Trust from proceeding with potentially politically damaging evictions and avoid the consequences of press criticism of the government. The eviction of widows was a sensitive issue for the de Valera Government and the Trust sought to capitalise on it; Alexander proposed to use the eviction of the widow Slowey to 'emphasise to the Irish Government the seriousness

56 TNA, AP, 1/150, Browne to Meath, 2 May 1941; Browne to Phillips, 1 July 1941; Phillips to DO, around July 1941.
57 TNA, AP, 1/151, Browne to Brunyate, 9 October 1941.
58 TNA, AP, 1/151, Browne to Phillips, 15 March 1944.
59 TNA, AP, 1/151, Irish Ministry of Local Government to BLSI, 18 June 1947.
60 TNA, AP, 1/151, Trust report, 26 June 1947.
61 *IT*, 6 March 1940; TNA, AP, 1/151.
62 NAI, TSCH, 3/S11344A, Trust/Shannon Report.

of the general position'.[63] Franks wrote to the Private Secretary of the President of the Executive Council in November 1935 that the Trust had no power to give preferential treatment to widows over the claims of unhoused ex-servicemen. He also noted that there were some 140 widows in similar cases with ex-servicemen pressing their claims to take possession.[64] The Trust responded to de Valera's requests, for example, in not evicting widows, in the hope of gaining his support, but in each case the wider negotiations with the Irish Government failed and were most likely only under consideration in the first place to delay the evictions.

Brady and Lynch write,

> the relationship between the Irish authorities and the Trust was always going to be complex. The fledgling Irish State could hardly be expected to welcome an entity which was funded and governed by the Imperial Government from whom a bloody independence had recently been wrested. At the same time, there was a lot of sympathy in the government of the day for the servicemen who had gone to fight in France.[65]

The attitude and involvement of Cosgrave and de Valera in the affairs of the Trust and its tenants were in marked contrast and indicative of changing priorities. Cosgrave was personally involved, worked closely with the southern trustees and the BLSI, and used his experience in housing administration to write detailed critiques of rental levels in support of the ex-servicemen tenants. Cooper said in the Dáil Éireann, 'The (Cosgrave) Government have always been accessible and ready to listen to these grievances and to do their best to remedy them'.[66] Cosgrave seemed concerned about the disruptive influence of the ex-servicemen on a still fragile state. He also welcomed what was a significant contribution to the housing problem. In contrast, the de Valera administration's ultimate lack of interest, either in enacting legislation or in helping to reach a negotiated settlement with the tenants, precluded a resolution to the legal ambiguities arising out of the Leggett ruling. The Irish Government engaged actively only when seeking to halt politically sensitive evictions such as the Cork widows. In 1937 Brunyate wrote that 'the deceased Chief Justice and the present President have possibly between them dealt us an irretrievable blow'.[67] That the Irish Government could easily have resolved the problem was indicated by its willingness to enact

---

63 TNA, AP, 1/30, Alexander to Ross, 15 November 1935.
64 TNA, AP, 1/30, Franks to Private Secretary of the President, 21 November 1935.
65 Brady and Lynch, 'The Irish Sailors' and Soldiers' Trust and its Killester Nemesis', 285.
66 *Dáil Éireann*, Vol. 21, 16 November 1927.
67 TNA, AP, 1/147, Brunyate to Ross, 14 February 1937.

legislation to overcome other court rulings to ensure the payment of rates by the Trust's tenants. The refusal to publish the findings of the Shannon Report demonstrated de Valera's intention to take no action.

Fianna Fáil inevitably lacked political empathy with the ex-servicemen, while the hostility arising out of the economic war with Britain was not conducive to the republican government helping its agencies. But de Valera's attitude was not antagonistic; indeed, he had seemingly cordial relationships with Trust representatives. There were other reasons for the disinterest. The political influence of ex-servicemen had lessened. Using Trust information on the number of widows and emigration, and assuming these were representative of all ex-servicemen, their ranks would have decreased considerably, and with the passage of time the war had become an increasingly distant memory. The financial motivation had diminished. When de Valera came to power, the Trust was nearing the end of its building programme; the Leggett ruling in any event ensured its curtailment. The confrontational tactics of the Killester Tenants' Association also diminished sympathy. In 1935 they approached Cosgrave, then leader of the opposition, and members of the Dáil Éireann, including the Minister for Local Government, for support, and all refused, one TD stating that they had quite enough to do to look after their own people in slum and rural districts.[68]

Attitude of the Government – Reaction to Grievances

The Irish Government's reaction to the grievances expressed by the ex-servicemen was indicative of its attitude towards them. It is notable that the ex-servicemen were confident enough to lobby to have their claims considered and the Irish Government felt a need to react. In November 1927 the Dáil Éireann voted to establish a committee (the Lavery Committee) to investigate the ex-servicemen's grievances against the British Government in relation to housing/land, pensions, and healthcare provision, and the Irish Government in relation to employment. The motion for the formation of the committee was proposed by William Redmond, who headed a small group of TDs and the National League, who sought to position themselves as representatives of the ex-servicemen. He stated that the complaints were predominantly directed towards the British Government and that the role of the Irish Government was to ensure that the grievances of its citizens were suitably communicated to its British counterpart. In the debate in the Dáil Éireann that led to the formation of the Lavery Committee, Redmond explained:

---

68 TNA, AP, 1/145; Killester Tenants' Association meeting, 5 September 1935 (a tenant sent the minutes to the Trust).

I am not blaming the Free State Government. They did not make promises. But what I am asking the Government to do by the setting-up of this Commission is to investigate and report with regard to the promises made by the British Government and the obligations which, I say, the British Government are under to these men, is that if this Commission reports favourably in regard to the claims made against the British Government, that then it should be their duty as an Irish Government to make immediate official representations to the British Government on behalf of a large body of the citizens of this State.[69]

During the debate there was no dissension over the point that the grievances should be examined, only with regard to the process. Cumann na nGaedheal, the governing party, opposed the motion, concerned at the reaction of the British authorities to the formation of a committee to investigate grievances against it, and the potential limitations of a committee without the right to call British Government representatives as witnesses. Cosgrave argued, 'this is a commission which is to try two governments, and in respect of which no case has been made for their trial'. Likewise, Ernest Blythe (Cumann na nGaedheal), Minister for Finance, opposed such a body as it would put the British Government 'in the dock' and the latter would not appear before a committee on which it had no representation, arguing that if the British Government had set up a committee to look at claims against the Irish Government 'we would be irritated and annoyed by it'. Michael Heffernan (Farmers' Party) was concerned that 'an official commission set up by the Executive Council to sit in judgment on the treatment that the British Government are meting out to the ex-members of its forces, is a rather dangerous direction'.[70] Trust chairman Brunyate, in a meeting in May 1928 with Cecil Lavery, who was appointed chairman of the committee, noted the sensitivity of a committee created by 'a Dominion Government asking questions of the Trust which was an imperial body created by the British Government, functioning in the Dominion as a result of a Treaty arrangement between the two Governments'. Brunyate was there of his own volition, the committee had no power to summon him.[71] Opposition to Redmond's motion also came from two TDs who were very active in their support of ex-servicemen: Bryan Cooper (Cumann na nGaedheal) worked closely with the British Legion and P.W. Shaw (Cumann na nGaedheal) was chairman of a pension advisory committee. Both argued that there were existing means to deal with the grievances. Cooper proposed an amendment

---

69   *Dáil Éireann*, Vol. 21, 16 November 1927.
70   TNA, PIN, 15/757; *Dáil Éireann*, Vol. 21, 16 November 1927.
71   TNA, AP, 1/121, Lavery/Trust meeting, 12 May 1928.

to the motion that associations authorised to speak on behalf of ex-servicemen (e.g. the British Legion) should bring the alleged grievances to the Executive Council. He argued that the Legion provided the best forum for addressing grievances as there were no concerns specific to Irish ex-servicemen, 'The laws and the code governing administration are the same in Great Britain as in the Free State'. He said that it was unimportant that many ex-servicemen were not members of the Legion as it still represented non-members, and 75% of its pension work was on behalf of non-members. Cooper stated that in addition to the Legion, 'the Government has always been accessible and ready to listen to these grievances and to do their best to remedy them'. Commending Cosgrave, he said:

The only satisfactory action that has been taken has been by this Government, and the only sure shield against injustice has been the influence of the Government of the Saorstát. I was with the President time and again on this matter [housing] when I was an Independent member of the Dáil. He was always accessible and was always anxious to help us.

He disputed Redmond's claim that the ex-servicemen did not have equal rights of citizenship: 'I heard no instance given of unequal treatment by the Legislature'. Shaw said, 'I am sure we are all agreed that something ought to be and could be done for the purpose of assisting ex-servicemen'. He outlined the Ministry of Pensions structure in the Free State stating, 'my reason for explaining the present machinery is to show that they (the ex-servicemen) are not, by any means, neglected'. Shaw said that in 1924 the Free State had appointed an advisory council with General Sir William Hickie as chairman and Sir Henry McLaughlin as vice chairman together with a large number of persons, well-known supporters of ex-servicemen, 'who met in Dublin regularly and undoubtedly did a great deal for ex-servicemen and had influence with the British Government and brought to the Ministry of Pensions all possible cases'. He said the pension area advisory committees effectively took over this work and there was no need for another committee. He concluded that the machinery exists 'to ventilate any grievances the ex-servicemen have got. We have a large number of responsible men all over the country connected with the Legion' who could report to the Executive Council if they were not satisfied with the treatment they had received from the British Government.[72] Ironically, those supporting Redmond's motion included two TDs who had fought in the British army in the Great War and on their return joined the IRA. Patrick O'Dowd (Fianna Fáil) said:

72 *Dáil Éireann*, Vol. 21, 16 November 1927.

The majority of ex-servicemen do not belong to the British Legion or any other ex-servicemen's organisation. There are in Ireland to-day many ex-servicemen in dire distress who, prior to the Treaty in 1921, took service with the IRA, and these men who, like myself, joined the IRA on their return from France, will not seek help through the British Legion to-day.

Frank Carney (Fianna Fáil), another ex-serviceman who joined the IRA, also supported Redmond for he disagreed that the Legion and other ex-servicemen's organisations could best deal with grievances, as 'there are hundreds and thousands of cases of ex-servicemen who do not belong to any of those organisations. It would be simply impossible for those organisations to deal with the cases of men who do not come on their roll'.[73]

There seemed to be considerable unanimity that grievances existed and that they should be looked into and the ex-servicemen treated fairly. Joseph Murphy (Cumann na nGaedheal) said, 'We all agree that there are grievances and they should be remedied', only the deputies had a different view as to the method. George Wolfe (Cumann na nGaedheal) commented, 'The substance of this debate will find favour with all Parties in the House, because there is no Party that does not reckon amongst its supporters men who have served in the Great War. It is a matter that concerns the whole country'. Richard Corish (Labour) said,

In the interests of the common citizenship of the country, everybody here should see that strong representations are made to the British Government, so as to make them realise that they cannot make promises to Irish citizens and break them as disgracefully as they have done.

Heffernan, who fought in the Dominion forces in the war, said,

I realise that owing to the political change which took place in this country between the time when Irishmen joined the British forces to serve in the Great War and the present time those men have become to a certain extent nobody's children, and that their grievances are not receiving the attention which they would have received if no change of government had taken place ... 'I am sure that there is general agreement here that the men who offered their services in the Great War are as good and as patriotic as those who did not'.[74]

73 *Dáil Éireann*, Vol. 21, 16 November 1927.
74 *Dáil Éireann*, Vol. 21, 16 November 1927.

The vote was therefore between Redmond's motion to establish a committee and Cooper's amendment, supported by Cumann na nGaedheal, that associations authorised to speak on behalf of ex-servicemen should bring alleged grievances of British ex-servicemen in the Irish Free State to the Executive Council. The amendment was defeated, 63 voting for it and 66 against. The motion was carried, 66 supporting it and 64 opposing.[75] The government was therefore defeated and Redmond succeeded with the support of de Valera and Fianna Fáil. The Lavery Committee presented its report in November 1928 and it was published the following January. The Irish Government produced a Government Memorandum on the Lavery Report, December 1929, with responses to claims against the Free State.[76]

Despite his opposition to the motion, the *Irish Times* acknowledged Cosgrave's support for ex-servicemen: 'He opposed Captain Redmond's motion for an enquiry into ex-service men's grievances,' as he 'held that the British Government would resent such an enquiry',[77] but 'Mr Cosgrave has no grudge against the ex-servicemen and is quite willing to help them'. In contrast, the motive of de Valera, who voted for the committee, was questioned: 'Here Mr de Valera would have a fine opportunity to make trouble between the British and Free State Governments, and we cannot doubt that he would employ it to the full'.[78] The *Morning Post* commented, 'De Valera and his Irish Republicans found the chance to attack the Government irresistible. But the crisis nevertheless suggests the unsuspected political strength of the British cause in Ireland'.[79] The press were critical of de Valera but the last point was most valid.

All parties in the Dáil Éireann spoke in support of examining the grievances of the ex-servicemen, differing only on whether this should be done through the auspices of the British Legion or a specially established committee. Fianna Fáil representatives highlighted the fact that many ex-servicemen had supported the republican cause and deserved a forum for their grievances other than 'imperialistic' organs such as the Legion. Support for the needs of the ex-servicemen was not perceived as support for Britain. Cosgrave opposed the formation of a committee only because of sensitivity to possible criticism of the British Government; he was otherwise supportive of the ex-servicemen. The fact that there was a debate on their grievances and that there was support from all parties was indicative of both the sympathy

75 TNA, PIN, 15/757; *Dáil Éireann*, Vol. 21, 16 November 1927.
76 TNA, PIN, 15/758, Lavery Committee.
77 *IT*, 24 November 1927.
78 *IT*, 18 November 1927.
79 *Morning Post*, 10 November 1927.

towards ex-servicemen and their considerable political influence. It certainly did not portray a marginalised segment of society.

Attitude of the Government – The Political Context

Ireland was governed by two parties with contrasting ideologies, one in each interwar decade. Cumann na nGaedheal under Cosgrave won the election of August 1923 and remained in power until 1932.[80] That the Cosgrave Government was supportive of the ex-servicemen is perhaps unsurprising. Perhaps because of their experiences defeating the republicans in the Civil War, the men who led the Free State Government, including Cosgrave, Blythe, and O'Higgins, became so conservative as to be seen by some as counter-revolutionaries from 1922.[81] There were few changes resulting from independence due partly to the unwillingness of Cumann na nGaedheal to erode the goodwill of the British Government who had helped them restore stability.[82] Cumann na nGaedheal prized this newfound friendship with Britain, and aped the manner and fashion of their former conquerors to the anger of republicans, Cosgrave wearing court attire for trips to Buckingham Palace. Republicans sneered in the 1920s that nothing much changed besides the painting of postboxes green.[83] The new government prioritised economic development over the redress of nationalist grievances. Positive relations with Britain, not revolutionary fervour would best achieve this. The administration was dominated by men who had run the country under Britain and who retained British values.[84] This explains why the Cosgrave Government did not support the idea of a committee to examine the grievances of ex-servicemen which may have embarrassed the British Government, but at the same time wished to be considered sympathetic towards those who had served Britain.

British agencies had anticipated that the republican election victory in 1932 would influence government attitudes to the ex-servicemen. De Valera was intent on loosening ties with Britain; the oath of allegiance to the Crown was abolished in 1933, followed by the abolition of both the right of appeal

---

80 Out of 153 seats Cumann na nGaedheal secured 63, the republicans (who did not enter the Dáil) 44, the Farmers' Party 15, Labour 14, and Independents 17. See Macardle, *The Irish Republic*, 982.

81 Townsend, Charles, *The Republic*, 453.

82 J.P. O'Carroll, 'Éamon de Valera: Charisma and Political Development', in J.P. O'Carroll and John Murphy (eds), *De Valera and His Times* (Cork, 1986), 19–20.

83 Ferriter, *The Transformation of Ireland*, 304–5.

84 Mary E. Daly, *Industrial Development and Irish National Identity, 1922–1939* (New York, 1992), 14–5.

to the Privy Council, and the right of the Governor General to withhold assent to bills passed by the Dáil. A new constitution in 1937, approved by a referendum, removed all mention of the monarch and his representative from the constitution. British control of Irish naval bases was relinquished following the Anglo-Irish Agreement of 1938, allowing De Valera to declare that the withdrawal of British military forces was an affirmation of Irish sovereignty.[85]

One of de Valera's first actions was to refuse to pay 'land annuities', annual instalments paid by tenant farmers purchasing their land through loans advanced by the British Government under the Land Purchase Acts. This led to the Anglo-Irish 'economic war' of 1932–38, with the British imposing a customs duty on Irish imports and de Valera withholding money for pensions due the Royal Irish Constabulary. Relations were not normalised again until the Anglo-Irish Agreement of 1938.[86]

However, while the political context changed considerably with Fianna Fáil coming to power, there was also much continuity, and many of the issues related to the development of cultural and political sovereignty were in practice a continuation of the state building of the previous decade. The same issues of stability and security remained equally relevant.[87] Fianna Fáil was pragmatic in its approach and had shifted to the centre, moving significantly away from its revolutionary origins, partly due to de Valera's own innate conservatism. A move to change Dublin street names, many named after British overlords, was abandoned for fear of offending the business community. Despite pressure from some in his party, de Valera did not make significant changes to the police, the army, the judiciary, or the civil service, even though some of the latter were considered Free Staters attached to the English interest and hostile to the new government.[88] If Fianna Fáil saw no reason to purge 'Free Staters', their bitter opponents, it is unlikely they would have wished to target ex-servicemen, many of whom supported them. This is evidenced by the British Ministry of Pensions, which anticipated that with Fianna Fáil in power there might be problems but instead found that the new government had 'gone out of its way to help not only the Ministry but also

85 D.G. Boyce, *The Irish Question and British Politics 1868–1986* (London, 1988), 82–89.

86 J. Peter Neary and Cormac Ó Gráda, 'Protection, Economic War and Structural Change: The 1930s in Ireland', *Irish Historical Studies*, 27/107 (1991), 250; Paul Canning, 'The Impact of Éamon De Valera: Domestic Causes of the Anglo-Irish Economic War', *Albion: A Quarterly Journal Concerned with British Studies*, 15/3 (1983), 179–205.

87 Ferriter, *The Transformation of Ireland*, 258–9.

88 Richard Dunphy, *The Making of Fianna Fáil Power in Ireland, 1932–1948* (Oxford, 1995), 19–24, 129–30, 143, 146, 211; Martin Maguire, *The Civil Service and the Revolution in Ireland, 1912–38: 'Shaking the Blood-Stained Hand of Mr Collins'* (Manchester, 2008), 207.

the children (of ex-servicemen) in whom we are interested',[89] although one motive may have been the continued inflow of Treasury money to Ireland.

The state's view, under both the Cosgrave and de Valera administrations, was that ex-servicemen should not be considered as a class, either to be discriminated against or to be given special privileges, but that as individuals they held the same rights and obligations as all citizens, and that it would not be in their interest to claim otherwise. Cooper said,

> I have always held that the British ex-serviceman is a citizen of the State and must regard himself primarily as a citizen of the State. It is not of any service to him to single him out specially [but] I heard no instance given of unequal treatment by the Legislature.[90]

Likewise, Redmond stated, 'I make no special claims on behalf of British ex-servicemen from the Irish Government. I want them to be regarded and recognised by the Irish Government of the day as Irishmen with equal rights of citizenship in this State'.[91]

A problem for the Irish Government, whatever its persuasion, was that despite their complaints about pensions, healthcare, and housing, British ex-servicemen received immeasurably more benefits than National army veterans, still more than anti-Treaty IRA veterans. Irrespective of the lack of any legal obligation, the Irish Government could not be seen to give practical support to British ex-servicemen when financial constraints and politics precluded it from providing for those with a greater claim because they had helped in the establishment of an independent Ireland. Cumann na nGaedheal was limited in the support it could give to National army veterans. The Military Service Pensions Act in 1924 was an effort to placate and ensure the loyalty of pro-Treaty soldiers within the National army in the aftermath of the army mutiny, and had it not been for these events it is doubtful that these pensions would ever have been introduced. The anti-Treaty IRA was excluded until 1934.[92]

89 TNA, PIN, 15/758, MoP report, 1936.
90 Dáil Éireann, Vol. 21, 16 November 1927.
91 Dáil Éireann, Vol. 21, 16 November 1927.
92 Marie Coleman, 'Military Service Pensions for Veterans of the Irish Revolution, 1916–1923', War in History, 20/2 (2013), 206, 207, 214–15, 220.

Government and Employment

The Lavery Committee investigated the nature and extent of claims against the Irish Government regarding alleged employment-related discrimination against ex-servicemen. These grievances covered several areas: central government departments, government-sponsored public works, local authorities, government agencies such as the post office, and government schemes aimed at influencing private sector employment. An underlying complaint was that there was no favourable treatment of British ex-servicemen and that they were disadvantaged against ex-National army servicemen. After the Civil War, the Free State Government was faced with the task of finding employment for large numbers of demobilised men, a not dissimilar position to that of the British Government in the aftermath of the Great War. Inevitably it used many of the same methods. Some grievances were consequences of Ireland becoming a separate state.

The issues related to government employment were parity with British salary levels and the position of temporary civil servants. Of the approximately 500 letters received by the Committee from individuals, 42 were complaints against the Irish Government regarding the civil service. In 1920 the Lytton Committee recommended that 75% of clerical grades in the British civil service should be reserved for ex-servicemen. Lytton entrants in Britain enjoyed a salary increase in April 1923, creating a differential to those employed by the Free State. The Lavery Report noted that the Free State Lytton entrants worked in 'conditions of service not less advantageous than those enjoyed at the date of transfer', and although they had suffered by the change of government they 'cannot be given conditions of service better than those given other civil servants, and that the Irish Free State service must be governed by Irish Free State conditions'. The attitude of the Free State Government as expressed in the Irish Government Memorandum on the Report was that Lytton entrants could not be granted better terms than those given ex-members of the National army.

The second category of complaint was in relation to temporary civil servants who had transferred from the British to the Free State Government and had subsequently lost their job. W.A. Haughton, General Secretary of the Association of Ex-Service Civil Servants, stated that his Association 'has been fighting the cause of ex-servicemen discharged from the Irish Free State Departments for the past three years'.[93] In the Dáil Éireann debate leading to the formation of the committee, Redmond highlighted one particular grievance:

---

93 Letter from Haughton, *Dublin Evening Mail*, 28 November 1927.

If there had not been a change of Government, they certainly would
have been in a much more advantageous position to-day. It appears
that there were 658 British ex-servicemen serving as temporary clerks
transferred to the Irish Free State; that there were 212 left in the
service, and that out of this number 158 sat for the qualifying
examination in June and July, 1925. They have a grievance in as much
as while they were not allowed to sit again for re-examination, those
who had served in the National Army were.[94]

The Lavery Report noted that after the War, the British Government
reserved all temporary civil service appointments for ex-servicemen and,
as Redmond stated, 658 such employees were transferred to the Provisional
Government. They were afforded no security of tenure or compensation for
dismissal and were disadvantaged against ex-National army servicemen and
younger, better-educated entrants from school, particularly in examinations
for permanent posts. Marks were given for answers in Irish, which likely
disadvantaged British ex-servicemen.

The Free State's intention to provide civil employment for men
demobilised from the National army inevitably led to the dismissal of
temporary civil servants, including ex-servicemen in order to make room for
them. By 1928 there was a considerable reduction of British ex-servicemen
serving as temporary clerks; some may have achieved permanent status,
resigned, or died, but although the Report did not mention the number
discharged it was likely significant. The Report noted that the British
Ex-Service Civil Servants' Association stressed that those discharged found
obtaining employment outside the civil service difficult, as preference was
given to ex-members of the National Forces. It was also claimed that many
temporary civil servants volunteered for the National army in 1922 but were
required to remain in their jobs and were thus precluded from the preferential treatment that service in the latter would have afforded. The Report
concluded:

> The position of ex-temporary Civil Servants, including British
> ex-servicemen, is undoubtedly a difficult one, and we have a great
> deal of evidence of the hardships endured by these men consequent
> upon unemployment. Many of them certainly suffered by the change
> of policy in the Civil Service consequent on the setting up of the
> Irish Free State. In the British Civil Service ex-servicemen were

94 *Dáil Éireann*, Vol. 21, 16 November 1927. The number of 658 ex-servicemen serving as
   temporary clerks comes from a letter from IFS Minister of Finance to Redmond, 15
   July 1927.

first in order of preference for absorption into the permanent service and last for dismissal, whereas, in the Irish Free State Civil Service, another class, ex-members of the National Forces, had certain limited advantages in examinations and had a preference for retention when discharges became necessary. It is hard to find the remedy.

The Irish Government Memorandum on the Report noted that before and after the change of government, a number of simple examinations were held for established posts and as those that remained in temporary posts had failed, or not taken the examination, then 'the capacity of this class may be taken to be below the average'. They had been given several opportunities to become established. Regarding the discharge of temporary clerks, the Memorandum commented that the steps taken by the Free State were less drastic than those previously take by the British Government, noting that it had been the British practice after the War to dismiss civilian clerks to make room for ex-servicemen:

Some of the British ex-servicemen who now complain of being discharged entered Government employment in such circumstances. In view of the precedent set by the British Government it could not have been held to be unreasonable if all the Temporary Clerks were discharged to make room for ex-members of the Defence Forces, but this course of action was not taken. It should also be remembered, moreover, that ex-members of the Defence Forces who entered the Civil Service comprised a percentage of British ex-Servicemen.[95]

An examination was held in July 1925, after which 651 (including British ex-servicemen) qualified, out of the 1,244 who entered. Ex-National army servicemen were given another opportunity in May 1927 to the exclusion of others, including ex-British army, as a result of which 128 entered the civil service. Ernest Blythe (Cumann na nGaedheal) argued that there was no discrimination against British ex-army temporary clerks but also no discrimination in their favour, and certain discrimination in favour of ex-National army candidates.[96] Blythe's comments encapsulated the problem for the ex-servicemen in the Free State. He was right that they were not discriminated against insofar as all non-ex-National army servicemen were excluded from a further opportunity to take the examination, but in Britain they would most likely have received preferential treatment.

In the Dáil debate that led to the formation of the Lavery Committee,

95 TNA, PIN, 15/758, Lavery Report, IFS Government Memorandum on Lavery Report.
96 *Dáil Éireann*, Vol. 21, 16 November 1927.

Redmond raised the issue of employment on public works under the grants made for road expenditure, claiming that even British ex-servicemen with large families and in poor circumstances had a lower priority for employment than National army veterans, who did not need to be either married or particularly destitute. British ex-servicemen had the same status as all other civilians.[97] After the Irish Civil War, the Free State army was reduced considerably in size and its former soldiers were given priority in connection with works carried out using public funds. The Lavery Committee received evidence that the policy of giving preference to ex-National army servicemen in connection with government grants for road and relief schemes resulted 'in hardship [for] British ex-servicemen, a very large proportion of whom are stated to be unemployed and in great distress'. The British Legion suggested that preference be given to ex-servicemen of both armies. The Lavery Report noted that the British Legion acknowledged that there was no discrimination against British ex-servicemen on the part of the Free State, although it was 'alleged that in the choosing of men locally, there was often discrimination by the foreman of works against British ex-servicemen', but stated that it was impossible to frame regulations against such incidents.

The Report concluded that the scale of the problem was not significant; the average number of men employed each month by county councils on roads and bridges between December 1926 and April 1928 and paid out of rates and government grants was 17,674, of whom 1,740 or only 9.8% were ex-members of the National Forces, and therefore as 'the average percentage of employment for such [ex-service] men is so small there appears no real foundation for the complaint' about discrimination with regard to employment on public works. The Irish Government Memorandum on the Report concurred, also noting that 'in so far as British ex-servicemen are also ex-National Irish sailors and army men, they share in the preference accorded to that class'.

There were also some complaints regarding post office employment; specifically the adverse effect of British army service in securing a permanent job, the preference given to ex-members of the National Forces, and the loss of employment to make room for ex-members of the National Forces. Similar complaints were made against local authorities. The Report also acknowledged the difficulty of partially disabled men with small pensions. The Free State was a predominantly agricultural country and such men could not work alongside farm labourers, and the opportunities of employment as watchmen, caretakers, and hall porters were far fewer than in Britain.[98]

As in the United Kingdom after the War, the Irish Government sought

97 *Dáil Éireann*, Vol. 21, 16 November 1927.
98 TNA, PIN, 15/758, Lavery Report, IFS Government Memorandum on Lavery Report.

the co-operation of private industry in giving preference to ex-members of
the National army. In October 1923, Cosgrave wrote to employers:

> The resettlement of all demobilised soldiers in civil life is an urgent
> problem and it is with confidence that I appeal for the most active
> co-operation on your part. Schemes for the absorption of ex-soldiers
> in the industrial and commercial life of the Nation are under consid-
> eration; but manifestly it is the first duty of employers to reinstate
> men who left their employment to join the National Forces in the hour
> of the country's need; and secondly, to set aside a fair proportion of
> vacancies for those who have rendered such loyal service to the people's
> cause.

The letter concluded, 'A record will in due course be prepared of the
provision for the re-establishment in civil life of demobilised men made by
employers, both public and private, and I trust that on that record you will
occupy a high and honourable position'. The reaction was monitored; a letter
from the Ministry of Industry and Commerce followed that of Cosgrave,
providing a questionnaire to be completed and returned to local employment
exchanges with an estimated number of the men to be re-instated, and new
vacancies to be offered.

Pressure was put on companies benefiting from supplying the government
by compiling a list of 'the names and addresses of firms holding government
contracts together with the amounts of the contracts in order that steps
might be taken to place before these firms the desirability of employing
demobilised ex-servicemen'. This list was provided to the Executive Council.
Letters were sent from the Ministry of Industry and Commerce to industrial
and commercial employers, the Ministry of Agriculture to agricultural
employers, and the Ministry of Local Government to public bodies.[99]

Plain-clothes forces such as the Civil Defence Force were treated similarly
to men who had served in the army. Disabled men who had been discharged
as medically unfit were given preference in terms of employment.[100] In
giving preference to National army veterans, the Free State Government
was fulfilling an obligation made while trying to recruit large numbers
of men to deal with the anti-Treaty threat. In July 1922, the Provisional
Government gave approval for 20,000 men to join the new volunteer army in

99 NAI, 3/S1956 Department of the Taoiseach, Resettlement in civil employment:
    President Cosgrave to employers, 12 October 1923; Memorandum from Ministry of
    Finance, 31 October 1923; Executive Council minutes, 11 October 1923.
100 NAI, 3/S1956 Department of the Taoiseach, Resettlement in civil employment:
    Executive Council minutes, 7 July 1923 and 16 July 1923.

addition to 15,000 regulars, promising that service would be for six months and 'arrangements will be made with employers whereby men who join the Volunteer Reserve will not lose their civilian occupation as a result'.[101] The pressure put upon the Free State Government by National army veterans and the challenge of dealing with high levels of unemployment partly explain the reluctance to give special consideration to British ex-servicemen. In January 1924 the Irish National Army Demobilised Soldiers' Federation wrote to the government that many of its members 'as you are aware are in dire circumstances owing to their inability to obtain employment'. In November 1924 a representative of the Association of Ex-Officers and Men, National Army wrote to the president and ministers of the Executive Council stating:

> I am directed by my Committee to put before you the present destitute position of our thousands of members. Perhaps you are not aware of the heart rending suffering they now have to endure; some of those men are demobilised since October, 1923 and have got neither a day's work nor the Dole with the result that little by little they have to sell out their home. You are aware that the Government has done little to help ex-National Army Men. After all considering what the British Government done [sic] for their ex-Servicemen we are not asking for much.

The Irish Government replied summarising the support on employment and benefits given to the 43,000 ex-National army servicemen, concluding that it had received a complaint from the 'Council of the Unemployed' that 'the Government is doing nothing for civilians and everything for ex-Army Men'.[102] As Minister for Local Government and Public Health, Mulcahy resisted job-hungry Free State army veterans' demands that British army veterans in public employment be dismissed.[103] The Free State Government was aware that anything it did to help British ex-servicemen or help the British Government fulfil its obligation to them would result in comparable demands from National army veterans. The Free State's

---

101 NAI, 3/S1302 Department of the Taoiseach, Army Recruitment 1922, Communication from Brigadier Niall MacNeill, Commanding No2 Brigade, 2nd Eastern Division, July 1922.

102 NAI, 3/S3555 Department of the Taoiseach, Irish National Army Demobilised Soldiers' Federation to Major General Price, Resettlement Section, 16 January 1924; Association of Ex-Officers and Men, National Army to President and Ministers of Executive Council, 25 November 1924; Irish Government reply to Association of Ex-Officers and Men, National Army, 24 December 1924.

103 Tom Garvin, *1922: The Birth of Irish Democracy* (Dublin, 1996), 168–9; see also 'Richard Mulcahy', *Dictionary of Irish Biography* (http://dib.cambridge.org/).

Minister of Labour, Gordon Campbell, would not accept any responsibility for the training of disabled British servicemen, even when paid for by the British Government.[104]

Complaints related to discrimination in favour of ex-National army servicemen during the period of mass demobilisation inevitability diminished over time and Fianna Fáil ended any preference upon its assumption of power.[105] Other issues occasionally arose. In the Dáil Éireann in March 1937, Peadar Doyle (Cumann na nGaedheal) said that married British ex-servicemen with families on small pensions were not eligible for employment on relief schemes and as a result were suffering severe hardships. Preference in such employment was given to recipients of the highest rates of unemployment assistance and, as pensions or other income were taken into account in the calculation of the latter, ex-servicemen with pensions were likely to receive lower rates of unemployment assistance, and as a consequence less likely to be eligible for employment on relief schemes.

While Seán Lemass's (Fianna Fáil) statement that 'British ex-servicemen in receipt of pensions were in precisely the same position as any other class in the community', was technically correct, it was probable that ex-servicemen were more likely to have disability pensions and therefore be more than proportionally affected.[106] A British Ministry report in 1936 noted that 'ex-servicemen in receipt of pensions were barred from work provided by County Councils and other Government Bodies, although the pension may only amount to 8/ per week'.[107] The case has similarities to the situation in which an ex-serviceman in receipt of a need pension from the British Government could be disadvantaged with regards to his Irish State old age pension.

Some of the ex-servicemen's complaints in relation to Free State civil service pay represented a failure to acknowledge the separation of Ireland from the United Kingdom. It was unrealistic to expect the Irish Government to retain parity for its civil servants in relation to their British equivalents, particularly as the cost of living was lower in Ireland. Although there was no official discrimination against ex-servicemen, nor was there any positive discrimination in their favour as with Great War veterans in the United Kingdom. One group that was prioritised over the ex-servicemen, and indeed all other segments of Irish society, was National army veterans, who were given preferential treatment regarding state employment and the government encouraged private companies to do likewise. National army

---

104 TNA, LAB, 2/528, MoL report, 6 July 1923, sent to the Treasury 27 July 1923.
105 Maguire, *The Civil Service and the Revolution in Ireland*, 207.
106 *Dáil Éireann*, Vol. 65, 11 March 1937.
107 TNA, PIN, 15/758, MoP report, 1936.

veterans were deemed to have played a critical role in the foundation of the state and, perhaps more pragmatically, as in Britain after the Armistice, employment had to be found for large numbers of these demobilising soldiers, and the methods used were the same. Ex-servicemen were recruited in large numbers into the National army. If figures indicating that they constituted half of its strength are correct then over 25% of the estimated British veterans saw service with it, and as such they would have enjoyed the employment privileges outlined above; those who did not were in the same position as all other segments of society.

Ex-Servicemen in Politics

The Houses of the Oireachtas (National Parliament) comprised the president and two Houses: Dáil Éireann (the House of Representatives) and Seanad Éireann (the Senate). Ex-soldiers were represented across the political spectrum. In the debate in November 1927 that led to the formation of the Lavery Committee, Cooper said, 'I think there is only one Party in the Dáil that has not amongst its members some person who served in the British Army during the period of the Great War. That Party, I think, is the Labour Party'.[108] Fianna Fáil members included Frank Carney, who on demobilisation from the British army, commanded an IRA Brigade during the War of Independence. Supporting the Treaty, he served as chief supplies officer in the Free State army. Standing at the request of de Valera, he represented Donegal from 1927 until his death in 1932. Though forthright in republican conviction, he worked energetically in the interests of former British servicemen. In the same debate he said,

In rising to support the motion of Deputy Redmond I may mention that I do not speak on this question of ex-soldiers as one who is entirely ignorant of the subject, because I happen to be an ex-soldier myself. As a matter of fact, the only brother I had in the world is buried three miles north of Cape Helles.

He also raised the issue of ex-Connaught Rangers who mutinied in India and had, he claimed, been 'disgracefully treated by the Free State Government'.[109] Patrick O'Dowd joined the IRA on his return from France and as a member

108 *Dáil Éireann*, Vol. 21, 16 November 1927.
109 *Dáil Éireann*, Vol. 21, 16 November 1927; 'Frank Carney', *Dictionary of Irish Biography*; Houses of the Oireachtas, Members Database (http://www.oireachtas.ie/members-hist/default.asp).

of Fianna Fáil represented Roscommon from 1927–32 and 1933–7, losing elections in 1932 and 1937. He supported Redmond in the debate, stating that many ex-servicemen had taken service with the IRA and would not wish to make their complaints through the British Legion.[110]

Bryan Cooper, a landowner, served in the British army until 1905. In the January 1910 election he became Unionist MP for Dublin County South, but was defeated in December 1910. His wartime experiences weakened his unionism, and as political unrest intensified he publicly advocated a settlement with Sinn Féin. In December 1922 the Irish Farmers' Union unsuccessfully recommended him for a nomination to the Senate. In August 1923 he was elected independent TD for Dublin County, unofficially leading a group of independent pro-business and ex-unionist TDs until 1927. A very active parliamentarian, he served on numerous committees and was supportive of the tenants in their conflict with the Trust. In August 1927, the Labour Party intended to offer Cooper a ministerial post in a Labour–National League cabinet. Cooper declared his support for the Cumann na nGaedheal Government and helped it survive a vote of no confidence before switching allegiance to the party in the September 1927 general election until his death in 1930. Fianna Fáil regularly cited him as exemplifying Cumann na nGaedheal's alleged subservience to British vested interests.[111]

In the debate on the Lavery Committee's Report in the House of Lords in June 1930, Lord Danesfort referred to William Redmond as 'the recognised leader of the ex-servicemen in Southern Ireland'.[112] Redmond, the son of John Redmond, the leader of the Irish Parliamentary Party, was elected to the House of Commons in 1910. After service in the war, he returned to Parliament in the 1918 election. He entered Irish Free State politics in 1923, when he was elected as an independent TD for Waterford in the general election and represented the town until his death in 1932. A prominent member of the British Legion, Redmond's promotion of the welfare of British ex-servicemen in Ireland was one of his principal political policies. In 1926 he helped form the National League party as a pro-Treaty opposition to Cumann na nGaedheal. With Redmond as its leader, the party won eight seats in the June 1927 election on a platform of increased welfare spending for the elderly and support for British ex-servicemen. An abortive attempt to form a Labour–National League coalition to replace Cumann na nGaedheal led to a loss of credibility and the National League was reduced to two seats in the subsequent September 1927 election. The League was dissolved

110 *Dáil Éireann*, Vol. 21, 16 November 1927; Houses of the Oireachtas, Members Database.
111 'Bryan Ricco Cooper', *Dictionary of Irish Biography*; Houses of the Oireachtas Members Database.
112 TNA, PIN, 15/758, Debate on Lavery Report, House of Lords, 25 June 1930.

in January 1931 and Redmond joined Cumann na nGaedheal, which as a pro-Treaty party was a more natural home for him than the republicans, and he successfully represented them in the 1932 general election. Upon his death shortly afterwards, he was succeeded as TD for Waterford by his wife, Bridget, who represented the seat until her death in 1952.[113]

Sydney Minch, soldier, politician, and businessman, was elected Cumann na nGaedheal TD for Kildare in the 1932 and 1933 general elections, and re-elected as a Fine Gael member for Carlow-Kildare in 1937, but was defeated in 1938.[114] Major James Sproule Myles was an independent TD for Donegal 1923–43.[115] Robert Barton was born into a wealthy Irish Protestant landowning family. Educated in England at Rugby and Oxford, he became an officer in the Dublin Fusiliers and was stationed in Dublin during the Rising but resigned his commission in protest at the heavy-handed British Government suppression of the revolt and joined the republican movement. In the 1918 general election he was elected as the Sinn Féin member for West Wicklow. He was elected to the Dáil Éireann in June 1922, but did not take his seat; he took the anti-Treaty side and was defeated in the 1923 general election.[116]

Several members were ex-soldiers from before the Great War. In the debate leading to the formation of the Lavery Committee, George Wolfe (Cumann na nGaedheal) said:

> although I served 11 years in the British Army, it is 38 years since I left it. My interest in the men's welfare still remains, and I am desirous that everything to which they are entitled by their service, and that was promised them by the British Government, should be obtained for them.[117]

Ironically, the politicians most associated with the support of ex-servicemen were in conflict in the debate leading to the formation of the Lavery Committee. Cooper and Redmond proposed opposing motions and Shaw commented that:

> although Deputy Redmond takes considerable interest in the ex-servicemen, and although it was mentioned at the last election that nobody should vote for persons except the National League candidates

113 'William Archer Redmond', *Dictionary of Irish Biography*; Houses of the Oireachtas Members Database.
114 'Sydney Basil Minch', *Dictionary of Irish Biography*.
115 Houses of the Oireachtas, Members Database.
116 'Robert Childers Barton', *Dictionary of Irish Biography*.
117 *Dáil Éireann*, Vol. 21, 16 November 1927.

who support ex-servicemen, I say we get no help whatever down the country from persons who may be supporters of Deputy Redmond.[118]

Though he was an advocate of ex-servicemen, Cooper disagreed that political loyalty should be based on such narrow factional interest as service in the British army, arguing that their interests were represented by all parties, and opposed Redmond's attempt to position the National League as the ex-serviceman's party. He stated in the debate:

I was peculiarly glad to hear Deputy Redmond say that this [ex-servicemen's grievances] is not a political question. It confirms a belief that I had, that he had no knowledge of a leaflet that was issued in the County Dublin during the June election. I shall quote a few words from it: "If you served in the Great War, or if you lost anyone dear to you in the Great War, then vote for ...," and there followed the names of the three National League candidates. I think reopening wounds and reopening sorrows for political purposes is a thing that Deputy Redmond would never have allowed.[119]

Ex-servicemen were also prominent in the Seanad, to which they could be elected or appointed by the President of the Executive Council. General Sir Bryan Mahon, a Protestant and unionist, commanded the 10th (Irish) Division and served as commander-in-chief in Ireland from 1916 to 1918, displaying a sympathetic attitude to nationalist grievances. He was appointed by the president in 1922 and 1925 and elected in 1928, and was an advocate of better treatment of ex-servicemen. He was the southern trustee nominated by the president for the Trust.[120] Sir William Hickie, a Catholic and a Home Ruler, was a British army general and commander of the 16th (Irish) division until 1918. During the Irish War of Independence (1919–21) he was critical of the indiscipline of the Black and Tans. Hickie became chairman of the BLSI in Ireland, tirelessly campaigning on behalf of ex-servicemen. He served as an elected senator from 1925 to his retirement from public life in 1936.[121] Commenting on Hickie's election in 1925 Lefroy wrote:

The ex-servicemen in Ireland during the Senate Elections have shewn in a very remarkable manner their power in electing General Hickie

---

118 *Dáil Éireann*, Vol. 21, 16 November 1927.
119 *Dáil Éireann*, Vol. 21, 16 November 1927.
120 'Sir Bryan Mahon', *Dictionary of Irish Biography*; Houses of the Oireachtas, Members Database.
121 'Sir William Hickie', *Dictionary of Irish Biography*; Houses of the Oireachtas, Members Database.

with an overwhelming majority at the head of the poll for 26 Counties and also General Sir E Bellingham to a very high place. No Government either British or Irish can ignore these very striking facts.[122]

Browne, however, believed that Hickie's support for the Trust's tenants was political, intended 'to court popularity' and secure the ex-serviceman's vote.[123] Brigadier-General Sir Edward Bellingham was a career soldier who was an elected member of the Seanad from 1925 to 1936.[124] Geoffrey Taylour, Marquess of Headfort, was a nominated member of the Seanad between 1922 and 1928.[125] Sir John Keane was a landowner, High Sheriff of County Waterford before the war, and was nominated to the Senate from 1922 to 1934. His unwillingness to act in concert with the ex-unionist group in the Senate led to his failure to win re-election in 1934. When de Valera reconstituted the Senate in 1938, he nominated Keane as a representative of the Protestant minority and of business interests. Keane retired in 1948. He was also a member of the Council of State and was noted as an outspoken Anglo-Irish critic of the increasingly restrictive Gaelic-Catholic ethos that dominated the first decades of the new Irish state.[126] When David Lubbock Robinson returned to Ireland from the War, he joined the IRA and opposed the Anglo-Irish Treaty. He was elected in 1931 to the Seanad, which he served as vice-chairman from March 1936 until its abolition in May that year. He sat in the new Seanad from 1938 to 1943 on the Taoiseach's nomination. As a Senator he often represented the government at Protestant functions.[127] Bernard Forbes, Earl of Granard, was a nominated member between 1922 and 1934.[128] Henry FitzMaurice, Marquess of Lansdowne, was a nominated member from 1922 to 1929, when he resigned.[129] As with the Dáil Éireann, some Seanad members were ex-soldiers but from before the Great War. Colonel Maurice Moore served in the British army from 1874 to 1906. By 1917 he was a supporter of Sinn Féin. He was a member of the Seanad from its establishment in 1922 until his death in 1939.[130]

---

122 TNA, AP, 3/7, Lefroy to Duckworth, 22 October 1925, Lefroy claimed his efforts were partly responsible for this success.
123 TNA, AP, 3/32, Browne to Duckworth, 15 March 1926.
124 Houses of the Oireachtas, Members Database.
125 Houses of the Oireachtas, Members Database.
126 'Sir John Keane', *Dictionary of Irish Biography*.
127 'David Lubbock Robinson', *Dictionary of Irish Biography*.
128 Houses of the Oireachtas, Members Database.
129 Houses of the Oireachtas, Members Database.
130 'Maurice George Moore', *Dictionary of Irish Biography*; Houses of the Oireachtas, Members Database.

Ex-servicemen were represented across the party spectrum in the Irish Parliament, albeit not in large numbers; some had served in the IRA or National army, and perhaps had thus 'redeemed' themselves. Others though had not served in either. War service was not a barrier to participation but nor did it define the politician; efforts to form a political party based, at least partly, on partisan ex-serviceman support ultimately failed.

The Courts and Judiciary

The Free State Government enacted legislation concerning compensation for injuries to property or person for which it was responsible. In 1923 it passed the Damage to Property (Compensation) Act dealing with the period 11 July 1921 to 12 May 1923. The compensation was limited and excluded most personal effects or consequential loss. In the same year the government also established the Personal Injuries (Compensation) Committee to deal with claims of non-combatants injured during the conflicts between the British Forces and the Irish National Forces and later the Free State and anti-Treaty armies, in incidents between 21 January 1919 and 12 May 1923. This new legislation restricted compensation that may have been obtained under the Criminal Injuries Acts of 1919 and 1920.[131]

Some of the ex-servicemen who applied to the IGC had first applied to the Irish courts based on the above legislation but had considered the compensations inadequate. Cornelius Donovan received an award of £25 from the Personal Injuries Committee for the death of his son James Donovan (an ex-serviceman shot by the IRA), his solicitor stating that they made 'hopelessly inadequate awards'. He later received £300 from the IGC.[132]

Ex-serviceman Benjamin Rose made a claim for the destruction of his mansion house in County Limerick in a conflict between Irish National troops and the anti-Treaty IRA in July 1922 through the Damage to Property (Compensation) Act 1923. He claimed £13,726, which was reduced to £3,250 as he did not want to rebuild or live in the country due to terrorism, but even this amount was not paid. Rose's London solicitor stated that, in common with many other Irish loyalists, he did not consider it useful to appeal and relied on the British Government to see that justice was done.[133]

Criticism of the Free State's compensation legislation, especially the Damage to Property (Compensation) Act, was particularly strident among

131 TNA, CO, 762/212, Final Report.
132 TNA, CO, 762/46/14; Donovan's solicitor to Trust, 16 May 1927.
133 TNA, CO, 762/41/2; Rose's solicitor to IGC, 11 January 1927.

the supporters of Irish loyalists in Britain.[134] The courts were restricted by the enabling legislation and the fiscal constraints of the Irish Government. A Free State judge acknowledging that redress was utterly inadequate commented, 'I have to confine myself within the law, and must administer the law and give compensation accordingly'.[135]

The legal processes related to compensation were open to other segments of society and were not therefore necessarily indicative of the attitude of the courts to ex-servicemen. In contrast, the numerous legal actions of the Trust and its tenants in both the Supreme and County courts provide an indication as to whether the judiciary reacted differently in cases specific to ex-servicemen. The Trust used the County Courts mainly to effect evictions in two periods; firstly up to 1933, particularly during the rent strike, entirely for non-payment of rent, and secondly as it reasserted its authority from 1937 for a range of irregular behaviours, including improper use of the premises for industrial purposes, unauthorised transfers, subletting, and prolonged absence.

There was some sensitivity in a British imperial body seeking evictions of Irish citizens. During the rent strike, Cooper warned against court proceedings that would result in the Irish Free State being 'asked to lend its forces to eject an Irishman at the behest of the British Treasury', as such a move would bring down Cosgrave's government. The BLSI and Cooper said that the situation had been made worse by the Trust using the Public Safety Act, a political measure previously used to expel republicans who had seized property, to remove tenants.[136] Duckworth argued that the Trust followed due process before evictions and therefore the judges upheld their position,[137] that they took 'meticulous care' regarding ejections, had received the commendation of Irish judges for the manner in which enquiries were conducted before ejections were sanctioned,[138] and that the Irish courts recognised the Trust had been fair and just in taking personal circumstances into account in seeking evictions.[139]

The Trust was successful in securing 98 evictions for rent arrears, often in cases in which two British institutions, the Trust and the Legion, took opposing sides. In one particular initiative in the course of the rent strike, the Trust took action against 15 tenants for arrears ranging from £7 to £45. The BLSI argued that 'the men did not want to evade payment of rents, but they were of the opinion that the rents were exorbitant, and that they should

134 Brennan, 'A Political Minefield', 410.
135 *Hansard*, HL Deb 02 July 1925 Vol. 61 cc 986.
136 TNA, AP, 1/84, Trust/BLSI meeting, 18 December 1924.
137 TNA, AP, 1/84, Duckworth, note, 29 October 1925.
138 TNA, AP, 1/98, Duckworth to BL, 1 March 1926.
139 TNA, AP, 3/32, Duckworth to Mahon, 13 May 1926.

be adjusted to a figure which would cover all essential costs'. The judge concluded that the Trust was 'anxious to administer the Act properly' and gave orders for the ejections.[140]

The courts were prepared to order evictions for comparatively small amounts or in what might appear accentuating circumstances with the tenant unemployed, disabled, or with a young family. This willingness to evict the ex-servicemen for rent arrears is understandable in the context that local authorities owned an increasing stock of social housing and it was important for them that there was a robust system of legal redress against undesirable or non-paying tenants. The legal process ensured that the tenant had time to comply; a notice to quit was given to the tenant, after which, if they refused to leave, an eviction decree for possession was issued, and if necessary enforced by the local sheriff and police.[141] The process could take considerable time even if the Trust's case appeared justified: Joseph O'Flaherty was provided with a cottage in June 1924 and never occupied it, instead installing relatives. After a long court case the Trust obtained an order for possession in November 1930.[142]

Although the Trust was successful with many evictions after 1937, it did experience difficulties with some judges. Following a case in 1937 in Wexford, Browne wrote, 'the judge was not in any way sympathetic to the Trust, and showed great reluctance in giving a decree in their favour', the Trust's solicitors noting, 'the Judge raised every conceivable point together with many points which were inconceivable'. The Treasury solicitor wrote to the Trust, 'I am afraid that the Trust may encounter rather a lot of unsympathetic treatment from the Courts'.[143] The Trust had a particular problem with a judge in Cork: Richard Grubb (Deputy Director, Dublin office) was advised to attend a court hearing by the Trust's solicitors because of 'the Circuit Judge's attitude towards the Trust'. The judge had previously given a ruling against the Trust, which was reversed on appeal.[144]

In the Circuit Court at Naas, R. Doyle of County Kildare appealed against a decree for possession. Doyle, a Boer War and Great War veteran, was living in England and his son and son's wife in the cottage. The judge said:

> On strict legal grounds I grant the decree for possession. Doyle would appear to have been a brave soldier. The Trust was in existence to

140 TNA, AP, 1/69; *IT*, 31 March 1925.
141 TNA, AP, 1/138.
142 TNA, AP, 3/16, Grubb to Alexander, 18 November 1930.
143 TNA, AP, 1/167, Browne to Phillips, 6 December 1937; Trust's solicitors to Trust, 1 December 1937; Treasury solicitor to Phillips, 11 December 1937.
144 TNA, AP, 1/167, Grubb to Phillips, 13 May 1938.

aid men who served as Doyle had served. I cannot assume that the Trust is blind to its responsibilities. I hope the Trust will act with compassion.[145]

In most cases, the police and sheriff enforced the decisions of the court when needed, although on one occasion in 1939 the sheriff in Limerick refused to remove the chattels of a tenant against whom a decree for eviction had been obtained. Browne wrote, 'clearly we cannot admit his contention, which revolutionises long established practice and would create difficulties all over the country'. Browne argued that as with the courts so with those who enforce their decisions, there had to be a uniform and consistent approach or all landlords would be detrimentally affected. The Trust decided to take proceedings to compel the sheriff to obtain possession of the cottage. The sheriff backed down when he realised that the Trust was in earnest and he carried out the decree without further trouble.[146] There was a general problem with the efficiency of the courts. Browne wrote that

owing to the extraordinary manner in which the Law Courts in this country are serviced, the case cannot be heard until next April at the earliest. This is only a specimen of what is occurring every day. The delays in hearing cases are not peculiar to us, but every litigant in the country is hampered in the same way by the ineptitude of the Ministry of Justice.[147]

In the 1930s there were cases of particular judges who were antagonistic to the Trust, perhaps as an imperial body, but the ex-servicemen appeared to be treated in a similar way to other tenants before the law, evictions being granted when due process was correctly adhered to.

That the tenants' associations were so aggressively litigious and ambitious in their aims indicated that they did not anticipate unfair discrimination in the courts. The Killester Tenants' Association launched an action (the Leggett case) against the Trust to prove it had no right to charge rent. Failing in the High Court, the decision was reversed by the Supreme Court in 1933, resulting in a judgement that was, according to the Trust chairman, 'so perverse and wrong that it passes the wit of the legal people to find any rational basis consistent with it on which to found decisions on the connected

---

145 TNA, AP, 1/167; *IT*, 29 July 1938.
146 TNA, AP, 1/168, Browne to Phillips, 21 March 1939; Browne to Phillips, 26 September 1939.
147 TNA, AP, 1/168, Browne to Phillips, 15 December 1942.

problems'.[148] The tenants then initiated a second action (the Callan case) for the return of rent paid, but failed in both High and the Supreme courts, resulting in a weakening of their legal position.

These actions were highly controversial as no landlord could contemplate that rent would not be paid. In these cases the legal premise was based on legislation specific to ex-servicemen. The court rulings were mixed, indicating that decisions were derived from legal argument rather than any intrinsic bias towards ex-servicemen. The judges' remarks in the summoning up of these cases indicate a fair measure of sympathy towards the ex-servicemen. In the Leggett case, the judge said that

> amongst those who suffered most from that dislocation of society for which the Great War was and is responsible were those men who served in His Majesty's Forces and who were thrown back in large numbers into civilian life with meagre resources and a very doubtful future.

He concluded that they 'required help which ought not be regarded as charity but more in nature of a right'.[149] The judge in the Callan case said that

> a good understanding should be arrived at between the Trust and the ex-servicemen so that as many ex-servicemen as possible should enjoy in peace and quiet in their declining years the cottages which the Trust has been able to provide.[150]

A Dublin-based official of the Ministry of Pensions wrote in 1936, 'I have often heard District Justices and judges in Law Courts give the greatest credit to ex-soldiers and make reference to the gallant part they played in the War'.[151] The courts also found in favour of the ex-servicemen in cases that were detrimental to the interests of the Irish Government. In Cork County Council versus Tuohy in July 1939, the Supreme Court found that tenants covered by the Rates on Small Dwellings Act, 1928 were not liable for rates. The Irish Government could not rely on the courts and passed legislation in 1941 imposing liability for rates on the tenants.[152]

148 TNA, AP, 1/168, Brunyate to Brown, 11 April 1939.
149 TNA, AP, 1/143, Leggett Case, 10 March 1932.
150 TNA, AP, 4/11, Trust Meeting, 15 April 1937.
151 TNA, PIN, 15/758, MoP, Report, 1936.
152 TNA, AP, 1/150, Note, 15 January 1940; TNA, AP1/162, Cork tenants, Tuohy case.

Before the law, the ex-servicemen were treated equally. The ex-servicemen's status was apparent in cases involving the Trust and there was no indication of discrimination towards them either positively or negatively. The County Court system was used by the Trust to evict tenants and there is little evidence that it operated any differently to any other landlord; tenants were evicted for cause. Cooper claimed that it would be sensitive to use the apparatus of the state to physically remove ex-servicemen tenants, but this was not the case; the police and the sheriff's office were used when needed. Both private landlords and the state with their social housing needed to be able to remove errant tenants and it would have made little sense to create unwanted precedents by taking an inconsistent approach to ex-servicemen. Trust tenant associations used the legal system to further their aims and were confident in pursuing their claims even though they were sometimes controversial. Court decisions went both for and against them, but with no indication of prejudice; indeed, the summing up of Supreme Court judges demonstrated a sympathetic attitude towards the ex-servicemen.

The Armed Forces

Under threat from anti-Treaty republicans, the new Irish Free State responded by rapidly establishing a National army which eventually numbered almost 60,000 men (O'Halpin estimates 50,000; Hopkinson, 52,000; and Lee, 58,300), twice the size of the British army in Ireland in 1914.[153] Initially, the National army had loosely followed the order of battle of the IRA in the War of Independence, but in October 1922 instructions to regularise enlistment, pay, organisation, and reporting were issued.[154] Its organisation was heavily influenced by that of the British army.[155] Even IRA members who supported the Treaty were, with their experience of revolutionary guerrilla warfare, less suited to the emerging National army than British ex-servicemen. Lee writes that to enable its rapid build-up, Richard Mulcahy, Minister of Defence and Army Commander, 'had naturally turned to the main reservoir of military experience in the country, British ex-soldiers and officers. These men were

---

153 Eunan O'Halpin, 'The Army in Independent Ireland', in Thomas Bartlett and
     Keith Jeffery (eds), *A Military History of Ireland* (Cambridge, 1996), 408; Michael
     Hopkinson, *Green against Green: The Irish Civil War* (Dublin, 1988), 265; J.J. Lee,
     Ireland, 1912–1985: Politics and Society (Cambridge, 1989), 96; Henry Harris, *The Irish
     Regiments in the First World War* (Cork, 1968), 202.
154 Donal MacCarron and William Younghusband, *The Irish Defence Forces since 1922*
     (Oxford, 2004), 4.
155 Peter Cottrell, *The Irish Civil War 1922–23* (Oxford, 2008), 23.

often more amenable to the discipline of normal army life than many who had flourished in the less disciplined ranks of the IRA'.

Republicans demanded that British influence in the army be curbed, but Mulcahy, in need of an efficient army, could not accept 'that because a man was an ex-British officer he should not be in the army'.[156] In addition to those demobilised after Armistice, the disbandment of the five southern Irish Regiments in June 1922 provided more manpower. These regular soldiers either transferred to British regiments or returned to Ireland. Many republicans remained with the anti-Treaty forces. Michael Davern, an IRA commanding officer (and from 1948 local TD) from South Tipperary, said the Treaty was a 'bombshell' and that almost the entire Tipperary brigade

> remained loyal to the oath of allegiance which they had given the republic, but a few who accepted the Treaty became active in organising the Free State Army and, to our grave concern they began to recruit ex-British soldiers and many others who were hostile to us during the War of Independence, into their ranks.[157]

In November 1922, Liam Lynch, the commanding officer of the anti-Treaty Forces, ordered the assassination of British army veterans who had joined the Free State army.[158]

This does not appear to have affected their recruitment. According to Leonard, it was officially estimated that approximately half of the 55,000 who enrolled in the National army were ex-serviceman.[159] Cottrell writes that 50% of its soldiers and 20% of its officers had served in the British army.[160] In the Dáil Éireann, Cooper said, 'It is, I believe, a fact that 50 per cent of the members of the National Army were men who served in the British Army'.[161] General Liam Tobin, an IRA intelligence officer who fought with the pro-Treaty forces, said the National army was, 'largely officered by and recruited from ex-British soldiers, some of whom had fought against us in the War for Independence'.[162] Its Officer Corps between 1922 and 1924 included more than 600 veterans of the Great War.[163] The IRAO, an

---

156　Lee, *Ireland 1912–1985*, 99–100.
157　IMA/BMH, WS1348, Davern, Tipperary.
158　Karsten, 'Irish Soldiers in the British Army', 54.
159　Leonard, 'Survivors', 219.
160　Cottrell, *The Irish Civil War*, 23.
161　*Dáil Éireann*, Vol. 21, 16 November 1927.
162　Karsten, 'Irish Soldiers in the British Army', 53–4, quoting from Major General Liam Tobin, *The Truth about the Army Crisis* (Dublin, 1924), 4, 11 (italics in original).
163　Leonard, 'Survivors', 219, based on Leonard's analysis of National army personnel files in the Department of Defence Archives, Dublin, *Iris Oifigiuil*, 14 October 1924.

organisation formed to represent members of the Old IRA, was concerned at a perceived preference for British ex-servicemen and claimed that 50% of National army officers had served with the British Forces.[164] According to Karsten, many of the National army's original officer corps were former British army NCOs, and had borrowed some distinctively British customs, to the annoyance of those among them whose military service had been fighting the British in the IRA.[165]

The appointment of British ex-officers to important posts caused friction with IRA veterans, who considered that they were 'overtaken in the military hierarchy by former foes'.[166] Some were decorated war veterans, including Dr B.J. Hackett, who served in the Royal Army Medical Corps. He was appointed by Lord French as Resident Medical Officer, Mountjoy Prison, Dublin and later served as a colonel commandant in the Free State army.[167] Others had served with the republican forces. William Murphy, a lieutenant colonel in the British army, returned in 1919 and worked initially as a school inspector before joining the IRA. On the outbreak of Civil War he was asked by Michael Collins to join the Free State army and served as commanding officer in County Kerry.[168] Emmet Dalton was a major in the British army who after demobilisation joined the IRA and then served as a major general in the National army.[169] George Adamson returned from service in the war to Westmeath and led an IRA flying column before the Treaty. A brigadier in the National army, he was killed near Athlone Barracks in April 1922. The overlap between the two wars was evident at his funeral when hundreds of local ex-servicemen turned out to pay their respects.[170]

After the Civil War, the Free State Government intended to reduce the National army to 28,000 by December 1923. Some 762 officers had left by this date, and 1,000 were yet to be demobilised. There was considerable criticism of this process, leading to a mutiny by the IRAO. An army enquiry was established to examine the accusation that British ex-servicemen received favourable treatment in comparison to pre-Truce volunteers; specifically, that they were more likely to be retained in the army and promoted. In 1923

164 John Regan, *The Irish Counter Revolution, 1921–1936: Treatyite Politics and Settlement in Independent Ireland* (Dublin, 1999), 165–7.
165 Karsten, 'Irish Soldiers in the British Army', 53.
166 O'Halpin, 'The Army in Independent Ireland', 408.
167 TNA, PIN15/663, note, 20 October 1922; Colonel Commandant Hackett of the IFS army to the Minister of Pensions, October 1922.
168 Karl Murphy, 'An Irish General: William Richard English Murphy, 1890–1975', *History Ireland*, 13/6 (2005), 10–11; Niall C Harrington, *Kerry Landing* (Dublin, 1992), 37 (according to Harrington he was in the IRA, but this was not in the *History Ireland* article).
169 'Emmet Dalton', *Dictionary of Irish Biography*.
170 Leonard, 'Survivors', 219.

the IRAO even issued death threats to British ex-army offices serving in the National army. Adjutant-General Gearóid O'Sullivan was accused of bias in favour of British veterans despite his impeccable republican credentials: he was a cousin of Michael Collins and took part in the Rising.[171] Valiulis disputes the claim that British ex-servicemen received preference and argues that those who were retained had particular skills that a 'professional' army needed.[172]

British veterans helped create a disciplined and professional National army and were one of the primary reasons for the defeat of the anti-Treaty forces. Their importance was such that pro-Treaty republicans who fought alongside them in the Civil War complained that British ex-servicemen were given preferential treatment, both with regard to promotion and retention. Service in the Civil War provided British veterans with an opportunity to demonstrate their credentials as supporters of the new state and gain absolution for service in the British army.

Commemoration and Remembrance

State and community remembrance are closely interrelated. The conflicts in the years immediately after the Great War inevitably restricted any commemoration, the *Irish Times* commenting that those years 'had not been favourable to all but the most unobtrusive celebrations'.[173] By 1922 poppy sellers in Dublin were 'literally besieged … stocks were cleared and replenished time and again, and soon everybody seemed to be wearing poppies'.[174] In the remembrance ceremony in Dublin in 1924, the first full year of peace, enthusiastic crowds of 50,000, wearing poppies and flying Union Jacks, cheered as 25,000 veterans, most wearing medals, marched through the city. A two-minute silence was followed by the Last Post. The event was marked by enthusiasm and the Union Jack was raised.[175] Watching republicans despaired; private correspondence written at the time, in contrast to later revisionism, indicated the scale of support for Britain and the ex-servicemen. Kathleen Barry Moloney knew Collins and de Valera and was from a staunch republican family. Her sister Elgin wrote to her:

But the worst shock of all was Remembrance Day. The Armistice

171 Hopkinson, *Green against Green*, 265; Regan, *The Irish Counter Revolution*, 170.
172 Maryann Valiulis, 'The "Army Mutiny" of 1924 and the Assertion of Civilian Authority in Independent Ireland', *Irish Historical Studies*, 23/92 (1983), 358–9.
173 *IT*, 15 November 1924.
174 *IT*, 13 November 1922.
175 *The Times*, 19 November 1924; *IT*, 15 November 1924.

celebrations were absolutely huge. Talk about the country being Free State or Republican or Mutineer or anything. It's British right through. There was never anything like the crowd that attended the ceremony. And red poppies, I dream about them now. If you didn't know how to count past ten, you could count the people who weren't wearing them during the weekend. Really I think we are rather wonderful to have the cheek to think that we could ever have made a republic out of this country.[176]

Remembrance ceremonies continued to be well supported in the 1920s by both ex-servicemen and the public. In 1925, services were attended by large crowds in towns across Ireland.[177] Leonard writes:

in 1927, 18,000 veterans were said to have paraded in the Phoenix Park before a crowd of 80,000. While such statistics need to be treated with caution, the visual evidence, police reports and records of poppy sales all suggest that Armistice Day in Dublin of the 1920s was even more widely observed than in Belfast.[178]

In 1925, 250,000 poppies were sold in Dublin,[179] considerably more than the 100,000 in Belfast.[180] Although the money raised was used to alleviate poverty amongst veterans, the wearing of a poppy was symbolic of British imperialism and 'poppy snatchers' were common.[181] In 1930, 5,000 ex-servicemen marched to Phoenix Park in Dublin, Union Jacks were flown, the crowd cheered, and God Save the King was sung.[182] The *Irish Times* wrote that 'in every town of note ex-servicemen paraded and marched to the churches where the special services were attended by large congregations'.[183] This included traditional republican areas. Describing Armistice Day 1930 in the city, the *Cork Examiner* wrote:

---

176 University College Dublin Archives, Papers of Kathleen Barry Moloney (September 1924/January 1926), 94/56, Letter to Kathleen from her sister Elgin, 13 November 1924. Jim Maloney was an IRA commander. Her brother Kevin Barry was executed by the British for his part in killing three British soldiers in 1920. Her grandson is Eunan O'Halpin, who deposited the papers in 1990.
177 *IT*, 12 November 1925.
178 Leonard, 'Survivors', 221.
179 *IT*, 11 November 1925.
180 *IT*, 12 November 1925.
181 BLSI annual meeting, *IT*, 4 February 1935.
182 *Cork Examiner*, 12 November 1930, 7–8.
183 *IT*, 15 November 1930.

The procession proceeded to the Cenotaph, where a large crowd of civilians were already assembled. The men made an imposing spectacle as they marched through the streets, the company numbered about 2,000 and the majority also displayed the poppy emblem. A touching feature was the number of young boys, wearing their dead father's medals, who took part. Yesterday's parade was undoubtedly the largest yet seen in Cork, and one of the most impressive.[184]

The paper also reported 'that the amount of money raised in Cork this year through the sale of poppies had exceeded all records', and that well-attended remembrance ceremonies took place at Tipperary, Athlone, Clonmel, and Nenagh.[185] According to Boyce, 'between 1919 and 1931 Armistice Day was celebrated throughout southern Ireland'. In addition to annual commemoration, memorials were raised locally, even in traditionally republican towns such as Dundalk and Cork.[186] In Cork there is a memorial to the Munster Fusiliers with an inscription noting that it was erected by the nationalist-leaning 'Cork Independent Ex-Servicemen's Club'.[187]

Although imperial symbols were discouraged at the advent of the republican Fianna Fáil Government, there was, according to Fitzpatrick, 'little effect on official attitudes towards Irish commemoration of the Great War'.[188] In 1933 the *Irish Times* wrote that permission was given by the de Valera Government for the British Legion to carry out its regular street sale of poppies on Remembrance Day, as well as the parade to Phoenix Park, Dublin.[189] In 1934 the remembrance service at St Patrick's Cathedral was attended by a congregation of around 3,000, including members of the Free State Senate and Dáil. The government also ensured that participants were protected from poppy snatchers: 'police arrangements were adequate, and a show of batons restored good order'.[190] In 1936, the *Irish Times* reported large attendances throughout Ireland with around 5,000 parading in Sligo.[191] In 1937, a great gathering attended the ceremony in Phoenix Park and the crowd sang 'God Save the King'. Local dignitaries continued to participate: in Sligo

184 *Cork Examiner*, 12 November 1930, 7. Until 1925 there were two remembrance parades in Cork, broadly divided by religion. See Jeffery, *Ireland and the Great War*, 129.
185 *Cork Examiner*, 12 November 1930, 8.
186 Boyce, 'Party Politics Should Divide Our Tents', 191, 201.
187 Keith Jeffery, 'Echoes of War', in John Horne (ed.), *Our War: Ireland and the Great War* (Dublin, 2008), 268.
188 David Fitzpatrick, 'Commemoration in the Irish Free State: A Chronicle of Embarrassment', in Ian McBride (ed.), *History and Memory in Modern Ireland* (Cambridge, 2001), 194.
189 *IT*, 25 October 1933.
190 *IT*, 12 November 1934.
191 *IT*, 14 and 16 November 1936.

the mayor delivered a speech at the town's parade, while the ceremonies in Cork, Drogheda, and Roscrea were well attended, and the latter 'witnessed one of the biggest Armistice Day parades during the past 10 years'.[192] In 1938 there were impressive ceremonies in Dublin.[193] From 1939 there was an 'absence of outward show or parade', but still in 1940, 'instead of being smaller in number the crowd seemed to have been swelled to many hundreds more' at the new Irish War Memorial.[194]

Great War commemoration was identified with unionist support and by association with Britain, and inevitably drew republican protests. In 1925 members of Cumann na mBan removed British flags from various buildings around Dublin marking Remembrance Day and burnt them, some outside Trinity College.[195] In 1926 the *Irish Times* reported that 40,000 people attended a remembrance ceremony in Phoenix Park, Dublin and over 3,000 ex-servicemen took part in a parade in Cork, while an anti-Remembrance Day protest was held against an 'unjust and unholy' war. Scenes of violence occurred as gangs of youths were seen picking poppies off pedestrians' clothing.[196] In 1927 the *Irish Times* wrote that a Fianna Fáil gathering in College Green, Dublin expressed their discontent at what they saw as the 'repetition of displays of British imperialist sentiment', while 'the largest ever crowds [were] seen at a Remembrance Day in Dublin'.[197] The *Cork Examiner* wrote that in the evening following a well-attended Armistice Day in the city, 'a party of young men, numbering it is believed 25, forced an entry into the park enclosing the Great War cenotaph and tore down a Union Jack which had been placed there in connection with remembrance ceremonies'.[198] In 1932, the *Irish Times* reported that large attendances were 'eloquent proof that the memory of those who fell in the Great War has not been dimmed by the passage of time', but there were also scenes of discontent in Dublin, where police fired shots in order to disperse the 'disorderly' crowd.[199]

What is apparent from these and other contemporary newspaper articles is that, despite the publicity these protests attracted, they were marginal in comparison to the considerable support for commemoration, from both ex-servicemen and the public, caused not least by the scale of Ireland's

---

192 *IT*, 12 and 15 November 1937.
193 *IT*, 12 November 1938.
194 *IT*, 18 November 1939, 12 November 1940.
195 UCD, Papers of Kathleen Barry Moloney, 94/56, Letter from Elgin to Kathleen, 13 November 1925.
196 *IT*, 12 November 1926.
197 *IT*, 9 and 12 November 1927.
198 *Cork Examiner*, 12 November 1930, 8.
199 *IT*, 12 and 17 November 1932.

participation in the Great War, with so many communities and families affected.

Republicans always stressed that they were not opposed to the commemoration of Ireland's war dead.[200] They claimed that they had nothing against ordinary ex-servicemen, only against the use of their sacrifice for the purpose of jingoism and making commemorations an annual excuse for the display of British imperialism in the streets of Dublin.[201] McGarry writes that because the Free State only attained an 'incomplete and unsatisfactory measure of sovereignty' it was inevitable symbols would be contested, specifically those of imperialism by republicans. The antagonism shown towards Great War commemoration thus has to be considered in the context of republican invective towards all the trappings of Britishness from Baden Powell scouts to the Royal Dublin Horse Show; a defensive response to aggressive British imperialism.

But some republicans considered commemoration illegitimate not only because of the way it was conducted, but because they objected to the war itself and Ireland's participation. McGarry argues that one powerful reason for republican anti-imperialist protests was that of mobilising popular support against the Free State, rather than specific antagonism of ex-servicemen, and that by forcing the pro-Treaty Cosgrave Government to defend poppy-wearers, republicans could depict them as defenders of British interests in Ireland. The advent of a republican government under de Valera, intent in any event on diminishing the British connection, removed this motivation and explains why there was a more sympathetic attitude to ex-servicemen's commemoration, minus the symbols of imperialism, from republicans in the 1930s.[202] As Hanley notes, Fianna Fáil's accession to power resulted in a Free State, which Republicans were not supposed to attack.[203]

The BLSI was sensitive to the exploitation of remembrance by unionists. In 1935 Hickie said there were people who were trying to make 11 November into a 12 July and promised, 'we will prevent the 11th November from being a political demonstration'. Referring to the waving of the British flag the previous year, he said, 'it was unfortunate that the Union Jack was a political emblem', and that Armistice Day should be of a 'reverent nature'.[204] A British Ministry of Pensions official wrote in 1936 that 'displays and

---

200 Fearghal McGarry, 'Too Damned Tolerant: Republicanism and Imperialism in the Irish Free State', in McGarry (ed.), *Republicanism in Modern Ireland*, Republicanism in Modern Ireland (Dublin, 2003), 67.
201 Brian Hanley, 'Poppy Day in Dublin in the '20s and '30s', *History Ireland*, 7/1 (1999), 5.
202 McGarry, 'Too Damned Tolerant', 62–4, 68–9, 74–75, 80.
203 Brian Hanley, *The IRA: A Documentary History* (Dublin, 2010), 82.
204 *IT*, 23 September 1926, in TNA, AP, 1/98.

parades which gave publicity to the British connection', caused problems for the ex-servicemen.[205] Many ex-servicemen were Fianna Fáil supporters and did not associate remembrance with unionism. They sometimes spoke at demonstrations against 'imperialistic displays'. In 1935 the *Irish Times* and *Irish Independent* were accused of suppressing a letter from an ex-serviceman who spoke at such a gathering.[206]

That Free State governments needed to take a cautious approach to commemoration was inevitable given the need to reconcile the remembrance of the Great War, the Anglo-Irish War, and, perhaps the most sensitive, the Civil War. Commemoration was controversial as it involved not only the challenge of confronting the losses endured during the War but also of dealing with conflicting allegiances, of endorsing an existing political culture or creating a new one.[207] There was an alternative tradition of remembrance among republicans who had fought against the British. In unveiling a 'glorious monument' to the men of the Limerick Brigade killed in action against the British in the war of 1920–1, in December 1922, Dr Hearty, Archbishop of Cashel and Emly, said 'to these men we are paying a nation's tribute of respect'.[208]

The government's ambivalence was reflected in its attitude towards a national memorial for those who had died in the Great War. Justice Minister Kevin O'Higgins argued in the Dáil Éireann that it should not be located in Merrion Square in front of the seat of government as, 'it is not on their sacrifice that this State is based'. Yet this did not indicate personal animosity; in the same speech O'Higgins said:

> I want it to be understood that I speak in no spirit of hostility to ex-servicemen. Two members of my family served throughout that war – one who did not survive. No one denies the sacrifice, and no one denies the patriotic motives which induced the vast majority of those men to join the British Army to take part in the Great War.[209]

His comments probably reflected a common view; so many families had been touched by the war. The government had an additional motive: ex-servicemen formed a substantial part of the electorate and successive Irish governments had to respect their needs. Jeffery writes, 'in the 1920s the Cumann na nGaedheal Government was represented every year in the wreath-laying at

205 TNA, PIN, 15/758, MoP report, 1936.
206 *IT*, 11 November 1935.
207 Johnson, *Ireland, the Great War and the Geography of Remembrance*, 57.
208 M. O'Callaghan, 'Language or Religion: The Quest for Identity in the IFS' (University College Dublin MA dissertation, 1981), 1.
209 *Dáil Éireann*, Vol. 19, 29 March 1927.

the Cenotaph in London'.[210] In 1923, Cosgrave was amongst the congregation in an Armistice Day service in Cork.[211] Cosgrave's sensitivity was indicated by his declining to attend a memorial ceremony in London in 1926, instead sending O'Higgins, whose two brothers had served in the War.[212] In 1929, thousands of veterans marched in Phoenix Park and a representative of the Free State laid a wreath. 'God save the King' was sung.[213]

Under de Valera, the Free State was also represented at Cenotaph ceremonies in London. In a time of fiscal restrictions, de Valera's government continued to subsidise the completion of a national memorial. A site was eventually chosen at Islandbridge outside of Dublin after much procrastination by Cosgrave. Ex-servicemen from both the British and National armies worked on its construction.[214] Jeffery writes that de Valera was well disposed towards its completion and initially planned to attend the opening in 1939 although war tensions postponed the dedication.[215] He argues:

> The real turning point was the Second World War, when the Free State remained neutral and any commemoration of the Great War could become identified with support for the British war effort, so much so that Armistice Day parades in Dublin were banned.[216]

Boyce writes that it was Irish neutrality that 'opened up a great emotional and political gap between Britain and Éire'.[217] The isolationism of the war years and the breaking of the final historic links with Britain in 1949, when Ireland became a republic, caused both the state and national consciousness to become even more distant from a British association and First World War commemoration.[218] In the 1950s, veterans attended remembrance ceremonies at Islandbridge although there were attempts to blow it up and gradually it fell into serious disrepair.[219] According to Jeffery, 'official silence was compounded by a growing public reticence to commemorate the Great War openly, especially with the onset of civil conflict in Northern Ireland in 1969'.[220] As Boyce writes, 'ex-servicemen, and their cause, simply sank

210 Jeffery, 'Echoes of War', 270.
211 *Weekly IT*, 17 Nov 1923.
212 Jeffery, *Ireland and the Great War*, 125–6.
213 *IT*, 12 November 1929.
214 Fitzpatrick, 'Commemoration in the Irish Free State', 192–4; Johnson, *Ireland, the Great War and the Geography of Remembrance*, 109.
215 Jeffery, *Ireland and the Great War*, 122–3.
216 Jeffery, 'Echoes of War', 272.
217 Boyce, *The Irish Question and British Politics*, 93.
218 Interview with Professor John Horne, Trinity College, Dublin, 6 August 2008.
219 Fergus D'Arcy, *Remembering the War Dead* (Dublin, 2002), 356.
220 Jeffery, 'Echoes of War', 272.

into political oblivion, as nationalists applied a sort of field dressing, in the shape of a national amnesia, to the Great War experience'.[221] Yet these later restrictions distort the reality that 'thousands ... participated in the annual Remembrance ceremonies throughout the interwar period in the Free State'.[222]

221 Boyce, 'Party Politics Should Divide our Tents', 201.
222 Jeffery, 'Echoes of War', 270.

6

Integration into the Community

Employment and Housing

Economic conditions in Ireland in the interwar years meant that many, particularly the working class, suffered from unemployment and poor housing. In 1926, there were 800,000 living in overcrowded conditions.[1] The question is whether the conditions of the ex-servicemen reflected those of the general population or whether they were worsened by discrimination. Employment and housing problems were raised in the 1927 Dáil Éireann debate on the claims of British ex-servicemen. Redmond said that Colonel Crosfield, the Chairman of the British Legion, who had just toured Ireland and met both Legion members and ex-servicemen unconnected to it, 'gave a fearful description of the condition of many of the ex-servicemen'. Redmond added, 'it has reached such a stage that Field Marshal Earl Haig has made an appeal in Great Britain for the destitute and suffering ex-servicemen in this country'. Shaw illustrated the conditions of ex-servicemen with reference to an ex-Irish Guard who had a 12s per week disability allowance, was unable to obtain work and lived with his wife and five children in a house with practically no roof.[2]

Commenting in 1927 on the need to examine ex-servicemen's complaints, the *Irish Times* wrote that 50,000 ex-soldiers were unemployed, of whom nearly 30,000 were in the City of Dublin, and that 'thousands of ex-servicemen in the Free State are in dire distress', and are helped by the Saint Vincent de Paul Society, the British Legion, the United Services Fund, and the Soldiers' and Sailors' Help Society, 'but thousands are dependent on poor law relief'.[3] The previous week the *Morning Post* had written, 'There are

1 Ferriter, *The Transformation of Ireland*, 319 (based on the 1926 census).
2 *Dáil Éireann*, Vol. 21, 16 November 1927.
3 *IT*, 15 November 1927.

in all about 186,000 British ex-servicemen in Southern Ireland, and of these approximately one third are unemployed and without any hope of getting employment'.[4] In 1928, Crosfield claimed that there were 800 unemployed ex-servicemen in Wexford alone, who existed mainly on a parish relief of 6s per week per family.[5] *The Times* reported in 1931 that ex-servicemen were finding it difficult to get employment or houses.[6] The Legion estimated that in 1933/34 an estimated 20,000 ex-servicemen were in need of work.[7]

In contrast, Trust surveys indicated that many of the ex-servicemen were in employment and that some of those who were not had chosen not to work. The Trust produced a report on the employment of tenants for a meeting held in December 1924 (the survey excluded a number of large sites, including Cork City, Mullingar, Naas, and Limerick), which stated that most tenants were in employment, many with the Free State Government or state run organisations such as the railways, others were employed in trades. The evidence was only based on Trust tenants, but it can be argued that they were a representative sample. The tenants ranged from the officer class to the ordinary soldier and were geographically dispersed and located in both urban and rural areas.[8]

Table 25: Employment of Trust tenants 1924

Location	Houses	Employment
Killester, County Dublin	247	Civil servants, postmen: 57; mechanics, artisans: 39; Guinness brewery: 22; clerks: 14; watchmen, warehousemen: 12; railway, tram workers: 9; stewards/managers: 9; tailors, shoemakers: 5; carters: 4; commercial travellers: 4; policemen: 3; motor vehicle owners: 2; miscellaneous e.g. journalist, watchmaker, chemist: 14; pensioners: 6. The remainder in employment included serving soldiers in the Free State army, labourers, and other trades. Unemployed: 15.

4 *Morning Post*, 10 November 1927.
5 *Morning Post*, 6 January 1928, Letter from Crosfield, Chairman BL.
6 *The Times*, 15 December 1931.
7 *IT*, 19 February 1934 in TNA, AP, 1/144, reporting on BLSI annual meeting.
8 TNA, AP, 1/54, Report for Trust meeting, 17 December 1924.

Location	Houses	Employment
Clontarf, County Dublin	38	Free State or British Government employees: 21; various trades: 10; GN railway officials: 2; secretaries of the Legion: 2; pensioners: 2; unemployed: 1.
Bluebell, County Dublin	32	With 3 exceptions, all were in good employment at for example the Guinness brewery, Great Southern and Western Railway, or working for the Free State Government.
Kells, County Meath	28	All farm labourers.
Castleknock, County Dublin	28	Free State Government clerks: 17; Guinness brewery: 6; self-employed contractors: 3; ordinary labourers: 2.
Kingstown, County Dublin	20	Labourers in good employment (railway porters etc.): 14, British Government clerks: 2; Free State Government clerks: 2; secretary of the local Legion: 1; unemployed: 1.
Dundrum, Dublin	15	Free State Government clerks: 3; British Government clerks: 3; labourers: 2; unemployed: 7.
Palmerstown, County Dublin	14	Free State Government clerks: 11; labourers: 2; unemployed: 1.
Thomastown, County Kildare	14	Farm labourers: 14.
Raheny, County Dublin	12	Free State Government clerks: 3; railway officials: 3; clerks: 2; school master: 1; sailor: 1; tailor: 1; labourer: 1.
Trim, County Meath	10	All farm labourers.
Edenderry, County Kildare	3	Farm labourers: 2; 1 cottage vacant.
Puckstown, County Dublin	2	Grave digger: 1; Free State Government clerk: 1.

Source: TNA, AP, 1/54, Report on employment of tenants
prepared for Trust meeting, 17 December 1924.

In December 1932, the Trust conducted a further survey of 2,202 tenants (the figure excluded tenants who paid rent directly to the Dublin office rather than through rent collectors), which indicated that 666 were without work and 73 were on 100% disability pensions, with many others on lesser allowances. Some 30% of the tenants were therefore seemingly unemployed, but the accompanying comments of the rent collectors, who as neighbours had first-hand knowledge, show the difficulty of relying on such figures.

One rent collector from Cork commented, 'a good number of the cases would not accept work if offered to them'. A colleague wrote, 'The majority are in receipt of a big pension, plus insurance benefit, plus family earnings, and are in no way a deserving case. I have got very few deserving cases to be classed as genuine unemployed'. It was also claimed that others left employment temporarily in order to obtain a medical certificate to prevent the pension board from docking their pension. The Dublin office wrote in a memo accompanying the figures, 'taking Devlin, the 5 unemployed are not really unemployed at all; taking Navan, of the 14 unemployed, really only 1 could be placed in that category'.[9]

Ex-servicemen in receipt of pensions were less willing to work, particularly if in so doing such pensions were jeopardised. Captain Whitehead, a resident of Birr, stated that problems also arose in building houses 3 to 4 miles outside of towns (as at Birr) as ex-servicemen were unwilling to face the journey and were prepared to live on a small pension.[10] War pensioners resident in the Free State benefited from higher pensions and allowances set in the context of the more expensive cost of living in the United Kingdom. As they were not reduced for a lower cost of living in Ireland it was possible for an ex-serviceman to live on less than a full pension, more so if he lived in a rent-free cottage. Trust records show that in a number of cases, particularly in the 1930s, after children were old enough, other members of the family contributed to the family finances, or that lodgers were taken in to provide additional income. These factors limited the need and/or willingness of ex-servicemen to work and unemployment data has to be considered in this context. It was also reflected in the attitude of employers: private employers preferred a workman without a pension who was solely dependent on his income and therefore more likely to be motivated.

Ex-servicemen often suffered from poor housing. *The Times* wrote in 1927 that housing schemes had been handicapped by the civil disturbances of recent years and as a consequence, 'thousands of ex-servicemen throughout the Free State are living in one-room tenements, for which they pay exorbitant rents, and the provision of decent accommodation for them is long

9 TNA, AP, 3/17.
10 TNA, AP, 1/84, Trust/BLSI meeting, 12 May 1924.

overdue'.[11] The *Cork Examiner* interviewed Brooke Brasier, a local politician, who said that ex-servicemen lived in 'small and unhealthy dwellings', men were deprived of their disability allowance, and little employment was to be had. 'Emigration has taken the skilled away, leaving the ineffective behind'.[12] Trust reports indicate that its tenants had previously paid higher rents for significantly inferior accommodation. A 1930 Trust survey in Dublin found 1,182 ex-service families were each living in one room. The popularity of the Trust houses, irrespective of the comments of their more antagonistic tenants, indicates that alternative accommodation was inadequate and in short supply. In the last Trust scheme completed in Dublin there were 2,666 applicants for 66 houses.[13]

In some aspects ex-servicemen were in a comparably advantageous position compared to the general population. The ex-servicemen who received pensions, set for a United Kingdom cost of living, and housing, free of rent after 1933, were better off than much of the population and this may have incurred some resentment.[14] The BLSI claimed there was some resentment towards those living in Killester, who were viewed as 'Crown colonists' with favourable housing.[15] Children of pensioners had the advantage of an assured income and parents were thus able to keep them longer at school, while the children of ex-servicemen living in housing colonies enjoyed a higher standard of health.[16] Nevertheless, the fact remains that most ex-servicemen did not benefit from either a Trust house or a pension.

Discrimination

In the 1927 Dáil Éireann debate on the claims of British ex-servicemen, Redmond argued that that the employment problems of ex-servicemen were caused by discrimination:

> there is not a day passes when I ask a man, who comes to me and says he is a British ex-serviceman, why he does not go to the Labour Exchange, that the inevitable reply is not: 'what is the use of my going there? I am a British ex-serviceman and I will be told to stand down'.

11 *The Times*, 16 November 1927.
12 Brooke Brasier, *Cork Examiner*, 1 November 1927.
13 TNA, AP, 1/121, BL to DO, 18 June 1930.
14 The Ministry of Pensions argued in 1936 that 'rent free Trust houses and the compara-tively high monetary value of our pension scale places him [the ex-serviceman] in a better position than the civilian of his own class in the Irish Free State'.
15 TNA, AP, 1/84, Meeting Trust/ BLSI, 12 May 1924.
16 TNA, PIN, 15/758, MoP report, 1936.

Cooper disagreed:

> I know of many cases of British ex-servicemen, who were also
> ex-National army men, who have been unable to get employment
> through the Labour Exchange. But I do not think the state of affairs
> is peculiar to them. I think you will find in every section of society
> complaints that there was nothing doing at the Labour Exchange.

Shaw argued that the position of the ex-servicemen was no different to
others: 'no doubt a large number of them are unemployed but they are no
worse off than all the other unemployed'. Carney said that the Connaught
Rangers who mutinied in India were recognised as having fought for Irish
freedom, but those who survived were almost all unemployed. According to
Shaw, on his tour of Ireland Crosfield 'could not find one single concrete
case of a man being victimised because he was an ex-soldier'. Shaw added,
'as far as my experience is concerned, I have never found any discrimination
in the counties I represent against ex-servicemen'.[17] Duckworth also refuted
the existence of discrimination, 'my fellow Trustees tell me that very little of
the original feeling against them now remains'.[18] Mahon said that he had not
been able to substantiate a single case of alleged victimisation:

> a lot of humbug is talked about their being badly treated and kept
> out of positions because they served with the British Forces. I have
> enquired into many cases myself and have never found yet an instance
> of hostility to anyone because he was an ex-Service man.

He stated that Hickie had similar views.[19]

The Trust, the Legion, and the TDs had good contacts throughout
Ireland and therefore were well placed to understand what was happening
at a local level. The Legion in particular would have had little reason
to downplay any accusations of discrimination. The Trust's survey of
employment in 1924 offered the insight that many of its tenants worked for
the Free State Government or its agencies. One explanation for the lack of
discrimination against ex-servicemen was that many had republican leanings
(see below). Yet in the case of the Trust's tenants, the majority were members
of the Legion but even this closer association with Britain did not seem to
count against them.[20]

---

17 *Dáil Éireann*, Vol. 21, 16 November 1927.
18 TNA, AP, 1/98, Duckworth to Ruggles-Brise, 17 June 1926.
19 Mahon, *Daily Mail*, 22 November 1928; *IT*, 3 February 1925.
20 TNA, AP, 1/54, Report for Trust meeting, 17 December 1924; TNA, AP, 1/84, Trust/

In 1924, Duckworth and Walker both stated that ex-servicemen were disadvantaged in applying for local authority housing; Duckworth said that ex-servicemen had no chance of finding a house elsewhere when in competition with a man who is not an ex-serviceman.[21] One explanation may have been that, knowing that ex-servicemen had an option for housing excluded to others, local councils gave them a lower priority. Walker wrote, 'service houses in many districts render the men ineligible for houses at the disposal of the local authorities', and that Killester ex-servicemen had been turned down by the Dublin Corporation and had no chance of transferring to local authority housing.[22] The Lavery Committee investigated the issue and found that in September 1926, 547 British ex-servicemen were tenants of the Dublin Corporation. The Committee's report also concluded that while the ex-servicemen had grievances regarding lack of employment and bad housing, these were common to all members of the community, particularly the 'labouring classes', to which many ex-servicemen belonged, and were in no way peculiar to British ex-servicemen.[23]

With the advent of a Fianna Fáil administration discrimination may have been anticipated, but reports from British agencies again indicated that this was not the case. The British Ministry of Pensions was present throughout Ireland with its network of area committees, and was in regular contact with large numbers of ex-servicemen. In 1936, the ministry asked its local offices to ascertain whether ex-servicemen or their children were subject to discrimination, and if this varied either by location or whether the ex-serviceman was a pensioner or not. The request was made in response to a claim by an 'official lady visitor' to a minister that ex-servicemen were subject to discrimination with regard to employment and assistance. Ten replies were submitted to the ministry's head office giving a cross-section of views. The ministry's concluding summary of the report noted that 'the consensus of opinion is that there is no general discrimination against ex-servicemen'.

Many of the local managers had considerable experience in working with ex-servicemen and their submissions provided further detail. One, who had worked for the ministry since 1921 and visited every town in the Free State, stated in his submission that he had, 'never known a pensioner or ex-soldier to be victimised because he was a British soldier'. He knew several republicans who employed ex-servicemen and their children and who assisted ex-soldiers. He claimed that British ex-servicemen in the Free State

BLSI meeting, 18 December 1924.
21 TNA, AP, 1/84, Trust/BLSI meeting, 14 May 1924.
22 TNA, AP, 1/39, Walker to Lefroy, 22 July 1924; TNA, AP1/84, Trust/BLSI meeting, 14 May 1924.
23 TNA, PIN, 15/758, Lavery Report, 1928.

were much more popular than men serving in the Free State forces, and concluded that as a servant of the British Government he was considered a 'somebody' and 'every attention and courtesy is paid to me'. Another manager who worked in Counties Meath and Wexford wrote, 'I have never known one proved case of victimisation of an ex-serviceman or his family'. A manager from Dublin reached a similar conclusion to the Lavery Committee a decade earlier when he said that an ex-serviceman's difficulties, 'do not spring from his war service but are indigenous to the economic conditions of the country and are shared by all other members of the same community'. Another wrote that since leaving the armed forces in 1922 he had been in close contact with ex-servicemen in Limerick, both due to his ministry role and as a member of the Legion and, 'I have not heard any complaints of victimisation', and 'the majority of the employers of any consequence employ our men as a rule'. He claimed a 'good man' would find employment but the one who is indifferent to work 'scrounges on every fund and charity known to him'. The implication is that many men who were not working falsely claimed discrimination to be the cause of their failure to find employment, that this was just an excuse for not seeking work. One manager wrote, 'regarding victimisation of the men, most of this seems to exist in the mind of the complainant'.

The report did however note other reasons for unemployment, including those related to age, lack of training, and the economic conditions of the country. Some 90% of ex-servicemen sought employment in the unskilled labour market. In this regard, by the 1930s, they were significantly disadvantaged as they were older and less educated than those against whom they competed. The typical ex-serviceman was 'less capable of adapting himself to the requirements of the new industries that are being nurtured under the high tariff wall'. In addition, ex-servicemen in receipt of pensions were sometimes denied employment. Given two men of equal merit, private employers preferred a workman who was solely dependent on his income and therefore was more likely to be motivated, but such decisions were commercial not political. One manager within the Ministry of Pensions commented, 'the average employer seeks only to get best value for his money by securing the man best suited to his requirements and no other consideration is allowed to apply'. On the other hand, men with pensions had an advantage; their assured fixed incomes gave them standing in the community. According to the report, ex-servicemen were considered equally with others for government appointments and the majority of those with local authorities and public bodies.

The one exception was the preference given to National army veterans, the report noting that 'De Valera has been more successful in impressing these views on employers in general than his predecessor in office', perhaps a surprising claim given that he had fought against the National army veterans.

Only one respondent claimed that discrimination existed and that it was caused by ex-members of the National army and the IRA. He cited a case in which an ex-serviceman obtained a job because of his republican credentials and was concerned that the ministry would approach his employer when he was admitted to hospital and his war service would become known.

The report also stated that children of ex-servicemen were not handicapped in seeking employment or apprenticeships. The ministry provided financial support to help dependants obtain training through the payment of premiums, which 'has undoubtedly been the means of obtaining many an ex-serviceman's child a job'. The likely result of such payment was the reduction of cost of wages to the employer. One submission stated that 90% of applicants seeking work for their children claimed that no one would give employment to them because of their father's army service, but the writer could not produce any concrete case of such treatment. He continued that the apprenticeships recognised by the ministry were with long-standing, reputable firms who were pro-British and provided openings for the children because of their father's service. He also gave the example of Monument Bakery, which earned money to erect monuments for fallen Sinn Féiners, and received the ministry's representative 'most courteously' and provided an apprenticeship. The writer noted, however, that in some country districts or republican counties problems could arise; the county council and university in Galway were considered anti-British.

The report also stated that no difficulties were placed in the way of ex-servicemen seeking voluntary or charitable help, 'the sole criterion applied by such organisations is the real need for assistance and the urgency meeting it'. One submission concluded that there was no 'organised boycott' but a 'definite lack of interest in, and sympathy for, ex-servicemen', but only in exceptional circumstances did that feeling impact upon his employment prospects. The report also explains that one reason the ex-servicemen were not affected by prejudice was that 'the majority of ex-servicemen are stated to be members of the Fianna Fáil Party and supporters of the present [Fianna Fáil] Government', and 'being anti-British in sentiment themselves are in no way hampered'. Several of the respondents emphasised this point.[24] In reference to the above report, Bourke writes that many ex-servicemen took refuge in the Fianna Fáil party but even this could not safeguard them from prejudice, particularly in the western counties. The segment of the report she quotes stated the opposite; that prejudice from officials was the 'exception, not the rule', and was in any event mainly confined to the western counties.[25] As with Leonard in the case of Michael Shannon, the

24 TNA, PIN, 15/758, MoP report, 1936.
25 Joanna Bourke, 'Shell-Shock, Psychiatry and the Irish Soldier', in Adrian Gregory and

example used to demonstrate that ex-servicemen were subject to intimidation or marginalised is questionable. The Trust also refuted the notion that prejudice existed under the Fianna Fáil Government. Edward Godfrey of Cork left for England in 1935 and obtained a permanent job, his wife and daughters remaining in the cottage. Browne wrote in 1937, 'Godfrey's statement that he could not get work in Cork on account of antipathy to ex-servicemen is pure nonsense'.[26]

Perhaps one important indication of a lack of discrimination is that recruitment to the British army continued and, according to O'Connor, in the 1930s, 'in most communities around the country there was little hostility shown towards those who joined up, and … in some areas British military service was explicitly valued and respected as a legitimate career outlet'. Such recruitment had at least tacit governmental sanction, O'Connor continues: 'both the Cosgrave and de Valera governments permitted the Garda Síochána to cooperate with recruit-related inquiries from the British military authorities'. Such recruitment escalated dramatically with the Second World War; Girvin estimates between 60,000 and 70,000 volunteered from southern Ireland.[27] These were not just new recruits, but Great War ex-servicemen re-enlisting; their experiences following the Great War did not stop many of them from serving Britain again. The Trust noted, 'A considerable number of tenants have re-joined HM Forces or are engaged on work of national importance'. Some 461 tenants were absent for reasons related to wartime service.[28] Perhaps also for economic reasons many worked in Britain's wartime industries.

Support and Integration

The ex-servicemen's problem was not that they were discriminated against but, as the Lavery Report concluded, 'all the grievances and disabilities complained of were grounded on claims to special treatment by reasons of promises given or of war service'.[29] There were in Ireland many large employers, such as brewers, distillers, and manufacturers of biscuits, sweets,

Senia Pašeta (eds), *Ireland and the Great War: 'A War to Unite Us All?'* (Manchester, 2002), 163. TNA, PIN, 15/758, MoP, report 1936, sub report from Dublin, 22 June 1936, 2.

26 TNA, AP, 1/167, Browne to Phillips, 29 May 1937.

27 Steven O'Connor, *Irish Officers in the British Forces, 1922–45* (Basingstoke, 2014), 13, 144; Brian Girvin, *The Emergency: Neutral Ireland 1939–45* (London, 2006), 274–5.

28 TNA, AP, 1/177, Browne to Phillips, 4 October 1939; Browne to Phillips, 20 January 1948.

29 TNA, PIN, 15/758, Lavery Report, 1928.

and cigarettes, including the Guinness Brewery and Jacobs Biscuits, that adopted the principle of the King's Roll; 542 brewery men returned to the Guinness. Such firms gave preferential treatment to ex-servicemen, handicapped or not, and their children.[30] But the ex-servicemen were disadvantaged in comparison to their counterparts in Britain, where the level of societal support was considerably greater, more employers of all sizes were sympathetic, and the government encouraged them to give preference to veterans.[31] Mahon accepted that 'the Free State Government cannot be expected to single out ex-servicemen from other unemployed men for preferential treatment'.[32]

One manager in the Ministry of Pensions' report wrote that, unlike their British counterparts, the ex-servicemen did not enjoy the support of the public as there was 'no wide appeal to public sympathy backed by Church and State, no claim on their fellow countrymen for services rendered'. Another wrote that the Free State refused to regard itself as having participated as a nation in the War and had repudiated responsibility for the costs of its after-effects and, as a consequence, 'the Great War and its aftermath does not enter into the ethical conscience of the Free State, with the result that those who volunteered their services excite neither interest nor sympathy'. It was noted that the ex-serviceman was only disadvantaged by his own indiscretion; if he persisted to plead war service as a reason for obtaining employment the likely response was 'go to the British for compensation'.[33] Bourke argues that the ex-servicemen endured the psychological trauma of returning to a much-changed Ireland that no longer recognised their motives for fighting. She writes that as with returning Vietnam veterans, Irish ex-servicemen suffered from an absence of 'purification rights' from a grateful populace willing to bestow understanding and forgiveness on uneasy consciences.[34] The Ministry of Pensions' report from 1936 noted that the ex-serviceman 'suffers from a sense of inferiority and helplessness born of his isolation from England and the apathy and lack of interest that surround him'.[35] As O'Higgins made clear, theirs was not the sacrifice upon which the Free State was founded. Mentally disabled Irish veterans suffered further disadvantages. Bourke writes, 'not only were they outcasts for having fought

---

30   TNA, PIN, 15/758, MoP report, 1936; Tom Burke, 'The Royal Dublin Fusiliers: Who Were They and Where Did They Come From?' in Eoin Magennis and Crónán O' Doibhlin (eds), *World War One and its Impacts* (Armagh, 2005), 30.
31   Report on BLSI, Annual Meeting, *IT*, 24 February 1936.
32   Mahon quoted in the *Daily Mail*, 22 November 1928.
33   TNA, PIN, 15/758, MoP report, 1936.
34   Bourke, 'Shell-Shock, Psychiatry and the Irish Soldier', 155, 158.
35   TNA, PIN, 15/758, MoP report, 1936.

for England instead of Ireland, their maddened minds debarred them from "making good" in the War of Independence and the Civil War'.[36]

It was not, however, service to the British Crown but the Civil War that ostracised those that fought on the wrong side. The civil conflict created a legacy of hostility and bitterness that pervaded Irish society, separating parties, interests, and even families, and creating the basis for political divisions that endured.[37] Those who opposed the Treaty were subject to social, economic, legal, and religious sanctions, excluded from public life and employment, and forced to emigrate.[38] The 15,000 republican internees released by 1924 were faced with unemployment, competition from demobilised National army soldiers who were given preference for jobs and social benefits, and discrimination by the Treatyite Government.[39]

In 1923 the Free State Government passed The Army Pensions Act of 1923 catering for wounded soldiers from the National army, and in 1924 the Military Service Pensions Act, which was based on service alone rather than disability. Applicants had to have served in the National army during the Civil War and in the pre-Truce IRA. Anti-Treatyite veterans did not receive pensions on grounds of disloyalty to the state, and this was not remedied until 1934, when Fianna Fáil extended the benefits to its supporters.[40] A proposal to allocate land to members of the IRA was discussed in the Dáil Éireann in March 1922 but plans were superseded by the Civil War, which did much to change the notion that IRA veterans were entitled to land; the Land Act of 1923 established a priority for land allocation but excluded the IRA.[41] Ultimately, Fianna Fáil proved as disappointing to land-hungry IRA veterans as Cumann na nGaedheal.[42] An IRA veteran complained to de Valera in 1957 that 'we are convinced more and more of the hostility of successive governments to the pre-Truce IRA. This was very evident in the allocation of land and positions in which we did not even get equal treatment with the rest of our countrymen'.[43] O'Brien compares the experiences of two relatives: Eugene Sheehy, who served in the Great War, was pro-Treaty, and became a Circuit Court judge, and Hanna Sheehy-Skeffington, who supported the republicans in the Civil War and as a consequence lost her job

36 Bourke, 'Effeminacy, Ethnicity and the End of Trauma', 68.
37 Foster, *Modern Ireland*, 511.
38 Hopkinson, *Green against Green*, 274–5.
39 Fearghal McGarry, 'Too Damned Tolerant', 62.
40 Coleman, 'Military Service Pensions for Veterans of the Irish Revolution', 201–3, 207, 214–15; O'Halpin, 'The Army in Independent Ireland', 414.
41 Dooley, *The Land for the People*, 84–85.
42 Terence Dooley, 'IRA Veterans and Land Division in Independent Ireland, 1923–1948', in Fearghal McGarry (ed.), *Republicanism in Modern Ireland* (Dublin, 2003), 102.
43 Dooley, 'IRA Veterans and Land Division', 103.

as a teacher.[44] Even the pro-Treaty IRA felt aggrieved; General Liam Tobin established an organisation, the Old IRA, in response to grievances that they had been disadvantaged against ex-British servicemen in the National army and excluded from employment opportunities and land distribution.[45]

Hart comments on the negative stereotype of Irish soldiers. But Great War veterans differed significantly from pre-war regular soldiers. The Ministry of Pensions made this distinction in their report, stating that in contrast to the reintegration of Great War veterans, the 'old time serving soldier', through many years of service had lost touch with family and friends and their 'lot is a pitiful one', as they are 'unwanted aliens in their own country'.[46] Those who had volunteered for the Great War were more representative of Irish society, far greater in numbers, not an isolated minority, and not absent for such a long period, so making their assimilation back into the community easier. Based on Hickie's estimates, they constituted between 20% and 40% of the male population of many towns. Referring to Cork, Borgonovo wrote that ex-servicemen 'were engrained in the city's social fabric'.[47] They were part of the community and received support from it. In 1926 the *Irish Times* reported that 'various churches had thoughtfully decided to hand over one day's collection to Earl Haig's Fund'.[48] In 1936 the Lord Mayor of Dublin attended the British Legion dinner.[49] Voluntary organisations such as the St. Vincent de Paul Charitable Society helped ex-servicemen.[50] A British Legion meeting held in Ennis, County Clare in December 1927 to discuss housing problems indicated the extent to which the ex-servicemen were part of the local community. The meeting was presided over by Lord Inchiquin (a local peer), and attended by the local clergy, the Reverend Canon King, and TD Patrick Hogan. It was reported in the *Irish Times*. Hogan's background may have suggested he would have little empathy for ex-servicemen, yet he was sympathetic to their problems. He was a member of the Labour Party, was active in the Gaelic League, and had served with the local IRA.[51] Other TDs were also supportive of the ex-servicemen at a local level. Patrick Shaw represented Longford-Westmeath for Cumann na nGaedheal from 1923 until his retirement in 1933 and sat on local pension committees. Brooke Brasier was a member of Cork county council (1925–40) and represented

---

44   C.C. O'Brien, *States of Ireland* (London: 1972), 104–5.
45   Dooley, *The Land for the People*, 86–88.
46   TNA, PIN, 15/758, MoP report, 1936.
47   See Chapter 2 for details of Hart's and Borgonovo's comments.
48   *IT*, 13 October 1926, in TNA, AP, 1/98.
49   Report on BLSI, Annual Meeting, *IT*, 24 February 1936.
50   TNA, PIN, 15/758, MoP report, 1936.
51   *IT*, 12 December 1927; 'Patrick Hogan', *Dictionary of Irish Biography*.

local constituencies from 1932/33 as an independent and from 1937/43 as a Fine Gael candidate. He was prominent in both the Trust and the BLSI.[52]

Ex-servicemen attained positions of prestige within the community and followed successful careers. The Ministry of Pensions' report from 1936 stated, 'many of the higher posts in the Civil Service, Army and Police (the Gardai) are held by British ex-servicemen', and that quite a number of the non-commissioned officers in the Free State army were ex-servicemen.[53] William Murphy, after his service with the National army, was appointed Chief Commissioner of Dublin Metropolitan Police in May 1923 until its amalgamation with the Garda Síochána in 1925, when he was appointed a deputy commissioner of the latter. For political reasons he was never awarded the position of commissioner, but this was due to the bitter legacy of the Civil War, not his service in the Great War. Murphy was a friend of Kevin O'Higgins. During the Second World War, de Valera asked Murphy to organise an auxiliary force that was to number 65,000 men as a backup to the army and Gardai. He retired from the police force in 1955, his career having encompassed service to the state under different regimes. He was an active organiser of amateur boxing and was instrumental in having the National Stadium built. He died in 1975 and was given a state funeral.[54] Robert Barton re-entered public life on Fianna Fáil's accession to power in 1932, holding a number of public appointments, including membership of the banking, currency, and credit commission (1934/38), and chairman of the Agricultural Credit Corporation (1933/59).[55] Captain J.C. de Lacy, the Trust's representative at Killester, was a successful candidate for Fine Gael in the Dublin municipal election of 1936. The Trust allowed him to stand but emphasised that he was not representing them and that the Trust could not be associated with any political party. De Lacy wrote 'it was a very hard fight for an Ex-British Officer but I came out victorious'.[56]

Their integration into society was not defined by war service. The term ex-servicemen implied a homogeneity which in reality, beyond attendance at remembrance ceremonies, did not exist. Most were not members of veteran associations. The Lavery Report concluded that they were 'distributed through all classes of the community'.[57] Redmond failed to develop a political party, the National League, one of whose defining messages was that it represented all ex-servicemen. Wolfe said, 'There is no Party that

52 'Brooke Wellington Brasier', *Dictionary of Irish Biography*; Houses of the Oireachtas, Members Database.
53 TNA, PIN, 15/758, MoP, report 1936.
54 Murphy, 'William Richard English Murphy', 10–11.
55 'Robert Childers Barton', *Dictionary of Irish Biography*.
56 TNA, AP, 1/163; De Lacey to Alexander, 8 July 1936.
57 TNA, PIN, 15/758, Lavery Report, 1928.

does not reckon amongst its supporters men who have served in the Great War'. Redmond's attempt to portray the National League as a party for all ex-servicemen was condemned.[58] Nor did unionism or loyalty to Britain define them, indeed the reverse; the majority supported the republican Fianna Fáil.

Even issues unique to ex-servicemen resulted in divisions between them; there was in many instances a lack of comradeship. Those who had secured houses did little to help the majority without. The cost of the rent strike caused the Trust to transfer £10,753 (the equivalent of 18 houses) from its capital fund to the reserve. Browne noted, 'morally this is a deplorable illustration of the "comradeship" of the men, the Trust are prevented from building for innocent men, who are in sore need of houses'.[59] The BLSI's attitude to the tenants changed over time as it became clear that the aims of the more extreme agitators were against the interests of the majority, who were without housing, as building work was suspended after the Leggett ruling. Its chairman, A.P. Connolly, said that the Legion 'did not agree that it was in the best interests of the ex-service men community as a whole' for no rent to be paid. He continued that if comradeship was not to be a 'hollow mockery', then those who had the advantage of a house should pay sufficient to cover maintenance and that '3,000 out of 200,000 ex-servicemen should have the abnormal benefit conferred upon them of having these cottages without paying anything at all was, frankly, absurd'. The remarks were made at the Legion's annual meeting in 1934 to the cheers of the audience.[60] Even those with houses were in conflict with each other. The Killester Tenants' Association representatives claimed they represented 65% of the tenants although other tenants' associations refuted this.[61] Browne commented that 'the better class of tenant had never had much sympathy with the tenant associations; it is a lower class of tenant who belongs to these organisations'.[62]

Large numbers of ex-servicemen returned and were distributed through all strata of the community. War service brought no special understanding or privilege, but nor was it an impediment to re-integration into the community.

58 *Dáil Éireann*, Vol. 21, 16 November 1927.
59 TNA, AP, 3/32, Browne to Duckworth, 20 April 1926.
60 *IT*, 19 February 1934, in TNA, AP, 1/144, reporting on BLSI annual meeting.
61 TNA, AP, 1/146, Franks to Alexander, 21 July 1936 and Browne to Alexander, 24 July 1936.
62 TNA, AP, 1/151, Browne to Phillips, 15 March 1944.

Ex-Servicemen's Associations

The majority of the ex-servicemen were not members of the British Legion or other veterans' organisations. In the debate on the grievances of the ex-servicemen, Redmond said that 'the great bulk of British ex-servicemen are not connected with the principal (ex-serviceman) organisations – they do not represent anything like a sufficiently large proportion of the ex-servicemen to say that they are authorised to speak for them'.[63]

Estimates of the number of members in southern Ireland varied. The *Irish Times* wrote in 1927 that 'we believe that fewer than one-quarter of them are members of the British Legion and that a majority belong to no organisation at all'.[64] In 1929 Hickie said that the Legion represented only 3% of the ex-servicemen in the Free State.[65] According to the BLSI annual conference in 1934, 10% of ex-servicemen were members of the Legion.[66] Barr estimates that between 1925 and 1939 membership varied between a high of 4,285 in 1929 and a low of 2,850 in 1925, the year the League of Irish Ex-Servicemen became affiliated to the British Legion.[67] Hickie, its president, who assumed the same role in what became the BSLI, said it had been a struggle to keep the League alive the previous eight years and that it had been forced to join the British Legion because of debt.[68]

The BLSI's continued low membership was not only due to geographical dispersal; membership was low even when there was a high concentration of veterans in a particular area. Of the 3,000 ex-servicemen in Waterford, only a small portion were members of the Legion.[69] The Legion was imperialist, conferences concluded with 'God Save the King', and this must have deterred republicans.[70] According to a Ministry of Defence report of 1936, the majority of ex-servicemen fell into this category and it was therefore unsurprising that so few were members. Patrick O'Dowd, the

---

63 *Dáil Éireann*, Vol. 21, 16 November 1927.
64 *IT*, 24 November 1927, reporting on Dáil Éireann debate on claims of ex-servicemen, 16 November 1927.
65 TNA, AP, 1/121, Trust, Browne to Alexander, 29 November 1929.
66 *IT*, 19 February 1934, in TNA, AP, 1/144. The percentage of ex-servicemen in the BL in the UK was also comparatively low; male member in the 1920s remained below 300,000 (with some exclusions), see Wootton, *The Official History of the British Legion*, 305. In comparison in France in 1930s, around 50% of the ex-servicemen were in a veterans' associations, see Antoine Prost, *In the Wake of War: 'Les Anciens Combattants', and French Society* (Oxford, 1922), 44.
67 Barr, *The Lion and the Poppy*, 59–6. Based on affiliation fee receipts, actual membership may have been 10–20% higher as the ill/unemployed paid no fees.
68 *IT*, 23 September 1926, in TNA, AP, 1/98.
69 *IT*, 7 July 1926.
70 *IT*, 19 February 1934, reporting on BLSI annual meeting, in TNA, AP, 1/144.

Fianna Fáil TD who had joined the IRA after service in the British army, in referring to men such as himself said in the debate on the claims of British Ex-servicemen that:

> this house should not ask these men to go back to the British Legion, or any other ex-servicemen's organisation, because they are in want ... they will not submit to such a display of Imperialism again. I could refer Deputy Cooper to many hundreds throughout the country.[71]

The associations of the disbanded southern Irish regiments were sometimes considered more congenial than the Legion.[72]

Hickie said the BLSI had three aims: to foster comradeship, to look after those in need, and remember the fallen.[73] He wanted the Legion to be 'non-religious, non-political and non-sectarian', and questioned a Legion band joining a political meeting organised by Redmond in Waterford as it was 'against the spirit of the Legion'. He maintained that it was the business of all parties to look after the interests of the ex-servicemen and therefore the Legion could not declare for one party and that there should be no political meetings in Legion Clubs.[74] Hickie's comments reflected many of the sentiments expressed in the debate on the claims of the ex-servicemen; that their political allegiance was not specific to one party and that correspondingly all parties had a responsibility to them. Leonard claims that the Legion never became a political force in the Irish Free State.[75] But that was not the case. While it may not have had allegiance to any particular party, the Legion was intensely involved in political lobbying and enjoyed close contact with government ministers, particularly under the Cosgrave Government, and was successful in prosecuting its case, both in relation to the lowering of Trust rents, and in highlighting grievances generally (although this was mostly to the extent of putting pressure on the British Government, who had responsibility for the ex-servicemen). The BLSI claimed that 'the relations between the Service organisations and the Government are of the friendliest nature'.[76] It had close associations with TDs such as Redmond, Cooper, and Shaw. Redmond and Cooper were both vice presidents of the Legion.[77] Hickie himself was a senator. Cooper said

71 TNA, PIN, 15/757; *Dáil Éireann, Vol. 21, 16 November 1927.*
72 Leonard, 'Survivors', 220–1.
73 *IT,* 23 September 1926, in TNA, AP, 1/98.
74 *IT,* 23 September 1926, in TNA, AP, 1/98.
75 Leonard, 'Survivors', 220.
76 Mahon, *IT,* 3 February 1925.
77 *IT,* 23 February 1926, in TNA, AP, 1/98.

that as the Free State was not represented in the Commons there was no constitutional line to bring criticism on the Trust, hence the importance of the Legion in representing the ex-servicemen to the Trust.[78]

Ironically, it was in the UK that the Legion never became a powerful advocate for the ex-servicemen; British politicians displayed great intolerance for legitimate Legion pressure.[79] Due to its independent origins, the BLSI had a very different character to that of the London headquarters: confrontational and aggressive, particularly in the 1920s. Many of the Trust's antagonists in the Killester Tenants' Rights Association were also members of the BLSI. The Trust sought initially to work with the BLSI, but the latter's confrontational tactics led to a breakdown in relations. Many of the Trust's tenants were in the Legion and the Trust thought that the BLSI's Dublin headquarters was deliberately antagonistic in order to gain their support. Browne wrote:

> the Legion is seeking to dominate the Trust and the local branches are encouraged by headquarters. The latter are losing their influence and find it difficult to get financial and moral support from the ex-servicemen in the country and Mr Walker [the then Chairman of the BLSI] is seeking to make his office popular by supporting the extremists.[80]

De Lacy, the Trust Superintendent at Killester, reported that he visited the tenants regularly during the rent strike, claiming they said that they would pay their rent when the Legion told them to. He concluded that the BLSI's headquarters was 'directly responsible for nearly all the rent trouble'.[81] The tactics of the BLSI were not welcomed by all the tenants. Browne said that many were critical of Hickie's interference.[82] An unnamed ex-serviceman and Legion member wrote in the *Irish Truth*, 'the Legion in Ireland is split into factions. There is no common policy; no unity about its decisions; no reciprocity between it and organisations that should be allied for the common good'. The writer noted that the Head Office of the Legion in Ireland fought the Ministry of Pensions and the Trust: 'the whole of the relations between

---

78 TNA, AP, 1/84, Trust/BLSI meeting, 18 December 1924.
79 Barr, *The Lion and the Poppy*, 146. Barr writes that for much of its history in the interwar years the British Legion was a failure, never developing into a mass movement, and lacking the political influence of its counterparts in Germany, France, and Italy, 1,193.
80 TNA, AP, 1/39, Browne to Duckworth, 1 October 1924.
81 TNA, AP, 1/84, De Lacy to Trust, May 1925.
82 TNA, AP, 1/98, Trust meeting, 30 March 1926.

the Legion and the Trust are bitter'.[83] Following the publication of the Lavery Report, Browne commented:

> Hickie and Connolly [the then Chairman of the BLSI] want to make capital out of the very colourless report of the Committee. Their influence, never very great, has been waning, and they will take to themselves the credit for the reduction of rent recently passed by the Trust, and try to recover some of their lost ground by showing themselves hostile to the Trust.

Browne considered there was little need to respond to the Legion's continued lobbying.[84]

By the end of 1924 there were 118 branches in the Free State, and by comparison 55 in the north. In 1934 there were 119 in the Free State, so the numbers do not appear to have grown, and 23 women's branches.[85] But the number of branches did not necessarily reflect activity (details of membership by branch is limited, but local poppy sales, see below, give an indication). The Legion's objective to foster comradeship and to serve as a centre for social activity was not always successful. Elizabeth Whitham of London travelled to Ireland in 1927 with a view to establishing an ex-servicemen's club in memory of her son, who was killed in the war. After a three-week tour she concluded:

> I visited the clubs for ex-servicemen in Youghal, Cork, Bandon, Kinsdale, Kilkenny etc. With two exceptions, I found these clubs a hopeless failure; comfortless, miserable rooms, never cleaned or swept, old crazy forms to sit on, no fires, old newspapers on the floor, mismanagement, disorder, chaos. No wonder that the membership has dwindled from two to three hundred to less than ten or at most twenty men.[86]

A British Legion conference in 1939 acknowledged that 'Ireland should follow more closely the example of England where the British Legion was looked upon as a social centre of the community'.[87]

83 *Irish Truth*, 5 March 1927, in TNA, AP, 1/98.
84 TNA, AP, 1/121, Browne to Alexander, 13 June 1929; Browne to Alexander, 29 November 1929.
85 *IT*, 19 February 1934, in TNA, AP, 1/144, reporting on BLSI annual meeting; BL Annual Report and Accounts 1924/5.
86 *Northern Whig*, 21 November 1927.
87 TNA, AP, 1/149.

THE COUNTY RECORDS.

The collections in all Ireland amounted to
£19,934 7s 1d., and the county totals were
as follow : -

	£	s	d
Northern Ireland Area	£10.211	18	9
Antrim	£5.174	10	7
Down	2,263	13	1
Londonderry	987	2	8
Tyrone	922	9	1
Armagh	545	4	11
Fermanagh	318	18	5
Irish Free State Area	£9.722	8	4
Dublin	£3,608	1	0
Cork	1,485	5	5
Wicklow	627	14	8
Limerick	410	3	0
Tipperary	321	12	5
Meath	269	12	8
Kildare	268	18	6
Wexford	217	14	11
Louth	202	0	0
Kings's County	198	16	11
Waterford	186	11	11
Donegal	181	13	7
Queen's County	175	4	9
Westmeath	171	19	1
Monaghan	166	10	4
Sligo	164	7	11
Galway	158	1	5
Mayo	140	15	4
Cavan	130	9	6
Kerry	129	3	0
Clare	125	19	8
Kilkenny	108	9	9
Carlow	82	2	6
Leitrim	81	17	11
Roscommon	66	8	6
Longford	43	3	8

Figure 3   Poppy Collection Records for Irish Counties, 1930[88]

The BLSI played a supportive role in providing need grants, helping find employment, and resolving pension issues. The Legion had 130 local committees of its Relief Fund, and claimed that 75% of those helped were not in the Legion.[89] In the 12 months up to September 1926, the Dublin Relief Fund helped nine legionnaires and 1,234 non-legionnaires.[90] Cooper in the Dáil Éireann said, 'I think three-fourths of our pensions work is done on behalf of men who are not members of the Legion'.[91] That ex-servicemen did not need to be a member to obtain benefits perhaps contributed to its low membership. In the year to September 1933, the BSLI administered grants to the amount of £31,142, an increase of £4,000 on the previous year, and its

88 *IT,* 18 September 1931.
89 *IT,* 3 February 1925, 1 May 1926.
90 *IT,* 13 October 1926, in TNA, AP, 1/98.
91 *Dáil Éireann, Vol. 21, 16 November 1927.*

employment bureau in Dublin had secured 588 jobs, 322 permanent and 266 temporary positions, while local branches were responsible for 134 permanent and 1,087 temporary placements.[92] The Legion placed 637 permanent, 1,446 temporary, and 821 casual jobs, a total of 2,904 in 1933–34.[93] It used Poppy Day to raise funds. In 1925 the BLSI collected £5,000.[94]

Newspapers

The considerable newspaper coverage the ex-servicemen received indicates that they were high profile and that the majority of the mainstream press was sympathetic towards them. The key events in the ex-servicemen's calendar, Armistice Day and the annual meeting of the British Legion, were extensively reported even though there was some republican pressure not to do so.

The press also covered the ex-servicemen's numerous complaints, for example, against the Trust or in lobbying to establish a committee to examine their grievances, and in general the largest circulation newspapers were supportive of their aims to the extent that the republicans considered the *Irish Times* and *Irish Independent* as reactionary.[95] In 1926 the *Irish Times* noted that 1,000 Trust houses had been completed but '2,500 houses remain to be built, while men who risked their lives for their country are living in the squalor of single-roomed tenements'.[96] The many meetings the ex-servicemen and their representatives had with the Irish Government were extensively reported. When the BLSI met with Cosgrave in May 1925, the *Irish Times* published their demands:

> The Council of the British Legion, Southern Ireland has asked the President of the Free State to receive a deputation to explain their grievances and ask him to request the British Government to inquire into the workings of the 1919 Housing Act and the Trust appointed to carry out its provisions, and hold in abeyance eviction notices against tenants withholding rent, or paying provisional rent pending a readjustment of charges.[97]

---

92 *IT*, 19 February 1934, in TNA, AP, 1/144, reporting on BLSI annual meeting.
93 BLSI annual meeting; *IT*, 4 February 1935.
94 *IT*, 23 September 1926, in TNA, AP, 1/98.
95 TNA, AP, 1/163.
96 *IT*, 26 June 1926.
97 *IT*, 8 May 1925.

> ·   A CHARA, – I have been instructed by
> the Executive of the above to forward you
> copy of resolution passed at last meet-
> ing:
>   "That this Federation, comprising
> the following organisations – Sean
> Oglaigh   na   hEireann,   Clan   na
> nGaedheal (pre-Truce I.R.A.), Old
> I.R.A. Association (Dublin District),
> Association of Old Dublin Brigade,
> Associated   Easter   Week   Men,   Old
> Republican Soldiers' Rights Associa-
> tion, Association of Old Fianna –
> calls upon you not to publish in your
> paper any picture dealing with 11th
> November celebrations.
>   "Mise le meas,
>   "P. Byrne, p.p. Runaide."

Figure 4   Letter to *Irish Times* November 1935

The meetings Cosgrave had with Mahon and Hickie during the rent strike were 'broadcasted' all over Ireland.[98] In the period leading to the formation of the committee to examine the claims of British ex-servicemen, their grievances received extensive press coverage and most publications were supportive that an enquiry to investigate their concerns was needed. The perspective of the different newspapers had much in common; an understanding that the ex-servicemen had returned to a changed Ireland, sympathy for their living conditions, and a view that the obligation to improve them was with the British not the Irish Government.

The *Irish Times* wrote that when the soldiers returned from the War, 'the British Government was engaged in fighting for its existence in this country', and 'that it had no time to think of the men who had fought its battles in France and Flanders. At home the ex-soldiers found that a new generation had grown up, and that their own people had lost sympathy with the ideals which had inspired them in their great adventure'. It continued, 'The British Government has primary responsibility for housing and overseas settlement, and no ex-soldier can blame the Free State Government for neglect of his interests in these respects', and the ex-servicemen were considered worthy of help as the 'vast majority are excellent citizens'.[99]

The *Westmeath Independent* wrote that the *Daily Mail* had sought to give the impression that the ex-servicemen were victimised because of past affiliations but that the Lavery Committee, 'will, we hope, effectively expose

98 TNA, AP, 1/98, Trust Meeting notes, 30 March 1926.
99 *IT*, 15 November 1927.

such a calumny and prove to the British people the delinquency of their Government'.[100]

The *Dublin Evening Mail* said many of the ex-servicemen were suffering acute distress after years of unemployment and

> they are undoubtedly deserving of sympathy. When their heroic services ended, the Irish ex-servicemen came home to find their country in the throes of a political upheaval. They found the British Government was too busy to carry out the great housing and overseas settlement schemes which had been promised them, but what was worse, they found that their heroism, too, had been forgotten by many of their own people.[101]

The *Morning Post*, which claimed it had 'frequently pleaded' the cause of ex-servicemen, wrote that sources of employment were lost with the withdrawal of the British army and with many of the gentry driven out, creating 'a desperate economic situation', and with a 'general population struggling for mere sustenance, it was inevitable that the political friends of the new regime should be served first, and their enemies should go to the wall'.[102]

The press in republican areas were also sympathetic. The *Cork Examiner* wrote, 'forming a substantial proportion of the population of the Free State, the position of the British ex-serviceman is far from enviable. His position as a citizen calls for the intervention of the Irish Government' to bring pressure to bear on the British Government.[103]

The press coverage, particularly at the time of Armistice Day, drew a cynical response from one ex-servicemen:

> we have 'walked with death' and the glories of this 'great death' are generally raked up at this time of year, coming on to the 11th of November. *Mails, Expresses, Chronicles, Times, Independents*, Irish and otherwise, are sadly perturbed regarding the many grievances of the British ex-serviceman, or what is now left of him.[104]

But there was no bias against ex-servicemen in the mainstream newspapers, indeed the reverse: they gave sympathetic coverage both in publicising their grievances and during the Armistice commemorations.

100 *Westmeath Independent*, 26 November 1927.
101 *Dublin Evening Mail*, 15 November 1927.
102 *Morning Post*, 10 November 1927.
103 Brooke Brasier, *Cork Examiner*, 1 November 1927.
104 Article by ex-serviceman, *Honesty*, 2 November 1929.

Conclusion

Heroes or Traitors?

The reaction to returning Irish soldiers was significantly influenced by the changes the War had wrought on Irish society. The violent suppression of the Easter Rising and the intended introduction of conscription meant that they came home to a much-changed Ireland that no longer recognised their motives for fighting and was in conflict with the country in whose army they had served. Leonard claims that the ex-servicemen were subject to 'extremes of intimidation', that of the estimated 120 ex-servicemen killed by republicans during the Civil War, 'the vast majority appear to have been killed simply as a retrospective punishment for their service in the Great War', and that they 'formed a marginalised and unwelcome group in Irish society'. The reality was more complex and multifaceted. Intimidation generally occurred for reasons other than war service; it was geographically focussed and occurred within a limited time period. After the civil conflict, ex-servicemen were not marginalised by the state or the community. Though perhaps not to the extent of the more unrealistic claims made on it, the imperial power largely fulfilled its obligations, certainly with benefits that compared favourably with their ex-servicemen counterparts in Great Britain, and which were provided despite extenuating circumstances.

Although encouraged to do so, comparatively few ex-servicemen made claims to the IGC for loss or damage and of those who did less than a third claimed that the actions against them were due to war service, even though it was an obvious demonstration of loyalty. In republican strongholds there were cases of IRA intimidation of veterans during the conflict but, in almost all cases, the causes of their intimidation had reasons other than war service *per se*, and were mostly applicable to other members of the population. Ironically, bogus claimants were the ones most likely to claim persecution due to army service. Given the devastating impact of spies on IRA ranks, extremes of violence were reserved for those who informed. In a vicious war the IRA targeted anyone they suspected of collaborating; some happened to be ex-servicemen, although their military background did make them more likely suspects. In most cases the IRA witness statements give reasons as to why these men were suspected of spying and appear to give incriminating evidence. But there was no campaign specifically against veterans. If the IRA had wished to undertake one, there were many high-profile ex-officers to target. Most victims of violence were from the same community background as IRA members, and it was the local knowledge arising from this that made them such a threat. The geographical distribution of violence of all types was highly focussed, with most taking place in Munster. Violence and intimidation towards ex-servicemen and the population in general closely correlated, indicating that ex-servicemen were not disproportionately singled out as a group. There were considerable areas of Ireland where violence was minimal. Support for extreme republicanism, and even more so its methods, was limited, varied by geography and decreased over time. Loyalty to Britain did not define those who volunteered at the outset of the Great War, even less so did it define them on their return. Many were disillusioned, often to the extent of joining the IRA.

Legal, moral, pragmatic, and political pressures combined to ensure that the British Government was faced with the need to fulfil a special obligation to Irish ex-servicemen in the south, which was reflected in the provision of land and houses; pensions, training, and health care for the physically and mentally disabled; and, until the formation of the Free State, employment programmes. The British Government and its agencies were remarkably persistent in discharging this obligation in a time of conflict and thereafter in a country in which they had limited and decreasing jurisdiction. In an initiative unique to Ireland, ex-servicemen's cottages were built, including garden city developments that were not emulated by Free State housing projects for many years. In November 1927, the Dáil Éireann established a committee to investigate the complaints of ex-servicemen, which concluded that 'nothing was brought to our notice to suggest that such ex-servicemen form a class with grievances or disabilities common to them as a class', they were 'common to all members of the community'. Their grievances were also similar to those of ex-servicemen in Britain. Although pension issues caused most complaints, the Irish ex-serviceman was far more generously treated than his British counterpart. Those ex-servicemen in receipt of pensions and housing enjoyed benefits in excess of veterans in Britain, which also gave them an advantage over their fellow countrymen.

Many though did not receive such benefits. Although in housing and pension benefits the Irish ex-servicemen compared favourably with their counterparts in the United Kingdom, in general the British state's treatment of its veterans was inadequate, particularly in comparison to that of other participants in the Great War, notably Germany. In Britain this deficiency was compensated for by a societal effort that had no equivalent in the Free State. In this respect, Irish ex-servicemen's experiences mirrored those of German veterans, who became hostile towards the state because of the dearth of societal support. In Ireland veterans directed their antagonism to the British Government and its representatives. The lack of societal support meant not just the absence of practical assistance, but the loss of reconciliation with those who had sent them to fight. After a bitter war they lacked the 'purification rights' derived from appreciation of their sacrifice by state and community. The ex-servicemen were considered equal citizens of the state but participation in the Great War brought no special favouritism; that was reserved for National army veterans. The Free State Government followed the precedent set by the British Government in giving priority to its own demobilising soldiers. However, perhaps a quarter of all ex-servicemen served in the National army; they made up half its number and in addition to employment preferences would have had the redemptive experience of helping to ensure the survival of the new state.

The ex-servicemen in Ireland had no claim on their fellow countrymen for services rendered and lacked the level of communal support enjoyed by their counterparts in the United Kingdom, a particular disadvantage for the large majority who received neither pensions nor housing. But there is a difference between a state and society that does not recognise motives for fighting and one that discriminates against those who fought. War service brought no privilege from the state or community, but nor did it result in discrimination. Following the creation of the Free State there is little to indicate that ex-servicemen were marginalised either through the state apparatus or in the local community. All parties in the Dáil Éireann supported examining the grievances of the ex-servicemen. Consideration for the ex-servicemen was not synonymous with support for Britain.

That ex-servicemen were not subject to discrimination is evidenced by the reports and comments of the British Legion, the Trust, politicians, and the British Ministry of Pensions. All had good contacts throughout Ireland and none a vested interest in such a conclusion, perhaps even the reverse. It may have been anticipated that the Cosgrave Government, with its desire for close ties with the British Government, would be supportive of British ex-servicemen, but they were not subject to unequal treatment under the republican de Valera Government either. A report in 1936 by the British Ministry of Pensions stated that 'there is no discrimination against ex-servicemen', a similar conclusion to that reached by the British Legion a decade earlier. Ex-servicemen held many of the higher posts in the civil service, army, and police. The ex-servicemen were no cowered segment of society and were prepared to lobby aggressively for their interests with the Irish and British governments and through the courts, often with success and mostly supported by a sympathetic press.

The majority of ex-servicemen were Catholic. Their position

compared favourably with their counterparts in the north, where sectarianism resulted in discrimination and exclusion. There, a network of official institutions and policies advanced the supremacy of Protestant-Unionists whilst those outside this hegemony faced exclusion. The Catholic community was left in a position of frustration, detachment, and justifiable paranoia. Participation in the War was lauded but when it came to remembrance, Unionist society excluded those not in the Protestant 36th (Ulster) Division.[1]

Another comparison is provided by those who returned from the Second World War. Irish recruitment into the British army continued during the War of Independence and throughout the interwar years and, despite Irish neutrality, an estimated 60,000 men and women from the 26 counties of independent Ireland joined the British armed forces during the Second World War. Some 9,000 were killed and the majority of survivors remained in Britain, only an estimated 12,000 returning home. For these latter the experience of returning shared some similarities to that of Irish soldiers returning from the Great War. Once again, the Irish Government did not accept responsibility for them, their economic and physical well-being was not the focus of government policy. Once more it was ex-members of the Irish forces, greatly expanded during the 'Emergency' (Ireland's term for the period encompassed by the Second World War) to a peak of over 40,000, who were shown post-war preference in terms of jobs and support. The returning ex-servicemen were not officially discriminated against by the government, with the exception of the estimated 6,000 who deserted the Irish army during the conflict to join the British Forces. Of this group, those who returned were subject to a seven-year disqualification from government-funded employment.[2] Both sets of ex-servicemen were excluded from the historiography of a republican Ireland and therefore could not expect state or community recognition for their sacrifice. Both gave emphasis to an unwanted British connection and, in the case of Second World War, volunteers undermined Irish neutrality. But there were significant differences. First World War veterans returned to a country in conflict, and the participation of many in the IRA, and particularly the National army, provided a redemptive experience. They were also much larger in numbers and, particularly as the new state was less secure than it would be 25 years later, were in a position of considerably greater political influence. Additionally, at least in the first decade after the formation

---

1 Jane G.V. McGaughey. *Ulster's Men: Protestant Unionist Masculinities and Militarization in the North of Ireland, 1912–1923* (Toronto, 2012), 159, 179, 196.
2 Bernard Kelly, *Returning Home: Irish Ex-Servicemen after the Second World War* (Dublin, 2012), 2, 3, 4, 90, 177, 184.

of the Free State, the influence of the British Government remained considerable.

The view that ex-servicemen were persecuted and marginalised became persuasive following the Second World War. An understanding of the everyday experiences of the ex-servicemen in the interwar years has been distorted by the success of loyalist propagandists, the dictates of republican historiography, and a reliance on the prism of commemoration. Loyalist lobbying groups such as SILRA had a vested political interest in portraying the ex-servicemen as subject to distress and highlighted any perceived discrimination or victimisation against those who had fought for Britain as it brought a sympathetic and well-publicised response from both the press and politicians, perhaps more so than an absentee landowner suffering damage to his property.

After the Great War, Irish society remained multifaceted but the historiographies developed by the nascent states in both north and south were uncomplicated and non-inclusive, giving a sense of purpose and identity to their respective supporters to the exclusion of others. In the south, with the advent of a republican government, a historiography was developed based on the idea of republican predestination; a linear path to a republic free of British association, which its supporters claimed reflected the nationalist aspirations of the majority of its citizens. The northern Irish state also found it convenient to propagate a simple historiography, this one, in contrast, based on Protestantism, unionism, and loyalty to Britain. The Ulster Protestants returned from the war to a hero's welcome, the political situation accentuating the need to laud their achievements. In 1966 Northern Ireland and Ireland commemorated the fiftieth anniversary of the events that so defined their historiography, the Somme and the Rising respectively. These events had achieved a mythological status far outweighing their original relevance and both dismissed the contribution of nationalists who had served in the British army. Irish state building distorted the past by foregrounding the winners while consigning the losers, the thousands of nationalist Irishmen who had fought in the War, to a 'national amnesia'.[3] Myers writes, 'all public ceremonial and utterance were dedicated towards another vision, of the Ireland which had taken up arms against Britain, not the other and, in fact, larger Ireland which had worn the uniform of the Crown'.[4] The Second World War and Irish neutrality led to restrictions on Armistice Day remembrance. The breaking of the final historic links with Britain in 1949 distanced both state and public consciousness even further from a British association and First World War commemoration, as

---

3 Boyce, 'Party Politics Should Divide Our Tents', 191.
4 Myers, 'The Irish and the Great War', 107.

would the onset of civil conflict in Northern Ireland in 1969. But although there were republican protests in the interwar years, they were marginal in comparison to the considerable support for commemoration, caused not least by the scale of Ireland's participation in the Great War, with so many communities and families affected. Ultimately, Irish ex-servicemen were excluded from nationalist historiography and their sacrifice ignored in state commemoration, but this does not mean that they were marginalised from Irish society or subject to discrimination. It would be misleading to consider the experiences of the ex-servicemen in the interwar years only through the perspective of republican historiography and commemoration. Fitzpatrick writes, 'Irish public life continues to dwell in imagined pasts as well as an equally fictionalised present, the link being most powerfully expressed through commemoration'.[5]

The term ex-servicemen suggests a homogeneity that did not exist. Unlike pre-war soldiers, they formed a large segment of the population and were part of the social fabric of their communities; they were distributed through all classes and across the political spectrum. Attempts to form a political party to represent their interests failed. War service did not define them; nor did loyalty to the Crown. Only a minority were members of ex-servicemen's societies and the BLSI, with its imperial connotations, struggled to survive. Many had fought in the IRA, more in the National army. A majority became Fianna Fáil supporters. It seems unlikely in daily life that the ex-servicemen would have been marginalised because of affinity to Britain. The one occasion where they might have been considered a group, Great War remembrance ceremonies, perhaps contributed to a false perception of loyalty. The displays and parades emphasised the British connection and promoted the association of ex-servicemen with the Crown, and it was on such occasions that ex-servicemen were most in the media spotlight. Many ex-servicemen though would have preferred to remember fallen colleagues without the trappings of imperialism.

The Rising may have become the defining event in southern Irish historiography but it was those who most adhered to its principles who found themselves excluded from public life and employment and forced to emigrate after the conflict. National servicemen, some half of whom had fought in the British army, were given precedent over IRA soldiers who had opposed the Treaty. It was not service to the British Crown that divided society; rather it was the Civil War that split families and communities, creating rifts that never healed. Later republican historiography found the ex-servicemen a more acceptable target than the group truly isolated by the conflict, the anti-Treaty republicans. Both loyalist lobbying groups and republicans found

5 Fitzpatrick, 'Commemoration in the Irish Free State', 186.

reason to portray the ex-servicemen as marginalised; it was a convenient collusion but at odds with the evidence.

The perception of the ex-servicemen continued to change with the political climate. Hutchinson refers to 'disillusionment with the legacy of nationalism emerging in the late 1960s as a result of the resurgence of sectarian violence in Northern Ireland and the sense of failure of the Irish Republic as a state'. He writes, 'Irish historians have called into question almost all the verities of the nationalist perspective: the idea of a pre-conquest Irish nation, the conception of Ireland as a victim eternally set against a ruthless and manipulative British oppressor'.[6] The Anglo-Irish Agreement in 1985 started the peace process that allowed a reassessment of Ireland's role in the Great War. Its exclusion from Irish historiography and the attitude of the state towards commemoration of the ex-servicemen was questioned. Reconciliation and remembrance became intrinsically linked with the intention of 'using the Great War dead as a means of healing the wounds of the contemporary Northern Ireland Conflict'.[7] The change was caused not only by an end to conflict; Ireland became more confident and cosmopolitan, defining itself as a member of the European Community rather than in conflict with Britain.

Research into the experiences of ex-servicemen remains comparatively limited. Cronin and Regan write that for many years even the professional historical community did not venture far outside the parameters of republican historiography.[8] Neither university courses nor school textbooks made mention of Irish participation in the Great War, reflecting the hegemony of republican Irish identity; postgraduate research was absent until the beginning of the peace process. The final section of *The Educational History of Ireland* (1947) covering the period from 1905 to 1921 did not contain even a subsection on the First World War. It was briefly mentioned in the context of the Volunteer movement and the conscription crisis and their part in the rise of republican nationalism.[9]

Since the 1990s there have been a number of studies on violence and intimidation during the Anglo-Irish and civil wars. These have inevitably focussed on the main areas of republican activity in Munster, but it is misleading to consider that the events that took place there were representative of much of Ireland. In many studies, such as Hart's detailed assessment of violence in County Cork, ex-servicemen were included tangentially.

6 Hutchinson, 'Irish Nationalism', 103.
7 Boyce, 'Party Politics Should Divide Our Tents', 212.
8 Mike Cronin and John Regan, 'Introduction', in Mike Cronin and John Regan (eds), *Ireland: The Politics of Independence, 1922–49* (Basingstoke, 2000), 4.
9 Myers, 'The Irish and the Great War', 107–8; Jason R. Myers, *The Great War and Memory in Irish Culture, 1918–2010* (Palo Alto, 2012), 200.

Leonard's interviews of surviving veterans were an important contribution to an oral record, but they were insufficient basis for a generalised conclusion that ex-servicemen were intimidated and marginalised. Her work was influential for two reasons. As one of the first academics to focus specifically on ex-servicemen, she was much quoted. Also, her work was timely. With the advent of the peace process, the 'rediscovery' of the War led to a more sympathetic appraisal of the ex-servicemen and a feeling that they had been forgotten and mistreated. This was not confined to the academic world but also reflected in extensive courage in the media. Myers, a journalist who had helped Leonard with the interviews, wrote not only of their exclusion from nationalist historiography and commemoration, but that in their daily lives they were, 'almost non-persons in many rural Irish communities, living in a condition of semi-boycott and often in one of permanent fear'. Myers and Eoghan Harris, another journalist, supported Hart's argument that the IRA targeted specific groups such as Protestants and ex-servicemen. Harris wrote, 'Tragically, hundreds of Cork servicemen came home to find themselves objects of suspicion', referring to ex-servicemen and Protestants as 'forgotten victims' of the IRA. Their views received considerable publicity and brought a vehement response from nationalist historians as they undermined their fundamental tenet that the IRA was non-sectarian, and that its actions were the result of military necessity.[10]

Perceptions of the ex-servicemen remained hostage to contemporary debate, the conflict between nationalist and revisionist historians played out in the media. The views popularised by journalists such as Myers and Harris, that ex-servicemen were victimised, have been as influential as earlier nationalist historiography in shaping perceptions of them. Few researchers have gone beyond the period of conflict, except in the area of remembrance, and this has precluded a more holistic understanding of the experiences of ex-servicemen, particularly with regard to their everyday lives in the interwar period.

Loyalist propagandists, the dictates of republican historiography, a reliance on the prism of commemoration, and perhaps the narrow focus of academic research have combined to distort our understanding of the experiences of Irish ex-servicemen, not only during the conflict but also in the interwar decades, following the formation of the Free State. They were not neglected by the imperial power. They may have lacked the emotional and practical support from within their own communities that war service might otherwise have brought, but they were not persecuted in the time of conflict for service in the British army, and in the period thereafter they

10 Myers, 'The Irish and the Great War', 105–8; Eoghan Harris, 'In memory of Peter Hart', *Irish Independent*, 25 July 2010.

were not marginalised in Irish society. Some ex-servicemen suffered the economic hardship characteristic within their class; many as individual citizens prospered in society and public life. Indeed, they did not even define themselves as a homogeneous group outside of remembrance. They were neither heroes nor traitors.

Appendix
Sources

The analysis of the violence and intimidation directed towards ex-servicemen contained in Chapters 1 and 2 is based on the records of the victims and the perpetrators in contrast to most other research, which has used newspaper articles and police reports.[1] The perspective of the victims is based on the files of the Irish Grants Committee (IGC), which convened in the second half of the 1920s, and represent the most comprehensively documented archive of violence and intimidation by republicans against loyalists. It was established to provide compensation for the victims.[2] The perspective of the perpetrators is derived from the Irish Military Archives, Bureau of Military History (IMA/BMH) files, which contains 1,773 witness statements by republicans recording their experiences during the period from 1913 to the end of the War of Independence. IGC claims were mostly made for reasons other than killings, whereas in contrast the IMA/BMH files provide details of executions for spying. The two repositories therefore cover the full spectrum of violence and intimidation.

The IGC files represent the 'voice of the victim', and provide first-hand

---

1 E.g. Royal Irish Constabulary (RIC) police reports (TNA, CO 904).
2 The ICG was established in October 1926 to consider claims related to hardship and loss by personal injury, or malicious destruction to property in the area of the Irish Free State between 11 July 1921 and 12 May 1923. The hardship and loss had to result from the claimants' loyalty to the Crown prior to 11 July 1921 (the IGC's terms of reference specifically allowed that proof of loyalty could be demonstrated overseas to allow for war service to be taken into account). The 212 boxes contain detailed documentation on each of the around 4,000 claims. Many applications were made due to perceived inadequate compensation from the Irish Free State, including those made under the Damage to Property (Compensation) Act, and therefore cover claims that may be inadequately documented in the NAI files. Many of the claims predate July 1921. Claims related to incidents that occurred exclusively before July 1921 received no compensation, but the details were still recorded and are included in this analysis. In addition, many incidents that prompted complaints after the Truce were a continuation of incidents that started beforehand. All the files related to other compensation processes established in the aftermath of the conflict should in theory provide additional source material, but archival limitations restrict their usefulness.

accounts of incidents of violence and intimidation, in some cases over a
long period of time. The majority of the files contain substantial records,
including confirmatory evidence from witnesses, testimonials from local
people in authority, and the IGC commentary on the submissions. They
provide background details on the victim and his circumstances, including
in many cases his family situation and the reactions of the community. They
'bring alive' the period in terms of personal experiences and local sentiment
in a manner perhaps lacking in official reports. Perhaps two caveats are
needed; it appears that an industry developed around the submission of
claims with, in some cases, the same solicitors representing claimants and
inevitably managing the process to optimise the possibility of compensation.
In addition, claimants to the IGC were seeking money and consideration has
to be given as to whether this reduces their value as a source of information.
What is clear from the files is that although the IGC was investigating
events that took place several years previously, and did not have judicial
authority, it was diligent in its investigations, particularly if there was any
suspicion of fraud. Arguably, the passage of time also allowed for a more
balanced depiction of events. The IGC's thoroughness is indicated by the
fact that only 2,237 of 4,032 claims were successful, 895 were ruled outside
the scope of the Committee's terms of reference, and compensation was
refused in 900 cases. The IGC disbursed almost £2.2 million, obliging it to
investigate more thoroughly than newspapers, whose reporting could also be
influenced by loyalist lobbying groups; and perhaps with less bias than the
RIC's reports.[3] In any event, the disbandment of the RIC in 1922, and the
passage of time before the effective establishment of a Free State police force,
limited official recording of incidents during the Civil War.

The IMA/BMH witness statements represent the 'voice of the
perpetrator', and again provide first-hand accounts of incidents of violence
and intimidation. They were only recorded from January 1947 and should
therefore be considered bearing in mind the passage of time, and the
possibility that those involved may have colluded in their preparation.
As an example, three officers from the same location in Athlone, County
Westmeath, Thomas Costello, Harry O'Brien, and Frank O'Connor, all
submitted statements referring to the same incidents in December 1955.[4]
The IRA wished to present itself as fighting a campaign that was law bound,
targeted, and proportionate, in contrast to the British military and Ulster
Loyalists.[5] There is therefore the possibility of bias and self-justification,

3 TNA, CO 762/212; CO 762/2/Admin; CO 762/86/5.
4 IMA/BMH, WS1296, Costello, Westmeath; WS1308, O'Brien, Westmeath; WS1309,
   O'Connor, Westmeath.
5 Eunan O'Halpin, 'Problematic Killings', 319.

a desire to portray incidents of violence as legitimate actions of war, and executions as the result of a quasi-legal process, perhaps to salve consciences. Ferriter notes, however, that 'the tone of the statements is measured, and while a number of witnesses were determined to settle old scores and indulge in hyperbole, many others seem to have been highly scrupulous in their testimony' and, 'where there was evidence of unreliability through "failing memory" or "self-glorification", a report to that effect was to be appended'. The statements are often very comprehensive and, although sometimes contradictory in points of detail when more than one officer described the same event, they are broadly consistent.[6] The records offer a large enough sample to be considered representative; if we accept O'Halpin's estimate of the total number of ex-servicemen killed by the IRA, the files provide details of about one-third. The files were only opened to the public in 2003, and were therefore not available to earlier studies.

The files of the British departments or agencies operating in Ireland, particularly after independence, proved extremely useful in relation to the chapters in Parts 2 and 3. Not only did they have comprehensive networks in Ireland – the Trust with their rent collectors for each estate, the Ministry of Pensions with their Area Committees, and the Ministries of Labour and Transport, which established Irish offices before independence – but also their reports and meetings were well documented, as might be expected from British bureaucracies. Extensive use has been made of the Trust files. Although only around 3% of the ex-serviceman population was awarded houses, the tenants were a representative cross-section, including officers and men, able bodied and disabled, and were geographically dispersed throughout the Free State. The files not only contain details of housing issues (building policy, rent policy, rent strikes, and tenants' associations) but also illustrate the attitudes of both the British and Irish governments towards the ex-servicemen and, particularly in terms of the latter, how this varied over time. They also provide an insight into the daily life of the ex-servicemen, notably with regard to employment, pensions, and veteran organisations.

6 Diarmaid Ferriter, 'The Opening of the Bureau of Military History', http://www. rootsweb.ancestry.com/~irlcar2/Bureau_Military_History.htm.

Bibliography

1. Manuscript and Archival Sources
Imperial War Museum, London
First World War, Private Papers, 1674, 10861, 7421
Irish Military Archives, Cathal Brugha Barracks, Rathmines, Dublin (IMA)
Bureau of Military History (1913–21), Witness Statements (WS1-1773, selected files)
The National Archives, Kew (TNA)
Files below contain reports, minutes, correspondences, and notes of meetings:
AP 1-4 Irish Sailors' and Soldiers' Land Trust
CO 762/1-212 Irish Distress Committee and Irish Grants Committee
CO 904 Royal Irish Constabulary (RIC)
DO 35/343/3 Dominions Office and Commonwealth Relations Office
LAB 2 Ministry of Labour
MT 47 Ministry of Transport
PIN 15/757-8 Commission to enquire into condition of British ex-servicemen in the
    Irish Free State
National Archives of Ireland, Dublin (NAI)
Records of the Department of the Taoiseach
Returns of the Census of Ireland (1911/1926), http://www.census.nationalarchives.ie/
    (online database)
Central Statistics Office (Ireland), Skehard Road, Cork, Ireland
Public Record Office of Northern Ireland (PRONI)
Papers of the Southern Irish Loyalist Relief Association
University College Dublin
Papers of Kathleen Barry Moloney (September 1924/January 1926), 94/56
University of Leeds
Liddle Collection, GS 1056

2. Printed Primary Sources
Contemporary Books and Journals
Barry, Tom, *Guerrilla Days in Ireland* (Tralee, County Kerry: Anvil, 1971).
Ewart, Wilfrid, *A Journey in Ireland 1921* (London: Putnam, 1922).
Harrison, Henry, *Ireland and the British Empire, 1937: Conflict or Conciliation* (London:
    Robert Hale, 1937).

MacDonagh, Michael, *The Home Rule Movement* (Dublin: The Talbot Press, 1920).

Martin, Hugh, *Ireland in Insurrection* (London: Daniel O'Connor, 1921).

O'Malley, Ernie, *On Another Man's Wound* (Dublin: Anvil Books, 2002; original edition 1936).

Pritchett, V.S., 'A Glimpse at a Southern Irish Town', *Christian Science Monitor*, 6 March 1923.

Prost, Antoine, *In the Wake of War: 'Les Anciens Combattants' and French Society* (Oxford: Berg, 1922).

Tobin, Liam, Major General, *The Truth about the Army Crisis* (Dublin: Irish Republican Army Organization 78A Summerhill, 1924).

Newspapers
British Library, Colindale: National Library of Ireland, Dublin
Cork Examiner
Daily Mail
Daily News
Dublin Evening Mail
Dundalk Democrat
Evening Herald
Freeman's Journal
Honesty
Irish Independent
Irish News (and Belfast Morning News)
Irish Press
Irish Times
Irish Truth
King's County Chronicle
Manchester Guardian
Midland Tribune (Birr)
Morning Post
Northern Whig
The Times (British)
Westmeath Independent
Wicklow Newsletter

Parliamentary Records
Dáil Éireann/Seanad Éireann Debates/Members Records, see online sources.
Houses of Parliament, see online sources.

3. Printed Secondary Sources

Aalen, F.H.A., 'Homes for Irish Heroes: Housing under the Irish Land (Provision for Soldiers and Sailors) Act 1919, and the Irish Sailors' and Soldiers' Land Trust', *Town Planning Review*, 59/3 (1988), 305–23.

Augusteijn, Joost, *From Public Defiance to Guerrilla Warfare: The Experience of Ordinary Volunteers in the Irish War of Independence* (Dublin: Irish Academic Press, 1996).

Barham, Peter, *Forgotten Lunatics of the Great War* (New Haven, CT: Yale University Press, 2004).

Barr, Niall, *The Lion and the Poppy: British Veterans, Politics and Society, 1921–1939* (Westport, CT: Praeger, 2005).

Borgonovo, John, *Spies, Informers and the 'Anti-Sinn Féin Society': The Intelligence War in Cork City, 1920–1921* (Dublin: Irish Academic Press, 2007).

Bourke, Joanna, 'Shell-Shock, Psychiatry and the Irish Soldier', in Adrian Gregory and Senia Pašeta (eds), *Ireland and the Great War: 'A War to Unite Us All?'* (Manchester: Manchester University Press, 2002), 155–70.

———, 'Effeminacy, Ethnicity and the End of Trauma: The Sufferings of "Shell-Shocked" Men in Great Britain and Ireland, 1914–39', *Journal of Contemporary History*, 35/1 (2000), 57–69.

Bowman, Timothy, *Irish Regiments in the Great War: Discipline and Morale* (Manchester: Manchester University Press, 2003).

Boyce, D.G., '1916, Interpreting the Rising', in D.G. Boyce and Alan O'Day (eds), *The making of Modern Irish History: Revisionism and the Revisionist Controversy* (London: Routledge, 1996), 163–87.

———, 'That Party Politics Should Divide our Tents: Nationalism, Unionism and the First World War', in Adrian Gregory and Senia Pašeta (eds), *Ireland and the Great War: 'A War to Unite Us All?'* (Manchester: Manchester University Press, 2002), 190–216.

———, *The Irish Question and British Politics 1868–1986* (London: Macmillan Education, 1988).

Boyce, D.G. and O'Day, Alan, 'Revisionism and the Revisionist Controversy', in D.G. Boyce and Alan O'Day (eds), *The Making of Modern Irish History: Revisionism and the Revisionist Controversy* (London: Routledge, 1996), 1–14.

Brady, Joseph and Lynch, Patrick, 'The Irish Sailors' and Soldiers' Land Trust and its Killester Nemesis', *Irish Geography*, 42/3 (2009), 261–92.

Brennan, Michael, *The War in Clare 1911–1921: Personal Memoirs of the Irish War of Independence* (Dublin: Four Courts Press, 1980).

Brennan, Niamh, 'A Political Minefield: Southern Loyalists, the Irish Grants Committee and the British Government, 1922–31', *Irish Historical Studies*, 30/119 (1997), 406–19.

Burke, Tom, '"Poppy Day" in the Irish Free State', *Studies: An Irish Quarterly Review*, 92/368 (2003), 349–58.

———, 'The Royal Dublin Fusiliers: Who Were They and Where Did They Come From?' in Eoin Magennis and Crónán O' Doibhlin (eds), *World War One – and its impacts* (Armagh, Northern Ireland, Cumann Seanchais Ard Mhacha and the Cardinal Tomás Ó Fiaich Memorial Library and Archive, 2005), 27–68.

Campbell, Fergus and O'Shiel, Kevin, 'The Last Land War? Kevin O'Shiel's Memoir of the Irish Revolution (1916–21)', *Archivium Hibernicum*, 57 (2003), 155–200.

Canning, Paul, 'The Impact of Éamon De Valera: Domestic Causes of the Anglo-Irish Economic War', *Albion: A Quarterly Journal Concerned with British Studies*, 15/3 (1983), 179–205.

Coffey, Leigh-Ann, 'Loyalism in Transition, Southern Loyalists and the Irish Free State, 1921–37', in James W. McAuley and Graham Spencer (eds), *Ulster Loyalism after the Good Friday Agreement: History, Identity and Change* (Basingstoke: Palgrave MacMillan, 2011), 22–36.

Cohen, Deborah, *The War Come Home: Disabled Veterans in Britain and Germany* (London: University of California Press, 2001).

Coleman, Marie, *County Longford and the Irish Revolution, 1910–1923* (Dublin: Irish Academic Press, 2006).

———, 'Military Service Pensions for Veterans of the Irish Revolution, 1916–1923', *War in History*, 20/2 (2013), 201–21.

Cox, Catherine, *Negotiating Insanity in the Southeast of Ireland, 1820–1900* (Manchester: Manchester University Press, 2012).

Cronin, Mike and Regan, John, 'Introduction', in Mike Cronin and John Regan (eds), *Ireland: The Politics of Independence, 1922–49* (Basingstoke: Palgrave MacMillan, 2000), 1–12.

Daly, Mary E., *Industrial Development and Irish National Identity, 1922–1939* (New York: Syracuse University Press, 1992).

D'Arcy, Fergus, *Remembering the War Dead* (Dublin: Irish Government Publications, 2002).

Dooley, Terence, 'IRA Veterans and Land Division in Independent Ireland, 1923–1948', in Fearghal McGarry (ed.), *Republicanism in Modern Ireland* (Dublin: University College Dublin Press, 2003), 86–107.

———, *The Land for the People: The Land Question in Independent Ireland* (Dublin: University College Dublin Press, 2004).

Dunphy, Richard, *The Making of Fianna Fáil Power in Ireland, 1932–1948* (Oxford: The Clarendon Press; New York: Oxford University Press, 1995).

Dwyer, T. Ryle, *Tans, Terror and Troubles: Kerry's Real Fighting Story* (Cork: Mercier Press, 2001).

Englander, David, 'The National Union of Ex-Servicemen and the Labour Movement, 1918–1920', *History*, 76/246 (1991), 24–42.

Fanning, Ronan, et al., *Documents on Irish Foreign Policy, Volume I: 1919 –1922* (Dublin: Royal Irish Academy, 1998).

Farry, Michael, *The Irish Revolution, 1912–23: Sligo* (Dublin: Four Courts Press, 2012).

Fedorowich, K. 'Reconstruction and Resettlement: The Politicisation of Irish Migration to Australia and Canada, 1919–1929', *English Historical Review*, 114 (1999), 1143–78.

Ferriter, Diarmaid, *The Transformation of Ireland, 1900–2000* (London: Profile Books, 2005).

FitzGerald, Thomas, Earls, 'The Execution of "Spies and Informers" in West Cork, 1921', in David Fitzpatrick (ed.), *Terror in Ireland, 1916–1923* (Dublin: Lilliput, 2012), 181–93.

Fitzpatrick, David, 'Commemoration in the Irish Free State: A Chronicle of Embarrassment', in Ian McBride (ed.), *History and Memory in Modern Ireland* (Cambridge: Cambridge University Press, 2001), 184–203.

———, 'The Geography of Irish Nationalism 1910–1921', *Past & Present*, 78 (1978), 113–44.

———, 'Militarism in Ireland, 1900–1922', in Thomas Bartlett and Keith Jeffery (eds), *A Military History of Ireland* (Cambridge: Cambridge University Press, 1996), 379–406.

————, *Politics and Irish Life, 1913–1921: Provincial Experience of War and Revolution* (Cork: Cork University Press, 1998; first published 1977).

————, 'The Price of Balbriggan', in David Fitzpatrick (ed.), *Terror in Ireland, 1916–1923* (Dublin: Lilliput, 2012), 75–101.

Foster, R.F., *Modern Ireland: 1600–1972* (London: Penguin Books, 1989).

————, 'The Problem of Writing Irish History', *History Today*, 34/1 (1984), 27–30.

Fraser, Murray, *John Bull's Other Homes: State Housing and British Policy in Ireland, 1883–1922* (Liverpool: Liverpool University Press, 1996).

Garvin, Tom, *1922: The Birth of Irish Democracy* (Dublin: Gill & Macmillan, 1996).

————, *Nationalist Revolutionaries in Ireland 1858–1928* (Oxford: Oxford University Press, 1987).

Girvin, Brian, *The Emergency: Neutral Ireland 1939–45* (London: Macmillan, 2006).

Hall, Donal, *The Unreturned Army: County Louth Dead in the Great War, 1914–1918* (Dundalk: County Louth Archaeological and Historical Society, 2005).

————, *World War One and Nationalists Politics in County Louth: 1914–1920* (Dublin: Four Courts Press, 2005).

Hanley, Brian, 'Poppy Day in Dublin in the '20s and '30s', *History Ireland*, 7/1 (1999), 5–6.

————, *The IRA: A Documentary History* (Dublin: Gill & Macmillan, 2010).

Hannan, A.J., 'Land Settlement of Ex-Service Men in Australia, Canada, and the United States', *Journal of Comparative Legislation and International Law*, Third Series, 2/3 (1920), 225–37.

Harrington, Niall, C., *Kerry Landing* (Dublin: Anvil Books, 1992).

Harris, Henry, Edward, David, *The Irish Regiments in the First World War* (Cork: Mercier Press, 1968).

Hart, Peter, *The IRA and Its Enemies: Violence and Community in Cork, 1916–1923* (Oxford: Clarendon Press, 1998).

Hart, Peter, *The IRA at War 1916–1923* (Oxford: Oxford University Press, 2003).

Henry, William, *Galway and the Great War* (Cork: Mercier Press, 2007).

Herlihy, Jim, *The Royal Irish Constabulary: A Short History and Genealogical Guide with a Select List of Medal Awards and Casualties* (Dublin: Four Courts Press, 1997).

Hopkinson, Michael, *Green against Green: The Irish Civil War* (Dublin: Gill & Macmillan, 1988).

————, *Irish War of Independence* (Dublin: Gill & Macmillan, 2002).

Horne, John (ed.), *Our War: Ireland and the Great War* (Dublin: Royal Irish Academy, 2008).

Hutchinson, John, 'Irish Nationalism', in D.G. Boyce and Alan O'Day, *The Making of Modern Irish History: Revisionism and the Revisionist Controversy* (London: Routledge, 1996), 100–19.

Jackson, Alvin, *Ireland 1798–1998: Politics and War* (Oxford: Blackwell Publishers, 1999).

Jeffery, Keith, 'The British Army and Ireland since 1922', in Thomas Bartlett and Keith Jeffery (eds), *A Military History of Ireland* (Cambridge: Cambridge University Press, 1996), 431–58.

————, 'Echoes of War,' in John Horne (ed.), *Our War: Ireland and the Great War* (Dublin: Royal Irish Academy, 2008), 261–75.

————, 'The Great War in Modern Irish Memory', in T.G. Fraser and K. Jeffery (eds), *'Men, Women and War'* (Dublin: Lilliput Press, 1993), 136–57.

————, *Ireland and the Great War* (Cambridge: Cambridge University Press, 2000).

Jeffery, Keith, 'The Irish Military Tradition and the British Empire', in Keith Jeffery (ed.), *An Irish Empire? Aspects of Ireland and the British Empire* (Manchester: Manchester University Press, 1996), 94–122.

Johnson, Nuala, *Ireland, the Great War and the Geography of Remembrance* (Cambridge: Cambridge University Press, 2007).

Karsten, Peter, 'Irish Soldiers in the British Army, 1792–1922: Suborned or Subordinate?' *Journal of Social History*, 17/1 (1983), 31–64.

Kee, Robert, *The Green Flag: A History of Irish Nationalism* (London: Weidenfeld and Nicolson, 1972).

Kelly, Bernard, *Returning Home Irish Ex-Servicemen after the Second World War* (Dublin: Irish Academic Press, 2012).

Kenny, Tomás, *Galway: Politics and Society, 1910–23* (Dublin: Four Courts Press, 2011).

Kissane, Bill, *The Politics of the Irish Civil War* (Oxford: Oxford University Press, 2005).

Kowalsky, Meaghan, 'This Honourable Obligation: The King's National Roll Scheme for Disabled Ex-Servicemen 1915–1944', *European Review of History*, 14/4 (2007), 567–584.

Larsson, Marina, 'Restoring the Spirit: The Rehabilitation of Disabled Soldiers in Australia after the Great War', *Health and History, Military Medicine*, 6/2 (2004), 45–59.

Lawler, Sheila, *Britain and Ireland 1914–23* (Dublin: Gill & Macmillan, 1983).

Lee, J.J., *Ireland, 1912–1985: Politics and Society* (Cambridge: Cambridge University Press, 1989).

Leonard, Jane, 'Facing the Finger of Scorn: Veterans' Memories of Ireland after the Great War', in Eoin Magennis, and Crónán O' Doibhlin (eds), *World War One and its impacts* (Armagh, Northern Ireland: Cumann Seanchais Ard Mhacha and the Cardinal Tomás Ó Fiaich Memorial Library and Archive, 2005), 87–107; first published in Martin Evans and Ken Lunn (eds), *War and Memory in the Twentieth Century* (Oxford: Berg, 1997).

————, 'Getting Them at Last: The I.R.A. and Ex-Servicemen', in David Fitzpatrick (ed.), *Revolution? Ireland 1917–1923* (Dublin: Trinity History Workshop, 1990), 118–29.

————, 'Survivors' in John Horne (ed.), *Our War: Ireland and the Great War* (Dublin: Royal Irish Academy, 2008), 209–23.

Lyons, F.S.L., *Culture and Anarchy in Ireland 1890–1939* (Oxford: Clarendon Press, 1979).

Macardle, Dorothy, *The Irish Republic: A Documented Chronicle of the Anglo-Irish Conflict and the Partitioning of Ireland, with a Detailed Account of the Period 1916–1923* (Dublin: Irish Press, 1951).

MacCarron, Donal, and Younghusband, William, *The Irish Defence Forces since 1922 (Men-at-arms)* (Oxford: Osprey, 2004).

McManus, Ruth, *Dublin, 1910–1940: Shaping the City and Suburbs* (Dublin: Four Courts Press, 2002).

Maguire, Martin, *The Civil Service and the Revolution in Ireland, 1912–38: 'Shaking* the Blood-stained Hand of Mr Collins' (Manchester: Manchester University Press, 2008).

McGarry, Fearghal, 'Too Damned Tolerant: Republicanism and Imperialism in the Irish Free State', in Fearghal McGarry (ed.), Republicanism in Modern Ireland (Dublin: University College Dublin Press, 2003), 61–85.

———, The Rising Ireland: Easter 1916 (Oxford: Oxford University Press, 2010).

McGaughey, Jane G.V., Ulster's Men: Protestant Unionist Masculinities and Militarization in the North of Ireland, 1912–1923 (Toronto: McGill-Queen's University Press, 2012).

McIntosh, Gillian, The Force of Culture: Unionist Identities in Twentieth-Century Ireland (Cork: Cork University Press, 1999).

Meehan, Niall, 'Distorting Irish History', Spinwatch (November 2010).

———, Troubles in Irish History: A 10th Anniversary Critique of Peter Hart's The IRA and its Enemies (Aubane: The Aubane Historical Society, 2008).

Morrison, Eve, 'Kilmichael Revisited', in David Fitzpatrick (ed.), Terror in Ireland, 1916–1923 (Dublin: Lilliput Press, 2012), 158–80.

Murphy, Karl, 'An Irish General: William Richard English Murphy, 1890–1975', History Ireland, 13/6 (2005), 10–11.

Murphy, Michael, 'Revolution and Terror in Kildare, 1919–1923', in David Fitzpatrick (ed.), Terror in Ireland, 1916–1923 (Dublin: Lilliput, 2012), 194–205.

Myers, Jason, R., The Great War and Memory in Irish Culture, 1918–2010 (Palo Alto: Academica Press, 2012).

Myers, Kevin, 'The Irish and the Great War: A Case of Amnesia', in Richard English and Joseph Morrison Skelly (eds), Ideas Matter: Essays in Honour of Conor Cruise O'Brian (Dublin: Poolbeg Press, 1988), 103–8.

Neary, J. Peter, and Ó Gráda, Cormac, 'Protection, Economic War and Structural Change: The 1930s in Ireland', Irish Historical Studies, 27/107 (1991), 250–66.

O'Brien, Anthony, 'The Soldiers' Houses in Limerick: The Story of the Irish Sailors' and Soldiers' Land Trust', The Old Limerick Journal, 35 (1998), 3–5.

O'Brien, C.C., States of Ireland (London: Hutchinson, 1972).

O'Callaghan, John, Revolutionary Limerick: The Republican Campaign for Independence in Limerick 1913–1921 (Dublin: Irish Academic Press, 2010).

O'Carroll, J.P., 'Éamon de Valera: Charisma and Political Development', in J.P. O'Carroll and John Murphy (eds), De Valera and His Times (Cork: Cork University Press, 1986), 17–34.

O'Connor, Steven, Irish Officers in the British Forces, 1922–45 (Basingstoke: Palgrave Macmillan, 2014).

———, 'Forgotten Soldiers: Ireland's Great War Veterans in the Irish Revolution, 1919–1921', paper presented at the conference of the French Society for Irish Studies, Ireland: Identity and Interculturality, Toulouse 1 Capitole University, 21 March 2014.

Ó'Corráin, Daithi, 'The Dead of the Irish Revolution 1921–25', The Blue Cap (Journal of the Royal Dublin Fusiliers Association), 12 (2005), 1–4.

O'Halpin, Eunan, 'Counting Terror: Bloody Sunday and the Dead of the Irish Revolution', in David Fitzpatrick (ed.), Terror in Ireland, 1916–1923 (Dublin: Lilliput, 2012), 141–57.

———, 'Problematic Killings during the War of Independence and its Aftermath:

Civilian Spies and Informers', in James Kelly and Mary Ann Lyons (eds), *Death and Dying in Ireland, Britain and Europe, Historical Perspectives* (Dublin: Irish Academic Press, 2013), 317–48.

———, 'The Army in Independent Ireland', in Thomas Bartlett and Keith Jeffery (eds), *A Military History of Ireland* (Cambridge: Cambridge University Press, 1996), 407–30.

O'Mahony, Ross, 'The Sack of Balbriggan', in David Fitzpatrick (ed.), *Terror in Ireland, 1916–1923* (Dublin: Lilliput, 2012), 58–74.

Oram, Gerard, *Worthless Men: Race, Eugenics and the Death Penalty in the British Army during the First World War* (London: Francis Boutle, 1998).

Pašeta Senia, 'Ireland's Last Home Rule Generation: The Decline of Constitutional Nationalism in Ireland, 1916–1930', in Mike Cronin and John Regan (eds), *Ireland: The Politics of Independence, 1922–49* (London: Palgrave Macmillan, 2000), 13–31.

———, 'Thomas Kettle: An Irish Soldier in the Army of Europe', in Adrian Gregory and Senia Pašeta (eds), *Ireland and the Great War: 'A War to Unite Us All?'* (Manchester: Manchester University Press, 2002), 8–27.

Pennell, Catriona, *A Kingdom United: Popular Responses to the Outbreak of the First World War in Britain and Ireland* (Oxford: Oxford University Press, 2012).

Price, Dominic, *The Flame and the Candle: War in Mayo 1919–1924* (Cork: Collins, 2012).

Regan, John, 'The "Bandon Valley Massacre" as a Historical Problem History', *History*, 97/325 (2012), 70–98.

———, *The Irish Counter Revolution, 1921–1936: Treatyite Politics and Settlement in Independent Ireland* (Dublin: Gill & Macmillan, 1999).

Shaw, Father Francis, 'The Canon of Irish History: A Challenge', *Studies*, 61 (1972), 113–53.

Sheehan, William, *A Hard Local War: The British Army and the Guerrilla War in Cork, 1919–1921* (Dublin: The History Press, 2011).

Strachan, Hew, *The First World War* (London: Simon and Schuster, 2003).

Townshend, Charles, 'Policing Insurgency in Ireland', in David M. Anderson and David Killingray (eds), *Policing and Decolonisation: Politics, Nationalism and the Police 1917–65* (Manchester: Manchester University Press, 1992), 22–41.

———, *The Republic: The Fight for Irish Independence 1918–1923* (London: Penguin Books, 2013).

Valiulis, Maryann, 'The "Army Mutiny" of 1924 and the Assertion of Civilian Authority in Independent Ireland', *Irish Historical Studies*, 23/92 (1983), 354–66.

Walsh, Maurice, *The News from Ireland: Foreign Correspondents and the Irish Revolution* (London: I.B. Tauris, 2008).

Ward, Stephen R., 'Intelligence Surveillance of British Ex-Servicemen, 1918–1920,' *The Historical Journal*, 16/1 (1973), 179–88.

Winter, J.M., *The Great War and the British People* (London: Macmillan, 1985).

Wootton, Graham, *The Official History of the British Legion* (London: Macdonald and Evans, 1956).

———, *The Politics of Influence: British Ex-Servicemen, Cabinet Decisions and Cultural Change (1917–57)* (London: Routledge and Kegan Paul, 1963).

4. Unpublished Dissertations/Theses

Brennan, Niamh, 'Compensating Southern Irish Loyalists after the Anglo-Irish Treaty, 1922–32' (University College Dublin Ph.D. thesis, 1994).

Clark, Gemma, M., 'Fire, Boycott, Threat and Harm: Social and Political Violence within the Local Community. A Study of Three Munster Counties during the Irish Civil War, 1922–23' (University of Oxford D.Phil. thesis, 2011).

Kowalsky, Meaghan, 'Enabling the Great War: Ex-Servicemen, the Mixed Economy of Welfare and the Social Construction of Disability, 1899–1930' (University of Leeds Ph.D. thesis, 2007).

McNamara, Conor, 'Politics and Society in East Galway, 1914–21' (St Patrick's College, Dublin Ph.D. thesis, 2009).

O'Callaghan, M., 'Language or Religion: The Quest for Identity in the Irish Free State, 1922–1932' (University College Dublin MA dissertation, 1981).

Staunton, Martin, 'The Royal Munster Fusiliers in the Great War, 1914–1919' (University College Dublin MA dissertation, 1986).

5. Online Sources

Dáil Éireann/Seanad Éireann Debates/Members Records, Office of the Houses of Oireachtas, Leinster House, Dublin, http://debates.oireachtas.ie/dail/ or http://historical-debates.oireachtas.ie/en.toc.dail.html (accessed frequently); Members Database, http://www.oireachtas.ie/members-hist/default.asp.

Dáil Éireann Debates, http://www.oireachtas-debates.gov.ie/en.toc.dail.html (accessed frequently).

Dictionary of Irish Biography, Cambridge University/Royal Irish Academy, http://dib.cambridge.org/.

Ferriter, Diarmaid, 'The Opening of the Bureau of Military History' http://www.rootsweb.ancestry.com/~irlcar2/Bureau_Military_History.htm.

Houses of Parliament Debates, Commons (HC) and Lords (HL), *Hansard 1803–2005*, Hansard Digitisation Project, Hansard Millbank Systems, http:/hansard.millbank-systems.com (online database).

'Island of Ireland Peace Park', website, http://en.wikipedia.org/wiki/Island_of_Ireland_Peace_Park.

The History of the Royal Hospital Kilmainham, website, http://www.rhk.ie/history.aspx.

Index

Note: Individuals from the primary sources such as the IMA/BMH WS and the TNA CO 762 IGC files are only referenced if the individual can be identified by first name and surname. It should be noted that the spelling of personal and place names can vary in historical sources. Authors' names are only included in the index if they are explicitly referred to in the body of the text, otherwise they are cited in the bibliography.